Italy

The Best Travel Writing From

The New York Times

Italy

The Best Travel Writing From

The New York Times

Introduction by Umberto Eco

Articles by Olivier Bernier, Rachel Billington, Burton Bollag,
Beth Archer Brombert, Frank Bruni, Paul Chutkow, E.J. Dionne Jr.,
Sarah Ferrell, Michael Frank, Shirley Hazzard, Paul Hofmann,
Dan Hofstadter, Bernard Holland, Cathy Horyn, Louis Inturrisi,
Nancy Harmon Jenkins, David Laskin, Carol Lettieri, Susan Lumsden,
Alison Lurie, Malachi Martin, Alastair McEwen, Michael Mewshaw,
Jan Morris, William Murray, Elisabetta Povoledo, Frank J. Prial,
Francine Prose, Frederika Randall, Robert Riche, Jane Shapiro,
Mary Taylor Simeti, Muriel Spark, Alexander Stille, James Sturz,
Susan Allen Toth, Barry Unsworth, William Weaver, Jo Broyles Yohay

Captions and boxes by Alessandro Frigerio,
Michele Micheletti, Angelo Ramella

Translation by Alastair McEwen

Harry N. Abrams, Inc., Publishers

Editor: Mitchel Levitas, *The New York Times*
Jacket design: Michael Walsh
Translation of Umberto Eco's essay: Alastair McEwen

Library of Congress Cataloging-in-Publication Data

Italy: the best travel writing from the New York times / Olivier Bernier... [et al]; introduction by Umberto Eco.
p. cm.
Umberto Eco's contribution translated from the Italian.
Includes bibliographical references and index.
ISBN 0-8109-5905-4 (alk. paper)
1. Italy--Description and travel. I. Bernier, Olivier. II. Eco, Umberto. III. New York times.
DG430.2.I845 2005
914.504'92--dc22

2004020646
Rev.

Travel articles written for and/or originally appearing in *The New York Times* copyright © 2004 The New York Times Company

All other content copyright © 2004 De Agostini Editore S.p.A.

Published in 2004 by Harry N. Abrams, Incorporated, New York
All rights reserved. No part of the contents of this book may be reproduced without the written permission of the publisher

Printed and bound in Italy by Officine Grafiche Novara 1901 S.p.A.

10 9 8 7 6 5 4 3 2 1

Harry N. Abrams, Inc.
100 Fifth Avenue
New York, N.Y. 10011
www.abramsbooks.com

Abrams is a subsidiary of
LA MARTINIÈRE GROUPE

Acknowledgements

Most books involve an author and publisher who speak the same language, literally and metaphorically. This book was different. Surprisingly, the cross-cultural, bilingual, transatlantic project, which includes no fewer than 40 contributors to The New York Times and four institutional participants, made the publishing process not only unusual but genuinely rewarding and creatively collaborative.

The prime mover in this endeavor was the Italian Government Tourist Board, which originally suggested this book and whose financial support made it possible. We owe thanks in particular to its president, Amedeo Ottaviani, general manager Piergiorgio Togni and Eugenio Magnani, the director of North American operations, who was ably assisted by the staff New York. Their generous spirit of cooperation and tireless attention to detail is deeply appreciated.

In Milan and Novara, the technical and human resources of the De Agostini publishing group were remarkable. Davide Gallotti, chief of public-sector special projects, was an essential presence, getting the work underway and miraculously keeping it on schedule. Luca Serafini's impeccable editorial standards encouraged everyone to do their very best work. Ada Mascheroni, chief of De Agostini's photographic department, used her formidable knowledge and imagination to hunt down in the huge electronic archive the many rare, spectacular and surprising images that make this book so striking. Meanwhile, Federica Savino, editorial coordinator, synchronized the many moving parts – articles, sidebars, photographs, captions, corrections, substitutions – without once losing patience or purpose. Luca Finessi's fluid design, with the help of Maria Chiara Balduchelli, created a visually coherent journey that is also unpredictable and stimulating. In a different voice, the sidebars, boxes and captions written by Michele Micheletti, Alessandro Frigerio, Angelo Ramella, and translated by Alastair McEwen, deepen the work by adding a fresh historical and cultural perspective. Finally, The Times project manager for this complex enterprise, Tomi Murata, chased a slew of essential data and kept it all on track.

De Agostini will publish the book in English and Italian editions. We are pleased, moreover, that the fourth participant in this venture, Abrams, the distinguished publisher of art books, will distribute the English language version. While the editorial content and process has been the responsibility of The Times, the outcome was made possible by a shared goal to which all participants were dedicated: a well-written travel book that appeals to the eye as well as the mind.

MITCHEL LEVITAS
New York Times
Book Development

Contents

By Umberto Eco

Many ITALIES

In the film *The Third Man*, while Harry Lime is riding the Ferris wheel in the Prater park in Vienna, he says to his friend Holly Martins that Italy, for centuries plundered, torn by interminable wars, massacres and tragedies of all kinds, nevertheless produced Leonardo, Michelangelo, Raphael and the like, while Switzerland, despite centuries of peace, produced no more than the cuckoo clock.

Apart from the fact that Harry Lime makes two mistakes (Switzerland has produced eminent men – which we often fail to remember because they wrote in French, German or Italian – while the cuckoo clock was invented in Bavaria), underlying his statement about Italy is a Darwinian concept of natural selection, a quasi-racist and eugenic idea, of the "races improve races" variety. Moreover Harry Lime uses this argument to justify his lack of moral scruples and to pose as an *ubermensch*. A product of the horrors of World War II and the will-to-power, Harry Lime perhaps possessed a certain criminal genius but he died in a sewer without having created anything.

Are the Italians creative because they have suffered a great deal? I could mention other peoples, who have suffered horribly over the centuries and whose culture has not developed, remaining unchanged for millennia. So we must look elsewhere for the reasons for Italian creativity.

If you take a car and visit the United States you can travel for days and days through a splendid, immense landscape framed by boundless horizons; if you travel through Northern Europe you can see horizons that are just as boundless as you drive along highways from which all you can see are magnificent fields of rye – and of course this is not to mention journeying through Siberia, the Central Asian steppe, the Sahara or

Gobi deserts, or through the vast expanses of Australia, in the center of which stands Ayers Rock. It was this experience of contact with the immensity of nature that produced the idea of the Sublime.

In its modern form, the idea of the Sublime developed in the 18th century, an age of travelers with a taste for things that were exotic, interesting, curious, different and amazing. This period marked the birth of what we might call the "poetics of mountains:" the traveler bold enough to venture to cross the Alps was enthralled by impervious cliffs, endless glaciers, bottomless chasms, and boundless stretches of land. Even before the end of the seventeenth century, in his *Telluris theoria sacra* Thomas Burnet saw in the experience of the mountains something that uplifted the soul toward God, something imbued with a hint of infinity and capable of arousing great thoughts and passions. In the eighteenth century, in his *Moral Essays* the Earl of Shaftesbury wrote that even the rugged crags, the mossy caves, the caverns and the waterfalls, adorned with all the graces of the wilderness, struck him as all the more fascinating for they represented nature in a more genuine manner and were enveloped in a magnificence far superior to what he described as the "ridiculous counterfeits" of princely gardens.

In his essay on the Sublime, Edmund Burke said: "Whatever is fitted in any sort to excite the ideas of pain and danger, that is to say, whatever is in any sort terrible, or is conversant about terrible objects, or operates in a manner analogous to terror, is a source of the Sublime; that is, it is productive of the strongest emotion which the mind is capable of feeling." And in order to celebrate the Sublime he went against an idea that had been accepted for thousands of years, that Beauty was first and foremost proportion. On the contrary, the Sublime allows us to enjoy vastness of dimensions, solidity, even massiveness and darkness. The Sublime comes into being with the unleashing of passions like terror, it flourishes in obscurity, it calls up ideas of power, and of that form of privation exemplified by emptiness and silence. Predominant aspects of the Sublime are nonfinite things, difficulty and sometimes magnificence.

The most famous theory of the Sublime is that of Kant, who draws a distinction between the mathematical and the dynamic Sublime. A typical example of the mathematical Sublime is the sight of the starry sky. Here we have the impression that what we see goes far beyond our sensibilities and thus we are induced to imagine more than we see. A typical example of the dynamic Sublime is a storm. Here, what shakes our spirit is not the impression of infinite vastness, but of infinite power: in this case too our sensible nature is left humiliated and, again, this is a source of a feeling of unease, compensated for by the sense of our moral greatness, against which the forces of nature are powerless. Perhaps it is over-doing things to spend more than a page on a description of experiences and feelings that have little to do with Italy, but this is precisely the point I wanted to make: you don't go to Italy in search of the Sublime. You don't go to Italy to find the dizzying pinnacles of Gothic cathedrals, the immensity of the pyramids, or the Niagara Falls. Once you have crossed the Alps (where you may well have an impression of sublimity, but exact-ly the same experience is to be had in France, Switzerland, Germany or Austria) you begin to have a different experience.

The horizon never opens up to attain titanic dimensions, because it is always limited to the right by a hill, or to the left by a small mountain ridge, while the way is continuously interrupted by small townships, at least one every five kilometers. And at every stretch of road (except in certain parts of the Po valley) you will find a bend, a change of course, and the countryside changes too, so that not only from one region to another but even within the bounds of the same region you will always find a different landscape, with infinite gradations from the mountains to the sea, as you pass though hills of various conformations. There are few similarities between the hills of Piedmont and those of the Marche or of Tuscany, sometimes it suffices to cross the Apennines, which run the length of Italy like a spinal column, from east to west or vice-versa to get the impression that you have arrived in another country. Even the seas are different, the Tyrrhenian coast offering panoramas, types of beaches and coastlines that are different from those of the Adriatic coast, not to mention the seas around the islands.

In this journey through absolute diversity, where the horizon never extends to form "sublime" dimensions, but where everything is always on a human scale, architecture, too, conforms to the landscape and makes no attempt to do it violence, which is why even Gothic architecture in Italy already heralds the proportion of the Renaissance.

And so we are faced with a country dominated by difference and by a taste for proportion. This variety is not solely a matter of the land but also of its inhabitants. Lots of people are probably aware that Italy has many different dialects, which vary from region to region, so that if a Sicilian listens to a Piedmontese from the northwest he cannot under-stand a word of what the other is saying. But few foreigners could imag-ine that these dialects change from city to city, even within the same region, and sometimes, albeit minimally, from village to village, every five kilometers. I realize that I have used the measure of five kilometers already, but it strikes me as a useful piece of advice for those who trav-el that distance: they will find a new country every time.

An analogy that anyone can understand may be found in the variety of Italian cuisine. Of course those who try it in other countries find themselves in the same situation as a westerner who eats Chinese food in Europe or America, because by now all the restaurants conform to a common standard. All you have to do is go to China to realize just how many different schools of cuisine they have there. It's the same in Italy. If I may be permitted a personal recollection, I first tasted pizza when I was almost twenty: being a northerner born and bred, I had not tasted that Neapolitan prodigy until then. Today, naturally, you find pizza everywhere in Italy, just as you find it in Paris or New York, but this is a phenomenon of globalization and pizza has become like blue jeans. But try the taste of "bagna cauda" from Piedmont, or "cassoeula" from Lombardy, "tagliatelle" in the Bolognese style, or "abbaccchio," roast spring lamb from Rome, or genuine Sicilian "cassata" and you will feel as if you have moved from China to Peru, and from Peru to Timbuktu. This variety of tongues (and of cuisines) depends on the variety of the population. Let's try to imagine Italy before it was unified by the Romans. The north, as far as Bologna at least, was populated by Celtic tribes — but in their midst there lived an extremely different people, the Ligurians, barbarians more closely related to the peoples of Catalonia, while to the east of the Celts there were the Illyrians. Central Italy was home to the Italic peoples (but there were other Illyrian settlements in Puglia), a series of tribes all different from one another, with different languages. These were the peoples subjugated by the Romans in the early years of the city's history. But that same area was also populated by the Etruscans, whose origins are still obscure but whose language and culture were quite unlike those of the other Italic peoples. Finally, in the south there was Magna Grecia, in other words the Greek colonies, and not many people know that some of the greatest Greek thinkers and scientists were born in Italy. It suffices to mention Pythagoras (who was born in Samos, but founded and developed his school in Italy), Parmenides and Archimedes.

The Roman Empire would seem to have given all the peoples of Italy a single language, but all we need do is take a look at how pre-existing ancient languages merged with classical Latin and we can see how modern Italian came to attain its present form over the centuries following the collapse of the Roman Empire. Then, with the fall of the Empire, Italy became a land formed by the states known as Romano-Germanic and was hybridized by Goths, Lombards and Byzantines, while the south of Italy was settled first by the Arabs and later by the Normans. This was quite a cultural leap, and to this day you find small, dark-skinned

Sicilians of Arab origins and others of Norman descent who are tall and blond with blue eyes. Finally, for about 14 centuries, various regions of Italy, which had never managed to become a nation state (like France, England or Spain – and was only to attain this status less than 150 years ago), were invaded and dominated by France, Austria and Spain.

The Fascist movement attempted to construct the myth of a pure Italian race, of Arian stock, in imitation of Nazi racism, but perhaps no other country had been so thoroughly hybridized. Indeed in the closing centuries of the Empire, Rome was something very like New York, a melting pot in which different populations had been meeting and interbreeding for at least four centuries, and in fact many emperors hailed from the provinces of the Empire, Africa included.

So, in order to reply to Harry Lime, it may be that the Italians were forged by massacres and invasions, but they sprang first and foremost from the phenomenon of ethnic pluralism and thus they are the result of a blend of many cultures.

This ethnic, cultural and territorial diversity has also produced political diversity. Political diversity has always been one of the endemic evils of Italy, forever divided up into cities that battled one against the other – and just as certainly there is a trace of this inheritance in the typically unruly nature of modern Italian politics. For centuries, this political fragmentation has deprived Italians of any sense of the State, and this also explains their skepticism and undisciplined attitude to any government. But at the same time this process engendered a sense of many proportionate identities. The sense of political affiliation had nothing to do with the sense of the sublime that fascinated the subjects of the immense Russian Empire, or the infantry that Napoleon led on his bid to conquer the world. Italians saw themselves as belonging to a city, to a region, to very limited territories, and they projected this sentiment into the balanced concepts of their architecture. Palazzo Vecchio in Florence or the nearby church of San Miniato al Monte, the Venetian palazzi, and the masterpieces of the Baroque never have the dimensions of Chartres Cathedral or the gardens of Versailles. I would say that the only exceptions are San Marco in Venice (which was inspired by Byzantine models), Milan cathedral (which is an imitation of French and German Gothic) and St. Peter's in Rome, where the papacy needed a visible symbol of greatness. Everything else is in proportion with a small city.

The cities were divided among themselves, but the Italians traveled from one to the other, and therefore these differences in culture, taste and aesthetic ideals produced new hybridizations.

So, when we talk of Italian creativity, from the arts to literature, from cuisine to fashion, from architecture to the construction of the simplest everyday objects, I think that we ought to bear in mind this principle of variety. Italian creativity is due to the diversity of places, languages, of ancient history and even local interests.

It may be that, seen from a distance, this plurality reveals some common elements. And this is natural, because I have been talking about continuous hybridization, of a cultural and ethnic multiplicity that engendered countless internal migrations. But I believe that it is equally important to reveal, underlying all that seems "Italian," from Leonardo to pizza, from Monteverdi to Fellini, the network of differences, the manifold roots of a creativity that we might define as "polytheistic." Italy is a country of many gods – and many of them dwelt there, as had been the case in Greece, before the advent of Christianity, and many continued to dwell there even afterwards – a fact that can be seen in many forms of the popular religious tradition. Thus a journey to Italy (which for the foreign travelers of the 18th and 19th centuries was usually a journey to Naples, Rome, Florence or Venice and to these places alone), should always be seen as a journey of discovery that will reveal not one, but many Italies.

UMBERTO ECO is the author of four novels as well as numerous works of criticism, philosophy and literary theory. His fifth novel, "The Mysterious Flame," will be published in June (Harcourt Brace). He is Professor of Semiotics at the University of Bologna. This essay was translated by Alastair McEwen.

By Nancy Harmon Jenkins

Italy's
GREAT CUISINES

May 2003

**VARIETY OF SHAPES
AND FLAVORS**

Spaghetti, macaroni, penne, fusilli, farfalle... when it comes to pasta the Italian imagination seems to know no limits. The plain dish par excellence, pasta is made of flour, water, salt and occasionally egg. Its richness comes from the sauce, which doesn't necessarily have to be elaborate but must brim with flavor, like "pesto" (above) or "ragù alla bolognese" (top).

Ask any Italian about Italy's cuisine and you're bound to get a bemused response. The happy truth is, there's really no such thing. Instead, there are any number of Italian cuisines, at least 20 of them, one for each of Italy's 20 regions, and some would say many, many more, one for each mountain range and river valley, and one at least for each major city, not to mention islands great and small, Sicily and Sardinia, Elba, Ischia and Pantelleria among them. Indeed, you could say there is a cuisine for every town and village, maybe for every household therein.

In fact, Italy's long and varied history, from Etruscans to Romans to invading Arabs, Normans, Spanish, French and Austrians, and the peninsula's extremely diverse geography, from high alpine peaks to the rich bottom lands of the Po valley, the wheat-growing plains of Puglia and Sicily and 4,000-plus miles of coastline, has resulted in a cornucopia of culinary traditions that are imaginative, artful and full of extraordinarily varied flavors and textures.

Italy is still deeply divided regionally, more so than any other country in the developed world. The divisions go way beyond the regions into which the country is officially carved, and they show up in many ways. Despite a half-century or more of television and compulsory education, for instance, regional dialects are still strong. Equally robust are regional foodways. In fact, I've observed with interest that at very point on the map where one regional dialect fades and another kicks in, food customs change too. In my mountain village in a remote part of Tuscany overlooking the Upper Tiber in Umbria, the locals speak with a south Tuscan accent and are careful to avoid anything that might misidentify them as Umbrian. Just so, the flat griddle-baked bread called "torta al testo" of the Upper Tiber valley, just 15 kilometers away, is considered a foreign invasion up here in the Tuscan hills where our flatbread focaccia is baked in the oven.

"Campanilismo" is what Italians call this phenomenon. It comes from the word "campanile," meaning the bell tower of the local church and a feeling that only within the sound of those bells can people be trusted to do things, and cook things, the right way. Take ragù, for example, the rich meat-and-tomato based sauce that is served on pasta throughout the country, north to south. A properly made ragù differs not only from one region to another but from one town to another, even from one kitchen to another. And each cook will boast that hers (or his) is the only true, original, authentic, genuine ragù, made the way it has always been made, with all others but pale imitations. In the Abruzzo, cooks make ragù with lamb, in Naples they use pork, and in Bari, capital of Puglia, the heel of the Italian boot, good cooks go all out with lamb, pork, veal and beef combined, while in Bologna, not to be outdone and Bologna calls itself the home of ragù, a glass of rich milk is thrown in at the end to cook down and give the sauce the requisite creaminess.

Or take pasta itself, the very symbol of Italian food. Tell me what you eat and I will tell you who you are, goes the adage. In Italy it's more precise: Tell me what pasta you eat, how you make it, sauce it, serve it, eat it, and I will tell you where in Italy you come from. In the north, it's soft-wheat pasta enriched with eggs, perhaps wrapped around a stuffing of meat, fish or greens and cheese, with a butter- or cream-based sauce; in the south, pasta is made from the flour of hard durum wheat, no eggs, often sauced with nothing but garlic,

White Truffles

Autumn is white truffle season when the penetrating fragrance of this rarest of all underground tubers perfumes restaurants all over northern Italy.

There have been periodic efforts to cultivate white truffles but so far without success. Instead, they are foraged in the most primitive way imaginable, one man and a dog (I have never heard of a female "trifolao," as the truffle-hunter is called), scouring the countryside in the dark of misty autumn nights. When the dog stops beneath a tree, his astute nose having assessed the telltale aroma, man and dog carefully dig together, sifting the damp earth to find the prize. It's all very secretive, very ritualistic, and that's part of the game. But the monetary prize can be considerable too, up to $500 a pound for prime examples that are shipped off to fancy restaurants and gourmet shops like Peck in Milan.

Northwestern Piemonte is the most famous region for tartufi bianchi, as white truffles are called, with the early morning truffle market in Alba a must for anyone curious about them. But in fact, truffles are available in many other parts of Italy too, in Tuscany, for instance, the area around San Giovanni d'Asso south of Siena is a treasure trove, as is the Marche, the region that borders the Adriatic south of the Po, while Umbria, long famous for less prestigious black truffles, is rapidly becoming a destination for white truffle-lovers as well.

And there is a difference. Black truffles have their place in the world but Italian black truffles are not on a par with the white ones, which have a redolence that is both indescribable and unmistakable, penetrating and delicate, earthy and sexy, all at the same time. White truffles are only eaten raw. Typically, in a restaurant, the proprietor himself will approach your table with his truffle slice and a large, dense, dirty-gray colored, misshapen blob that is the precious tuber. He weighs it beforehand, then proceeds to shave it in rapid, precise strokes over a dish of rich egg pasta, a buttery risotto or a fonduta of melted Fontina cheese, then weighs it again. You, the diner, are charged for the amount consumed and it's up to you to raise your hand to signal a halt to the slicing.

White truffle oil, by the way, on sale throughout the year all over Italy, is disdained by true truffle-lovers.

SEDUCTIVE HAMS
In Western culture the pig is known as an animal none of whose parts is wasted, something like the llama in parts of South America and the buffalo in North America. But the noblest part of the pig is beyond a doubt the ham. Whether boiled, baked or cured, ham has earned its place among the meats of the world.

oil, a spoonful of tomato paste and crumbled hot chili peppers. If you sprinkle your pasta liberally with grated parmigiano cheese, you're from the north, but if the topping is breadcrumbs, toasted in a little olive oil, you're deeply southern and proud of it.

That breadcrumb topping is a definition of "la cucina povera," poor folks' cuisine. But what was once the mark of poverty has become, in recent years, a mark of savvy triumph as the Italian version of the Mediterranean diet has swept the world. Lots of vegetables and legumes, not much meat, pasta and bread as the principal carbohydrates, olive oil as the principal fat, and, most importantly, food that is freshly prepared from seasonal ingredients and enjoyed around the table with family and friends, and plenty of time to savor it, that's the Italian way of eating, and anecdotal evidence alone shows that it's a solid route to good health, both physical and mental.

But there is also a "cucina ricca," a rich cuisine, in Italy and it's not to be disdained either. Good farm-churned butter, lush cheeses, cream from pasture-fed cows, the well-braised meat of young veal and plump capons, wild game and fat sausages grilled on the embers of a wood fire, and delicacies like the incomparable white truffles and real aceto balsamico, these are the hallmarks of a cuisine that is distinctively urban yet based in the agricultural traditions that pervade throughout the peninsula. The rich cooking of the bourgeoisie is omnipresent.

Eating anywhere in Italy is a serious business, which is not to say it isn't also a joyful experience. Italians take their food very, very seriously, more so, in my experience, than any other culture in the world including the French. Nowhere else do people talk about food the way Italians do, nowhere else are people so obsessed

with the quality of the oil, the bread, the cheese, the very salt on the table. My New England grandmother said you shouldn't talk about food at the table, but Italians talk about nothing else but the food on the table right now, the meal we ate yesterday or the day before, the meal we're going to be having this evening, the wild mushrooms we bought in the market this morning, the prosciutto that Zio Vittorio has promised to send after he slaughters his pig, the way Nonna Adelina flavors her rabbit with fennel pollen, all are subjects of the most intense discussion.

Perhaps that's the reason why Italy unquestionably has the best food in the world. That's my opinion, based on 30 years of living, working and traveling here, much of that time spent cooking and eating, but it's an opinion I share with many other people. And it holds for all levels from elegant, expense-account restaurants in Rome,

Florence and Milan down to the mom-and-pop osterias tucked away in unassuming hill towns. Even industrially made ice cream, like the ubiquitous chocolate-coated vanilla bar on a stick, is far superior in Italy to what's found elsewhere in the world.

How a person negotiates this bounty is something you can only learn by experience. But what an experience! It's easiest to understand if you divide the country into north, central and south. North, which is to say the regions from the Po valley to the Alps, is a cuisine based on butter, pork fat and cream. It's exemplified by dishes like osso buco milanese, wherein the fat shanks of veal are braised in red wine and served with a risotto enriched with saffron and veal stock. In the center, in regions like Tuscany, Umbria and the Marche, the cooking is plainer, more straightforward, with food tasting rigorously of what it is: T-bone steaks of local chi-

A HOST OF DELICACIES

A display of Italian foodstuffs. Top left, petal-thin rosettes of bresaola, a salted, air dried beef from Valtellina (Lombardy). Top right, polenta. Bottom left, "tome," typical Alpine cheeses. Bottom right, various types of bread rolls. Above, plump rounds of parmesan, the prince of Italian hard cheeses.

Pizza,
in all shapes and flavours

You'll find pizza all over Italy in a multitude of shapes and flavors that I've seen, but never tasted, such as chocolate pizza in Rome. But Naples claims, with considerable justification, to be pizza's real home. For years Neapolitan pizza-boosters have been promoting a Denomination of Protected Origin for "la vera pizza napoletana" but the bureaucrats in Brussels have yet to bite.

A true Neapolitan pizza, according to the boosters association, has a crust made simply from flour, water, salt and yeast (no oil or other fat); it must be kneaded and shaped by hand and baked directly on the floor of a very hot (750 °F.) wood-fired oven for a couple of minutes, no more; the topping, ideally, should be either "marinara" (simply tomato sauce with garlic and origano) or "margherita" (tomato sauce with mozzarella or fior di latte cheese and basil). Some latitude is allowed for variations. But not much. I don't know how many pizzerie there are or ever have been in Naples but if I said there's one on every block, I don't think anyone would dispute it.

AN IMPERIAL DINNER
A tasty delicacy becomes unforgettable when enjoyed in the right setting, for example, in front of the Pantheon in Rome (facing page). Or, for another example, in a street market (below) where a shopper can enjoy the flavors of a time when "organic" wasn't merely a trendy adjective but a way of life.

anina beef grilled over embers, accompanied by wild porcini mushrooms and "fagioli al fiasco," stewed garlic-flavored white beans garnished with the lush green olive oil of Central Italy, are hallmarks of both urban and country restaurants. In the south, "la cucina povera" comes into play and the innovative fantasy of cooks produces dishes like "incapriata," an unassuming but delicious puree of dried fava beans with steamed chicory greens, or "zuppa di pesce," an assembly of freshly caught seafood of the humblest sort, seasoned with garlic, red chili peppers and robust Southern oil.

Food like this is not just to be found in restaurants. One of the greatest thrills for the food-fixated traveler is to be found in the open-air markets and food stalls that proliferate still throughout the country, despite the incursions of huge "ipermercato" supermarkets. Even these last can be the source of enormous interest as you stroll the aisles examining the varieties of canned tomatoes, olive oils, boxed pastas, the meats, the seafood, the produce sections wherein each vegetable is marked with its place of origin. But true joy is in street markets like Venice's great Rialto fish market or the Sant'Ambrogio market in Florence.

Street food is another grand opportunity for adventurous travelers to sample local wares only in Florence, for instance, will you find sandwiches of tripe ("trippa") or pancreas ("lampredotto") being sold like Coney Island hot dogs; only in the coastal towns of Liguria can you appraise the virtues of "farinata," a flat cake of chickpea flour baked in a fiery oven and garnished with olive oil (much more delicious than it sounds, believe me!); only in Palermo and its environs can you taste the charm of "arancini," saffron-scented rice balls stuffed with a dol-

lop of ragù, then deep-fried unless it's Naples and Rome where you'll find street vendors and "tavole calde," cooked-food shops, selling arancini's close cousins "supplì al telefono," similar rice balls with mozzarella in the middle, so that when you take a bite the melted cheese strings out like telephone wires.

Beyond Leonardo, beyond Michelangelo, beyond the Greek temples of the south, Italy's greatest treasure, I believe, is her food. But wherever you go, be sure to allow plenty of time to enjoy it. It's no accident that Slow Food, the international movement to counter McDonald's-style fast food, was founded and is still based in Italy. Slowness defines the very essence of eating in Italy. It's an insult to your host, an insult to the restaurant chef, an insult even to the street vendor, to expect to grab a bite and eat on the run. Time to enjoy a morning cappucino with a little sweet pastry, time at the very least two hours to linger over lunch or dinner, time for the early evening aperitivo in a neighborhood bar, time to chat (even in broken Italian mixed with English) with the woman who sells fresh porcini mushrooms in the market or the folks sitting at the next table in the trattoria. It's time well spent. Always.

_____

NANCY HARMON JENKINS is a widely published food writer who specializes in Italy and the Mediterranean.
Her most recent book is "The Essential Mediterranean" (HarperCollins). She lives in Tuscany and Maine.

Olive oil
Where the olive is king

The olive harvest, which begins late in autumn, is the last of the year's crops to be brought in. It's an anxious but joyful time, anxious because farmers are on the watch for icy winds and chill rains that inhibit the harvest, joyful because the olive tree, along with its fruits and its oil, have been symbols of bountiful abundance since Mediterranean farmers first began its cultivation thousands of years ago.

Everywhere south of the Po, and even in a few districts north of the great river, the olive is king, the most important crop in the field and the most important ingredient on the table. Italy is the world's second largest producer of olive oil, right behind Spain, and may well be the Number One producer of extra-virgin olive oil, truly the finest kind (extra-virgin oil is produced solely by mechanically expressing oil from the olives, without any chemical solvents or other refining processes).

While American chefs are leery of cooking with extra-virgin olive oil, Italian cooks use almost nothing else, even for deep-fat frying, indeed, they say that for a perfectly fried "fritto misto," that extravagant combination of meats, fish, vegetables and something sweet, crisp and crunchy but without a trace of grease, there's nothing better than extra-virgin oil. That's because, when heated to the correct temperature (about 180 °C, 350 to 360 °F), the hot oil sears the outside and cooks the inside rapidly and consistently. At lower temperatures, the breading or batter will absorb the oil; at higher temperatures, the outside will burn before the inside is cooked through.

Freshly pressed olive oil, available in late autumn into winter, is a revelation in flavor, something most Americans will never be able to taste without being on the spot. This is one food product that is perfectly legal to bring back to the U.S. and food-loving travelers are well-advised to do so. Poke your nose into a "frantoio" or olive mill and you may well come across a stunning local oil that can't be found outside the town where it's pressed. Buy a five- or ten-liter plastic "bidone" at a hardware store, rinse it thoroughly and let it dry, then take it to the "frantoio" and fill it up. You may curse your purchase as you struggle to get it on the plane (olive oil has to be hand-carried) but you'll bless your foresight over and over again once you get it home.

THE TEARS OF THE OLIVE
For climatic reasons the Mediterranean basin is the homeland of the olive grove; the oldest olive presses date from several millennia before Christ. The importance of the olive and olive oil in many Mediterranean cultures is borne out by the legends that surround its origins and the holiness associated with it. According to the Greeks, the olive was a gift of Athena; the Jews consecrated their kings by anointing them with olive oil; and the olive branch has remained a symbol of peace ever since its origins in early Christian times. Favorably reassessed by modern dieticians, olive oil rules the table with regal equanimity, granting its blessings to every dish.

By Frank J. Prial

The Wines
of Italy

June 15, 2003

A DELIGHT FOR THE SENSES
While it is true that wine connoisseurs must have good palates, it is equally true that the quality of good wine does not reside solely in its taste. The first approach is visual (above), in order to appraise the color and the clarity, followed by an assessment of the bouquet and, finally, the taste.

Right, the castle at Badia a Passignano is the backdrop to the vineyards of Chianti. In the 19th century Baron Bettino Ricasoli was the first to perfect the grape varieties of Chianti – the full body of Sangiovese, the smoothness of Canaiolo and the perfume of Malvasia.

To a visitor, Italy can appear to be a single vast vineyard. For all practical purpose, it is. From the Alpine fastnesses high over the Valle d'Aosta to the rugged, sun-seared hills of Sicily, from the Alto Adige in the northeast to remote Sardinia, vines grow everywhere but on the faces of cliffs. In an area smaller than California, Italy currently produces a staggering 5.9 billion liters of wine, or about 160 million cases, a year. And this in spite of the fact that production has been declining for decades. The record crop, in 1980, came to 8.6 billion liters. Since then, per capita wine consumption in Italy has dropped from around 100 liters a year to 60.

Italy is a great vinous paradox. Its wine history goes back before recorded time. Wine has been an integral part of Italian life since the age of the Etruscans, long before the Roman era. The Greeks cultivated vines and made wines all over the Italian peninsula. The Greeks are gone, but their grapes remain: Greco bianco and Greco nero still thrive in Calabria in the far south, as does Grechetto, sometimes called Greco bianco di Perugia, in Umbria. In the heyday of the Roman empire, Italy was too small for all the grapes the Romans wanted to plant. Eventually, Rome's vines were found as far north as the Rhinegau, as far east as Mesopotamia, and in Spain and France to the west. Bordeaux was a center of Roman winemaking – they called it *Burdigala*. In the 4th century, Ausonius, the poet, consul and tutor to emperors, owned vines near what is now St.-Emilion, not far from the site of present-day Château Ausone.

But Italy is a young wine nation, too. In the 1950's, it was still known mostly for raw Chianti in "fiaschi," straw-covered bottles shaped like bowling balls. In the

A TRAIN AMONG THE VINES
Nowadays, grapes are harvested
mostly with the aid of machines
that reduce manual handling
of the boxes of grapes to
a minimum. In the Cinque Terre
the steep terrain rules out the
use of tractors, so farmers have
turned to unusual little
monorail trains (top left).
Top right, the grape harvest in
Franciacorta, an important wine
making area in the province
of Brescia that produces
a fine spumante.

cellars and in the vineyards, from Piedmont to the heel of the boot, little had changed since Charlemagne. Then it all changed, seemingly overnight. The wine critic Burton Anderson, who has lived in Italy for more than three decades, has watched with fascination as the country leaped into the modern era. "Techniques have evolved from antiquated to avant-garde with stunning rapidity," he wrote recently. "The challenge has been to keep abreast of the relentless changes during an era that has been characterized as Italy's modern renaissance of wine."

Anyone with the vaguest interest in wine can recall a time, not that long ago, when aside from the Chianti fiaschi, Italian wine meant bland Soave and Valpolicella and a handful of indifferent sparkling wines. Only a few specialists had a clue as to what the important grapes were. The modern era for Italian wines can be divided into three parts. In the first one, in the 50's, 60's and 70's, the new middle class in Europe and the Americas was discovering wine for the first time and becoming more sophisticated and demanding.

Faced with losing out to more advanced France and later California, the Italians updated their vineyard and cellar techniques as fast as they could. In the second period, serious Italian winemakers who had adopted French techniques and standards took what seemed at the time to be the next logical step; they planted French grapes: Cabernet sauvignon, Chardonnay and Sauvignon blanc, to name just three. Thus were born the so-called "super-Tuscans," blends of Cabernet and the traditional local grape, Sangiovese.

As the vintners grew bolder, some of the new — and very expensive — Tuscan wines were 100 percent Cabernet sauvignon. For a time it appeared that Cabernet and Chardonnay would one day edge out all the traditional Italian grapes and reign supreme in Italian vineyards. However, not all Italian winemakers bought into the fad for French grapes.

Even while he was winning plaudits for super-Tuscans like Tignanello and Solaia, the influential Tuscan winemaker Piero Antinori was saying that, ultimately, the region's reputation — indeed, Italy's reputation — would stand or fall on great wines made from indigenous grapes. That began the third period. All sense of inferiority dispelled, Italian producers began to take a second look at the native grapes and pronounced them good.

The Cabernet based super-Tuscans are still much in demand (and still expensive), but more and more, they have come to be rivaled by wines made entirely from Italian grapes. Since there are some 400 varieties of Italian grapes, that is not much of a limitation.

Some regions, Piedmont, for example, never totally succumbed to the temptation to use foreign grape varieties. The powerful Nebbiolo grape has always prevailed. It is the basis of all Barolo, one of the finest and longest-lived red wines in the world, and of Barbaresco, which often approaches Barolo in strength and finesse. But for all the depth and power in the wines made from Nebbiolo, which gets it name from "nebbia," or fog, it is not a prolific producer; it rarely provides more than three percent of Piedmont's annual grape crop.

The other famous, if lesser, Piedmont grapes are Barbera and Dolcetto, both of which are made into substantial wines that should be drunk within a few years after the harvest. In Tuscany, the great red grape — some say the only red grape — is Sangiovese. It is the only red grape permitted in Brunello di Montalcino and is always part of the blends for Chianti and Vino Nobile di Montepulciano. It is widely planted in Umbria and in the Marches and it can be found in Lombardy and south in Campania. It is used in most of the super-Tuscans, those that are not not entirely Cabernet, and it is part of Carmignano, usually a Cabernet-Sangiovese blend, which predated the appearance of the first super-Tuscans in the 1970's.

The name Sangiovese is derived from *sanguis Jovis*, or "blood of Jove" which hints at great antiquity. The writer Jancis Robinson has suggested that it may even have been known to the Etruscans. At the same time, she notes that the first historical mention of Sangiovese was in the 18th century when it became part of the first formalized recipe for Chianti. Other grapes in the original Chianti formula included Canaiolo, Mammolo and Colorino along with the white grape Trebbiano.

The current generation of Chiantis, especially the Chianti Classicos, bears little relation to the wines in the straw-covered bottles. For one thing, there is no longer any Trebbiano in the blend.

Trebbiano, it should be noted, is the most widely planted white grape in Italy. There are also immense plantings of Trebbiano in Southern France, where it is known as Ugni blanc. Perhaps familiarity does breed

IRRESISTIBLE APPEAL

The cultivation of roses among the vines (top right) may be practiced in order to attract certain insects: an agri-biological stratagem aimed at encouraging pollination. As it grows, the vine is "trained" and controlled in various ways, whose development depends on the characteristics of the climate and the terrain.
Top left, a Sicilian vineyard cultivated in the "ad alberello" style so that the overhanging crown of leaves protects the lower parts from the fiercest sunlight.

25

contempt because hardly anyone has anything good to say about it. A blending wine that is often shipped off in bulk, it is virtually unknown in the wine world when compared with Pinot grigio. Catarratto and Garganega are two other important Italian white wine grapes that are used mostly in blends or for making brandy.

The renewed interest in Italian grapes has sparked a renewed interest in Italy itself. There are disadvantaged regions in the south, in Campania, in Basilicata, in Apulia and Calabria, in Sicily and Sardinia too, where wines have always been made – and ignored by the sophisticates in Piedmont, Veneto and Tuscany. The powerful, intense, high-alcohol wines of the south had since time immemorial been shipped off and used to fill out and strengthen pale northern wines in poor or mediocre vintages. But modern winemaking techniques brought new life – and investors – to these regions and more local producers wanted to put their wine in bottles rather than tank trucks.

They were not without precedent. Wineries like Mastroberardino in Campania and Cosimo Taurino in Apulia had long been making big but complex wines in Southern Italy. The Duca di Salaparuta in Sicily and

Sella & Mosca in Sardinia had done the same. Beginning in the 80's, good wines began to flow out of these forgotten provinces, red wines, mostly, with structure and character and exceptionally reasonable prices. Importers and wine writers had to add new grape names to their vocabularies: in Southern Italy, Negroamaro, which means "black and bitter," and Aglianico which is said to derive from *vitis hellenica*, or Greek vine. In Sardinia, the most popular grape is Cannonau, a relative of Spain's Garnacha, and in Sicily, the current star is a grape called Nero d'Avola.

Winemakers from the north, even the prestigious Antinori clan, have flocked to these long underrated regions to buy up cheap land and start making strong wines at modest prices. If anything won new respect for Italian wines – other than the improvements to the wines themselves – it was the adoption of stringent quality control laws beginning in the 1960's. Before that, all of Italy was thought of as a producer of cheap wines with little or no heritage. The introduction of the DOC laws, followed by the DOCG changed all that. DOC stands for "denominazione di origine controllata;" DOCG for "denominazione di origine controllata e

**FROM THE FRUIT
TO THE BOTTLE**

Treading on grapes barefoot, although no longer done, is the method most respectful of the grape and its precious juice. The wine press, however, is an invention that dates back to ancient times; long before anyone thought of hygienic problems there was a need to invent an instrument capable of extracting the greatest possible quantity of must from the marc. Top right, an old wine press in the Museo del Vino at Torgiano in Umbria. Top left, a "marmonier" wine press, used for Champagnes and, in Italy, for sparkling white wines of the "champenois" variety. Facing page, a vineyard near Barolo in Piedmont.

**IN THE DARKNESS
OF THE CELLAR**

Long is the road that great
wines must take before they
arrive to enliven the table.
It is a route of repose and slow
maturation amid shadows
and silence. While modern
fiberglass, steel and cement
containers are rapidly gaining
ground, the strong point of the
traditional barrel (top left)
or the more modern barrique
keg (top right) lies
in their scented woods.
Bottom left, the cellar
of a restaurant;
right, a well stocked
"enoteca", or wine shop.

garantita." Just like France's AOC laws, DOC sets out
geographical zones such as Chianti. Basically, to qualify
for the DOC rating , a wine must come from where the
DOC name says it does. Valpolicella, for example, must
come from the Valpolicella DOC area in the Veneto
region in Northeast Italy. To get the DOCG rating, a
wine must meet certain quality standards that are higher than those required for the DOC rating. There are
lots of qualifiers of course, but the basic rules here hold
true. The word "classico" on a label means that the wine
comes from the place within the DOC zone where that
type of wine was first made. As the DOC zone grows,
more wines are allowed to use the rating. Only those
from the original zone can call themselves "classico."
As more sections of Italy get into the fine wine business,
there are more and more DOC and DOCG appellations
created. The laws, like most laws, become extremely
complicated. What is not complicated is the name and
reputation of the person who makes the wine. Famous
names in Italian wines are the best and the simplest
guarantees of quality. Names Like Antinori, Biondi
Santi, Ricasoli, Volpaia and Coltibuono in Tuscany; Aldo
Conterno, Vietti, Gaja and Bruno Ceretto in the

Piedmont; Masi and Quintarelli in the Veneto;
Lungarotti in Umbria, Mastroberardino in Campania,
and Cosimo Taurino in Apulia are guarantees of quality
and enjoyment that supersede any governmental or
quasi-governmental rating systems.

Lastly, there is the matter of price. It can be said
that, over the years, Italy has been responsible for the
best values in the world on good table wines. Italy has
its $300 Barolos and equally expensive old Chiantis. It
has its duds, too. No one can be considered truly well
versed in Italian wines until he or she can quote the
prices of rare examples of those wines in the market
that day. At the same time a wine enthusiast with only
$10 in his pocket will almost certainly find more wor-
thy bargains among the Italian wines than among any
others. Italy is the greatest source of wine bargains,
true wine bargains, in the world today.

———

FRANK J. PRIAL *has written the "Wine Talk" column in* The
New York Times *for three decades. "Decantations," a collection
of his recent columns, was published in 2001 (St. Martins Press).*

WINE IN THE BOTTLE,
WINE IN THE CARAFE

The dark glass of the bottles protects the wine, while the colors of the caps and the labels emphasize its qualities. An ample and well ordered cellar is a pleasure to behold. Laying bottles down horizontally is the best way to ensure long ageing, since the wine keeps the cork moist and prevents it from drying out or cracking.

Above, the sign outside an old hostelry in Lazio showing the typical "liter," the glass carafe used for pouring a guaranteed quantity of wine from the cask.

29

By Burton Bollag

Paradise in an
ALPINE WILDERNESS

September 10, 1989

In northern Italy, within sight of Mont Blanc, is the country's oldest natural reserve, the Gran Paradiso National Park. The park is named for one of the mountains within its confines, the highest entirely on Italian soil. And the name is particularly fitting. For the park is a paradise of unspoiled Alpine wilderness, filled with an incredible variety of plants, flowers and animals.

Throughout the summer and fall any reasonably fit visitor armed with a pair of hiking boots can see gentians, edelweiss, anemones, violets and literally hundreds of other wildflowers, including some species that exist nowhere else. Those willing to walk for several hours have a good chance of seeing chamois, ibex and marmots. The park extends into France, where it becomes the Vanoise National Park. The two reserves slope away on opposite sides of the ragged Alpine spine that runs southward from the Mont Blanc range to the Mediterranean, forming the border between France and Italy. Situated on the eastern slope, the Gran Paradiso is a two-and-a-half hour drive from either Milan or Geneva, in Switzerland, and a little less from Turin.

A friend and I went to the town of Cogne, the most popular gateway to the park, last June. There we met one of the park wardens, Luigi Fachin. Each of the 60 wardens is assigned to a particular area of the park, whose valleys, waterfalls and wildlife he comes to know intimately. Three years ago Mr. Fachin gave up a career as a computer analyst. Now his job is to monitor the park's animals in his sector and insure as best he can that visitors do not harm the park's environment. Mr. Fachin invited us to join him and a friend on a daylong hike through part of his sector. We met at 5:30 A.M. in the village of Lillaz and headed off toward the wide, U-shaped glacial valley of Urtier.

The warden said the valley through which the park boundary runs attracts botanists and flower lovers from around the world because of its rich, sometimes unique Alpine flora, like Haller's anemone. The valley is marred only by the high tension line that runs its length, bringing electricity from a French nuclear power plant to industry in Tuscany.

Our guide was an inexhaustible source of information. As we climbed past a natural pool showered by a powerful little waterfall that shot out of a rock gorge, Mr. Fachin pointed out a juniper sabine. This low evergreen bush has little blue poisonous berries. It used to be brewed as a herbal tea, taken to induce abortions, but the mixture sometimes proved fatal to the mother. He pointed out small carnivorous plants that digest insects to compensate for the lack of nitrogen in the soil. The pinguicole vulgaris has small purple flowers; the pinguicole alpine has white ones. We saw the small gentians with their blue five-petaled flower. A much taller red or yellow variety is harvested in the Alps to produce a liqueur.

Mr. Fachin showed us a rocky cliff, where the park's biggest nighttime predator, the le duc owl, had its nest. And he explained that another winged predator, the brown and white royal eagle, lives in pairs that change their nesting site every several years. We also learned that the ptarmigan, ermine and hare are the three animals living in the Gran Paradiso National Park that change the color of their coats from brown in summer to white in winter.

ON THE EDGE OF THE ABYSS

The ibex (facing page) is the true master of the rocks. Its hooves can cling to the slightest ledge, permitting it to make acrobatic leaps to and from the most unlikely ridges. Above, a rock grouse in its white winter plumage; top, its tracks in the snow.

We left the open, grassy Urtier Valley to enter the park proper and climb to higher ground. Our path took us first through a wooded area. Evergreens and larches predominate in the park. In autumn the large needles turn red and then golden yellow before falling. We had started at an altitude of about 5,000 feet. By 11 o'clock, at an altitude of about 7,500 feet, we reached the top of a grassy, rocky shoulder. Suddenly, Mr. Fachin called us over to the edge in a hushed voice. On the steep slope below us was a herd of about 80 chamois with their characteristic small black curved horns. They were females with their young, some no more than a week old.

The chamois, which are always more timid than ibex, were quickly aware of our presence and began running away. With great speed they crossed the slope below us and began climbing a much higher mountainside opposite us. In a few minutes we could see them crossing a snowfield several hundred yards above us. It would have taken a fit mountaineer more than an hour to cover the same distance.

We headed down by a different route. About a half-hour later we came upon a group of about 10 male ibex. The heavy, slightly curved horns of the oldest were almost a yard long. The biggest males let us approach as close as two or three yards. Mr. Fachin told us that after last winter's mild weather the park's population had increased to almost 4,000 ibex, 8,000 chamois and perhaps 7,000 marmots.

Hunted almost to extinction at the beginning of the last century, the ibex are now strictly protected. Like other European natural reserves, the Gran Paradiso allows no hunting to cull the herds, even though animal predators no longer exist. Instead, when a growing population puts too much pressure on the food supply, animals leave the park's boundaries in search of better grazing and are killed by hunters. Poaching, a constant problem, is severely punished. Mr. Fachin told us that two poachers had recently been fined about $ 80,000 – equivalent to about four years of an average salary – for having killed two female ibex that were suckling young.

We returned in the afternoon to Cogne, from where a visitor can head out in various directions. The most popular trip takes a visitor two miles up a gentle side valley, toward the permanently snow-covered Gran Paradiso Mountain, to the hamlet of Valnontey. It is the trailhead for a number of walks and has several simple hotels and good restaurants. There is also an interesting Alpine garden there, a naturalist's delight, with a large variety of labeled Alpine plants and flowers. The less ambitious can stroll along the almost flat valley floor in the direction of

**ETERNAL SNOWS
AND SPONTANEOUS FLORA**
The Gran Paradiso (left, an aerial view of the massif) is considered an "easy" peak by mountain climbers, as is proven by the feat accomplished by a certain abbot Henry in 1931, who said: "To persuade everyone to climb the Gran Paradiso and to prove that all can gain its summit, I made a fully convincing experiment. Guess what I had climb up there? A donkey. Yes, a donkey in flesh and blood. And that donkey climbed to the top very easily and got back down to the bottom again very easily too!" (For the record the animal's name was Cagliostro). But this episode hardly proves that the climb is kid's stuff. The Gran Paradiso is a tough, harsh environment, enlivened in the brief Alpine summer by the brilliant colors of the perennial flora. Above, *Gentiana asclepiadea*.

33

the boulder fields and glaciers that rise sharply toward the majestic 13,324-foot Gran Paradiso summit. For those with more stamina, one of the more popular outings is a roughly two-and-a-half hour hike, 3,000 feet up an old mule trail to the mountain refuge of Vittorio Sella. The refuge, formerly a royal hunting lodge, offers dormitory accommodations and hot meals in the summer and an unattended shelter for the rest of the year. This walk affords one of the best chances of seeing chamois and ibex. But there is a wide choice of trails to choose from. Although the trails are not usually well marked, orientation is not difficult. The visitor is soon above the tree line, which is at about 6,000 feet, and it is usually obvious in which direction the deep valley floor lies. However, licensed Alpine guides are available to lead climbers up a mountain peak or across the glaciers, which start at around 10,000 feet. Trained mountain

"accompaniers" offer nature walks at lower altitudes. Information can be obtained at the tourist bureaus or at the guides' offices in Cogne, Aosta or the ski resort of Courmayeur, near the southern entrance to the Mont Blanc Tunnel. In addition there is a cooperative of accompaniers whose specialty is something called "agritourism." They organize visits to mountain barns where cattle and goats are taken for summer grazing. The program includes demonstrations of cheese-making and a rustic meal.

The Gran Paradiso summit is a very popular destination for the casual alpinist. It is a long walk presenting no particular difficulties, but it can be strenuous and one must be equipped with crampons, ice pick and a rope, because a good part of the way is along glaciers. The most common approach is to spend a night in the

**LAND OF SAINTS
AND ROYAL HUNTERS**
Some of the old royal hunting
lodges (facing page, below)
now house the park rangers,
others are refuges for walkers,
hikers and climbers
(facing page, top,
the Vittorio Sella refuge).
Left , the mighty Roman bridge
at Pondel, near Aymavilles.
Above, the Romanesque
cloister of Sant'Orso in Aosta
(12th century), renowned
for its columns embellished
with carved scenes.

35

Sentinels of the Valley

The Valle d'Aosta's long feudal history has left many physical traces: fortresses, castles, fortifications, towers and aristocratic mansions, often splendidly conserved. This historic and architectural heritage includes about 150 buildings, generally located on dominant sites-- guarding the valleys or points of strategic importance-- which are important examples of medieval military and residential architecture.

The castle of Cly, for example, constructed in 1250 by Boniface of Challant and finally abandoned in the 17th century, is perched on a spur standing 782 meters above sea level and overlooks the town of Chambave. Its outer walls, still in good condition, enclose the keep, the chapel, the guardhouse and the residential buildings. The castle's decline was set in motion by the last owners, the Barons Roncas, who used part of the material to build their house in Chambave.

A double ring of crenelated walls defended by tall towers of various shapes encloses one of the best known castles in the Valle d'Aosta, the castle of Fénis, whose origins are unknown. The location, apparently not ideal for defense, has led to suggestions that the original construction, later transformed into a castle, was intended as a residence. Certainly, however, it went through numerous changes until taking on its current aspect in the 13th – 15th century under the counts of Challant. The interior, which contains some valuable frescoes, reflects the old owners' refined sense of luxury.

The castle of Issogne is also famed for its frescoes. From the outside the castle seems massive, severe, almost anonymous, but all visitors have to do is walk through the small entry and they are projected into the Middle Ages. The entrance hall and the inner portico are decorated with frescoes that reproduce with extraordinary freshness expressive scenes of everyday life and craft activities (the tailor's workshop, pharmacy, butcher shop, guardhouse, the fruit and vegetable market, as well as stores selling bread, meat, cheese and groceries).

The austere guardian of the Valle d'Aosta, the fortress of Bard controls access to the region from a high crag, carved out by the erosive power of the Dora Baltea river at the narrowest point of the valley floor. Built in the 11th century by Ottone of Bard as a toll station on wayfarers, it was fortified in the 13th century by Amedeo IV of Savoy and assumed a growing military importance in the centuries that followed. But today's construction is not the original structure. In May 1800 the garrison of the fortress put up stiff opposition to advancing French troops led by Napoleon Bonaparte. The French took 16 days to overcome this resistance and then only by trickery; they spread the road surface with manure and wrapped the wheels of the cannon with straw to muffle the sound. Once they defeated the beleaguered garrison, they razed the fortress to the ground to wipe out the sign of their humiliation. In 1830 Carlo Felice decided to have it rebuilt, creating one of the most interesting and best preserved works of 19th-century military architecture.

DEFENDING THE VALLEY

The Valle d'Aosta, an essentially mountainous region, frontier zone and crossroads, played a particular strategic and economic role over the centuries. From the 12th to the 15th century the counts of Challant, Bard, and Vallaise, feudal vassals of the House of Savoy, built defensive positions perched on the mountainsides and later constructed large complexes in which residential requirements prevailed over those of defense. From grim sentinels, in fact, many castles in the Aosta area were transformed into comfortable aristocratic palaces. Above, a fresco in the castle of Fénis that portrays Saint George battling the dragon. Right, the castle of Cly.

Vittorio Emanuele II refuge – a two-hour walk from the neighboring Valsavarenche Valley – and then leave early the next morning for the three-and-a-half hour trip to the summit. In the summer the refuge is almost always filled and reservations should be made several months in advance.

The Gran Paradiso National Park, established in 1922, was formerly a hunting reserve of Italy's kings. One of the most fascinating legacies of that period is the remaining stretches of hunting roads built to facilitate the kings' hunting forays.

Two years ago we made a three-day trip in the park, spending two nights in one of the unattended bivouacs, small huts with sleeping space for about a half-dozen people that dot the park. On the long return leg of the trip we had an unforgettable experience.

After crossing a difficult pass in intermittent fog, we saw before us a wide, boulder-strewn and desolate mountain plateau. But instead of the slow, painful going that we expected, we discovered a largely intact royal hunting road that made our advance an absolute pleasure. It was built of rock and earth and raised about a yard off the ground to negotiate the rough terrain in an almost straight line.

We imagined with awe the thousands of man-hours that had been spent during the 19th century, building such roads at these desolate altitudes, so that King Vittorio Emanuele II could more easily pursue his favorite pastime.

Although it is possible to enter the park from Piedmont in the south, the more common approach is from the Aosta Valley in the north. It is well worth combining a visit to the park with a trip through the valley.

This historic route of north-south passage through the Alps encompasses about a hundred castles and fortresses, displaying a rich variety of styles, along its 50-mile length. It also has a gambling casino at St. Vincent.

The valley offers a rich program of concerts and exhibitions in the summer. And in the region's capital, the city of Aosta, the visitor can see ruins of Roman buildings and monuments.

Tourism came late to the region, which helps explain why most towns and villages have retained their rustic Alpine appearance, including their ubiquitous heavy slate roofs. However tourism has been expanding steadily since the completion of the Mont Blanc Tunnel in 1964, two years after the completion of the St. Bernard Tunnel.

If the visitor looks backward on the climb out of the valley, there is a striking sight. On the opposite side of the valley, which climbs steadily and interminably to distant summits, are many dozens of rows of old terraces, still clearly discernible on the steep grassy slopes. Here grapevines, wheat and rye were grown, often with the help of complex networks of narrow irrigation canals, called "ru," which can still be found and hiked along. They are mute reminders of the great efforts that the inhabitants of this densely populated, rugged mountain region had to make in order to feed themselves in previous centuries.

_____

BURTON BOLLAG is a reporter for the Chronicle of Higher Education, *in Washington DC. He was a journalist in Europe for more than 20 years.*

**STONE AND WOOD
TO PROTECT FROM THE COLD**
In days gone by the austere mountain economy required that only local materials be used for construction. Facing page, rustic stone foundations support a chalet made of larch trunks. Above, a woman's hand has embroidered the drapes and placed flowers on the old window-ledge burnished by time.

The "Four 4000s"

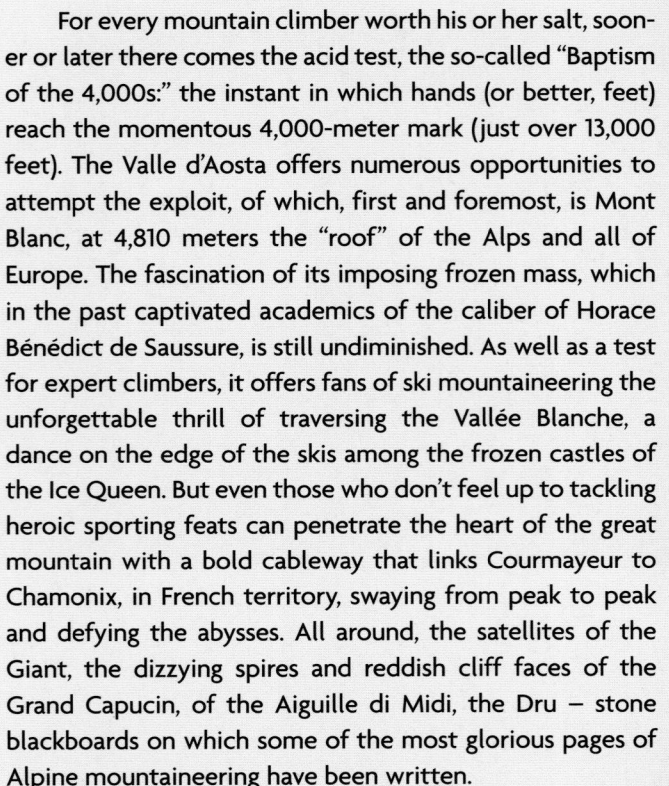

For every mountain climber worth his or her salt, sooner or later there comes the acid test, the so-called "Baptism of the 4,000s:" the instant in which hands (or better, feet) reach the momentous 4,000-meter mark (just over 13,000 feet). The Valle d'Aosta offers numerous opportunities to attempt the exploit, of which, first and foremost, is Mont Blanc, at 4,810 meters the "roof" of the Alps and all of Europe. The fascination of its imposing frozen mass, which in the past captivated academics of the caliber of Horace Bénédict de Saussure, is still undiminished. As well as a test for expert climbers, it offers fans of ski mountaineering the unforgettable thrill of traversing the Vallée Blanche, a dance on the edge of the skis among the frozen castles of the Ice Queen. But even those who don't feel up to tackling heroic sporting feats can penetrate the heart of the great mountain with a bold cableway that links Courmayeur to Chamonix, in French territory, swaying from peak to peak and defying the abysses. All around, the satellites of the Giant, the dizzying spires and reddish cliff faces of the Grand Capucin, of the Aiguille di Midi, the Dru – stone blackboards on which some of the most glorious pages of Alpine mountaineering have been written.

In Italian the word rosa usually means "pink," but not in the case of Monte Rosa. In fact this mountain, which is actually a massif that rises to the 4,633-meter peak called Punta Dufour, probably owes its name to the Celtic term *roiza*, which means "ice." On the top of Punta Gnifetti, Europe's highest mountain refuge stands firm. Visible with good binoculars even from the plain, it is dedicated to the mountain-climbing queen who tackled Alpine ascents – Queen Margherita of Savoy. The Monte Rosa massif also boasts the highest rock face in the Alps on its stern eastern side, soaring to a height of 2,500 meters.

From imposing massifs to the elegance of "the noblest rock in Europe," as the English writer and mountaineer John Ruskin defined Monte Cervino. On its treacherous rocks the local guide Jean Antoine Carrel and the Englishman Edward Whymper battled to win the honor of making the first ascent. Victory went to the Englishman, but the price was a high one: four of his companions did not return. The unmistakable outline of Monte Cervino, which dominates the Breuil basin, also forms the backdrop for the acrobatic maneuvers of the skiers on the slopes of the Plateau Rosa and the Piccolo Cervino, the big mountain's "little brother" which can be reached by cableway.

Finally there is the "Easy 4,000," the Gran Paradiso, so easy that some climbers with a touch of recklessness and a lot of imagination even scale it by mountain bike!

THE INTOXICATING THRILL OF THE HIGH COUNTRY
The rarified air leaves contours more marked and colors sharper, and climbers more short of breath. The environment of the high mountains has an irresistible appeal. Who could resist the fascination of the looming slopes of Monte Cervino, also known as the Matterhorn (right, top) or a thrilling ski run (right) amid the silence of eternal snows? Facing page, ski mountaineers beneath the Dente del Gigante (the Giant's Tooth), in the Mont Blanc group.

By Beth Archer Brombert

PIEDMONT'S
Many Pleasures

July 29, 1990

GREAT WINE COUNTRY

The rolling hills of Le Langhe (facing page) are covered with vineyards that produce some of Italy's noblest wines, including Barolo. Until the mid 19th century Piedmontese wines were generally sweet and the tables of aristocrats proudly featured the products of Bordeaux and Bourgogne. Then the marchioness Falletti of Barolo asked Louis Oudart, a renowned French enologist, to transform her wine and to bring it on to a par with French wines. Thus Barolo was born. Above, night view of Alba Cathedral.

Even if Piedmont did not have truffles, or one of the great national parks of Europe (Parco del Gran Paradiso), or the Borromean Islands, or the more refined and most varied regional cuisine in Italy, it would still be top of my list for travelers to Italy who have already made the grand tour between Rome and Venice. There are many ways of enjoying Piedmont: as a lover of alpine sports or, at less cost and less risk, as a walking nature lover, as a lover of wine, or of what the French call *vieilles pierres* – old buildings. Since I no longer consider snow and sliding pleasurable, I'll take my mountains in warm weather. A week's stay in late summer revealed the bucolic serenity of Lake Orta, where the loudest noise was an outboard motor; the wine country of "Le Langhe;" the pleasure palaces of the Savoy dynasty; striking medieval towns such as Saluzzo, Cherasco and Alba, and the Benedictine monastery of San Michele, a stone aerie perched 3,000 feet above the plain of Turin.

Driven by gluttony, we hastened first to the wine country in southern Piedmont, hoping to work off the acquired calories as we moved north. Le Langhe, lying south of the Tanaro River, is the home of the noble Nebbiolo grape that evolves into Barolo and Barbaresco wines. The famous Barbera wine comes from a grape of the same name. The term Langhe refers to the strange conical hills that rise and fall across the landscape. Ringed on three sides by ascending curves of terraced vines, these hills display an extraordinary geometry of half circles and verticals. There is also a Bassa Langa, where the hazelnut tree is as prevalent in the higher altitude and colder climate as the vine-stock lower down. Indeed, the hazelnut tree is to Piedmont what

the olive tree is to Tuscany. Immediately northeast of the Bassa Langa and separated from it by the Tanaro River is the region called Roero, similarly wine-producing, with which the two Langhe are generally coupled.

Descriptively named *Pedemontium*, "at the foot of the mountain," in the early Middle Ages, Piedmont does indeed unfold from a half circle of perennially snow-covered Alps. Beneath them, stretching eastward, is a variegated landscape of hills and valleys, alpine lakes and rice paddies, fabled vineyards and medieval fortresses. Piedmont was integrated into Charlemagne's Holy Roman Empire in the eighth century, was repeatedly raided by Saracens and Hungarians in the 10th, became the fief of the Duke of Savoy in the 15th and eventually a kingdom ruled by the House of Savoy. Its possessions once included Nice, the Mediterranean coast as far south as Genoa, and Sardinia. In 1861 Piedmont's king became the first sovereign of a united Italy.

Piedmont has long since retreated from its royal past into its present regional boundaries, but each of its eight very distinct provinces still inspires chauvinistic allegiance to its dialect, its geography, its folklore. On the main routes to Italy from France and Switzerland since ancient times many more tourists drive through than stop, which means Piedmont is one of the few regions of Italy not overrun by foreigners; Italians comprise the majority of its visitors.

In the 18th and 19th centuries, the carriage trade of Europe built villas on Piedmont's lake shores, and Italophiles like Stendhal and Balzac wrote rapturously about the region. "What is there to say about Lake Maggiore and the Borromean Islands," Stendhal asks, "except to pity those people who are not crazy about them?"

DELICACIES FROM ALBA

The words surrounding the coat of arms say "Order of the Knights of the Truffle and the Wines of Alba" – a fraternity of gourmets and wine lovers that, by dint of tastings and dinners, fights its battle in favor of two of Alba's best known products. These last include at least a third, nougat, displayed like jewelry in the window of an old bar-patisserie in the capital city of the Langhe (top).

One of our first destinations was the truffle and wine capital of Piedmont, the late medieval town of Alba, which stands between the Langhe and Roero. It boasts a Romanesque cathedral whose lofty dimensions suggest Alba's early importance. Verduno, surrounded by vineyards, is a village of some 400 souls, nestling beneath its early 16th-century castle. The few rooms open to guests are in the section of the castle rebuilt in 1740 by Filippo Juvara, the architect associated with most of the palaces commissioned by the House of Savoy. The walls are covered with delightful memorabilia of the Sabaudi, as members of the Savoy dynasty are known. In 1838 King Charles Albert bought the castle to serve as a hunting lodge and restored its vineyards, which today produce Barolo and the much rarer Pelaverga, a spicy ruby-red, deeply fragrant and drunk young. Except for modern plumbing, the rooms have changed little since the Sabaudi hunted and held their assignations there. Even if the castle was once owned by royalty, it was far from regal, more like a country villa, and now very much family style. If an elevator is more important than atmosphere, better to stay in Alba. From either Verduno or Alba, one can easily do what the locals call "Andar per Langhe," wander up and down the territory. Following are some highlights.

Walking through the broad curbless streets of Cherasco one has the impression that time stopped after Napoleon came through in April 1796. More than a century earlier, noble families fleeing the plague in Turin built their fine houses along the arcaded main street and rebuilt the town on the Roman grid pattern. A collection of splendid buildings, some predating this period, makes for a delightful half-day's visit.

A handsome avenue of sycamores precedes the 14th-century Visconti Castle, whose square brick towers stand at the periphery of the town. Notice also the Romanesque church of St. Peter, with heads of saints in the niches of the facade, the 1672 church of St. Augustine, whose altar is considered a Baroque masterpiece, and, from the same period, the Madonna del Popolo and its gorgeous cupola. On the main street, the Confetteria Barbero is a landmark for delicate pastries and baci di Cherasco, toasted chopped hazelnuts in dark chocolate. Headquarters of the International Snail Breeders Association, Cherasco is also the place for tasting snails, "alla Cherasca," in one of its attractive restaurants.

The castle of Barolo dates to the 10th century and offers a panoramic view of the countryside and famous vineyards.

Continuing south to Dogliani, one comes to the Alta Langa. By cutting across to the parallel eastern arm of the road to Alba, one can make a lovely loop along the strada panoramica through Bossolasco. Along the

way are the majestic towers and unscaleable brick walls of Serralunga d'Alba, as perfect a castle-fortress as one could imagine outside the pages of a tale of chivalry, which was built around 1350 to protect the castle of Barolo.

The austere castle of Grinzane Cavour, dating from the 13th century, and in the 19th the home of the great statesman Camillo Cavour, stands six miles north of Serralunga. Surrounded by terraced vineyards, it now houses an excellent restaurant devoted to Piedmontese specialties, an extensive enoteca and a hall devoted to the truffle and to its first scientific investigator, Alfonso Ciccarelli.
Along the Salita di Castello (easier downhill; take the slightly less steep Via Valoria, on the left, going up), are the monuments that make Saluzzo a major discovery. Make sure to see the little 13th-century church and cloister of San Giovanni on a cobbled square with a well at its center, and the Renaissance mansion known simply as Casa Cavassa, in memory of its former proprietor, Galeazzo Cavassa, vicar general of the marquisate. All along the Salita al Castello are narrow medieval houses sandwiched between grander Renaissance dwellings with frescoed facades, the 1482 Municipal Palace and bell tower, and below, flowering terraces and inviting cafes and antique shops.

During our trip, two nights in the luxurious wooded quiet of Villa Sassi, on the hilly east bank of the Po, afforded easy access to Turin's suburban monuments without having to fight the city's heavy midtown traffic. Above Villa Sassi is the royal basilica and burial crypt of Superga, the 1716 masterwork by Filippo Juvara. The crypt, like the church above it, in the form of a Greek cross, has floors and walls covered in illusionistic yellow and black marble designs.
About 22 miles due west of Turin is the amazing Benedictine construction known as the Sacra di San Michele. Take the tangenziale (connector) out of Turin 1.8 miles from the toll booths, then go right toward Rivoli and from there toward Avigliana and Susa. At the sign for Laghi di Avigliana, turn left. At the railroad crossing is a sign for San Michele, 7.5 miles up a wooded winding road whose speed limit of 6.25 miles per hour should be taken seriously. Once at the top, park and continue walking; it will be worth it.
However intrepid Benedictine builders were elsewhere in Europe, San Michele surpasses anything I have seen, from Mont St.-Michel in France to Pannonhalma in Hungary. Hewn into the summit of a peak towering over the valley floor, the abbey commands the entire countryside between Susa and Turin, with vertiginous views through the church's flying buttresses. Access to the church is up the forbidding "scalone dei

THE STATESMAN FACTOTUM
The great architect of Italian unification, Camillo Benso, Count of Cavour, had a host of interests. In the rural peace of Castle Grinzane he pursued the latest developments in agricultural innovation and wine making techniques. Today the castle is home to the Enoteca del Piemonte, a regional body for the promotion of local wines.

"A delightful little lake at the foot of Monte Rosa, an island... coquettish and simple..." This was how Honoré de Balzac described the Lago d'Orta (on the following pages). A few strokes of the oars away lies the island of San Giulio, where the Basilica di San Giulio is the venue for classical music concerts organized by the celebrated "Settimane musicali" event based in nearby Stresa.

morti," the staircase by which deceased monks left the abbey, carved out of the raw rock face beside it. Go on a clear day.

The last days of our stay in Piedmont were given over to Lago d'Orta, a tiny chip, so to speak, off the block of nearby Lago Maggiore. The village of Orta sits on a tiny promontory above this little finger of a lake ringed with thickly wooded hills, its few narrow streets passing beneath charming old houses and opening onto the lakefront Piazza Motta, which is more like a large terrace. A 16th-century town hall faces the lake, and all around are outdoor cafés. A walk up the cobbled street perpendicular to the piazza leads 1,312 feet above it to Sacro Monte (one can also drive along the main road), where 20 rococo chapels contain life-size terra cotta figures depicting scenes from Scripture. Just opposite the piazza is the miniature island of San Giulio rising out of the water like a mirage. Small boats make frequent crossings in 10 minutes to the reality of

a few stunning private villas, palm trees, magnolias, three year-round families who run the shops and restaurant, and 32 Benedictine nuns who remain for life in the convent attached to the 12th-century Romanesque basilica of San Giulio. It is a perfect place for lunch and a walk along the Via Alla Basilica that circles the island.

Piedmont cannot yet compete with Tuscany in the realm of three-star restaurants and charming inns. But it certainly holds its own when it comes to landscapes, monuments, refined food and great wine. Few regions can offer a range of pleasures that include high mountains, authentic villages, historic towns, ravishing lake resorts and ancient abbeys within so small an area.

———

BETH ARCHER BROMBERT, author of "Edouard Manet: Rebel in a Frock Coat, *spends summers in a village near Siena. She is presently working on a memoir of her years in Italy.*

PIEDMONT'S
MANY PLEASURES

THE SACRA DI SAN MICHELE
Perched on the summit of Monte Pirchiriano (facing page), the Sacra di San Michele watches over the mouth of the Valle di Susa, a few kilometers from Turin. The abbey was founded around 1000 A.D. by Benedictine monks. In spring, when the rice fields are flooded, the plain is transformed into an immense stretch of water made dazzlingly bright by the sunlight. Every so often a heron spreads its wings and takes to flight. The scene may look like the Far East it is actually southern Piedmont.

By Alexander Stille

The Two TURINS

August 19, 2003

**UNDER THE ARCADES
OF OLD TURIN**

A typical feature of
Piedmontese cities, the arcades
are a great convenience
because you can stroll, shop
and meet a friend even
if it's raining or cold.
The arcades that surround
the main avenues and squares
of Turin offer some truly special
temptations: the patisseries,
where for centuries they have
been using cocoa to produce
irresistible handmade chocolate
confectionery; and the old
cafés redolent of the days
of the Savoy dynasty.
In one of these cafés, toward
the end of the 18th century,
they invented Vermouth,
the traditional aromatic wine
that conquered the world.
Not to be missed is a visit
to the "Al Bicerin" café to taste
the eponymous chocolate- and
coffee-flavored drink.

Although one of the largest and most handsome cities in Italy, Turin is unknown to most people visiting Italy, the equivalent of Edgar Allan Poe's "Purloined Letter," a well-kept secret left out in plain view. This may well be because, at first glance, Turin seems so little "Italian:" its wide elegant boulevards, long and straight, in rational, grid formation, lined with imposing 19th century apartment buildings with Mansard roofs and French doors, remind people more of Paris than the labyrinthine tangle of narrow medieval alleyways characteristic of the center of so many Italian cities. Its best museum hosts a collection of Egyptian mummies and artifacts rather than works of Italian art. Turin is best known as the home of the Fiat car company and the Italian automobile industry rather than as the city of Michelangelo, Raphael, Leonardo or Bernini. Yet, paradoxically, Turin is at the same time the most Italian of cities. It was the home of Italy's royal family, the House of Savoy; it led the drive for the unification of Italy and it was Italy's first national capital, between 1861 and 1865, when the seat of government was moved, first to Florence, and then to Rome, when the whole of Italy was unified in 1870.

The "otherness" of Turin, however, is not purely imaginary. Nestled against the Alps on Italy's northwestern extreme, the region of Piemonte (of which Turin is the capital) shares a border with France and in its long history as the Duchy of Savoy was closely tied to France in the centuries before there was an Italy. Indeed, until the second half of the 19th century, the city's educated classes were more likely to speak French than Italian. Count Camillo Cavour, Italy's first prime minister, is reported to have had a rather uncertain grasp of the lan-

...guage. The Piedmontese pride themselves on their difference from other Italians, emphasizing their efficiency, promptness and love of organization. Strict Turinese families of the old school sometimes used to force their children to sit up straight at table by making them hold up a stick placed between their back and their chair throughout meals – a far cry from the care-free, easy-going, rule-breaking Italian that most people associate with Italy. And other Italians complain that the Turinese are cold, stiff and unwelcoming.

But Turin's differentness is, in fact, one of the things that makes it extremely Italian. Since Italy was a patchwork of different city-states, principalities, duchies, kingdoms and republics for centuries before being united, each has its own peculiar history, most as "impure" and "un-Italian" as Turin and Piedmont's, many having spent centuries living under foreign domination (the Arabs, the Spanish, the Austrians) and speaking dialects incomprehensible to most Italians.

Despite Turin's fame as an industrial city, its pleasures are not to be underestimated. The city has one of the most favorable natural settings in Italy. It is located at the juncture of two rivers, the Po and the Dora as well as in the foothills of the Alps, so water runs through the city and one has magnificent views of snow-capped mountains in the distance. Even though it is a city of a million people, nature seems very close: in about ten minutes drive from the city center you find yourself in green hills and rolling countryside. Piedmont makes some of the very best wines in Italy – Barolo (the "king" of Italian wines), Barbaresco, Barbera and Gattinara, to name a few. And its food is equally good, arguably better than the much ballyhooed food of Bologna. Turin is the seat of Italy's premier food show, Il "Salone del Gusto," sponsored by the Slow Food movement, which brings together small, traditional food makers from around the world Italy with restaurateurs and food importers the world over (the food show is held in the former Fiat factory on the edge of the city, which was converted during the 1980's by the architect Renzo Piano into an exhibition space, and serves as convention center, art gallery and a movie complex with 11 screens).

Those put off by Turin's label as the "Detroit of Italy," will miss a city center with a rich and important architectural core. Like many Italian cities, Turin was founded in Roman times, as *Augusta Taurinorum*, and two of the four ancient Roman gates to the city survive. The city enjoyed a major revival in the 16th century when the dukes of Savoy moved their capital here from Chambéry, France. One of the Roman gates was incorporated into a medieval castle in what is now Piazza Castello, in the heart of the city. But the city's principal

A FUTURISTIC "BUBBLE" The roof of the Fiat plant at Lingotto used to house a test track for the cars. Today it is topped by architect Renzo Piano's innovative construction known as the "bubble," a glass and steel meeting room from which you can enjoy the spectacular panorama of the Alpine chain. The Lingotto plant also houses the Pinacoteca Gianni e Marella Agnelli, a valuable collection of paintings that Turin's most famous son gifted to his city in 2002. Among other works, the gallery contains six canvases by Canaletto, seven by Matisse, two by Picasso and some exceptional examples of Italian Futurist art.

architectural masterpieces are Baroque buildings from the late 17th and early 18th centuries. Indeed, Piedmontese baroque, much of it concentrated in and around Turin, may be the most interesting and innovative answer to the Roman Baroque architecture of Gianlorenzo Bernini and Francesco Borromini.

The great court architect of Turin, Guarino Guarini (1624-1683), who was also a brilliant mathematician, created extraordinary geometries of architectural form. His greatest masterpiece is probably the Cappella della Sindone, the Chapel of the Holy Shroud, created to house the shroud in which the body of Christ was supposedly wrapped. Built in an unusual triangular form, the chapel is sheathed in black marble, which is then flooded with light through the dome. The ribbing of the dome rises in a dizzying series of circles, semi-circles and hexagons that criss-cross one another, rising toward the star-shaped base of the lantern of the dome. Tragically, the chapel was severely damaged in an electrical fire in 1997; the shroud, which was not stored in Guarini's chapel, was unharmed. While conservators attempt to restore Guarini's masterpiece, visitors can console themselves by visiting Guarini's church of San Lorenzo, with an almost equally complex geometrical dome, as well as the Palazzo Carignano, a handsome brick palace with an undulating Baroque façade, which served as Italy's first parliament.

Of equal interest are the buildings of Filippo Juvara, who became the court architect of the Savoys in 1714. Juvara built several churches in Turin, and designed the façade of Palazzo Madama, a royal residence in Turin's central square which encapsulates much of its history. Its core is the two towers of the city's ancient Roman gates which were then incorporated into the medieval castle, on to which Juvara added a rich and elegant Baroque façade. But perhaps the most spectacular example of Juvara's work in Turin is the royal hunting lodge just outside of town at Stupinigi, the Savoys' equivalent of Versailles, a huge, yet graceful palace with four long arms extending like spokes from a circular structure at its center topped by a magnificent statue of a stag with antlers. The city grew rapidly in the 19th century when it became the political center of Italy as well one of the country's few industrial centers, growing from 200,000 to half a million people in the second half of the 19th century. The city's medieval and Baroque buildings were suddenly linked together on a rectangular grid of straight streets and avenues, lined with porticos, hosting elegant shops and cafés. Via Roma — generously named after the new national capital — became the city's central artery, going from the Savoys' old Royal Palace to the train station at Porta Nuova (the new gate). The street knits together many of the city's grandest old palaces and squares, Palazzo Madama, Palazzo

RESERVED FOR THE LADIES

The name Palazzo Madama goes back to the 18th century when, having lost its defensive function, the building became the residence of the royal "Mesdames," Christine of France and after her Maria Giovanna of Savoy-Nemours, the wife of Carlo Emanuele II.

The Turinese poet Guido Gozzano (1883-1916) wrote that Palazzo Madama "is a synthesis in stone of Turin's entire past, from the days of its origin and the Roman period to the days of our Risorgimento."

In fact the building includes the towers of the Roman Praetorian Gate, the 15th-century castle and the extensions designed by Filippo Juvara.

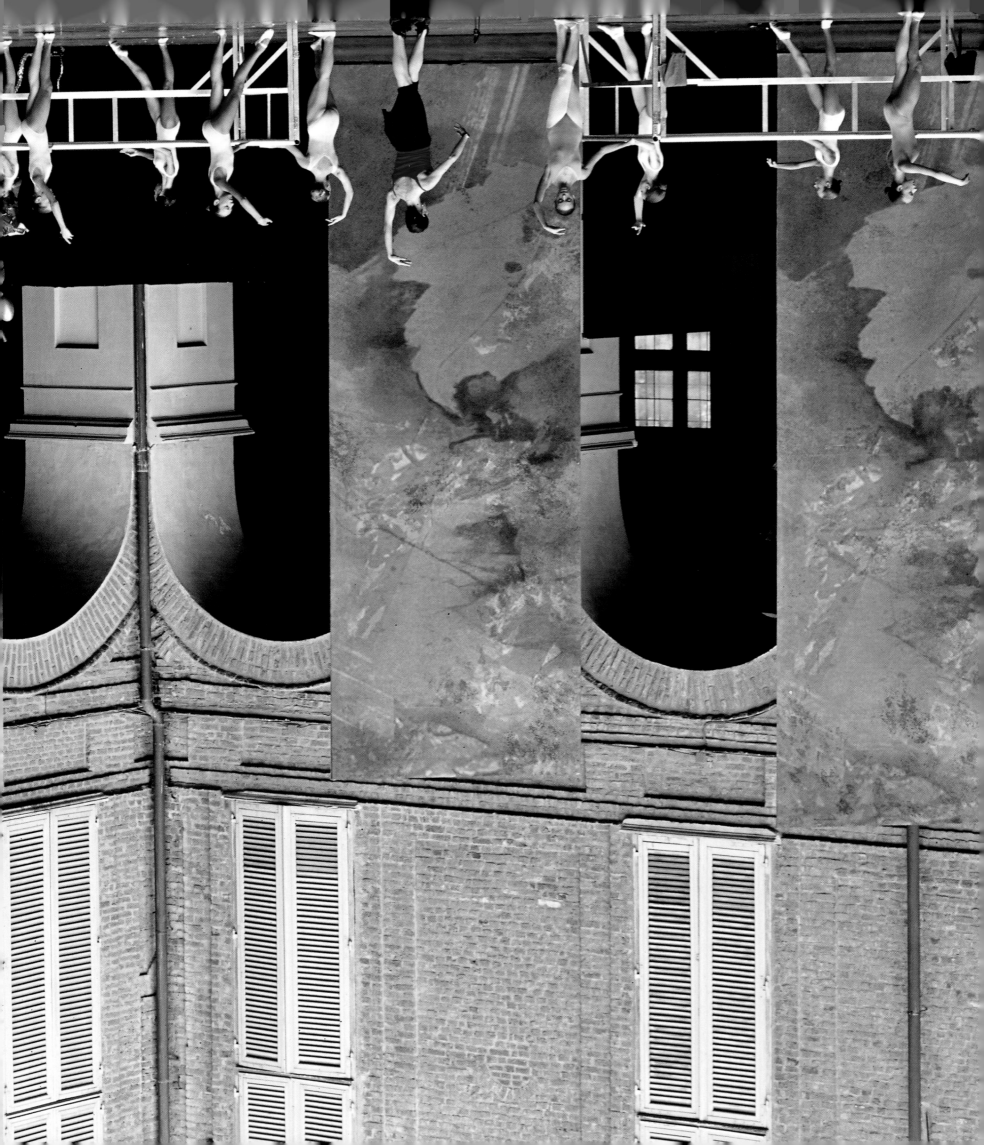

Carignano, the Egyptian Museum and Piazza Carlo Felice along a grand new axis.

For all the seeming rationality that 19th century urbanism tried to impose on the city, there are strange and dark elements to Turin that greatly add to its fascination. The philosopher Frederick Nietzsche was living in Turin when he suddenly went insane in 1889. Of course, it was a symptom of a degenerative case of syphilis but somehow the setting seems fitting. Turin was one of the favorite subjects of the great surrealist painter Giorgio De Chirico, who called Turin a "monarchical and fluvial city:" fluvial because of the rivers winding through it, monarchical because of the countless reminders of the House of Savoy. De Chirico's surreal cityscapes, with long empty boulevards and grand, heroic monuments are paintings of Turin.

Turin is known for its esoteric leanings, famous for its mediums and magi. Perhaps because it houses the Shroud, Turin has always been the object of much mystical speculation. Some believe that the holy grail and the true cross are buried somewhere here. The Savoys hosted the so-called prophet Nostradamus in the 16th century and sponsored alchemical experiments in the basement of Palazzo Madama (the "alchemical grottoes" where these took place are open to the public). The royal family began its world-class collection of Egyptian antiquities in the 18th century because of a legend (propagated by a bogus Renaissance "translation" of Egyptian texts) that the ancient Egyptians had founded Turin. To this day, followers of the occult consider Turin a "magic city," strategically placed on the corner of a "white magic" triangle together with Prague and Lyon as well as on a "black magic" triangle with San Francisco and London.

This somewhat mad, extravagant element of Turin's personality finds its physical expression in its largest and most famous architectural monument, the Mole Antonelliana, a pioneering, 19th-century skyscraper that soars some five hundred feet in the air. The building's name literally means "Antonelli's Pile," named for its architect Alessandro Antonelli. Almost half the height of the Empire State Building in New York and built more than half a century earlier, the Mole Antonelliana was the largest stone structure in Europe until relatively recently. Its design is highly eccentric, resembling fantasy renditions of ancient Mesopotamian architecture rather than any real building. It has a broad, rectangular base, out of which rises a massive rectangular cupola that slopes gradually into a cone shape, topped by a structure that looks like two ancient Greek temples stacked on top of each other hundreds of feet in the air, out of which rises a stone spire.

The building was originally conceived in 1863 as the syn-

SYLPHS BEFORE
THE ANCIENT WALLS
Left, the graceful pirouettes
of a corps de ballet against
the austere background of the
courtyard of the Palazzo Reale.
This 17th-century building was
the residence of the dukes
of Savoy, the kings of Sardinia
and, until 1865, of the kings
of Italy. The gardens were
designed by André Le Nôtre,
the architect who also created
the gardens of Versailles.

agogue for Turin's Jewish Community, which accounts for its neo-Mesopotamian air. The city's Jews wanted a grand new building to celebrate their emancipation from the ghetto and their status as citizens, but Antonelli spun wildly out of control. The original design called for a building about 150 feet high (47 meters), and the local Jews were alarmed to discover that Antonelli had set about building something more than twice that height, well beyond both their means and needs. The project took about thirty years to complete as Antonelli had to search for new sponsors for the project as he continually modified the design to make the building bigger. Finally, he convinced the city of Turin to complete it as a monument to King Victor Emanuel. To make it worthy of this honor Antonelli added another 120 feet (40 meters) in height to the building, which was completed in 1899 by Antonelli's son 16 years after the architect's death. Finding a proper use for the building — much more impressive from the outside than the inside — has been a headache for the city. For many years it housed a museum of the Italian Risorgimento and now holds a Museum of the Cinema.

Yet Antonelli's grand folly shows a side of impractical dreaminess to a city much dedicated to work and industry and which became, along with Milan and Genoa, part of Italy's industrial triangle in the early 20th century. With a large working class population, Turin became a center of radical politics and remained something of a bastion of anti-fascist culture during the years of fascism. The Einaudi publishing house became the center for a number of anti-fascist writers and intellectuals, including Cesare Pavese, Leone and Natalia Ginzburg, Carlo Levi, Italo Calvino and Primo Levi. Turin lost its last connection to the royal family in 1946, when Italy voted to get rid of the monarchy and the Savoys went into exile. The city continued to grow after World War II, its factories attracting hundreds of thousands of Southern Italians who migrated North in search of work. But from a peak population of 1.1 million in the 1970's, Turin has lost about 150,000 residents as some Italian sectors moved from industrial to post-industrial. Fiat has let go tens of thousands of workers. The city's bid for the 2006 winter Olympics is part of an ambitious plan to refashion Turin's economy, make international culture and tourism a more important economic element and to open up a city that has been content to keep its pleasures and its beauties to itself.

ALEXANDER STILLE is the author of "Benevolence and Betrayal: Five Italian-Jewish Families Under Fascism" *(Picador) and* "Excellent Cadavers: The Mafia and the Death of the First Italian Republic" *(Vintage). He is a frequent contributor to* The Times.

THE FACE OF THE REDEEMER
Since 1578 Turin Cathedral has been home to one of the holiest and most controversial relics in Christendom: the Shroud. Since then the sacred winding sheet that is said to portray the features of Jesus has left the city on only two occasions. In 1706 it was removed to Genoa upon the approach of a French army about to lay siege to Turin and between 1939 and 1946, in anticipation of the outbreak of the Second World War, it was transferred to the sanctuary of Montevergine, in Campania. The photographs show the outside and the inside of the dome of the Chapel of the Shroud.

The splendors and riches of the Savoy residences

TURINESE BAROQUE
In 1729 Vittorio Amedeo II commissioned Filippo Juvara to create the Palazzina di Caccia at Stupinigi. The architect's design reflects all the fundamental concepts of his art, which was inspired by a clever use of light and space. In addition, Juvara personally supervised the design of the interiors and the selection of paintings and sculptures.

A disconsolate Venetian ambassador, describing the condition of Piedmont in the mid 16th century, lamented: "This part of the country, most beautiful not long ago, is now in such poor case that there remains no trace of what it once was." Such was the portrait of a region that had become little more than a battlefield, ruined by the incursions of the French and Spanish armies and unable to get back on its feet. The long-awaited revival came about under Emanuele Filiberto of Savoy, nicknamed "ironhead" for his stubborn determination, who managed regain possession of his lands under the terms of the 1559 peace of Chateau-Cambrésis. Four years later the royal court was transferred from Chambéry to Turin, thus launching one of the most ambitious urban renewal plans in Europe, which continued for another two centuries.

With the construction of the Palazzo Reale, Palazzo Madama and Palazzo Carignano it soon became obvious that these important centers of political, military and administrative power had to be linked by roads. Then it became equally evident that these links would have to be extended to the sumptuous villas — used for hunting, social occasions, and relaxation by the royal family — scattered here and there in the surrounding countryside.

Some of these country residences involved modernizing pre-existing structures, such as the castles of Rivoli, Racconigi, Moncalieri and Agliè, while others were built from scratch by talented architects. In 1659 Carlo Emanuele II called in Amedeo di Castellamonte to create a complex devoted to his favorite pastime, hunting. The choice fell on a small town just outside Turin, which was renamed Venaria Reale ("the royal hunting estate"). This luxurious building, named for Diana the goddess of the hunt, was the model for Versailles.

The 18th century Palazzina di Caccia (Hunting Lodge) at Stupinigi, only four miles outside Turin, is one of architect Filippo Juvara's masterpieces. "Hunting Lodge" is something of an understatement, given that had 137 rooms and a huge area of well over 33,000 square yards. On the top of the domed roof stands the statue of a stag, perhaps to emphasize the original purpose of this building; but, by a twist of fate, the surrounding park is now a nature reserve whose woodlands are full of hares, squirrels, foxes and weasels, all finally safe from lethal pursuit.

Today Stupinigi is the home of the Museum of Art and Furnishings, with furniture, paintings and objects of the finest quality from the Palazzina as well as from other residences once owned by the Savoy family.

LIFE IS A SHOW

Inside the Mole, the Museo del Cinema plunges the visitor into a timeless, dream-like ambience. Period posters, reproductions of famous sets, cult objects that belonged to famous stars, images on screen that trace the history of the 20th century as seen through the lens of the movie camera – a pleasure not to be missed for devotees of the silver screen.

By Sarah Ferrell

The Idyllic Islands of
LAKE MAGGIORE

July 19, 1981

By and large, the Borromeos are a lucky lot. Over the centuries the family has been rich (banking), powerful (politics) and certifiably pious (St. Charles Borromeo, whose relics are in Milan Cathedral, was one of their number). Perhaps best of all, they have, since the 12th century, been the proprietors of the Borromean Islands, a handful of tiny specks of land afloat in northern Italy's Lake Maggiore, within sight of the bustling resort town of Stresa.

Of the three major islands (insofar as anything so small can be major), two – Isola Madre and Isola Bella – remain Borromean domains, although the Borromeos will let tourists play on them. The third, Isola Superiore, better known as Isola dei Pescatori, is now part of the Commune of Stresa, but fishermen lived here as long ago as Neolithic times and established effective ownership long before the Borromeos arrived.

Now Stresa and its lakefront neighbors have many attractions – easy access to Milan, hotels in all categories, a glamorous history (royalty used to holiday on Lake Maggiore, before the age of mass tourism), even a certain lingering international glitter. But my husband and I share a taste for the slightly down-at-the-heel. We wanted something less chic. Pescatori seemed to be just the right size (the island is roughly rectangular, and about one New York City block in area) and to offer just the right number of accommodations – there is a small hotel at each end, and a half dozen cafes in the middle. Frequent boat service in all directions would allow us to poke around the other islands and the shore resorts at our leisure.

Since it was early afternoon we decided to stay on our own island, about which we had already begun to feel proprietary. We strolled past umbrella-shaded souvenir stalls offering long scarves of ersatz silk and statues of the Virgin, Jesus and Pope John XXIII framed in seashells. A few fishing boats, with the elongated prows and halfcanopies of canvas typical of this part of the world, were drawn up on the shingle-and-broken-tile beach near a breakwater adorned with a green Madonna. Pink and green nets were hung out to dry, and brightly patterned silk scarves flew as banners from masts. It was a scene of idyllic picturesqueness, marred only by a small girl wearing a sweater emblazoned "Alcatraz College."

We sat and drank beer in a cafe adjacent to the public boat pier and watched the boats come and go, bringing in groups of tourists who fell upon the souvenir stalls. There were cats to watch, too – the cat population of Pescatori would seem to be several times that of the human population of 80 or so. A ratty-looking French poodle worked valiantly to keep them in line, but each cat he started would disappear up a steep, narrow alley, and another would take its place. An enormous sidewheeler passed, coming, we guessed, from Switzerland since it appeared on no local schedules. We ordered more beer.

The next morning, after we had watched fish jump as we sipped our coffee on the terrace, we set out for a close look at Isola Bella. We were on an early boat, and it was just as well – Isola Bella fills up fast. The ice-cream and souvenir vendors were still rubbing the sleep out of their eyes when we arrived and we passed them unnoticed.

ON THE TRAIL OF THE GRAND TOUR

Italy has many lakes, but there is only one Lake Maggiore, a fact well known to the travelers of earlier centuries. The cosmopolitan Englishman Samuel Butler called it "the most beautiful of all lakes" and Stendhal compared it to the bay of Naples. In fact, Lake Maggiore offers visitors a triptych of thrilling colors – the deep blue of the water, the green of the hills and the dark hues of the mountains. In the center lies the small, yet highly singular archipelago of the Borromeo Islands.

Although by now only few
residents on the Isola dei
Pescatori (Fishermen's Island)
still engage in the activity that
gave the place its name,
the local restaurants still offer
mainly fish dishes,
plus a view of the lake.
Above, fish drying in the sun.
Top, right. A view
of the island's old houses.

The greater part of Isola Bella is taken up by a 17th-century palace and gardens built by Count Vitaliano Borromeo, who also named the island in honor of his wife, Isabella. The exterior of the palace is restrained – for baroque – its blockiness relieved by classically ordered cornices. Once inside, it is necessary to join a group, but since group follows fast upon group, it is easy to drift from one to another to proceed at your own pace.

The tour opens with the Armory, which contains no surprises, then proceeds upstairs to the Medallion Room, named for the carved and gilded ornamental plaques that show scenes from the life of St. Charles (who, among other things, was made a cardinal in 1560, when he was 22). The Grand Hall is next, an imposing space that was only recently completed according to the original design. There is pretty plasterwork (including a blind window with a cherub holding for dear life onto a stucco drape) and a terrazzo floor with a compass rose. There are other rooms, all fairly grand, but none exceptionally so. The palace, up to this point, seems fairly workaday.

The surprise awaits down another flight of stairs. Here, in a lowceilinged basement, are what served as the guest rooms. This is not as inhospitable as it sounds, for here is baroque theatricality and fantasy unleashed: the entire suite of six rooms has been transformed into Neptune's grotto. The walls are inlaid with rough stones that surround panels of red marble. Great twisted plaster seashells surmount lintels, while vaults are outlined in a coarse stucco that looks like white coral. The floors are worked in a mosaic of small pebbles, washed smooth by the sea. The lighting is almost sufficiently dim to obscure the Asian sculptures that look silly in this submarine context.

This is baroque excess at its most glorious, and there is even more to come. The gardens of the palace are constructed on 10 terraces, piled atop each other in a truncated pyramid. They are as much architecture as horticulture; although there are trees and flowers in abundance, they are only a small part of the greater plan.

An astonishing folly, in the same mode as the grotto rooms, crowns the next-to-the-highest terrace. This structure, clearly the product of a fevered imagination, is composed of three stories of artfully rusticated stone interspersed with pools and niches, cornices and balustrades, pediments broken and intact. The niches harbor more giant stucco seashells, and a dozen or

THE CINDERELLA
OF THE ARCHIPELAGO

The Isola dei Pescatori, probably
the first of the Borromeo
Islands to be inhabited, boasts
an ancient village that serves
as a counterpoint
to the opulent aristocratic
mansions on the larger islands.
The church, dedicated to Saint
Victor, was founded
in the 11th century.

**GRAND HOTEL,
COMINGS AND GOINGS**
Built in 1861 on the lakefront
in Stresa and continuously
renovated until modern times,
the sumptuous Grand Hotel
et des Îles Borromées (left) calls
up the refined luxury of the
Belle Époque and an exclusive
clientele of nobles, bankers,
artists, and intellectuals.
In 1870, one melancholy rainy
day, an esteemed client used
a diamond to inscribe her name
on a window in the hotel:
"Alexandra, Grande Duchesse
de toutes les Russies."

Above, the gardens of Villa
Taranto, near Pallanza.
In springtime, its wealth of over
20,000 plant species envelops
visitors in a cloud of colors
and scents.

**ISOLA BELLA, BEAUTIFUL
IN NAME AND IN FACT**
After a tour of the baroque
palazzo built by Vitaliano
Borromeo (above, the
underground rooms), the balmy
climate of the lake tempts
tourists to visit the gardens
(facing page).
Terraced like those of ancient
Babylon, the gardens were
designed to guarantee that a
certain number of the various
species will be in continuous
bloom from spring to autumn.

more pedestals support statues of gods and goddesses, Atlases (themselves supporting nothing) and Cupids. The entire heap is flanked by staircases and obelisks and more statues; it is surmounted by yet another Cupid mounted on a unicorn, the crest of the Borromeos. For some reason, this superb excrescence is called the Amphitheater. One remembers that Wagner, standing on the terrace of Isola Bella, is supposed to have said that it was the first place he had ever felt his soul at peace. He must have been facing some other direction.

An afternoon's excursion took us to Stresa. We window-shopped for fishing equipment and coral jewelry and strolled along the lakefront, with its flower-decked turn-of-the-century villas. Feeling slightly depraved, we dropped into the bar of the Grand Hotel et des Îles Borromées and ordered martinis – the kind made with gin, rather than the aromatic Italian aperitif. The Grand Hotel is to hotels what Stresa's lakeside villas are to villas, a manifestation of the Belle Epoque at its most belle. It is also something of a literary monument: it was a favorite of Ernest Hemingway's, and it may be remembered that Frederick Henry, the hero of *A Farewell to Arms*, not only ordered martinis here, but also borrowed from the barman the boat in which he rowed to safety in Switzerland.

We had saved Isola Madre for last. It seemed to need some working up to – Flaubert described it as "Terrestrial paradise… the most voluptuous place in the Gulf that I have seen; nature charms you there with a thousand strange seductions." Nature has not been altogether unassisted, however. There is another palace – an 18th-century one this time – and a family chapel on Isola Madre, and its gardens are again arranged in terraces. Lest one forget whose it is, the harbormaster wears a T-shirt with the three interlocked rings that are another emblem of the Borromeos.
We toured the palace first. Its exterior is austere to the point of looking institutional; its interior surprisingly domestic. There is a small polygonal drawing

A LOVING MOTHER
The largest of the three islands in the Borromeo group is enveloped in a heady atmosphere of silent meditation. The 18th-century Palazzo Borromeo (above) houses interesting museums, including a display of puppet theaters from the 17th through to the 19th century.

room, frescoed in yellow with trompe l'oeil columns and vine-covered trellises, in which it would be pleasant to breakfast on a sunny morning, and an even smaller room that houses a collection of 19th-century dolls, many of which look well used. Even such important spaces as the grand staircase, the library and the dining room are of manageable proportions. The palace is light and airy, delicately rather than oppressively gilded; its mood is summery. Another Borromeo motto, "Humilitas" looks less absurd here than it might.

One wanders at will through the palace on Isola Madre. Furnishings are well displayed and clearly labeled, and there are mannequins in 18th-century dress representing servants in Borromean livery and various important Borromeos. They can give you a nasty start if you are not expecting them.

Flaubert's thousand strange seductions are the bounty of Lago Maggiore's semitropical climate. There are orange and grapefruit trees, a palm-bordered walk (and a single Chilean juba palm that is said to be the largest in Italy), magnolias, weeping cypress, flowering clematis and wisteria. Azaleas, rhododendrons, camellias and roses blossom in mass and in season. The largest and most exotic trees are labeled, and the grounds are stocked with birds of every description, from gaudy bantam chickens to even gaudier Chinese pheasants, both golden and silver (the birds, especially the larger ones, are bold – if you hear the pitter-patter of little feet on the gravel behind you, it means that a pheasant is sneaking up). A small restaurant near the boat landing offers refreshment for those who choose to while away the day here.

We found that Pescatori offered superior facilities for loafing, however. In addition to hanging out in the cafés, we waded, skimmed stones on the water and watched amateur as well as professional fishermen (the rule seemed to be that nothing was ever too small to keep – if you could see it, you could take it home and eat it.) We looked into the little church, modestly redecorated in the Baroque style, whose low steeple is yet higher than anything else on the island. Like the resident cats, we prowled up and down the alleys and in and out of the shops on the island's more-or-less main street, the claustrophobically narrow Via Ugo Ara (Ara was a musician and a friend of Toscanini; he also, in 1933, published a charming book on the island in which he quoted another musician, Gabriel Fauré: "Few quarters of Italy are so Italian." The souvenir stalls were not here in Fauré's

– or Ara's – time, but the description still holds). Our last evening on Pescatori we stood on our balcony and looked out on the lake, upon which a thin mist was settling. A single fishing boat, with a single light, slowly rounded Isolotto della Marghera, as we had learned the islet with the tree was called. A plan began to form in our minds. Surely the Borromeos could spare Isolotto della Marghera; it was so small they would never miss it. Perhaps we could buy it. We would then, of course, name it after me. Isola Sarah has a nice ring to it.

SARAH FERRELL is the associate editor of The Sophisticated Traveler, *a magazine of* The New York Times *that appears four times a year. She has traveled widely in Italy.*

EXOTIC GREEN ISLAND

Green is the color of the Isola Madre. From afar, in summer, it is almost concealed by its elegant turban of emerald green. But, once you land there, you find azaleas, camellias, rhododendrons and espaliers of citrons and lemons, while parrots, pheasants and peacocks evoke a refined and slightly *démodé* exoticism.

By Jo Broyles Yohay

On the Edge of a
TIME GONE BY

March 18, 2001

With an abrupt jog to the left, the trail climbed out of a gray-green olive grove and opened onto a staggering expanse of steep, rugged coastline and turquoise sea. Moments before, the footwide stone path had been benign and well behaved. Now it flung itself into thin air, following a cliff-side ledge a hundred feet above hard surf. I flattened my body against solid mountain and tried to reckon with the roiling ocean crashing recklessly onto the jagged rocks below.

This trail was the precise reason I had come to the Cinque Terre (Five Lands), Italy's isolated string of five villages on a stretch of wild Ligurian coast southeast of Genoa. Craggy mountains trap the region, an enclave about twice the size of Manhattan, between rock and sea, creating an islandlike solitude. Because its inaccessibility long insulated it from casual visitors, it stands a world apart from the dazzle of Portofino, a scant 45 miles to the north.

Compelled by a friend's description – "old fishing villages you reach by walking on a mule track" – I couldn't get there fast enough. The romantic in me pictured a place suspended in time, pure and uncluttered by the commercial icons of contemporary life, its people as weathered and rugged as the landscape, living alongside nature as their ancestors had for generations. I had commandeered my husband, Victor, and some friends to come along. Now I stood gulping in air to stoke my courage. We all breathed hard while we got our bearings.

Far below, in miniature, I caught sight of Corniglia, the thousand-year-old town, midway between the northernmost village of Monterosso al Mare and the southernmost village of Riomaggiore, that we'd left on foot a

PIRATICAL ATTACKS
Stacked in tight clusters and clinging to a promontory, the houses of Manarola (left) seem ready to withstand a pirate attack. The impression is not mistaken: during the Middle Ages Saracen raiders obliged the inhabitants along the coast to take refuge in the least accessible high ground.

THE POET'S BEACH

Above, the beach at Monterosso. Eugenio Montale, one of the greatest Italian poets of the 20th century and winner of the 1975 Nobel prize for literature, spent the summers of his youth in this village. His most famous work, *Ossi di Seppia* (Cuttlefish Bones), contains many poems that evoke the nature and the atmosphere of the Cinque Terre.

Kissed by the sun and the wind, the vineyards of the Cinque Terre (right) fill the wine casks with delicate aromas and flavors. The thing to do is to wear a pair of comfortable walking boots and head off into the dense network of timeless paths, immersed in an ancient silence, enjoying at every step the scent of the Mediterranean vegetation and the sea.

half-hour before. We'd picked it as home base for our three-day stay. A cluster of four-story houses, in cheerful shades of yellow, rose and burnt orange, were stacked along a ridge high above the sea. The narrow alleys, twisted stairways and windy belvederes that we'd had so much fun exploring the previous day had all but vanished, woven into the rocky promontory. On the near side of town, scrupulously terraced hillsides plunged to the sea; on the far side, they leapt hundreds of feet into the air.

Every possible inch of soil was held back by retaining walls, contoured over centuries at an unimaginable cost in effort and time. The hard-won plots of land, a scant 10- to 20-feet wide, held acres of vineyards, pocket-size olive groves, lemon orchards and kitchen gardens. Near Corniglia, we'd even spotted a lone pomegranate tree, covered with huge, firm fruits, each one utterly red. Plump hens scratched in the earth beneath.

I looked in the opposite direction, hoping to see the next village, Vernazza, our destination for lunch. Instead, far ahead, I saw the hazy crescent beach of what I guessed to be Monterosso al Mare. Vernazza was probably hiding behind the mountain spur just ahead. By the crow's reckoning, the total distance between the first hamlet and the last is only about six miles. But the

path that strings the five villages together runs longer, close to nine miles, as it winds among vineyards and climbs high into the hills before descending again to sea level.

We had driven our rental car to Riomaggiore, the first town in the series, parked in a public garage, and filled our backpacks with what we'd need for our stay. We planned to move on foot, hiking among towns at our leisure and returning to Corniglia in the evenings by train. The local La Spezia-Genoa line is a convenient way to get to and around the Cinque Terre. Frequent trains running along the sea stop at all the villages, which are just minutes apart by rail. In summer, a boat also ferries passengers between towns. Theoretically, it is possible to snake along a narrow, rough, tortuous road and park a mile or so above each town. But when we made inquiries, a seasoned Italian driver said that he'd tried it once and that he'd never do it again.

Hiking is the classic way to see the Cinque Terre, and, for much of its history, the only way except by boat. But the first day we were obliged to rely on the train because recent heavy rains had caused rocks to loosen and fall onto the footpath between Riomaggiore and Manarola, just down the coast. As is sometimes the case, the section had been closed temporarily to walkers to prevent an accident.

BORN FROM THE WATERS
Dominated by its 40-meter high octagonal bell tower, the 14thcentury church of Santa Maria d'Antiochia in Vernazza seems to have no fear of the salt spray. With its foundations sunk directly in the water, it is emblematic of a society whose roots have always been in the sea, the source of work and survival.

BETWEEN THE CINQUE TERRE
AND THE BAY OF LA SPEZIA
In the slanting light of the
sunset the island of Palmaria
looks like a great slumbering
cetacean. A narrow arm of the
sea separates it from the
promontory of Portovenere,
where the church of San Pietro
stands high on the cliff.
According to legend, in ancient
times this was the site
of a temple dedicated to Venus,
the goddess of love.

As we came to know the region, we understood that its environment was fragile. Every spare inch of land is under cultivation. The minuscule towns are old and weathered; harbors, scarcely larger than municipal swimming pools, are hemmed in by sheer cliffs. There is nowhere to expand to accommodate a growing number of visitors.

Even in mid-October, we encountered tourists. Some relaxed on sunning rocks, some whizzed in and out by train, ticking off each town as they went. Others had come to hike: the glorious young double-timed the footpaths in sneakers; the over-30's sported well-worn boots, assorted Alpine attire and the occasional sturdy walking stick. Ages ranged from an infant in a backpack to a group of rosy-cheeked British with white hair and oak-tree calves.

We had chosen Corniglia as home base precisely because it is the least visited of the five towns – and to our eyes, the prettiest. Those who arrive by train may walk to the town along an inclined roadway or face a stiff climb up 365 leg-breaking brick steps that zigzag back and forth in hairpin turns. Most visitors, lured by the small, pebbly beach below, never tackle these stairs to the actual town which offers two modest hotels, five restaurants, and a scattering of cafés and bars.

We opted to stay in a private flat. As elsewhere in the Cinque Terre, villagers rent out bedrooms in their homes, or even small apartments. We knocked on a door with a "Camere" (Rooms) sign, and were greeted by Maria, a mildly grumpy woman who spoke little English. As she led us through a maze of dark lanes and uneven stone staircases, I began to wish I were dropping a pocketful of bread crumbs along the way.

Maria unlocked a door with an iron key worthy of a medieval dungeon. Our second-floor rooms opened off a dim, shuttered sitting room with antimacassars, faux-crystal lamps, once-gaudy drapes. Then we threw back the shutters. The window of each bedroom framed a brilliant view over a stony precipice to the open sea, stretching out on three sides to the horizon. We could have been on a remote island, far from shore. We slept with windows opened to the pounding surf and moist night air.

To refuel after walking, we lingered in unpretentious trattorias and harborside cafes, sampling local specialties: anchovies, pale and delicate, taken straight from the sea and seasoned with fresh basil and a wedge of just-picked lemon; antipasti al mare with squid, calamari and scallops; risotto with seafood and local herbs; bread dipped in home-grown olive oil; crisp, local white wine. Investigating Corniglia, we sat outside the locked, 14th-century Church of San Pietro, admiring its marble rose window with a graceful deer carved in the center. Just then, a group of grandmotherly women, in print housedresses, walked by us, chattering companionably as they moved toward the church. They unlocked the door and disappeared inside. Welcoming the chance to see the interior, we crept in after them. They had gathered in a circle near the altar, preparing, we thought, to pray. To our surprise, they began to sing, their strong, clear voices filling the small space with what sounded like a hymn. We huddled close by the door, doing our best not to intrude, yet unwilling to give up this chance to savor an intimate view of Corniglian life. Luck had honored us with a moment of choir practice and we gave it our full attention.

People don't come to the Cinque Terre for museums and paintings, for grand hotels or for soft-sand beaches. They come because life on this coast has remained much the same for centuries. Laundry still flaps in the wind at open windows. Groups of men with work-hardened hands gather in the twilight to talk. Fishermen, bringing in the day's catch, haul up their boats to the quay because only a few vessels will fit in the harbor at one time. Farmers still climb to vineyards perched so precipitously that some are connected by ladders propped against the retaining walls.

I found myself wishing the Cinque Terre could stay the same forever. True, its charms are not for everyone. Some find its low-brow, unadorned demeanor gloomy and wonder what all the fuss is about. Others of us love the close of wild nature and earthy lifestyle. The region's placement on Unesco's world heritage list in 1997 and its status as a national park, acquired in 1999, should help save its stage-set beauty. On the other hand, what right have we to hope the residents will resist the pull of tourist cash when the rest of the world hasn't been able to? Why on earth would we expect the younger generation to fish, rain or shine, when they can open Internet cafés?

From my scary cliffside perch that first morning, I looked down at the crashing surf and decided that walking was the only reasonable way to approach the Cinque Terre towns. Personally, I loved the idea of encountering a new place on the strength of my own legs. But more important, these quiet villages deserve that gesture toward their history, that level of attention and respect. Driving or making quick visits by train does nothing to serve the area's fragile beauty. But the real cliffhanger was something much bigger: how would the Cinque Terre survive the modern world?

JO BROYLES YOHAY writes frequently for The New York Times travel section and other publications.

AUTOS WITH OARS

For the inhabitants of the Cinque Terre a boat is not only a source of work and amusement, it is also the most common means of transport. The old folks say that not all that long ago some vineyards could only be reached by sea. To be good winemakers they had to be good sailors, too!

ON THE EDGE OF A
TIME GONE BY

A PALACE FIT FOR A KING
The jewel of via Balbi, a venerable residential street in Genoa, the Palazzo Reale is an exhibition of sumptuous 18th-century elegance and the decorative splendors of the Baroque period. The monumental staircases by Carlo Fontana (right) give access to the throne room and audience chambers, as well as the Art Gallery, which has valuable paintings from the 17th and 18th centuries.

By Michael Frank

GENOA,
City of Contrasts

April 9, 2000

Not long ago I had the good luck to spend some time in Genoa in the company of some Genoese. The experience affirmed for me an old truism of travel: you cannot really know a city until people who live there invite you to dinner. And show you how they cook and dress and do up their houses; and tell you something about daily life; and teach you a few words, preferably racy, of the local dialect. And, after a glass of wine – in a living room befogged, as so many in Italy still are, with cigarette smoke – speak of the things they love about their city and those they love less.

The people I know in Genoa are the family and friends of my friend Elisabetta Beraldo, who is a costume designer for the movies. Her profession is pertinent. It supplies at least one metaphor for the compelling, layered, only slowly penetrated city that has been home to her family for generations. Genoa, Elisabetta said to me one day, is like an old nobleman who goes around in a plain cloth coat: threads may dangle from his hem, but underneath, you can be sure, his vest will be cut from damask.

This sense of aristocratic dilapidation, of finery and secrets tucked just out of view, pervades Genoa, once a thriving port on the Ligurian coast in northwestern Italy and for centuries a powerful, cosmopolitan, independent maritime republic. Its elusiveness is age old and much remarked, as is its mixture of beauty and plainness.

Charles Dickens, who lived in Genoa in 1844 and was one of the city's great fans, spoke of its "strangest contrasts." In *Pictures From Italy*, he wrote that "things that are picturesque, ugly, mean, magnificent, delightful, and offensive break upon the view at every turn." It is a

place, he added, that "'grows upon you' every day." And so it does still, 156 years later. Blissfully devoid of tour buses, information booths and souvenir hucksters, Genoa is a city to wander through; like Venice, it is best experienced when you allow yourself to lose your way. This is not difficult.

The essential thing to know about Genoa's topography is its compactness: the city, which hugs the curve of the port, fits itself into a relatively confined, fairly steep, naturally occurring amphitheater defined on one side by the Ligurian Sea and the other by a sweep of enclosing hills. Every inch of earth is prized, carved into and built upon, so that the characteristic Genoese street, called either a "vicolo" or a "carrugio," is narrow, crooked, unmappable, mysterious and rich with beauty and beguilements.

The carrugi are bordered by buildings dense as a palimpsest. This word, which is too often applied to old cities, might have been invented for the palazzi of Genoa, whose medieval and Romanesque underpinnings (black-and-white striped facades, braided columns, stylized overdoors carved of slate, a standard local building material) poke out from the lower levels of Renaissance and Baroque facades like a preliminary pencil sketch that lies beneath a finished chalk drawing. In Genoa, process – time, if you like – seems to unfold everywhere before your eyes.

The carrugi may be the prototypical Genoa, but there is also one grand street that is not to be missed: the Via Garibaldi, which was laid out in the 1550's by Bernardino Cantone, a pupil of Galeazzo Alessi, Genoa's premier and visionary architect of the

GENOA,
CITY OF CONTRASTS

GENOAN LUXURY

The Genoans are said to be very parsimonious (to use a euphemism). But for the Cathedral they spared no expense, utilizing marbles and sculptures for the exterior (below) and embellishing the interior with works of art.

Right, a pause for relaxation in front of the Palazzo Ducale, built at the end of the 16th century to house the government of Genoa.

Renaissance. Grand in Genoa is nothing like grand in Rome or Paris, however; the Via Garibaldi, despite the impressive – in places, flashy – 16th-century palazzi that flank it, feels human in scale.

This may have something to do with the origin of the palazzi, which were built as private homes for Genoa's premier families, among them the Brignole, the Sale, the Spinola and the Doria. By creating and colonizing the handsome avenue, these families sought to give Genoa an emphatic urbane street that could rival its counterparts elsewhere in Europe while at the same time affirming their oligarchic presence in, and hold over, local society.

While Genoa has no principal museum, it has unlocked the large, fortified doors of several of its palazzi and fitted them out as galleries. Two of the most prominent are on the Via Garibaldi, the Palazzo Rosso and the Palazzo Bianco. Their unfussy ambience is typically Genoese: when I visited the Palazzo Rosso, two young children sat in red velvet chairs, swinging their legs and looking with indifference upon a downright disturbing *Judith holding the head of Holofernes* by Veronese, while the view from rooms upstairs was of an appealingly regular (for Genoa) jumble of Baroque palazzi and more ordinary houses, TV antennas and flapping laundry, laundry being as fundamental to the city's identity as its lighthouse.

Genoa's early splendor is fully in evidence in the Palazzo Rosso's portraits of the local nobility by Van Dyck (who spent many years toting his easel from one local salon to the next), Hyacinthe Rigaud and Matteo Picasso, a painter from Recco, down the coast a bit, whose charming portrait of Maria Brignole features Genoa's landmark lighthouse, La Lanterna, visible through an open window in the background. There is no mistaking the message: all this good linen, red velvet and gilded wood are directly linked to profits generated by the republic's maritime trade.

Another grand house not to be missed, but easily overlooked, nestled as it is among the humbler carrugi, is the Palazzo Spinola, a property left by the family to the Italian state in 1958. There you get a vivid sense of how the patrician Genoese lived and decorated their private rooms in the 17th and 18th centuries. Maddalena Doria Spinola, who had (as one description put it) a "passione per il bello," ordered her mirrors from Paris and her chandeliers from Murano. She commissioned her share of Guido Renis and Van Dycks, too, and she or her relations had a fondness for old maps, bold faience and frescoed ceilings and the color red, which appears in damask, velvet, floor tile, porcelain.

For all its luxury, though, the house feels surprisingly relaxed: in one room, a sheet of paper had been folded over a picture frame, to catch plaster falling out of a moldy patch in the wall above, while in another, boxes (albeit attractive ones) of the family's correspondence and paid bills still stand on open shelves, as though the latest statement from the local electric company, might soon be dropped in.

A week alone could go to visiting the churches – my favorites, if I had to narrow them down, were probably Alessi's Santa Maria Assunta di Carignano and San Matteo, once the Doria family chapel, with its sleepy, silent garden. Half a day at least can be spent at the remarkable Staglieno, Genoa's cemetery, whose collection of marble Victorian funerary sculpture – narrative, sensual, exuberantly mournful – has acquired a chiaroscuro crust of dust and grime through which rainwater has cut channels that in some instances suggest blood, in others tears. This leave-things-as-they-are approach is typical of Genoa. Cleaned up, these monuments would look excessive, even vulgar; dirty, they display a likable patina of time, authenticity, endurance. Many of the younger people I spoke to told me that life in Genoa was, like these funerary sculptures, encrusted with the old ways; enduring, yes, but also conservative, inhibitory of change and innovation, limited in job prospects, and socially rather closed. These qualities, which can admittedly make full-time life problematic, have a more positive effect on a visitor, who can revel in the city's extraordinary intactness.

Nowhere was this more true, for me, than in the carrugi. In these narrow streets you experience the layers of a city that has grown up over centuries and frugally preserved generations of building materials, habits and traditions. You see this in the entrances to the tall palazzi, with their stunning marble and slate checkerboard floors, their arched windows and robust stone balustrades. You see it in the signage on the shops, elegant old script announcing the establishment of a tailor or a pharmacy in 1760 or 1823. You see it in the clusters of ladies of the night – or afternoon – in the Via del Campo, who seem rather less poignant in person, however, than they do in the songs of Fabrizio de André, Genoa's beloved balladeer. You see it in a place like "Sciamadda" (Genoese for flame), a bakery run by Liliana Sturla, which is not far from the Porta Soprana and thus the presumed birthplace of Christopher Columbus. Signora Sturla prepares such Ligurian staples as "torta di carciofi," "di cipolle," and "di bietole" (pies – though they're thinner and more refined than the word suggests – of artichoke, onion, Swiss chard) and "farinata," a delicious chewy bread

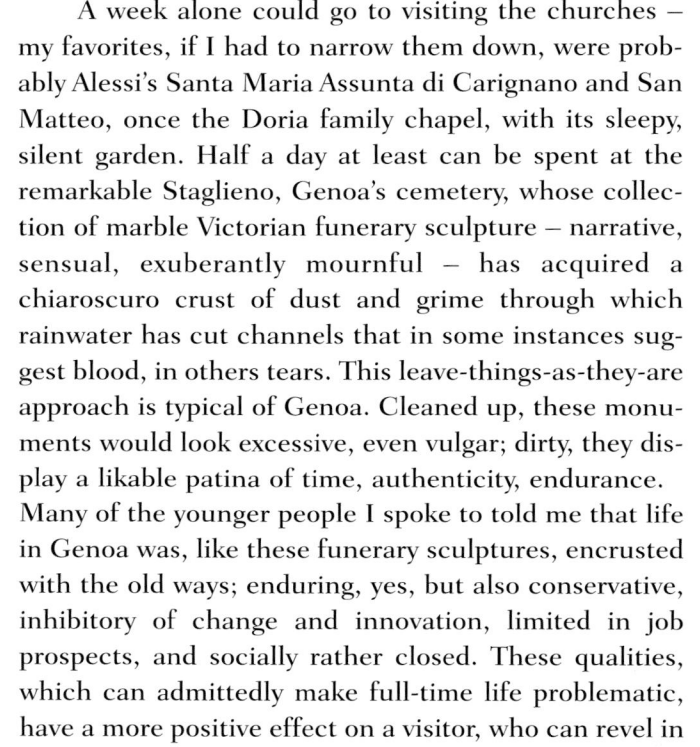

SIGNS OF THE PAST, EVER PRESENT

The frescoes that decorate the façade of the Palazzo San Giorgio evoke the splendor of the old Maritime Republic, when Genoa vied with Venice, Pisa and Amalfi for the control of trade in the Mediterranean. During that period the palace housed the Bank of Saint George, which administered the revenue from excise taxes.

79

FROM THE TIP OF THE YARD

In the innermost part of the old port of Genoa a singular structure rises up from the sea with seven metallic arms of unequal length radiating out from a central one. This is the Bigo, designed by the architect Renzo Piano on the occasion of the Columbus celebrations in 1992. In aspect and name it is intended to commemorate the maritime traffic that played an enormous role in the city's history. In fact, "bigo" is the local word for the cargo booms used to unload merchant ships.

GENOA,
CITY OF CONTRASTS

made of water, chickpea flour and oil. It is easy to make, she told me, "if you know what you're doing" — and if you have inherited special brass "tegami" (pans) from your great-grandmother, who had received them from her great-grandmother as part of her wedding dowry in the mid-19th century. Entering Signora Sturla's Sciamadda comes as close to stepping back in time as is humanly possible.

The same is true at Pietro Romanengo, a candy shop founded in 1780 that is the quintessence of the refined old Genoa. With its frescoed ceiling, ornate carved cabinetry and marble floor, the establishment is magnificently unmodernized. Romanengo still works chocolates with a granite stone, candies actual violets, and fills fondants and fruit drops with rosolio. (Rosolio? "But of course," a clerk told me. "The liquor ladies of the 19th century used to take when they felt faint. They were a favorite of Verdi's"). You half expect to look out through its bubbly glass windows and see flickering lanterns and gilded sedan chairs being carried through the carrugi.

Despite the presence of the annoying "sopraelevata," a modern raised roadway, walking along the port is still an essential way to experience Genoa. Under old arches of the Sottoripa Porticos, which were first built in 1100, the city's close connection to the water remains palpable. Fish markets with immaculate marble counters offer more varieties of sea creatures than you can ever name. Ship chandlers sell ropes, knives, hooks and floats. In the "friggitorie," the Genoese equivalent of fast-food joints, you can eat freshly fried shrimp, octopus and the ubiquitous sardines.

At the handsome Palazzo San Giorgio, you can see where that great explorer, Marco Polo, was held prisoner in 1298. Nearby, you can see thousands of species of fish at the modern aquarium, designed by the Genoa native Renzo Piano. And throughout the neighborhood, people of many origins and backgrounds and colors stroll along this same arcaded street as they have for 900 years.

In Lucarda, a clothing shop in the middle of the arcade, my friend Elisabetta (who knows a few things about clothes, after all) directed me to the sailors' T-shirts and Italian work jackets, cotton all and many in a blue as strong as the sea, that she and her brothers first wore as children, when their mother brought them there to be outfitted by the father of the father of the present owner. There were no damask waistcoats, but to me, the shirts and jackets were every bit as authentic, and rather more practical.

This Genoa, attuned to the water, thick with atmosphere and heritage, teeming and various and dense, was for Dickens "a bewildering phantasmagoria, with all the inconsistency of a dream." Petrarch, famously, dubbed it "La Superba." Chekhov had Dr. Dorn say (in *The Seagull*) that it is the kind of city that makes a man believe in a universal human soul.

I am not sure that I know it well enough yet to say that. "Yet" is key: Genoa shows you just enough of its treasures on an inaugural visit to ensure that you will return to discover the many you know you have missed.

———

MICHAEL FRANK's essays, articles, and short stories have appeared in The New York Times, Travel & Leisure *and* The Yale Review, *among other publications. He divides his time between New York and Italy.*

A fishing village where time has stopped, Boccadasse (a dialect word for "donkey's mouth") owes its name to the form of the bay on which it stands. Not far from city traffic, there is a little beach (below), clothes hanging out to dry, a few old boats – the ideal ingredients for a momentary flight from day-to-day worries.

IN THE LABYRINTH
OF THE OLD CITY

The medieval heart of Genoa
is enclosed in a maze of alleys,
known as "carrugi," whose
arcane and rather seedy charm
has inspired unforgettable songs
by the local folk singer Fabrizio
de André ("diamonds give birth
to nothing, from manure
the flowers grow...").
Today this area is a multi-ethnic
"casbah," in which one may still
find old-fashioned hostelries
and a few traces of the old days.

83

The Riviera of Flowers

Beaches and sun? Or mountains, old towns, archaeology and museums? Or again, superior wines, tasty local cuisine and amusements? All this plus the flowers that give the name to the stretch of coastline running from Cape Cervo to the French border, an authentic Mediterranean garden. For those who venture into this strip of land in the westernmost part of Liguria the points of interest are legion.

Sanremo first and foremost, a tourist and health resort of primary importance and Italy's biggest flower producer. Along the sea front – warm water even in winter – stands the new city center, with parks and gardens overflowing with luxuriant tropical plants. Also in the center is the Municipal Casino, designed in the early 20th century by the architect Eugène Ferret. Behind it, old Sanremo, known as La Pigna (the pine cone), a medieval town clinging to the sides of a hill dominated by the sanctuary of Nostra Signora: stone steps, narrow lanes and houses crowded together, almost in reciprocal defense.

In the hinterland of Ventimiglia is the village of Dolceacqua, divided by the river Nerva into two nuclei, known as the Borgo and the Quartiere della Terra, linked by the bold 33-meter span of the old bridge. The Quartiere della Terra is a typical example of medieval Ligurian townships; perched on the hillside, the houses are laid out in concentric arches to form a segment of a cone. Set slightly to one side of the tip of this cone stands the castle of the marquises of Doria. Built in the 12th century as a military installation, it was gradually transformed into a noble fortified residence, until it was seriously damaged by Franco-Spanish artillery fire in 1746. The land all around the town is terraced, each terrace supported by dry-stone walls, the work of generations and generations of peasants, thus enabling the cultivation of grapes and olives. From the prized grapes exposed to the sun and the sea breeze winemakers produce the splendid Rossese di Dolceacqua, a full bodied red that is the pride of the region.

Just northeast of Cape Mele, in the province of Savona, lies Alassio – founded, or so legend has it, by Adelasia, presumed to have been the daughter of King Otto I of Saxony. The town has the longest sandy beach in the western Riviera. Its fame as a tourist resort is borne out by the "Muretto," a retaining wall decorated by hundreds of ceramic tiles bearing the signatures of the city's most illustrious visitors.

ALASSIO AND SANREMO: THE PEARLS OF THE RIVIERA
Alassio (right) is an elegant tourist resort on the slopes of hills cloaked with olive groves. Its renowned "Muretto," inaugurated with a tile autographed by Ernest Hemingway , inspired the "Miss Muretto" beauty competition, still the big event of the tourist season. Facing page, the Municipal Casino of Sanremo, a torment and delight for lovers of the green baize.

By Paul Hofmann

PORTOFINO,
For the Rich and Less So

June 19, 1994

MEDITERRANEAN COLORS

Nestling in an enchanting bay and defended by a promontory (right), Portofino owes its inimitable charm to a happy blend of Mediterranean nature and the colorful harmony of its houses. Above, the ranks of buildings that line the "Piazzetta," the central square.

Several years ago, a few of the Italians ensconced in villas on Portofino's green slopes, from which they could see their yachts down at the marina, were in the habit of sending their helicopters to Genoa, 15 miles to the northeast, every morning to fetch the newspapers from Milan and Turin in time for breakfast. The rotor noise irked other guests of Portofino, so in 1991 the municipal council, representing the little harbor town's 650 year-round residents, banned all choppers from its vast territory. And thus ended air service to one of the most elegant resorts along the Italian Riviera.

The sheltered natural deep-water harbor at the south-eastern tip of the square, hilly peninsula was called *Portus Delphini*, or dolphin's harbor, by the ancient Romans — whence the name Portofino.

A lot was going on during the latest of my many visits to the resort last June. The cafés around the piazzetta, the theatrical little square hugging the harbor, had removed rows of tables to permit the erection of a platform on which models flaunted new creations by couturiers from Milan, Florence and Rome at an evening fashion show.

Next morning, while the piazzetta was being cleared of the fashion-show and TV paraphernalia, the low walls around the harbor were occupied by 200 students from Genoa University's architecture department. As part of their first-year exams, each had to select one of the narrow houses facing the water and render it in exact proportions on a large sheet of drawing paper.

The facades of the old fishermen's dwellings, in faded yellow, ocher, brown or blue, are all are designated as historic landmarks. Nobody would suspect that the interiors

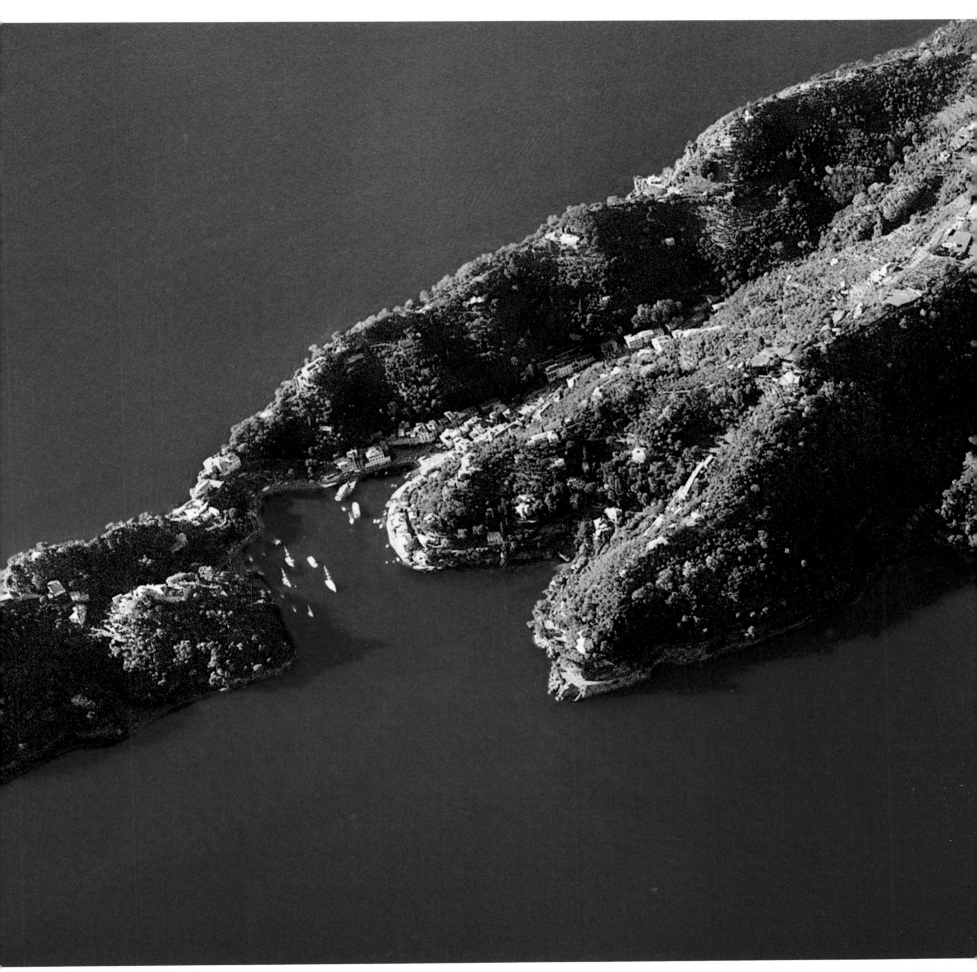

SMALL VILLAGE, BIG NAMES
"A little village spread out like
a crescent moon around a calm
basin." The famed 19th-century
short story writer
Guy de Maupassant was one
of the first celebrities to
discover Portofino, and he was
followed by many more –
movie stars, industrialists,
politicians and the powerful
from all over the world.
What fascinates the
international jet set is the fact
that Portofino is something
more than a fashionable
watering hole. It is a secluded
drawing room, simple
as a fishing village, evocative
as a set made for a great
director.

have long been gutted and restructured into small, smart apartments for people who live elsewhere most of the time. A studio looking out on the Portofino harbor costs more per square foot than a Park Avenue duplex in Manhattan. While the students tried to render the distinctive hues of the buildings, the passengers of a large Club Med cruise ship that had cast anchor off the promontory swarmed around the piazzetta and the nearby narrow streets. Meanwhile, the public-service boats from Rapallo and Santa Margherita Ligure disgorged sightseers at the embarcadero. Some visitors bought rolls and salami at the shop of friendly Signora Canale on the right side of the short Via Roma, which is Portofino's main drag. Others eventually dropped in at one or another of the several restaurants, filling their terraces.

In Portofino as elsewhere along the Italian Riviera, seafood dominates the menus. A regional specialty is pesto as garnish for pasta dishes. The green sauce contains olive oil, basil and other herbs, garlic, pecorino or Parmesan cheese, and finely ground pine nuts. Among the Ligurian wines, mostly whites, the vintages grown in the rocky Cinque Terre are particularly recommended. On my most recent visit, a few picnickers were sitting in

the shade on a long stone bench beneath a marble plaque that read "The writer Guy de Maupassant sojourned in Portofino for several days in 1889 aboard his sailboat *Bel-Ami*." The yacht's name was the title of the French author's frivolous and successful novel. Opposite the tablet, at a distance of no more than a dozen yards, a party of five around a table on the canopied afterdeck of an oversize cabin cruiser were having lunch, served by a steward in a white jacket. The gangplank had been half-withdrawn from the pier, insuring their privacy.

High above the port, on the crest of the promontory, a white flag with a red cross on a tall pole was fluttering in the breeze. It was Portofino's St. George's Cross (the same one that, together with the crosses of St. Andrew and St. Patrick, appears on the Union Jack). The adjacent parish church of Portofino treasures what is believed to be a relic of St. George, England's patron saint. The British have since the Middle Ages shown a particular liking for Portofino. King Richard the Lion-Heart of England sailed from here in 1190 for the Third Crusade. And, much more recently, distinguished Britons, like the Earl of Caernarvon, have bought properties on the peninsula. The gaunt old fort on the promontory was built by the seafaring Republic of Genoa centuries ago. The British Consul in Genoa bought it in 1870, and the Italian Republic acquired it in 1961.

Vistas from the height of the promontory are spectacular. On clear days one can see as far as the Capo delle Mele, a cliff 60 miles west of Genoa and the resorts and hills along the Gulf of Rapallo to the east. After visiting the Church of St. George, some visitors proceed on a footpath for half an hour to the lighthouse to take in the vistas of the sea and of the Gulf of Rapallo with the fantastically rugged Cinque Terre coast at its eastern end.

If you like trekking, take the marked path from Portofino to the ancient fishing port and abbey of San Fruttuoso on the south side of the square-shaped peninsula. The distance as the seagull flies is barely two miles, but the hike, up and down the rocky peninsula, may take two hours, affording beautiful views and a chance of seeing patches of the macchia, the dense Mediterranean underbrush that has long disappeared from most stretches of the Italian coastline. The footpath skirts a nature reserve and wildlife sanctuary. San Fruttuoso can also be reached, with less effort, by public-service boats that sail from Portofino's embarcadero several times a day. There is no road to the village.

However, most visitors, instead of climbing the steps to the parish church and the panoramic balustrades nearby, just stroll in the neighborhood close to the harbor. They tread the flagstones and pebbles of the Via Roma, which is bordered by fashion boutiques, jewelers' stores, art galleries, bank branches and souvenir shops. Works by contemporary artists are often shown in a deconsecrated chapel at No. 41.

The Via Roma, like most of the town, is closed to motor traffic. Autos arriving on the narrow, curving three-mile highway from Santa Margherita Ligure can only get as far as the elongated Piazza Libertà where the town hall stands. If they don't find a vacant slot in the town's only public parking garage, motorists must turn around and drive back all the way. In fact, almost all the excursionists take the evening boats back to the nearby coastal resorts or otherwise leave the peninsula around sunset, because Portofino can't accommodate too many guests. There is, of course, the Splendido. One of the most famous and expensive hotels in all of Italy, the Splendido is a former private villa on a luxuriant hillside a mile from town. Its own access road from the peninsula's only highway snakes up across a sloping park with pine and cypress trees and diverse plants from Mexico, South Africa,

China, Japan and other parts of the world. From the balconied rooms of the yellow-and-pink building and from its flowery terraces guests see an overwhelming panorama of the harbor, the forested spur of the promontory beyond it, and the sea. A wall near the dark-paneled reception desk displays portraits of celebrities who have stayed here, mostly show-business personages from Clark Gable and John Wayne to Larry Hagman, who as J.R. Ewing in *Dallas* won TV fame in Italy. The Duke of Windsor, Greta Garbo, Ernest Hemingway, Ingrid Bergman, Aristotle

Onassis – all stayed at the Splendido at one time or another, and dined in style on the terrace high above the heated outdoor swimming pool.

Each time I have visited Portofino I have been struck by the cordiality of the local people, who don't seem spoiled by the unflagging tourist boom. Visitors are greeted and thanked politely whether they have bought a soft drink out of the refrigerator in a hole-in-the-wall shop, or have ordered the seafood risotto at a posh restaurant and ask for the wine list.

"But make no mistake, one is always the outsider here," a white-haired, deeply tanned Italian told me. He was sitting at a neighboring table outside the Caffè Bellini in the piazzetta, and we had started talking. "The types in the deluxe pads all around here and in the villas and in the Portofino Yacht Club wait until the day trippers are gone. They entertain solely one another, and think they're the real Portofino."

PAUL HOFMANN is a former chief of The New York Times *Rome bureau. He is the author of 13 nonfiction books including* "Cento Città: A Guide to the Hundred Cities & Towns of Italy." *He lives in Rome.*

THE MONASTERY IN THE BAY
Justin and Procopius, disciples of San Fruttuoso (St. Fructuosus), the Spanish bishop and martyr, who fled from Spain in 259 B.C. with the ashes of their master, were hurled by a storm into a sheltered haven beneath Monte di Portofino. Here they were met by three lions who used their paws to mark on the ground the perimeter of the church the disciples were to build, and which in fact was erected in honor of the martyr. So much for the legend. Historical data records the foundation of the monastery in the year 711, when the ashes of San Fruttuoso were actually brought to this site by the bishop of Tarragona, Procopius.

By Alastair McEwen

MILAN,
the Italian Big Apple

February 1, 2004

**IN THE HEART
OF THE METROPOLIS**
The Galleria Vittorio
Emanuele II (above and right)
is a remarkable covered gallery
linking the Cathedral square
and piazza della Scala. It is the
"drawing room of Milan," the
heart of social and cultural life
and a favorite destination after
the customary Saturday
afternoon stroll among the
shopping streets of the city
center. The Galleria boasts
some famous cafés, such as the
Camparino, a historic
rendezvous for artists and
writers, and renowned
restaurants.

Few visitors arriving in Milan's domestic airport (Linate) notice the sign that says "Aeroporto Forlanini." Fewer still know that the eponymous Enrico Forlanini made a steam-powered model helicopter that flew almost twenty years before the Wright Brothers took to the air over the beach at Kitty Hawk, North Carolina one historic December day in 1903.

Milan is a place where people like to get things done – not only well, but fast. The powerhouse of the Italian economy, it is the capital of the country's wealthy Lombardy region. It is also one of the few places I know where some people actually run to work. Industrial, entrepreneurial and international, Milan has it all: from history to art, fashion to design, publishing to finance, universities to research centers, yesterday to tomorrow, and hustle to bustle. Like Sandburg's Chicago, Milan is a city with big shoulders. And there's no Italian Big Apple to rival it.

As far as we know, the first settlement in the area where the city now stands was built by a Celtic people known as the Insubres around 400 BC. A couple of hundred years later, this settlement was conquered by the Romans, who renamed it *Mediolanum*, which means "in the middle of the plain." Italy's largest lowland region, the Lombardy plain was once an extension of the Adriatic Sea, filled in over millions of years with the rich alluvial deposits that have made this the best farmland in the country. Thanks to this location Milan soon became the main industrial and commercial center in northern Italy, a fact that made it tempting for a long series of foreign invaders who made the city their own, often for centuries: the mixed bag of barbarian

A TROUBLED HISTORY

Behind the statue of Giuseppe Garibaldi stands the tower of the Sforzesco Castle, for whose construction Duke Francesco Sforza called in the Florentine architect Antonio Averlino, known as Il Filarete. The castle has known many vicissitudes. A military fortress during the Spanish domination (1535-1714), it was half destroyed by Napoleon, became a barracks later in the 19th century and was finally restored to its former splendor in 1893. The tower also had to be rebuilt, since the original one had been destroyed by an explosion.

Facing page, top, an early engraving of the Teatro della Scala, the temple of Italian opera. Below, a detail from the *Last Supper* by Leonardo da Vinci, a magnificent fresco in the church of Santa Maria delle Grazie.

tribes who looted and occasionally destroyed the city during the Dark Ages was followed in more modern times by the Spaniards, the French and the Austrians. What's all this got to do with the modern city? Plenty. A long and colorful history of this sort leaves a mark, and not just on the fabric of the city. On the character of its citizens too. If asked to define the folk of Milan, other Italians tend to portray a rather reserved workaholic suffering from delusions of grandeur. The Milanese, they say, think only of work, money and status. What's worse, they give themselves too many airs and feel superior to everyone else when in reality their city is grimy and ugly. But before you cancel your plane ticket, nothing could be farther from the truth. The Milanese may not be exuberant and outgoing like the Romans and the Neapolitans, but neither are they as self-important as the city's claim to be the "moral capital" of Italy might seem to suggest. And beneath that reserve there beats a big heart.

When, in October 2001, the city council decided to launch Milan's candidacy for the 2012 Olympic Games the official document contained a revealing proviso: "In the event, however, that the city of New York should confirm its bid for the 2012 Olympics, the city of Milan will postpone its own candidacy until 2016 in homage to the great civic courage shown by that city and as an expression of faith in dialogue and fraternity among peoples." This doesn't seem to fit with the stereotype at

all. So will the real Milanese please stand up? In fact, it's getting harder and harder to say if the Milanese as such really exist at all. A true-blue Milanese with, say, five generations of forebears in the churchyard is harder to find than a 3-dollar bill and there are very few families in the city that don't have at least one grandparent from some other part of Italy. Whereas a good 50 percent of the citizens of other Italian cities still speak their local dialect, hardly anyone under the age of 70 speaks the dialect of Milan these days. And this apparently insignificant fact speaks volumes about the way the city has developed in recent times. For the last 50 or 60 years, Milan and its thriving industry and commerce have been attracting people in search of work from all over Italy. In recent years, moreover, immigrants have been flooding in from China, Africa, the Philippines, South America and, most recently, eastern Europe.

Despite this influx of new blood, the essential character of the city has remained unchanged. Like all great cities, Milan has the power to absorb newcomers and mold them to its own standards. In Chinatown, for example, many of the teenage kids who hang out together speak in Italian with a marked Milanese accent. The magic of Milan: from Cantonese to Milanese in two generations.

Thirty years ago, for example, Milan offered a mere handful of Chinese restaurants and one Japanese restau-

93

rant, and that was about it as far as exotic cuisine is concerned. Nowadays anyone looking for something a little spicier than traditional local dishes such as "risotto" or "cassoeula" (both delicious, by the way) can choose from Indian, Thai, Greek, African, Mexican, Japanese and Chinese. And pretty much everything else in between.

But let's get back the stereotype about the grasping, status-conscious workaholic. When I came to Milan almost 30 years ago, I didn't speak the language and – what's worse – I didn't have a penny to my name. If I managed to avoid starving in those first six months, it was thanks solely to the generosity of many local people who not only invited me into their homes of an evening for a nourishing plate of pastasciutta and a restorative glass of red wine, but also offered me small sums of cash to be repaid "when you get set up." Which is the main reason why, unlike previous barbarian invaders, I decided not to destroy the city.

One of Milan's most charming districts is Brera. Built along the axis of two streets with poetic and mysterious names (via dei Fiori Chiari and via dei Fiori Oscuri, or the street of the bright flowers and the street of the dark flowers), it teems with intimate restaurants, bars and cafés, modern art galleries and antique shops. With its upmarket yet vaguely bohemian air, its street artists and fortune tellers, Brera is a small but cosmo-politan area much favored by celebrities from the worlds of television, the cinema and sport. It is also home to one of Italy's finest and perhaps most underrated art museums, the Pinacoteca di Brera, which houses works by Titian, Mantegna, Raphael, Piero della Francesca, Tintoretto and Caravaggio, just to name a few.

But my favorite part of the city is the district known as the "Navigli," or the Canals. If the historic city center, which spreads out from the Cathedral, is the heart of Milan, then the Navigli are the arteries that once provided the city with its lifeblood. Work on the canals began in the 12th century and by the 15th century barges laden with coal, cattle, cheese, hay, lumber, marble, granite, salt, wine and manufactured goods were gliding along the new waterways that linked the city with Switzerland via lakes Maggiore and Como. This immense network was finally completed in 1805, under Napoleon, and with the completion of the canal linking Milan and Pavia a centuries-old dream came true: Milan had access to the river Po and from there to the Adriatic sea – some 150 miles distant. As a result, a landlocked city was transformed into a busy port. No mean feat.

Today, the canals are no longer used for commerce but the picturesque area that grew up around them over the years is now home to artists' studios, craft shops, jazz

ALONG THE ANCIENT CANALS
The Navigli (Canals) area is one of Milan's trendiest neighborhoods that, despite its proliferation of pubs, restaurants and boutiques, still possesses a certain bohemian charm. In order to discover its real character, just venture into the courtyards of the traditional "case di ringhiera," old 4- or 5-storey tenement buildings with long balconies that lead to the apartments.

Italy's fashion capital

By Cathy Horyn
April 1, 2004

Situated in a smog-filled valley and plagued in summer by heat and mosquitoes, Milan is Italy's fashion capital by default. In the Sixties the international horde of dress buyers and status seekers flocked to Rome, as much for the couture designs of Valentino and Roberto Capucci as la dolce vita. Florence was known for leathergoods and gold, and it didn't hurt Florentine fortunes that Emilio Pucci and Salvatore Ferragamo were jet set favorites. But in the Seventies, with the advent of ready-to-wear and the demand for masculine-inspired clothing that women could wear to work, pragmatic Milan emerged as Italy's fashion center.

Within an hour's drive were factories and silk mills, which in time would produce high-quality clothes and fabrics not just for Italy but for the rest of the world, too, including France. And within the city's borders were banks, which would do their part to create Italy's fashion monopoly. By 1982, when Giorgio Armani appeared on the cover of Time, Italian fashion constituted bread and butter for stores like Neiman Marcus and London's Harrod's. Today, with the exception of the perennially tanned Valentino, who divides his time between Rome and Paris, when not sailing on his yacht, all of Italy's boss designers are based in Milan.

Perhaps because Paris is so persistently brainy and has harbored a string of superior talents, from Cristobal Balenciaga and Karl Lagerfeld to Azzedine Alaia and Rei Kawakubo — all of them foreigners — Milan is often accused of being insular, a small town in the guise of a metropolis. Armani, for instance, lives and works under one roof, in a palazzo on the via Borgonuovo, where, if you get past the security guards, you can see his cats prowling in the lush greenery of his walled garden. Patrizio Bertelli, the husband of designer Miuccia Prada, is probably happiest visiting his factories, which he reaches by private jet and which produce Prada's coveted fashion and handbags. The late Gianni Versace used to entertain Sting and Prince at his Lake Como villa. Yet, like his arch rival Armani, he preferred to live almost literally above the store.

Indeed, despite the city's propensity for competition, feuds of all kinds, and fashion that sells, there is an un-changing quality about Milan. To walk through the lobby of the Four Seasons Hotel during the collections or into Bice, a favorite restaurant of the fashion pack, is to experience a sense of deja-vu. One sees the same faces at the same tables. Even the chic Milanese on the street, with their somber cashmeres and flannel trousers (usually made by a local tailor), somehow look familiar. Paris, by contrast, is an ever-changing kaleidoscope of style and personality.

Paradoxically, as designers like Miuccia Prada and Tom Ford of Gucci created global brands in the Nineties, Italian fashion has suffered, to some extent, from globalization. Revenues from fashion were $53 billion in 2003, down from $62 billion in 1990, and the number of apparel jobs in Italy has also declined, as more manufacturing shifts to countries in Eastern Europe. Still, it is hard to beat the combination of Italian craftmanship and ingenuity. Prada is the most widely copied fashion label in the world, and recently a small factory near Florence developed the first pliable transluscent leather. Fendi plans to use it to make skirts.

CATHY HORYN is the fashion critic of The New York Times.

TWO OTHER TEMPLES
Above and top right, Peck,
a gastronomic landmark.
The enormous range
of products, artfully displayed,
include ready-to-eat dishes
of all kinds, cheeses, meats,
fish, fruits, vegetables,
desserts and wines.
Facing page, the Milan Stock
Exchange.

On the preceding pages, the
Duomo of Milan took a long
time to construct, from 1386,
when the first stone was laid, to
1812, when Napoleon ordered
the completion of the façade.

clubs, bookstores, bars, restaurants of every kind, and a whole lot more besides. Some of the old barges that used to ply these waters have now been converted into floating restaurants and it is a rare pleasure of a summer evening to savor a cocktail or a veal cutlet "alla milanese" as you watch the lights dancing on the water. But here I have to come clean. Milan is *not* Italy's most beautiful city. Venice, Florence, Rome, and Palermo, to name a few, are all very tough acts to follow. But it is not ugly. A better word would be discreet.

The elegant city center has some particularly fine Neoclassical and Art Nouveau buildings and the discerning stroller will find much to please the eye: the world's best dressed men and women, just for a start. In exchange for the traditional arm and a leg, the boutiques and jewelry stores in via Montenapoleone, via Manzoni and via della Spiga offer the best of Italian fashion and design while the smaller streets leading off Montenapoleone, like via Gesù and via Sant'Andrea, are lined with imposing residences whose enormous doors conceal courtyards of breathtaking beauty, filled with classical statuary, fountains and lush gardens.
At the heart of all this stands the Duomo, the world's third biggest cathedral, a marvelous Gothic pile with a myriad of spires and statues that took over 5 centuries to build. In a characteristically acid moment, D.H.

Lawrence dismissed it as "an imitation hedgehog of a cathedral," while Mark Twain called it "a poem in marble." But no one can deny that it is a spectacular sight and, as far as the Milanese are concerned, it is simply the soul of the city. On a clear day it's well worth climbing the 919 steps (or taking the elevator) to the cathedral roof, from where you can enjoy a peerless panorama of the city with the jagged peaks of the Alps in the background.
I still remember standing in a small piazza just behind the Duomo very early one foggy winter's morning. The fog, known locally as "scighera" (shee-gay-rah), one of the few truly beautiful words in Milanese dialect, had blanked out the base of the building so that the upper structure and its intricate crown of carved spires appeared to be floating on a cloud. The Madonnina, the famous golden statue of the Virgin that stands on the very top of the church, blazed in the morning sunlight. Had James Joyce been with me that morning he would have said "epiphany." Holden Caulfield would have said "it was so romantic it made me want to puke." As I was on my own, I didn't say anything at all. But I was thinking of all the legions of people that had probably seen this too and of the lady – a "harlot" according to the Cathedral records – who had given a few of her hard-earned coins toward the construction of this remarkable building almost six centuries before.

The Duomo is flanked on the one side by the Galleria, arguably one of Europe's first shopping malls, and on the other by the Palazzo Reale, a large Neoclassical complex that was the headquarters of the city's Spanish rulers in the sixteenth and seventeenth centuries. The building is now the venue for major exhibitions of classical and modern art.

Opened in 1867 by King Vittorio Emanuele, the Galleria is an imposing example of early glass and iron architecture that connects Piazza del Duomo and Piazza della Scala, home of the legendary opera house. The cosmopolitan atmosphere of the Galleria, which boasts sophisticated continental-style cafés and a truly historic restaurant, has made it one of the city's favorite meeting places. The elaborate inlaid marble paving of the concourse features a zodiacal Taurus sign right underneath the huge central glass dome. Some years ago, I was sitting at a table in a pavement café, sipping an outrageously expensive Manhattan and idly watching the world pass by, when I spotted an elderly gentleman rather furtively stepping, indeed almost hopping, on top of the most sensitive part of the mosaic bull's anatomy. The waiter told me that stepping on that spot brought good luck and guaranteed lasting virility.

A short stroll through the Galleria takes you to Piazza della Scala and the opera house. Il Teatro alla Scala, as it is officially known, is currently closed for much-needed restoration work and is scheduled to reopen on December 7, 2004, the traditional opening night.

Say La Scala and the mind immediately flies to an endless series of great names: Verdi, Puccini, Rossini, Caruso, Callas, Pavarotti, Domingo. But not many people know that the theater was also the scene of one of the most important technological advances in Italy's history. On the evening of December 26, 1883, to mark the première of Ponchielli's *Gioconda*, La Scala was illuminated by 2,880 electric lights. This enterprise was the work of Italy's first energy provider, the Edison company, which earlier that same year had constructed a generator for the continuous distribution of electrical energy - the first of its kind in Europe.

This is more than mere trivia, it is emblematic of the blend of art and technology that makes Milan unique among Italian cities. But if trivia is your thing, then you also might like to know that Thomas Alva Edison is Milan's most famous son. Milan, Ohio, that is.

About ten minutes stroll in a straight line from the Duomo stands the city's largest and in many ways most fascinating monument: the Castello Sforzesco, a military fortress that was transformed into one of Renaissance Italy's most splendid courts under Duke Lodovico il Moro.

Today the Castle houses many art collections as well as the impressive Museo d'Arte Antica with its large collection of sculptures. But the real treasure is to be found in one of the ground floor rooms of the Ducal Courtyard: the Rondanini Pietà, one of Michelangelo's most moving works. The great artist hammered away at this work for the last nine years of his long life, but he left it unfinished. Despite this, however, the Pietà possesses a haunting and strangely modern quality, as if the two figures were struggling to free themselves from the block of marble. It is arguably every bit as interesting as the city's best-known artwork, the renowned *Cenacolo* or "Last Supper," frescoed onto a wall in the church of Santa Maria delle Grazie by Leonardo da Vinci in 1497.

So there we have it, a few very brief stills taken from an epic movie with a cast of millions – painters, poets and sculptors, soldiers of fortune and men of letters, fashionistas and industrialists, soccer stars, TV personalities and outstanding chefs. All this is Milan, Italy's fastest moving and perhaps most "American" city and – in many ways – its best kept secret.

Born in Scotland, ALASTAIR McEWEN is a freelance translator based in Milan, where he has lived for nearly 30 years. He has translated works by some of Italy's leading authors.

OUT OF THE ASHES

The Torre Velasca soars above Milan like a medieval city tower. Completed in 1957, it immediately became the symbol of the city's rebirth after the destruction of World War II.

The "city on the hill"

If you take the freeway that connects Milan with the cities of the Veneto and the Adriatic Sea, on bright spring days or in the warm atmosphere of fall, Bergamo appears outlined in the air on the slopes of a hill. The first element that gradually begins to stand out is the 16th century wall that surrounds the contours of the old city with a dark color, followed by the silhouettes of the domes, the bell towers and the towers and finally the chiaroscuro of the rooftops clustered in distinct blocks around the citadel, set on the highest part of the hill.

The original nucleus of ancient Bergamo, which was founded by the Celts and became a Roman municipality in the 2nd century B.C., stood on the summit of the hill known as the Colle della Fara, and in fact the name of the city means "the place on the mountain" in the local dialect. The two-fold nature of Bergamo was a fact even in the distant past. The fortified Roman town, in its strategic position, was gradually joined by the suburbs that grew up along the access routes. To this day, lower Bergamo, the pulsing commercial and industrial heart of industrial Lombardy, is a counterpoint to the austere isolation of the old city center, the custodian of the history and traditions of the past that is connected to the lower city by a cable railway.

Visitors to Bergamo Alta, the upper city, will find beautiful monuments amid a magical atmosphere. The old Roman road takes you to Piazza Vecchia, the heart of the city, dominated by the Palazzo Nuovo – formerly the city hall and now a library – the Palazzo della Podestà and the Palazzo della Ragione (12th century). The lion of Saint Mark, a memento of Venetian rule, can be seen on the façade of this last building. To this day the "big bell" of the Torre del Comune still peals 180 times to mark the curfew and the closing of the city gates.

While Piazza Vecchia evokes the civil power of medieval Bergamo, Piazza del Duomo represents the center of religious authority. The eternal dichotomy of Italian cities is repeated in Bergamo Alta too. The 15th-century Cappella Colleoni, with its elegant façade clad in pink and white marble, was constructed by order of Bartolomeo Colleoni, the great soldier of fortune who led the army of the Venetian Republic. The interior, with frescoes by Tiepolo, houses the tombs of Colleoni and his daughter. In the basilica of Santa Maria Maggiore, with its dazzling wealth of stuccoes, gilt work, paintings and valuable ornaments, stands the tomb of the composer Gaetano Donizetti. Then there is the Cathedral, built over a period of four centuries on a site where a church dedicated to Saint Vincent once stood. And more: the 14th-century Baptistry, the Torre del Gombito; fountains, porticoes, palazzo and medieval workshops. In short, the ancient heart of modernity.

A MULTICOLORED MASQUERADER
Legend would have it that a very poor little boy by the name of Harlequin was unable to get himself a costume for a fancy dress party; so all of his friends gave him scraps of cloth left over from their colorful costumes, which his mother then sewed together to create a multicolored mosaic. Extravagant and mischievous, Harlequin (above) is the traditional masquerader of Bergamo.

Facing page, the Cappella Colleoni and the basilica of Santa Maria Maggiore. Two stone lions support the columns at the entry (top, left).

101

By Alison Lurie

A Moody Retreat
UNDER THE ALPS

April 3, 1988

**THE HOLY LAND
IN YOUR BACKYARD**

Starting from the 16th century, in order to provide a "surrogate" for the faithful who were unable to make the pilgrimage to the Holy Land, numerous "Holy Mountains" were established all over Europe, including one above Ossuccio. These were devotional itineraries that wound their way among chapels ornamented with paintings and statues (above) that reproduce on a minor scale the buildings in which the Passion of Christ unfolded. Facing page, the bell tower of the church of Santa Maria Maddalena, in Ossuccio.

Lake Como, where I spent some weeks last spring finishing a novel, is temperamental. In 10 minutes it can change from the rippling transparency of ginger ale to a simmering olive-green witch's broth beneath which you can almost glimpse the heaving and churning of the aquatic monsters some locals claim to have sighted on dark, misty mornings. This long, narrow, beautiful shimmer of water is the stem and western branch of an inverted "Y" that lies at the base of the Italian Alps (the eastern and shorter branch is Lake Lecco), less than an hour by train north of Milan. It is one of the deepest lakes in Europe and, at about 1,350 feet, could easily drown a 100-story skyscraper.

On clear days, the lake was ringed with mountains, and to the north rose the rocky, snow-flecked Alps, impossibly high and so sharply painted in white and burnt umber against the sky that I felt I could touch them if I reached out my hand. But sometimes, even as I watched, the air would begin to blur and thicken. Soon, though the sun still shone, an invisible blue haze would erase the mountains as if the artist, dissatisfied, had rubbed out this day's work.

I found Lake Como entrancing in all its moods. It has operatic scenery, ancient churches with strange, half-comic and half-devout frescoes and sculptures, classical villas, lush gardens, luxurious hotels, delightful pensions and delicious north Italian food. It also has a proud, generous people who have not forgotten the war in which many of them or members of their families fought as partisans or hid escaped Allied soldiers in remote farms and mountain caves. While I was in Bellagio, there was a lively all-day reunion and parade

of the local chapter of the famous Alpine Brigade, with two brass bands that became increasingly enthusiastic, and loud, as time went on.

You can circumnavigate the shore of Lake Como by car, driving from one town to the next; but the roads are narrow and tortuous, and in midsummer you may be backed up for miles in a procession of stubborn trucks and honking Fiats. It is far easier and pleasanter to explore the area by boat. Ferry and hydrofoil service connect the principal lakeside towns, and all-day trips leave from the Piazza Cavour in the city of Como, at the south end of the lake. I found the hydrofoil – a spouting white walrus – to be fast, but not very scenic (its seats are in its bowels next to small, water-splashed windows). The steam ferry took longer, but the views from its deck were spectacular. Also, it ran more often, so that one could get off for an hour or two to explore a garden or a villa or a town square that seemed intriguing and then catch another boat back to one's base.

From the center of the lake, the villages look much alike, with their ranks of red-roofed stucco houses in subtle shades of ocher, rust, pink, buff and umber clustering on the shore and ascending toward the mountain peaks. But some occupy the gentle, sloping banks of tributary streams; others climb streets so steep they soon become shadowy staircases. Some are lively, with crowded cafés and markets, others are sleepy and silent. There are primitive fishing villages where nets are spread to dry on the beach, and there are modern towns where you can buy Milan fashions or hand-carved and painted antiques.

My own exploration of Lake Como began with a trip to the ancient city of Como. Its most famous

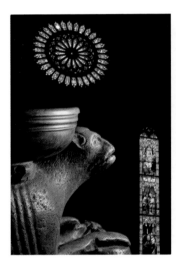

COMO CATHEDRAL
In 1740, after more than three
centuries of construction,
Como cathedral (right) was
finally completed. The building
is topped by an elegant dome
designed by Filippo Juvara, the
architect responsible
for the chapel of the Holy
Shroud in Turin.
Above, the interior of the
church with the rose-window.
Top, the statue of Pliny
the Younger on the façade.

natives were the Romans Pliny the Elder (A.D. 23-79) and his nephew Pliny the Younger (A.D. 62?-113). The younger Pliny had several villas on the lake. One, just north of Como, has a famous spurting spring, first described by its owner, that still amazes visitors. The villa was so close to the water, and the fish in Lake Como so abundant at the time, that Pliny claimed he could cast his line from his bed as if he were in a boat. Though they were pagans, the two Plinys are commemorated by statues on either side of the main door of Santa Maria Maggiore, the Como Cathedral, where they sit in niches below two ascending columns of stone saints and martyrs. I found it agreeable to imagine generations of unwitting visitors pausing to offer a prayer to the great naturalist or to the statesman who once assured the Emperor Trajan in a letter that Christianity was an absurd but harmless superstition that would soon die out. Inside the Cathedral there is much to see, including a series of 16th-century tapestries depicting scenes from the Old Testament and the life of the Virgin, and several remarkably good paintings, including a *Flight into Egypt* by Gaudenzio Ferrari. There is also a beautiful rose window, best viewed in the afternoon

when the sun is in the west. Not far from Santa Maria Maggiore is the 12th-century Church of San Fedele, less noticed by guidebooks, but remarkable for its celebration of the dark side of faith and human destiny. Just inside its door is a monument composed of what look like human skulls and bones, and nearby there is a graphic representation, in brightly painted wood, of surprised and unhappy souls in Purgatory.

Como is, and has been for many hundreds of years, a center of the silk-weaving industry. Brilliantly hued scarves, shirts and ties can be found at many elegant stores near the Cathedral; they are also available at a considerable discount from outlet shops. These shops are within easy walking distance of Como's broad main square, the Piazza Cavour, which opens onto the lake. The piazza is lined with hotels and outdoor cafes where one can rest after a tour of the city, watching the passing multilingual crowds and drinking iced coffee so rich it is almost a milkshake.

About halfway up the lake from Como on the west bank are two neighboring resort towns, Tremezzo and Cadenabbia, whose hotels have been favored by the

A MOODY RETREAT
UNDER THE ALPS

WEDDING PRESENT

Gracefully situated among luxuriant gardens, Villa Carlotta owes its name to Princess Carlotta of Nassau, who received the villa as a gift from her mother Marianna in 1847, on the occasion of her wedding to the Grand Duke Georg of Saxony-Meiningen. It has been the property of the Italian State since 1927.

English for over a century. Between them is the Villa Carlotta, an immense 18th-century palazzo with an art gallery and a garden remarkable for its collection of lollipop-hued flowers – camellias, azaleas, rhododendrons (best in May) – and its arbors of exotic fruit trees. Since the villa is on the western shore, it is most spectacular in the morning, before the shadow of the Monte di Tremezzo falls over the flowers. The art gallery is a monument to early 19th-century aristocratic taste: its piece de resistance, featured on postcards, is Antonio Canova's *Cupid and Psyche*, a sensual masterpiece sculptured in what looks like polished white soap.

Stendhal visited the Villa Carlotta in 1818. Twenty years later he made it the birthplace of Fabrizio del Dongo, the hero of *The Charterhouse of Parma*. The novel contains a long, enthusiastic description of the landscape. "All is noble and tender, everything speaks of love, nothing recalls the ugliness of civilization," declares Fabrizio's aunt, the Contessa; later, made careless by her romantic enthusiasm, she slips and falls into Lake Como in the middle of a storm.

Directly across from Cadenabbia, on the headland between the two branches of the lake, is Bellagio, a beautiful village that spills down a series of stone staircases onto a long plaza open to the water and lined with shops and cafes. Here I and my fellow tourists bought literary British paperbacks, luscious leather bags and finely cut cameos in pale pinks and salmons that matched the stucco houses. A shop in the Via Garibaldi sold the best homemade hazelnut ice cream I have ever eaten, piled generously into an old-fashioned sugar cone.

I stayed at the Villa Serbelloni above Bellagio, on the site of a house built by Pliny the Younger (ancient Roman ruins are still visible on the hilltop). The villa has colorful, elaborately terraced formal gardens, in which not a pansy is allowed to stray out of place, and from its grounds there are magnificent views of all three branches of Lake Como.

If, like me, you prefer flowers and trees in less mannered arrangements, the gardens of the Villa Melzi are just to the south of Bellagio, within easy strolling distance. The wide, rolling lawns and ornamental pavilions and pools of the villa stretch along the shore in a series of almost impossibly picturesque vistas. The Japanese maples are especially striking, and in May the silky, flaming stands of azaleas were a match for those across the water at the Villa Carlotta.

North of Bellagio, on the eastern shore of Lake Como, is the flourishing village of Varenna. It has a remarkable lakeside walkway, the lifelong dream and eventually the gift of one of its citizens, which runs

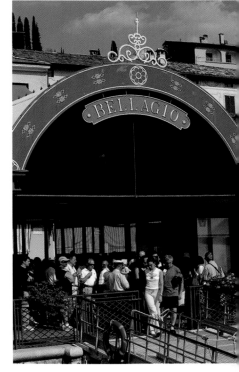

**THE NOBLEMAN AND
HIS ILLUSTRIOUS GUESTS**
Built at the beginning of the
19th century to accommodate
Duke Francesco Melzi d'Eril, the
vice president of the Cisalpine
Republic, Villa Melzi is one
of the pearls of Lake Como.
Its most illustrious guests
include the Austrian Emperor
Francis I and the composer
Franz Liszt. Left, the Coffee
House in the villa.

Above, Bellagio is linked
to all the principal towns
on Lake Como by a convenient
boat service. The landing stage
seems to herald the parade of
hotels in the Art Nouveau style
that characterize the lake front
of this enchanting little town.

107

**THE TWO BRANCHES
OF LAKE COMO**

Lake Como is shaped like an
upside-down "Y", whose arms
extend to the city of Como,
to the west, and to Lecco,
in the east (facing page).

Above, the tranquil lakeshore
at Varenna, a small town
on the eastern shore.
Even at a distance from the
splendor of the aristocratic
villas the serene calm
of the lake never loses
its evocative appeal.

along the cliffs directly above the water and is much used by local fishermen. Higher up, at the top of the steep stone staircases that serve as streets, are two interesting churches with ancient frescoes. Just to the south of the town, the beautiful but melancholy waterside gardens of the Villa Monastero, with drooping willows and pale lavender wisteria, and a view across the water to Bellagio, are a perfect background for moods of romantic longing.

A darker and more dramatic mood is evoked farther up, on the western shore of the lake, in the villages of Dongo, Gravedona and Sorico, which were once part of the separate republic of the Three Parishes (Tre Pievi). Even now, the local population is fiercely independent, and the area was a center of partisan activity during World War II. It was in Dongo that Mussolini and his mistress, Claretta Petacci, trying to escape to Switzerland as the Americans approached Milan, were captured by the partisans. According to one account, Mussolini was noticed because, unlike the shabby and exhausted Germans, he was wearing expensive, highly polished field boots. He was eventually recognized and taken to the mayor's office, where he was assured he would be safe. "I know," Mussolini replied, "The lake people are kindhearted." Then he made the rash (and for her fatal) admission that the "Spanish signorina" the partisans had in custody was his mistress, Claretta, and

he asked to see her. The two spent a wet, windy night together in a mountain farmhouse, south of Dongo, that had sheltered many escaping anti-Fascists. The next afternoon, they were taken down a road and shot. Today there is a plaque in the Dongo town hall to commemorate these events. Thinking of them, even on a sunny April afternoon over 40 years later, I felt a cold chill.

Another way to get a sense of the dramatic side of local life is to attend a religious service. I was lucky enough to be in Bellagio on the evening of Good Friday. San Giacomo was filled to overflowing. All the statues were draped in purple; the life-size wooden figure of Christ had been taken down from its cross, and lay on the altar as on a tomb. After the service the congregation marched in half-time down through the town to the harbor, accompanied by a band playing funeral music. Women in black chanted and wailed as if for the burial of a relative, and the figure of the dead Christ was displayed on a bier under an embroidered canopy. Behind it came altar boys dressed in white, carrying branches of laurel, and they were followed by what looked like the entire population of the town, including dogs, babies in strollers and ancient men and women in wheelchairs.

_____

ALISON LURIE is the author of nine novels, most recently, "The Last Resort." She is professor of English at Cornell University.

Where the lemons grow

THE OUTPOST ON THE LAKE

A slender promontory, slim as a finger, protrudes into the heart of Lake Garda from the south. On this peninsula stands a city: Sirmione (right). Its castle was constructed in the 13th century by Mastino I della Scala, the lord of Verona, as a strategic base for the control of the lake. The perfectly conserved "darsena," or basin, is a rare example of a fortified harbor.

Lake Garda, the largest lake in Italy, lies in a pre-Alpine basin bordered by the Lombardy, Veneto and Trentino-Alto Adige regions. The Roman poet Catullus, born in nearby Verona, described it as the blooming garden of Gallia Transpadana. At the southern tip of the Sirmione peninsula visitors can see the remains of what is traditionally considered to be the poet's villa, known as "The Grottoes of Catullus." It is a grandiose building, probably erected around the 1st century B.C.

On his travels through Italy, Goethe admiringly referred to the shores of Lake Garda as the "land where lemon trees bloom". It does seem amazing to find citrus fruits growing at the foot of the Alps, but a series of factors combine to create the lake's exceptionally mild climate, more Mediterranean than Alpine. The immense stretch of water ensures mild winters and summers that are never sultry, while the mountains bar the way to the cold north winds. In the early 14th century the cultivation of citrus fruits was introduced by Franciscan monks, who chose the southernmost areas where the trees are sheltered from the winds and where the water is deepest. Grown in greenhouses in winter, the lemons were in great demand in Venice and were even exported to northern Europe. Today the fruits that struck Goethe's imagination have been overwhelmed by competition from southern Italy; but visitors can still see what remains of the "limonaie" – the gardens where the lemons were grown – with their long rows of white pillars enclosed within stone walls. These gardens can be seen especially between Limone del Garda – a name that says it all – and the city of Salò. But while lemon production has all but vanished, the olive groves – which produce a flavorful but delicate olive oil – still flourish, and the local vineyards produce the famous Chiaretto del Garda and other quality-guaranteed wines. From one poet to another. Gabriele D'Annunzio was a man for all seasons. Writer, playwright, soldier and playboy, he was a major figure in Italian public life in the decades between the 19th and 20th centuries. In 1921 D'Annunzio elected Lake Garda as his "buen retiro" and, near the village of Gardone Riviera, he transformed a 17th-century villa into a monument to himself. A visit to the "Vittoriale degli Italiani", as the poet dubbed his home, is a sort of mystical journey among mountains of ornaments, souvenirs and mementoes. Half-buried in the garden is the prow of a ship, presented to D'Annunzio by the Italian Navy to honor him as a war hero.

By James Sturz

CASTLE
Country

April 2, 1995

THE CASTLE ON THE HILL
Excavations carried out in 1993 on the hill dominated by Castel Tirolo brought to light the remains of three churches, each built on the ruins of the previous one. Wrapped in the finest silks were precious reliquaries containing the remains of unknown saints; the papyruses, by then quite crumbled away, made identification of the poor bone fragments impossible. A tombstone behind the choir bore a dedication to "Lobecena of the white robes." Perhaps a humble girl newly baptized? Or a princess? It would seem that Castel Tirolo (right) has yet to reveal all its secrets.

Since the 12th century, the lush terrain of Alto Adige, a 3,000-square-mile stretch of the Tyrol in Italy's farthest north, has been studded with a king's ransom of castles, manor houses and monasteries. There are more than 350 of them today, overhanging rocky cliffs or lying, half-concealed, in primordial pine forests. Dozens are open to daytime visitors; some are ruins while others have become museums, hotels and restaurants.

I set out last November on a three-day tour of the region from Bolzano, the provincial capital, driving 20 miles north to the outskirts of Merano, where a battery of castles is clustered into its own unofficial duchy. As I followed the twisting contours of the Adige River a sea of grapevines poured down to the road, flooding over valleys and plains. The Dolomites rose up from the asphalt. Soon, faraway fortresses began to pop up in the countryside, their great stone facades towering above me.

Alto Adige became part of Italy in 1919, after perennial battles with neighboring Austria. Because of the years of hegemony, everything has two names, one in Italian and another in German (for German speakers, who make up two-thirds of the population, Alto Adige is known as the Südtirol). Some street names have changed position on the signs several times: the choice of which language comes first depends on whether the street is home to more Italian or German speakers, and that count is updated after each birth and death.

My first stop was the town of Tirolo, also known as Dorf Tirol. I took the Schlossweg footpath from the center of town, walking about five minutes past the flowered tombs and wrought iron crosses of the church

The elegant township of Merano has been a popular spa since the days of the Hapsburg emperors. In the 1930s these healthful natural waters were progressively exploited, while new buildings and hotels were constructed to create more modern spas. The Kursaal, in the Art Nouveau style (above), is among the latest of these.

of St. Johann Baptist to a small terrace overlooking the Passirio River Valley. There is a view from here of the massive Schloss Tirol and the turreted Gothic Schloss Brunnenburg, poised on hardy rock cliffs and dominating the mountains. I continued on, taking the high road where the path split off: 10 minutes later I arrived at an underpass burrowed into the hill and exited to find Schloss Tirol perched on a 2,000-foot peak.

With parts believed to date to 1095, Schloss Tirol is among the best preserved fortresses in Central Europe, although recent digging has uncovered the remains of an eighth-century church beneath it. A grass-covered cobblestone path leads from the trail to the mammoth rock-and-brick structure. Inside, magnificent marble doorjambs have been decorated with elaborate carvings of lions, dragons and eagles, along with depictions of the devil leading man into the depths of hell.

In the Middle Ages, this was the castle of the counts of Tirolo. In the 14th century the poet Boccaccio visited the castle as the ambassador from Florence. Today the furnishings have long since been removed, and the main rooms are used for concerts of medieval and

Baroque music and for art expositions. Of the half-dozen large rooms you can visit, the most imposing is the castle's chapel. There, stained-glass windows date to Boccaccio's time, as do frescoes of archangels and apostles on the walls of the apse. An enormous Gothic crucifix towers over the altar, and from the windows the views are wide and overwhelming.

It is less than a 10-minute walk from Schloss Tirol to Schloss Brunnenburg, which occupies a nearby summit. Built in 1250 (and restored in the early 1700's), the stone facade of the castle is enveloped in turrets. Nowadays, nearly 20 rooms of the compact residence have been converted to an agriculture museum. There's a formidable display of more than a dozen axes in the Gothic entrance hall. From there, a labyrinthine trail leads from chamber to chamber, each of which is devoted to a trade, such as blacksmithing, wine making or milling.

But the most astonishing sight is in the *rittersaal*, or knight's room, packed with copies of the works of the American poet Ezra Pound, along with an eerie collec-

tion of swords, daggers and African masks. Pound lived in the castle from 1958 to 1962, after his release from a psychiatric institution in Washington, and it was there that he finished writing his *Cantos*. Today the museum is owned and partly occupied by his grandson, and the *rittersaal* has become a paean to the poet's life.

When I left Brunnenburg, a red sun had begun to set beyond the hills, and the lights of Merano, Tirolo and the town of Lagundo were starting to fill the valley. It was about a 15-minute drive to Merano, where I had decided to spend the night. Each of the 30 rooms at the 12th-century converted castle is slightly different, and a few in the tower are truly palatial.

In the morning I set out for Merano. In the days of the counts of Tirolo, this was the capital of their realm (it wasn't until the 15th century that Innsbruck became the Tyrol's leading city). Since the late 18th century, the town has attracted visiting royalty, and grand Edwardian hotels now line the principal promenades. In the 1870's Empress Elizabeth of Austria was a frequent visitor; later Richard Strauss, Thomas Mann and

Franz Kafka all spent extended sojourns in the town. Since the 19th century, Merano has also been famous as a spa.

Surrounded by 10,000-foot peaks and bordered by the Adige and Passirio rivers, Merano claims to be the northernmost town in Europe where palm trees grow. The temperatures are so moderate that jasmine and allspice bloom even in winter. Spring brings magnolias, forsythia and pomegranates. The stained-glass windows of the 14th-century Gothic cathedral of St. Nikolaus, in the center of town, depict Merano's flowers at their most dramatic.

A short walk from the cathedral, the Castello Principesco, or Landesfürstliche Burg, guards the northern edge of town by the Tappeiner promenade, which is lined with laurel and oleander. Built in the 15th century, Castello Principesco was once home to visiting royalty during their stays in town. Today the crenelated fortress houses a permanent collection of antique musical instruments, arms and lapidarian devices. The interior has been maintained with period furnishings, including Gothic four-poster beds.

MERANO AND SISSI

A refined garden-city halfway between vine-clad slopes and glaciers, the origins of Merano's historic city center are lost in the meanders of time. It's well worth discovering mementoes of its past by strolling beneath the low arcades in the center, while imagining the presence of ancient Romans, emperors, counts and even the tragically ill-fated Empress Elizabeth of Austria. Sissi, as the empress was affectionately known, was a beautiful woman who was very popular with the common people, but less so at court where her progressive, liberal ideas met with deep disapproval. In 1898 she was assassinated in Geneva by an Italian anarchist.

115

THE MAN WHO CAME IN FROM THE COLD
Discovered in 1992 by two mountaineers on the Similaun glacier in Val Senales, on the boundary between Trentino Alto-Adige and Austria, he was nicknamed Ötzi (from the Austrian name for this mountain chain, the Ötztaler Alpen). Ötzi (in the reconstruction above) was the mummified body of a man who had lived over 5,000 years ago, perhaps a shepherd or a hunter who was surprised by a storm at an elevation of over 10,000 feet and drifted into a millennian sleep. His remains, his weapons and his equipment, now in the archaeological museum in Bolzano, are of exceptional scientific importance. Right, Schloss Korb.

I continued my castle tour in Scena, just three miles northeast of Merano. About half of the village of 2,500 is still forest, but along the Schlossweg, at the summit of the town, Schloss Schenna, a stocky stone castle, commands spectacular views. A wing of the castle is still inhabited by the descendants of the counts of Merano, who built Schloss Schenna in 1346.

A castle tour encompasses over a dozen rooms, and the first of them overflows with armored helmets, breastplates, spears, swords, maces and cannons. Rifles from 400 years ago, weighing more than 60 pounds each, are lined up along one wall, resembling primitive bazookas without the firing power. In the *rittersaal*, extravagantly carved Gothic furnishings and cabinetry date to the 1600's. The bedrooms have marvelous wooden doors with hinges that allow them to open from either side.

A drawbridge leads from the castle past a moat overgrown with trees and grass back onto the Schlossweg. I took that road back through Scena, and then south to Schloss Runkelstein (Castel Roncolo), on Bolzano's northeastern edge. Built in 1250, the castle is perched

on sheer rock above the Talvera River, along the Sarentino Valley gorge. After years of ruin, it was restored in 1880, when it belonged to Emperor Franz Josef of Austria, who also oversaw the repair of the many frescoes that filled its walls. Along a balcony overlooking a courtyard, frescoes depict the age of chivalry, with images from the early 1400's of an armor-clad Tristan battling a bloodied dragon and giants glowering at anyone who cares to look. Inside the half-dozen large rooms, the walls display a cavalcade of knights, musicians and fishermen, and Margarete Maultasch, the 14th-century Duchess of Tirolo, inviting guests to her gardens. Elsewhere, knights and their ladies in waiting are pictured in their best finery; a medieval fashion show captured eternally on the sturdy walls.

In the afternoon I drove to the hamlet of Appiano, six miles west of Bolzano. There, the hilly landscape teems with castles, offering enough to build an oversized chess set, with pieces to spare. Schloss Gandegg, a private palace now shared by three families, is a short

THROUGH THE ANCIENT ROOMS

Facing the mouth of Val Sarentina, just north of Bolzano, the 13th-century Castle Roncolo stages frequent exhibitions and cultural events. Its splendidly preserved medieval frescoes show King Arthur sitting at the Round Table with his Knights, Tristan and Isolde living out their tragic love story, knights making war and ladies simply languishing. Against this evocative medieval background the restaurant offers visitors typical dishes from the local culinary tradition.

**FOLK COSTUMES AND THE
ROSES OF KING LAURINO**
Proud of their traditions,
the people of the Alto Adige
jealously guard their
ethnic identity – a fact
demonstrated also by their
dress. Festivals, saints' days,
concerts: any occasion
is reason to display
the brightly-colored local
costumes (above and top).

Right, the vineyards
of the Isarco valley form
a gentle counterpoint
to the austere eastern face
of mount Catinaccio. Known
in the local tongue as the
Rosengarten, the rose
garden, it is the mountain
where the legendary
King Laurino cultivated
his rose bushes.

walk from Moos-Schulthaus, a 13th-century manor house that today functions as a private home and provincial farm-life museum. Set between them, Schloss Englar, a 15th-century castle sprung from a grove of pines. Out front, horses frolicked, and chickens and geese bustled about, and the view of vineyards spread to the horizon.

Schloss Sigmundskron, about a 15-minute drive from the Englar, is a 12th-century castle that was heavily restored in the 14th century and has since been converted into a hilltop bar and restaurant; it is also the largest castle in Alto Adige. Hulking stone doorjambs open onto a dozen long wooden tables. Horns from the local game adorn the walls. At nightfall, floodlights bathe the fortress's exterior. Through holes in the stone wall surrounding the castle grounds, I could see all of Bolzano below.

On my last day in Alto Adige I headed just north of Appiano, between the two tiny towns of Missiano and San Paolo. I stopped briefly at the 13th-century Schloss Korb, which commands mighty canyon views. Leaving my car, I took an hour's walk to Schloss Hocheppan (Castel d'Appiano), magnificent fortress ruins on a 2,000-foot rocky spur. About one-third of Italy's apples come from Trentino-Alto Adige, so I probably should not have been surprised when, at one point along my hike, an apple fell from a tree onto the path before me. I arrived at Hocheppan with pockets bulging with apples. An original castle underneath Hocheppan dates as far as 590 A.D. But ruins of the more recent structure, first built in 1131, with reinforcements throughout the next few centuries, are impressive enough. In its heyday, the fortress belonged to the counts of Appiano until the counts of Tirolo conquered it. Today a tiny chapel on the hilltop is still there. Inside, on richly colored walls, lions, knights and centaurs do battle under the gaze of pastel angels.

From Hocheppan's battlements, two dozen castles, fortresses and ruins cover the countryside, all in plain view. But even as Alto Adige's castles folded into the hills before me, I knew I had made a small dent in the region's 350 monuments to medieval Tyrol.

———

JAMES STURZ is author of the novel, "SASSO," set in the Basilicata region of Italy. His articles about Italy have appeared in The New York Times, Travel & Leisure, Condé Nast Traveler *and other magazines.*

A northern tradition

The Christmas markets (also known as "Advent markets") were born in northern Europe and gradually conquered almost all of the Old Continent. Particularly popular in German-speaking countries, they found fertile ground – especially in the province of Bolzano, which is closely linked to those countries by language, tradition and culture. Generally held from the end of November through to the beginning of the New Year, they are a joyful and popular celebration of the Christmas festivities, a ritual immersion in the mid-European past that, by commemorating symbolic figures from the collective imagination, delight children and bring out the child even in adults. Multicolored lights, Christmas trees, candles, pine branches, colored glass balls, decorations, music and folklore: all contribute to make these little festivals of the imagination an event not to be missed. The most important part is without a doubt the Christmas decorations. The stalls are laden with beautifully made hand-crafted items, such as carved wooden statuettes and all the things needed for making crèches, some of which are very large. On the streets various aromas lead to the products of the local cuisine, with the inevitable mulled wine and the delicious sweets of Alto Adige. And if the snow comes to lay a white blanket over the booths and the pine trees, then the magic is complete!

In Bolzano the heart of the festivities is the piazza Walther. There they sell crèches, toys and gift items while the bakers make *zelten*, the typical Christmas fruit bread made with dried figs, candied fruit, raisins, almonds and walnuts, a delicacy whose recipe is jealously guarded and passed down from one generation to the next. Many restaurants offer local cuisine at fixed-price menus and the hoteliers honor the region's tradition for hospitality by offering bargain prices. For the youngest visitors, guided tours through this magical "Land of Toys" are an irresistible attraction.

In Merano, tastefully decorated for the occasion and enlivened by Christmas melodies, visitors will find a series of stalls laid out in ordered ranks along the banks of the river Passirio. This market specializes in artistic colored glass items, pumpernickel bread made according to ancient recipes, iced sweets in the shape of Christmas trees *(baumkuchen)* and the traditional boiled wool slippers.

Those who pass the festive period in Bressanone would be well advised to forego the ski slopes of the Plose for a while in order to savor one of the liveliest moments in the life of the city. As well as offering the typical products of the South Tyrol, the traditional annual market is accompanied by exhibitions, musical performances, choirs and organ grinders. For all tastes.

THE MAGIC OF CHRISTMAS
The Christmas markets in
Bolzano (above and facing page)
and Bressanone (below).
The man playing the barrel-
organ transports visitors
to the fairy-tale atmosphere
of once upon a time.

By Carol Lettieri

Bringing Back the
PAINTED CITY

October 4, 1992

Crossing the Alps into Italy, 16th-century travelers were enchanted by the painted city of Trento. A convenient wayside along the Imperial Road from Vienna to Verona, this small but strategic crossroads in the Holy Roman Empire offered visitors more than a pleasant night's lodging beneath its Dolomite peaks. For Trento was one of the few sites in Italy where frescoes decorated the exteriors of public buildings and private homes. As wayfarers exchanged greetings in the Piazza del Duomo or strolled the elegant Via Belenzani, brightly colored images of garlands, emperors and goddesses met their gaze.

Visiting Trento for the first time several years ago, I, too, was taken by this cosmopolitan Alpine town of about 50,000 people near the Austrian border. At the Caffè Portici, I savored the crisp Tyrolean twilight. The Piazza del Duomo formed a delicate, civilized enclosure with a Baroque Fountain of Neptune near its center and a startling expanse of jagged mountains as backdrop. But unlike Renaissance visitors, I could behold only pale traces of the painted city. Trento's exterior frescoes had almost vanished. Across from the Duomo, on the facade of the Casa Cazuffi, a dim silhouette of a maiden's face remained where the Goddess of Fortune once reigned.

So it was with eagerness that I returned to see conservators at work on major restorations of Trento's frescoed facades. Part of a comprehensive plan to renovate the entire historic center, the project [now completed] has also included repaving streets in native stone and a two-year restoration and cleaning of the Fountain of Neptune, unveiled only days before my arrival. Emerging from the scaffolding was the luminous painted city that refreshed and delighted 16th-century travelers.

The concept of the painted city flourished in the late Renaissance, particularly in Venice, Verona and Mantua. When Bernardo Cles, bishop and Hapsburg prince, came to power in 1514, Trento was still architecturally a Gothic town. At his bequest, stone ornamentation and festive exterior frescoes – like those that embellished the Venetian palazzi along the Grand Canal – were used to create the fashionable look of a Renaissance capital.

The most striking of Trento's frescoed houses line the grand processional route from the Piazza del Duomo to the Castello del Buonconsiglio (Castle of Good Counsel), residence of the ruling prince bishops. In 1509, a ceremonial journey along this route was part of the coronation pageant of the Hapsburg Emperor Maximilian I. Here the bishops of Europe also passed when they convened for the counter-Reformation Council of Trent (1545-1563). Retracing their steps today offers the best views of the frescoes.

FRESCOES, FRESCOES EVERYWHERE

Toward the end of the 14th century Bishop Georg von Lichtenstein commissioned Wenceslaus of Bohemia to decorate his rooms in the Torre dell'Aquila, inside the Castello del Buonconsiglio; the frescoes (facing page, detail) are known as the *Ciclo dei Mesi.* Below, an evocative view of Trento, protected by its crenelated walls and by the natural barrier of the mountains.

123

THE FRESCOED SQUARE
All roads through the center
of Trento lead toward the
piazza del Duomo, one of Italy's
finest squares, thanks
to the picturesque façades
of the Cazuffi-Rella mansions,
frescoed in 1530
by Marcello Fogolino.

Entering the Piazza del Duomo in the morning Alpine sunshine, I was more appreciative than ever of its freshened colors: the pale green patina of the Cathedral of St. Vigilio's copper cupolas, the salmon and white stone checkerboard on the bishop's entrance to the church and the rosy-hued stone sea gods emerging from the fountain.

At the piazza's northeast edge, two adjacent four-story houses lead into the square, forming vividly painted polygonal facades that angle off toward Via Belenzani. Together they are called the Case Rella after their 19th-century owner. On the facade of the Casa Cazuffi (as the house on the left is also called), the Goddess of Fortune has regained her radiance. She is now clearly two-faced, with favorable and ominous profiles cleverly

split by the corner of the building. Her optimistic side regards the adjacent house, where polychrome scenes have appeared that were hidden beneath the accumulation of mineral salts, pigeon droppings and grime from the exhaust of cars that until recently circulated around the piazza.

Softly modeled and other-worldly white, Fortune and her companions float like clouds in an azure sky that we can now only imagine. Successful in recapturing the figures' sculptural quality, the restoration could revive only fragments of the luminous blue background.

The Wheel of Fortune appears often in Trento, echoing the fresco's own transience. Popular in the Renaissance, the motif was already established in the

piazza by the tracery of the Romanesque Duomo's rose window, where Fortune stands capriciously at the hub while helpless figures rise and fall around her.

On the Casa Cazuffi facade, the inexorable wheel appears three times: Fortune rides a deer-drawn carriage, holding the wheel in her left hand. Poised uncertainly on a sphere, she looks triumphantly forward — and gazes back in doubt. Opportunity balances the wheel for a precious moment, and thrusts her dagger. An ambitious cherub grasps her shoulder, another mounts the wheel, and those who failed to seize her fall aside. Finally, Justice stands firmly on the wheel, in perfect equilibrium. She faces us serenely, a contemplative lunar sphere upheld in one hand, a bridle for our wayward impulses in the other.

The white columns of the mullioned windows frame the figures vertically, while frescoed imitation cornices provide horizontal foundations. The medallion and lozenge shapes are bordered with Latin maxims and filled with moral emblems. Illustrating, for example, "tolerance for adversity," "shrewdness," or "the stupidity of conceit," the icons are taken from the *Emblematur Liber*, a book almost certain to have been in the library of the original owner, Tommaso Cazuffi. The Casa Cazuffi fresco has been attributed to the Vicenza artist Marcello Fogolino, who worked for Cles on the Magno Palazzo, a Renaissance addition to the castle. The fresco on the adjacent house, more mannerist in style, is now well established as a later work by a different artist. Its rainbow of colors – gold, orange,

125

magenta, green, blue, violet — barely visible before the restoration, now offers a startling contrast to the relatively monochrome Casa Cazuffi. Unlike the sea of space in which the Casa Cazuffi figures dwell, here the stage is teeming with characters, acting out didactic scenes like the Ladder of Virtue, the Triumph of Apollo and the Suicide of Lucrezia.

Walking through the piazza and into the Via Belenzani, the visitor reaches the beginning of the processional route to the castle. Dramatically aligned with the bishop's entrance to the cathedral and the Fountain of Neptune, the Via Belenzani proceeds along the same north-south axis as the original Roman road. This is the first stretch of the processional route to be renovated: the street in red-tinged porphyry and the sidewalk in rose and white stone. The stone is found nearby and was quarried in the Renaissance for the bishop's portal and the fountain.

On the street's west side is the Palazzo Alberti-Colico, whose facade is frescoed in a rare and remarkably well-preserved late Gothic motif. In this purely decorative fresco, overlapping red and blue crescents appear, each bearing a stylized spray of white leaves. Crossing over

GOOD AND BAD ADVICE
It is said that the rocky high ground overlooking the walls where the Castello del Buonconsiglio (Good Counsel Castle) stands was once called "Malconsey" (Ill-advised). The name was changed in the hope that good luck would attend the construction of the Prince-Bishop's new residence. Below, the arcades around the inner courtyard of the castle.

some wooden planks, one reaches the Palazzo Geremia. Michelangelo Lupo, the artistic consultant on the project, explained that the palazzo will be furnished with 17th-century pieces and used for exhibits and receptions.

Not far from the Palazzo Geremia, the Via Belenzani ends, and the processional route continues to the east on Via Manci, again following the original Roman road. At the corner of Via Suffragio is the Palazzo del Monte, whose frescoed facade still awaits restoration. Dating from 1515-1519, this faded fresco also honors Maximilian by depicting the Labors of Hercules, the emperor's heroic alter ego.

A short distance from the Palazzo del Monte the processional route ends at the Castello del Buonconsiglio, a governmental palace and strategic fortress commanding the Imperial Road. Construction and additions date from the 13th through the 17th centuries. In the era of Bernardo Cles, guests entered through the diamond-faceted, rusticated stone portal, strolled through the Italian garden and ascended the stairs to the loggia, frescoed by the spirited Brescian artist Gerolamo Romanino. In the loggia's blue vault, Phaeton recklessly drives the Sun God's chariot toward Zeus's fatal thunderbolt. On the floor above, in the reception room of the Magno Palazzo, Romanino's robust portraits of the Hapsburg Emperors Charles V and Ferdinand I continue the imperial theme of the Palazzo Geremia. More stately allegorical studies of Justice, Fortitude, Temperance and Prudence by the Ferrarese court painter Dosso Dossi are nearby in the Room of the Black Fireplace. A walk down a dim 14th-century corridor leads to the Torre Aquila, the castle's oldest structure. The tower's slim interior unfolds in the warm pastels of the Bohemian Venceslao's *Cycle of the Months* fresco, a candid recording in the bold International Gothic Style of nobles and peasants engaged in their seasonal activities.

Open to the public as the Museo Provinciale d'Arte, the Castello del Buonconsiglio, with its richly frescoed interior, provides the modern traveler with an interesting complement to Trento's external frescoed facades. The Renaissance traveler, with senses invigorated and perhaps with business beyond the Brenner Pass in Innsbruck or Vienna, would have headed north from the castle into the Alps, taking leave of the painted city until Fortune favored another journey.

CAROL LETTIERI *has translated three books of contemporary Italian poetry. She works in corporate communications, writing about architecture and technology.*

**THE SACRED
AND THE PROFANE**
The solemnity of the cathedral
of Trento (above, one of the
entrances) is mitigated by the
gracious Baroque work known
as the Fontana di Nettuno (left),
the work of Francesco Antonio
Giongo. Contrary to all
expectations, the architect
succeeded in making the water
flow without interruption,
as is borne out by the plaque
on the fountain: *"cum acquarum
perpetuo cursu..."*.

127

The Pale Mountains

ROCK GIANTS

Facing page, top. Against the backdrop of the Locatelli refuge, the Tre Cime (Three Peaks) of Lavaredo look like the fingers of a giant emerging from the ground.

Facing page, below. The rugged peaks of the Odle, where the renowned local mountain climber, Reinhold Messner, honed his skills as a youth.

Below, the light of dawn slips among cliff faces and ridges, barely skirting the frozen gullies and announcing its arrival on the snow-covered ledges.

A prince wanted to marry the princess of the Moon, but the young maiden would not resign herself to leaving her gleaming white home to live among the gloomy gray rock faces of the mountains of Earth. But then some industrious gnomes came to the rescue of the two lovers: in a single night the little creatures spun moonbeams and spread them out like a silvery blanket over pinnacles and peaks, ravines and cliffs. Enraptured, the princess married her beloved and came to live on Earth. Thus were born the Dolomites, which since time immemorial have also been known as the "Monti pallidi" (Pale Mountains).

The history of these magnificent peaks goes back hundreds of millions of years. In the abyssal depths of the first oceans, there accumulated an incalculable number of organisms, algae, and coral rich in calcium salts and magnesium. In the 18th century the geologist Dieudonné Gratet de Dolomieu accurately described the sedimentary rock whose origins lay in this gigantic submarine cemetery — vestiges of which are still to be found in the form of fossils — thus guaranteeing his place and name in history.

Pushed up from the depths, the rocks once lapped by the waters have become cliff faces, the towers eroded by wind and rain have been carved into curious shapes, the detritus carried away by the elements has accumulated to form boundless stretches of scree, small rocks and sand that collect to form fan-like configurations at the base of cliffs.

Bounded approximately by the rivers Adige, Brenta, Piave and Renza, the Dolomites lie between the Veneto and the Trentino-Alto Adige regions. They are not a single bloc, but are broken up into many groups and sub-groups. The best known of these are the Tofane, the Pale di San Martino, the Civetta, the Catinaccio, and the Sella, Pordoi, Brenta and Sassolungo groups. The highest peak is

the Marmolada (more than 10,000 feet), whose northern face is covered by the largest glacier in the Dolomites.

At the foot of the rocks, a paradise for mountain climbers, lie manicured pastures and vast conifer forests; hikers will find no lack of paths, "vie ferrate" (iron steps), and high climbing trails. And, in winter, the white rocks are enhanced by the ski slopes, a vast network of multiple connections that makes the Dolomites a skiing paradise. Cortina d'Ampezzo, nestling between the Tofane and the Cristallo, is a superb and fashionable spot, much favored by the international jet set.

At sunset, as the rays of the dying sun cast a warm reddish hue over the peaks, residents might recall a local legend. Laurino, the king of the dwarfs, disappointed in love, put a curse on the roses in his garden, transforming them into stone by day and by night. But at sunset, which is no longer day and not yet night, the magical rose garden blooms again.

By Muriel Spark

VENICE
in Fall and Winter

October 25, 1981

VENICE IN BLACK AND WHITE AND IN COLOR

The black of the gondolas, the white of the snow and the gray of the Palazzo Ducale (left) beneath a wintry sky: these are the ingredients of a melancholy charm that enfolds the "city on the lagoon." But inside the bars and restaurants, light and warmth and life are restored; above, the historic Café Florian, established in 1720 with the grandiose name, "Caffè della Venezia trionfante" (The Café of Venice Triumphant).

Most people who write about Venice do not tell you what they think of it but how they feel. Venice is a city not to inspire thought but sensations. I think it is something to do with the compound of air, water, architecture and the acoustics. Like the effect of these elements on the ear, there are acoustics of the heart. One can think in Venice, but not about Venice. One absorbs the marvelous place, often while thinking about something else. I have never been to Venice in summertime, or in festival time, nor at the time of any of the cinema and great art shows. My Venice belongs to late autumn and winter, the Venice of meager tourism, the Venetians' everyday city. I have never known Venice to be crowded or hurried. Perhaps for this reason, when I published a novel set in autumnal Venice, someone was puzzled by the facility with which some of my characters encountered each other in the street. It transpired he had only been in Venice during the crowded and stifling tourist seasons, when you could not very likely meet the same face two days running. In the winter it is quite different. After a week of walking around Venice – and one does have to walk a lot – or of waiting at the landing stage for the diesel-run vaporetto, the same laughing students are there, the same solemn goodwives with their shopping bags and wellpreserved fur collars, the same retired gentlemen with righteous blue eyes and brown hats. This is everyday Venice where the passers-by are sparse, where eventually they say good morning.

My first visit to Venice was on a cold, bright morning in February, with a friend who had been there before. However much one has read and heard about the visual impact of Venice, it never fails to take one by

surprise. After five visits I still gasp. It is not merely the architecture, the palaces, the bridges and the general splendor, it is the combination of architecture with water, space, light and color that causes amazement; especially, I think, the element of water. The first impression of the waterways of Venice is acoustic, so that normal sensations subliminally cease and new ones take their place. Voices, footsteps, bird cries, a cough from the window on the other side of the canal – all are different from the sounds of the land one has left. The traffic is entirely watery. A greengrocer's shop piled high with vegetables is a ship floating past your window.

After a few days of this estrangement from normal life I begin to feel at home with it. Some people tell me they can never settle down to a feeling of familiarity with Venice. Sometimes they are people who frequent the super hotels where everything is done to comfort and console the visitors who come with their usual bag of worries. I do not say that this is not a very good thing for a holiday. But the very nature of Venice is such that the things that usually preoccupy us, from which we are attempting to get away, undergo a shift of perspective after about three days.

I have known Venice in a mist and drizzle, where everything is depressed and soaking, every bridge is a bridge of sighs. But it is not the usual personal depression one is experiencing; it is something else, something belonging to Venice, it is collective. I think this is something like the reverse of Ruskin's "Pathetic Fallacy" in which he holds that artists and poets tend to attribute to nature our human responses; Venice would be "brooding" or "smiling," according to how we feel. On the contrary, I think we are sad when majestic Venice is in gloom; and if we are depressed already the fine thing about those gloomy days of Venice is that you forget what you are personally depressed about. Venice is a very good place to be sad. On days of mist, it is like a trip to the Shades. But winter often sparkles and these are the days one can sit warmly in Café Florian while outside the hardy musicians perform their nostalgic Palm Court pieces.

Venice has been declining for some hundreds of years. Decline is now of its essence, and I do not think it would be anything like as attractive to ourselves if it were on the way up in the modern sense and flourishing. The Venetians themselves talk little about Venice, never unless you ask. They are proud of their native city and attached to it, but it does not go to their heads as it does with the rest of us.

There was a time when wealthy foreigners like Milly in Henry James's *The Wings of the Dove* could take on a romantic palace, and play at princesses. Poor Milly got

THE RIALTO BRIDGE

With a single, short span the most famous bridge in Venice joins the two banks of the Grand Canal at its narrowest point. But the Rialto is not the first connection between the two banks; the boat bridges put in place here in the 12th century were replaced by wooden structures, sometimes movable in order to permit the passage of vessels with masts; the first fixed bridge was called the Ponte della Moneta (The Coin Bridge), because a toll was paid to use it. In 1444 the bridge collapsed under the weight of a crowd that flocked there to witness the passing beneath of the bride of the Marquis of Ferrara. The present day construction, finished in 1592, also houses various shops.

133

THE LOVE BOAT

The gondola, one of the symbols of the city, was first conceived to transport goods; its design is the fruit of centuries of improvements carried out by the city's shipwrights. The canals were jammed with 10,000 gondolas in Venice at the end of the 16th century but today there are only 500, and those are reserved solely for tourists and lovers (plus a few equipped as ambulances). The traditional black color was imposed by authorities in the 16th century in order to "moralize" the excessive sumptuousness of the boats.

POETIC AND LIBERTINE MASKS

While the origins of the Carnival of Venice are untraceable, it is known that the custom of wearing masks was not limited solely to the Carnival period. Many decrees (the oldest dating to the 13th century) inflicted severe punishments on those who wore masks in order to gamble incognito, avoid creditors, sneak into the homes of young ladies, or even into convents!

135

THE BRIDE OF THE SEA

Venice and water – an indissoluble union that has been celebrated since the 13th century with a Historic Regatta. First designed to train men in the use of oars, it is now a picturesque competitive event involving various types of vessels, all with equally picturesque local names: "pupparini," "mascarete," "caorlini" as well as the inevitable gondolas. At the head of them all, the Bucintoro (above), the sumptuous craft used by the Doges for the "Sposalizio del mare," an annual ritual celebrating the union of the Venetian Republic with the sea.

what she demanded, and this was, of course, how James made fun of his contemporaries in Venice: "At Venice, please, if possible, no dreadful, no vulgar hotel; but, if it can be at all managed – you know what I mean – some fine old rooms, wholly independent, for a series of months. Plenty of them, too, and the more interesting the better; part of a palace, historic and picturesque, but strictly inodorous, where we shall be to ourselves, with a cook, don't you know? – with servants, frescoes, antiquities, the thorough make-believe of a settlement."

Byron thought seriously of settling permanently in Venice to spend the winters there. Permanently is not a good idea; the city is bad for our bones, and also, the sort of infatuation a foreigner feels about Venice cannot last. Henry James's American girlfriend, if one can stretch a phrase, settled in Venice only to throw herself out of a window one dark night, to her death. Byron's Venetian girl, who threw herself into the canal, was careful to be rescued.

However, it is difficult not to be romantic about Venice. Myself, I arrived on one of my visits – it was early in November – close to midnight. All the river traffic including the taxis was on strike in solidarity with the gondoliers who had notices up demanding that gondo-

liers' claims should be dealt with "globally." There was a squall blowing in from the lagoon. It was quite a plight for me, there on the landing stage, for my luggage was heavy with some reference books (I was correcting the proofs of my Venetian novel *Territorial Rights*). But it was really exciting to strike a bargain with some men on a coal barge which rocked and plunged in the wind and surge, with me and my books among the sooty cargo, up the Grand Canal where doges and dowagers were once wont to ride in state.

The night porter at my lodgings showed no surprise; he merely came down to the landing stage to collect me and my goods, dripping rags that we were, and to make sure that the men had not overcharged me. I will always remember that midnight journey through the black water, and the calling of the bargemen, wild seabird noises, as every now and again they passed another laden vessel. The palaces were mostly in darkness with the water splashing their sides, the painted mooring poles gleaming suddenly in the light of our passing; the few lights from the windows were dim and greenish, always from tiny windows at the top. Nobody walked on the banks, and yet a strange effect that I can only describe as water voices came from those sidewalks and

landing stages. Perhaps they were ghosts, wet and cold. I usually stay at a charming, fairly old pensione near the Accademia, which sits on an angle of the Grand Canal and a side canal. In time, after I had taken in day by day all the sights and spectacles of Venice, the incredible St. Mark's Church, the happy square with its shops full of expensive junk, the Tintorettos, museums and galleries and all those already hyper-described stones of Venice, I began to form a Venice of my own. It is rather as one does with acquaintances when one goes to live for a length of time in a new country – eventually one whittles them down to an affectionate few. These I visit again and again in my winter walks and excursions, well wrapped up and wearing boots like everyone else. Most men and women wear warm hats, too.

Since one of the advantages of an off-season visit is that there are no crowds, it is possible to sit without interruption almost alone in the church of the Frari looking at Titian's *Assumption*. I love to walk around the Ducal Palace to see those four charming Tetrarchs, timid and proper and quietly influential, modestly embracing each other in a formal half-huddle. Giorgione's mysterious *Tempest* in the Accademia is another of my best-loved familiars. And I remember a sunny winter trip, and also

a cold bleak one, with a friend in the ferryboat to Torcello, one of the islands in the Venetian lagoon where very little goes on now except the magnificent Cathedral, part Gothic, part Byzantine. There is a vast biblical narrative done in seventh-century mosaics at one end, and a goldenbacked mosaic of the Madonna behind the altar, hypnotically radiant. But going behind the altar to snoop we waded into a deep pool of water that had seeped into that glorious building. We were glad of our boots. In winter there are no restaurants on the smaller islands, no bar on the ferryboats. But sweet visitors do not care, and the sour ones do not matter.

The art treasures apart, what I return to again and again are the more homely friends of my walks through the windy calles and the placid, sometimes leafy squares of Venice. These include a men's hat shop standing all alone in a small square house on the canal near Santa Maria Formosa; in the windows, and piled up inside, is a vast variety of men's hats; straw boaters, Breton sailors' berets, felt hats, black velour hats, fedoras, stetsons, hats for hunting, hats for going to funerals.

Funerals in Venice, of course, are a stately procession. The city lays on a great show, with gilt-edged barges and coffins carved within an inch of their lives.

A HINT OF THE ORIENT
Cupolas in wood and copper, gilded stuccoes, 13,000 square feet of Byzantine mosaics: is this Istanbul or Venice? Built by order of the Doge Giustiniano Partecipazio (9th century) as a resting place for the remains of St. Mark, the construction of the Basilica di San Marco was actually inspired by the ancient church of Constantinople and is a masterpiece of Romanesque-Byzantine architecture.

137

In vain the last two Popes set the example of being buried in plain pinewood boxes, there in St. Peter's for all the world to see. Venice sails on regardless. In Venice the ambulance service too is interesting: it provides a sedan chair to run a less-than-stretcher case down to the boat.

Often, in Venice, getting lost, as everyone does, I have come across a type of that high blank wall of James's *The Aspern Papers*: "...a high blank wall which appeared to confine an expanse of ground on one side of the house. Blank I call it, but it was figured over with the patches that please a painter, repaired breaches, crumblings of plaster, extrusions of brick that had turned pink with time; and a few thin trees, with the poles of certain rickety trellises, were visible over the top. The place was a garden and apparently it belonged to the house." I like the term "apparently." Because, in Venice, anything can or might lie behind those high blank walls. It is well to say apparently. One never knows.

And the bridges on the side canals are something I can gaze at for hours. Sometimes they are set in groups, obliquely, for no immediately serviceable reason, and this is all the more enchanting.

It is true that, for myself, I never cease to feel a certain amazement that all that sheer visual goodness and aural sublimity was in fact based on commerce. Culture follows gold, somebody said. Indeed, in Venice, it apparently has done so. Today in Venice you could never live and follow a culture in the sort of style that gave birth to it. In a Venetian palace you could never live a modern life: you would have to be serving the walls, serving the servants, giving orders for your private riverboat to be repaired, the mooring posts to be painted, the chandeliers to be cleaned piece by piece. To own a Venetian palace must be simply awful. Some people still do it.

It was only quite lately, in a much-traveled life, that I made my first trip to Venice. That was in 1975. I was vaguely saving it up for a romantic occasion. Special and romantic occasions were not wanting in my life but they never coincided with the possibility of a trip to Venice. So in the winter of 1975 I suddenly went. Venice itself was the romantic occasion: the medium is the message.

MURIEL SPARK is the author of 22 novels, most recently "Aiding and Abetting" and the forthcoming novel, "The Finishing School." Her most celebrated works include "The Prime of Miss Jean Brodie" and "Loitering With Intent." She lives in Tuscany.

LACE AND "MURRINE"
The skill of the lacemakers of Burano (top), a small island in the lagoon, is proverbial. According to legend, a Venetian sailor gave his sweetheart a piece of beautiful seaweed, picked up on his long sea journeys. In order to preserve the gift, the girl reproduced it with thread, copying its outlines in minute detail. Thus, lacework was born. On the nearby island of Murano, master glassblowers make bundles of multicolored glass "canes" to breathe life into ornamental patterns. The heat of the furnace composes the variegated mosaic of the traditional pendants known as "murrine" (above).

By Jan Morris

LIVELY
BIRTHPLACE
of a Fateful Word

December 13, 1981

CENTURIES OF SEGREGATION
On March 29, 1516 the Venetian government issued a decree ordering the large Jewish community to live in a designated area where the city's iron works once stood. This area became known as the ghetto, a word derived from the Venetian term "geto," meaning foundry. The decree marked the creation of Europe's first ghetto (aerial photo, right). It lasted until 1797, when Napoleon ordered the gates of the enclosure to be torn down.

A perpetually busy pedestrian thoroughfare, starting as the Lista di Spagna but changing its name repeatedly along the way, leads rumbustiously from the railway station at Venice into the heart of the city. Six or seven hundred yards along it, I suppose, beyond the great canal called Cannaregio, a smaller street takes off to the north: and if you follow this one, the Rio Terrà Farsetti, after a few minutes you will find yourself standing upon a wooden bridge before the looming back-quarters of a monumental row of buildings.

They are six, seven or eight stories high, very high for Venice, and they look from this side distinctly forbidding, for not only are their serried windows small and dark, but a canal runs all the way round them like a moat. Lines of washing flap cheerfully enough, it is true; there are canaries in cages and geraniums in pots, somebody's basket hangs on its long string waiting for the morning mail and here and there you may glimpse the movements of housewives in high kitchens. The tunnel-like entrance in front of you, though, looks grimly unwelcoming, and the sockets in its stonework, evidently meant for iron bars, make it look disturbingly like a prison gate.

Be bold. The tunnel is dark and dank indeed, but when you have passed through its shadows, and emerge through the doorway at the other end, you find yourself astonishingly in a very large, stony, airy kind of piazza, with a few young plane trees, three stone wellheads and marble benches dotted round about, and the fronts of those tall houses, not quite so cheerless from this side, towering high above it all.

Top, two miniatures from a Venetian collection of 15th-century Jewish sacred texts. They show prayer at home and the preparation of unleavened bread for Pesach, the Passover holiday, which commemorates the end of Jewish captivity in Egypt.

Tall houses built very close together (facing page) remain characteristic of the ghetto. Some of these buildings reach seven stories, unique in Venice. This vertical development of housing represented the only solution to the problem of keeping an expanding population within the limits established by law.

It feels quite different from any other Venetian square. It feels indeed only half-Venetian, with a particular tang or perhaps muffle in the air. And this is not surprising: for you are standing in a very particular part of Venice, the Ghetto – the first of all the world's enclaves to bear that fateful name, and physically perhaps the best pre-served of them to this day. Put away your guidebooks. Your instincts will be enough.

Jews were often powerful, rich, influential and admired in the Republic of Venice, but like Jews every-where in Europe they were frequently harassed, too, and in the 16th century they were all obliged to move them-selves lock, stock and barrel into this place. It had been an area of iron foundries, and was called "Geto Novo" – "New Foundry" in the Venetian dialect – and so a harm-less and necessary word went into all our vocabularies as a synonym for cruelty and intolerance. Its inhabitants were never physically harmed, but they were made to wear identifying badges and were confined to the ghet-to at night: sentries in boats patrolled the canal that completely surrounded the quarter, and barriers were placed at sunset in those ominous doorway sockets. The Jews of Venice flourished and proliferated all the same, their situation being much happier here than in most cities, and one's first instinctive impression of this remarkable place is not one of subjection – confine-ment, certainly, but confinement rather in the New York

manner, cramped but opportunist. Like Manhattan's skyscrapers, these tall buildings were designed to make the best use of limited space, and with the wide open square in front of them – one of the few campi in Venice, incidentally, to have no café tables in it – they possess a dour but undeniable excitement. One could hardly have sneered at the people who lived in this stern enclave, and indeed the life of the Venetian ghetto in its best years was lively, varied and creative.

Look up above your head now, and on the lintel there you will see the words "Banco Rosso". It is a pri-vate house now, but once it was one of the three Jewish banks that prospered here, and contributed largely to the financial stability of the Republic itself. The Jews were not allowed to own land, but they were indispen-sable as bankers and pawnbrokers, as ships' suppliers, as furnishers to diplomatic missions, as agents of many sorts. Though they were officially un-Venetians, and though this Ghetto was established in a part of the city largely reserved for aliens, still they often stood para-doxically close to the founts of power in the Republic. So we must not imagine this square, as we stroll over its somewhat bumpy flagstones, to have been a sullen or even a particularly introverted place. From the begin-ning of the Ghetto until its abolition at the fall of the Venetian Republic in 1797 it was a place more often than not full of vitality: merchants discussing deals or exchange rates, learned rabbis passing here and there, visitors no doubt from the adjoining foreign missions – scholars calling on the great publisher Daniel Bomberg, fashionable Venetians on their way to the salon of the poet Sara Copio Sullam or the consulting rooms of the famous ghetto physicians – sea captains organizing their provisions, poor folk come to hock their heirlooms, craftsmen of many kinds hammering and chiseling and sawing in ground-floor workshops all around.

The Ghetto soon expanded, and spread beyond the moat first to the south, to the area of an older iron foundry (Ghetto Vecchio), and then to the east, where it absorbed some handsome patrician mansions to form the Ghetto Nuovissimo. This was its limit until the end, and you may trace its presence exactly still, just as it was, untouched by war or pogrom.

High on the rooftops, among the bulbous Venetian chimneys, you may notice a couple of wooden cupolas, rather rickety and toppled now, but still elegant, like grace notes above the massive composition of the square below. Shortage of space made the first Jews of the Ghetto build their synagogues eyrie-like above their houses, shops and offices, nearer to God indeed than any other houses of worship in the city.

They built five in all during the first century of their segregation, three above the original square, two in the Ghetto Vecchio. All are still there, and even in this half-Eastern metropolis of the seas they are wonderfully exotic buildings to discover – so gilded still, so hung with elaborate lamps, so rich in memorial slabs, so mellow with woodwork, so grave with hanging textiles. In the Venetian manner they are called "Scuole" (Schools) and they remember in their names the particular communities that built them: the German School, the Italian School, the Spanish School, the Levantine School and the Canton School, which was named for the Canton family of bankers.

Though all have been rebuilt at one time or another, each remains different in style as in origin. The German School, for instance, the oldest of them all, is like a little opera house, trapezoidal in shape, surrounded by a delicately latticed women's gallery, and with a Bimah or pulpit of light and spindly gilt, like a sedan chair. The Spanish School on the other hand is tremendously imposing: It is said to have been rebuilt in the 17th century by Baldassarre Longhena, the architect of the great Salute church at the head of the Grand Canal, and is a showpiece of Baroque solemnity, marbled, classically detailed, heavy with brass candlesticks and hugely pendant chandeliers.

These structures were of course the foci of the ghetto, around which all else revolved, and while some fell into

IN ANCESTRAL HOMES
Even though the Jews of Venice are an integral part of the city's social fabric, the community remains fond of the ancient streets where their ancestors were confined and many still occupy the area assigned to them by the Doge long ago. Here, teachers hold courses in Jewish language and culture; also located here are the Jewish museum, the library, the nursery school and the synagogues (top).

decay in later years, some have never ceased to function. I went to Saturday service recently in the Levantine School, founded in 1538 in the Ghetto Vecchio, and marvelously moving I found it. There were perhaps a couple of dozen of us in the old building – a few women in the gallery, a handful of men below: but thrilling it was to think, as the ancient words sounded, as the cantor and his assistants huddled around their sacred scrolls like seers or navigators, that through all the miseries of exile and prejudice, through all the rise and fall of the very idea of Ghetto, that ancient sanctity had triumphed.

Though the Jews of Italy were guaranteed full civic equality by King Vittorio Emanuele II in 1866, a large community of Venetian Jews lived in the Ghetto until the precarious days of Fascism and Nazism in the 1930's, when many of them left. During the Second World War, in two terrible episodes, 200 were deported to Germany and never seen again. Today only some 20 Jewish fami-

lies live within the Ghetto area, but scattered through the municipality of Venice there are nearly 700 Jews in all, and their headquarters remain here within the old confines. The community council and the rabbinate have offices in the Ghetto Vecchio; the House of Rest for elderly Jews is in a corner of the Ghetto Nuovo; services are held every Sabbath in the Levantine School, and on special occasions in the Spanish School, too.

During the last few years the Ghetto has been noticeably reviving. I remember the place, 30 years ago, as melancholy indeed, its tall buildings crumbling, its great square rubbish-strewn and deserted, its Jewishness apparently hidden away behind locked doors – only an 18th-century stone slab of rules and regulations, and a somber 20th-century memorial to the dead of the concentration camps, honored the history of the first of all the ghettos. Today things are very different. There is a new and more assertive memorial to the victims of the holocaust, a series of bronze slabs by the sculptor Arbit

Blatas, but there is also a burgeoning of Jewish consciousness in a more hopeful kind.

For one thing those old synagogues are being restored one by one to glory, and are already becoming a tourist attraction fascinating even by Venetian standards. For another there is now a lively museum of Jewish art, beneath the German School. And for a third the Ghetto at large has found a new pride in itself, and attracts to its purlieus many kinds of craftsmen and their families – not to speak of Jewish visitors from abroad, many of whom are likely to be especially drawn there during the eight-day festival of Hanukkah. The old square rings again to the sound of saw and hammer, children kick footballs about the wellheads, and cheer up with their laughter the old people of the House of Rest, which has its own little oratory, by the way, besides an excellent kosher dining-room that is, I am told, very hospitable to visitors.

Jewish shops show themselves again. "Shalom!" is heard across the square. On one corner of the Ghetto Nuovo Gianfranco Penzo produces and sells works of art, in glass and enamel, that are an innovative blend of Jewish and Venetian forms – a union of styles, it seems, never achieved before. On another corner is the shop of the glassworker Gianni Toso: one of his chess sets, in which a team of Rabbis is matched against a team of Christian priests, was bought by the Corning Glass Museum, the ultimate accolade for craftsmen in glass. Then there are a couple of shops selling specifically Jewish souvenirs, candelabra, ornaments, postcards; and some Jewish furniture-restorers, following one of the oldest traditions of the Ghetto; and in the Calle del Forno, Oven Lane, a bakery still makes unleavened bread and Jewish sweetmeats. Sometimes there is a wedding in the Spanish School, and into the little square outside seep the wheezy strains of its venerable hand-pumped organ: and almost any day of the year, at about 10 o'clock in the morning, tourists from all over the world come trailing down the alley-ways on their guided tour of the synagogues, exchanging old Jewish jokes in Italian, Hebrew or Brooklynese. The Ghetto, a place of sad suggestion, has lost its sadness for now. Well, almost lost it. We entered the Ghetto at its northern end, where the silhouette of the square is an excitement in itself. We will leave it at the south, down the long narrow street of the Ghetto Vecchio, and there we may still feel some gentle emanations, wistful perhaps rather than tragic, of sorrows long ago.

The deportation memorial is sad, of course, and the list of names, on the wall of the Levantine School, of those Venetian Jews who died in the First World War – Aboaf, Boralevi, Foa. But it is something less tangible, something suggestive in the atmosphere or in the old gray walls that makes this thoroughfare a little dispiriting still. It feels so very tight, so shut-in, so introspective. Faces look pale down here in the shadowy light, eyes seem to look out a little suspiciously from the doors of workshops or the windows of houses up above. It feels, in short, just a little, just a tremor, like a living ghetto still.

Of course it is all imagination – the past is gone, the gates are open, the Jews of Venice are free as air: but still I think you may experience, as you pass through the

southern gateway of the Ghetto on to the sunlit quayside of Cannaregio, where the fish stalls are a babel of commerce and the espresso machines hiss hospitably in the cafés – I think you may experience, all the same, some faint sense of unease or even unreality: as though you have passed through a chamber of time, or wandered down that alley from one sensibility to another.

There was a happy sequel to this essay. A lady in New York was inspired by it to visit the glassworker's shop it mentions. She fell in love with Signor Toso and when they were married they invited me to a celebratory lunch in Manhattan. I took along my friend the actor Dick Cavett, and a great time we had of it.

JAN MORRIS, who lives in Wales, has traveled almost everywhere, and has also written extensively about Venice. She recently published her "final" work, "Trieste and the Meaning of Nowhere."

VILE PERSECUTION

The Holocaust that overwhelmed Europe in the 20th century did not spare the Jews of Venice or Italy as a whole. Mussolini's infamous "race laws," enacted by the Fascist government, forced Jews into a harrowing new exodus.

Above, a religious ceremony held on board the ship Conte di Savoia that, in 1940, took a large group of Italian Jews to America.

By Susan Lumsden

A Palladian Journey in
VICENZA

August 13, 1989

Palladio himself could not have designed a better view of the subtle symmetry of his 16th-century Villa La Rotonda than from a four-seater plane high in the sky above the province of Vicenza in northeastern Italy. La Rotonda, the architect's most celebrated building, appears as a giant crab grasping its Berici hillock at its highest and most logical point. Nearby, some of the province's other Palladian villas – Pisani, Malinverni, Piovene, Poiana and Saraceno – nestle naturally into the landscapes. Sublime architecture, they are also brilliant sculpture (Vicenza's villas are among 25 that are scattered throughout the larger Veneto region). Flying high in this judgmental fourth dimension, one almost hears the music of Mozart's opera *Don Giovanni*, filmed at La Rotonda in 1981.
Suddenly, there's another voice, that of the pilot who regularly flies the planes of an "aero club" that are available to tourists on sightseeing flights...

"On the left is Juliet's castle, now a restaurant of Montecchio Maggiore," he said of the tragic heroine whom Shakespeare placed in the area. "Over there is Romeo's castle, really more of a rockpile."

Andrea Palladio (1508-1580), who was born in nearby Padua, went to the city of Vicenza as a young stonecutter. His potential was recognized by Gian Giorgio Trissino, one of the local nobility, which had created a humanist court in the hinterland of Venice. Palladio wrote of Vicenza as "a city of no very large circumference, but full of noble intellects." As well as Trissino's, these included those of the counts of Thiene, Barbaro, Pisani and Chiericati, some of the names that still label the region's Palladian buildings. In 1614, they were visited by the English architect Inigo Jones who constructed the Banqueting House in London (1622) on Palladian principles.

THE INCARNATION OF HARMONY
Symmetry embodies the Renaissance ideal of perfection. Set on a piece of high ground, Villa Almerico Capra Valmarana, known as "La Rotonda", can truly be described as one of the queens of Palladian villas thanks to its sumptuous yet solemn interior décor and the purity of its lines. A masterpiece of Italian art.

THE SORROW OF THE DWARFS

Legend has it that the dwarfs on the walls of Villa Valmarana (top) are the servants of a prince, petrified by grief at the death of their mistress. Above, a detail of the garden of Villa Piovene in Lugo.

More important to Palladio's posterity were his *Four Books on Architecture* (*I Quattro Libri dell'Architettura*, 1570), arguably the best how-to series of all time, translated into English in 1737 at the instigation of the third Lord Burlington, whose own country seat, Chiswick House, near London, was a variation on La Rotonda.

By the time of the American Revolution, the Palladian belief in "natural" laws and proportions in architecture was easily transplanted in the 13 Colonies. Thomas Jefferson designed his own home, Monticello, on Palladian precepts. He also used the architect's unexecuted design for the Villa Trissino at Meledo for the University of Virginia. Although Jefferson's plan for a White House like the Villa La Rotonda was rejected, his own Memorial is a variation on that same porticoed temple of antiquity.

But perhaps the most beautiful of America's Palladian-inspired, antebellum mansions, real or imagined, was Ashley Wilkes's Twelve Oaks in *Gone With the Wind*, with its tall white columns and center hall open back and front to the greenery around. It was not surprising, then, to find that Palladio's presumed home in Vicenza had been restored by the American Institute of Decorators under the leadership of William Pahlmann in 1957.

Unlike his city palaces, which are derivative of Bramante and other Renaissance architects, Palladio's country villas are clearly classical. Their model was the old walled Roman villa recast by Palladio as a temple and liberated to the fields around. "Every architect finds his own antiquity," writes James Ackerman in *The Architect and Society: Palladio*. In point, Palladio's was the "stripped style of antiquity" lifted from the Rome of masons and engineers, not of architects and decorators influenced by Greek traditions. Particularly in Palladio's country villas, symmetry was the rule. Yet, within this rule, there was a fascinating flexibility as one can discover touring the villas of Vicenza province. Many were summer homes for wealthy Venetians escaping the malodorous Grand Canal and were unheated. They are still generally unheated, uninhabited and closed in the winter. The outstanding exception is the Villa Pisani which, at first glance, appears to be afloat in the long grass that grows right up to its foundations at Bagnolo di Lonigo, about 12 miles south of Vicenza. A rare stone villa of Palladio, it was completed in 1545 and features the rampant lion crest of the original Pisani family in its pediment.

The villa was restored a few years ago by its present owner, the Countess Maria Pia Ferri de Lazara, and her children. It had been subdivided by their tenant farmers into a rabbit warren of rooms. "We felt we just couldn't let this happen to Palladio," the Countess recently explained, waving toward the reopened central portion magnificently cross-vaulted and frescoed by an unknown 16th-century artist.

Outside, the Palladian villas appear to be perfectly, almost magically, grounded in nature. Inside, they seem to be reaching for Heaven. The latter effect is achieved by the lofty ceilings with frescoes in pastel, allegorical scenes that render the furniture almost insignificant. In the Villa Pisani, for example, the visitor's eye is drawn upward by happy scenes of typical villa activities – hunting, dancing, swimming and eating. Immediately south of Vicenza, the most celebrated but uninhabited Palladian villa, La Rotonda, features frescoes by Lodovico Dorigny, stuccoes by Lorenzo Rubini and an oil portrait of the wise, distinguished-looking Palladio.

Decidedly, the villa's 100,000 visitors a year do not have the warmth of a resident family. But La Rotonda was designed by Palladio for a retired cleric, Paolo Almerico, as a summer party house, in about 1567.

Guests could sleep in the second-floor bedrooms, closed to contemporary visitors but accessible by the four fetching staircases almost lost in the soaring center hall. The hall is flanked by four richly frescoed, although sparsely furnished, living rooms with fireplaces decorated by

FROM CASTLE TO ARISTOCRATIC VILLA

The Palladian Villa Pisani in Bagnolo di Lonigo was built about the middle of the 16th century over the ruins of the castle of the Nogarole family.
The frescoes inside, inspired by allegorical representations, are attributed to Bernardino India, a pupil of Raphael. Damaged during World War II, the villa underwent long, painstaking restoration, which brought it back to its former splendor. Above, the Music Room.

AN UNMISTAKABLE
SILHOUETTE
By night, Vicenza is dominated
by the unmistakable silhouette
of the Palladian basilica.
Once the Palazzo della Ragione,
the building was restored and
remodeled by Palladio in 1549.
Along the entire perimeter
are three-light windows,
known as "finestre serliane,"
named after Sebastiano Serlio
(1475-1554), who established
the canons for their design.

Ridolfi. This four-fronted monument is topped by a dome like those over the Roman baths that so fascinated Palladio.

Standing beneath the dome in the middle of the center hall open on four sides to the Berici Hills beyond is like levitating in a low flying saucer. Better still, the Villa La Rotonda can be rented for very rare and auspicious occasions, says the owner, Count Ludovico de Valmarana, who didn't miss a day's shooting of *Don Giovanni*. There are different ways of seeing the Palladian villas of Vicenza. For tourists with a car, the most obvious approaches are the north or south roads out of the city. Each direction's sites require at least a day, given the distances and incompatibility of certain villa schedules. For visitors traveling independently, an interesting, albeit circuitous, tour is the chronological approach to Palladio. His first job, as a young stonemason, was the restoration in 1537 of the Villa Trissino at

Cricoli on Highway 248 north from Vicenza to Lonedo di Lugo, the site of his first original work, the Villa Godi-Valmarana-Malinverni, in 1542.

The Palladian palaces and villas are named for their owners, and have been since their creation. Since basically the same families have commissioned, bought and sold the same villas over the centuries, there is some room for confusion. The Malinvernis, for example, are the present owners of Palladio's first and relatively massive villa. Its flanking tower blocks are clearly derivative of the still Gothic Villa Trissino. The Villa Malinverni's small central atrium would gradually blossom forth elsewhere into the graceful columned pronaos or porch of fame and imitation.

Characteristically the interior highlights of this villa are the frescoes reflecting the full evolution of painting by the late Renaissance. Executed by Zelotti, Del Moro and

attributed to Palladio, his hallmark, the central portico, was completed in 1587, seven years after his death. The two attached side buildings, called "barchesse," were completed in the 18th century. This second characteristic of Palladio, the attached dependence, is strangely missing in later English and American versions possibly because of the implied proximity of the slaves, servants, animals or maybe the guests. While the villa itself is closed to visitors, its garden and large neoclassical park with a 15th-century chapel to St. Gerolamo are worth the walk and the view. Another way of visiting some of the villas is through the back door. A few of the buildings are actually abandoned, at least unoccupied and partly open to the elements. In all fairness, Italy is strapped by its countless architectural monuments which, in turn, are tied up by laws preventing owners from altering them for easier living. One case is the Villa Poiana Maggiore, designed by Palladio and completed in 1566, between Noventa and Lonigo, 23 miles south of Vicenza. This small villa features an unusual atrium with five lunettes. It looks almost post-modern.

One day last winter, the only inhabitants of the Villa Poiana Maggiore were frightened birds one of which instantly killed itself by flying into the vaulted ceiling frescoed presumably by the great Giambattista Zelotti, who also adorned the Villa Malinverni. In a smaller adjacent room, the walls and ceilings are covered with whimsical characters known as grotteschi and probably painted by Anselmo Canera and Bernardino India of the 16th-century Veronese School. Not so curiously, the frescoed interiors so characteristic of the Palladian villas are better preserved than the exteriors, many of which were never completed. Missing a balancing left barchessa, the Villa Poiana is nevertheless striking with its external statues standing like guardians through time.

Palladio's similarly small and uncompleted Villa Saraceno (designed about 1545) can be seen nearby at Finale di Agugliaro off the Strada Statale 500, south of Vicenza. At the moment, its poor state of repair allows a look at Palladio unadorned. The ordinary red bricks visible through the crumbling stucco reveal another reason for Palladio's popularity in his own lifetime: he was affordable. His stucco facades were not only accessible to the medium rich but were also changeable, allowing the refined Venetians and their enlightened country cousins to experiment with color. Unmaintained, they look shabby but their harmonious structures, like good bones, save them 400 years later.

SUSAN LUMSDEN, a Canadian journalist and broadcaster, spent the last 15 years of her life as a free-lance journalist in Italy writing about travel and art history. She died in 1994.

Padovano, they are perfectly conserved historical and mythological scenes of the classical, pre-Christian world represented by the exterior, some of them quite witty. Perhaps the most exultant is the Room of the Muses and the Poets by Del Moro, with the pastel Grecian-robed goddesses seeming to support the entire room. In addition, this luxurious villa offers a gallery of 19th- and 20th-century Italian art, a collection of antique musical instruments, a 19th-century "English" park and a working tavern-restaurant.

A fine contrasting example of mature, full-blown Palladio is conveniently next door at the Villa Piovene-Porto-Godi. If ever a villa were enthroned in nature it is this one set into the pre-Dolomites like the original temple to the gods, particularly when seen from the approaching plain and in winter when snow rims the mountains. Although the design of this villa is usually

THE MAESTRO AND HIS LAST WORK

The last work of Palladio (above, in a 16th-century portrait), the Teatro Olimpico (top) was completed by Vincenzo Scamozzi, who enlarged the building with three new and large rooms, known overall as the Odeo Olimpico. The name derives from the Accademia Olimpica, an association devoted to the cultivation of the humanities, arts and sciences that built the theater for staging classical tragedies.

The city of Romeo and Juliet

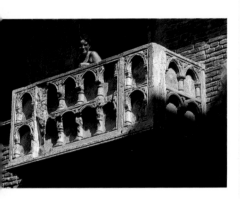

ROMANTICISM AND SPECTACLE
Above, the balcony of "Juliet's House," the romantic destination par excellence. Below, a performance of Verdi's *Aida* in the setting of the Roman Arena. Facing page, a view of the city.

On the banks of the river Adige, its back protected by the Lessini mountains and open on the west to the breezes of Lake Garda, lies Verona, one of the pearls of the Veneto plain. More than a mile of city walls, erected by the Scaligeri family in the 13th century and modified by the Austrians in the 19th century, enclose a city that is famous for three things: home of Romeo and Juliet, the cake known as "pandoro," and its Roman arena. To this day, crowds visit so-called "Juliet's House" (created in 1935 from a restructured 13th-century building) and move on to "Juliet's Tomb," located, naturally, in via Shakespeare. Patisseries offer delicious chocolate sweets called "baci di Romeo" and "baci di Giulietta" (Romeo's and Juliet's kisses).

Pandoro was first created in 1894 by Domenico Melegatti, a local confectioner. In that year, inspired by the famous sweets in the Viennese tradition, which is deeply rooted in Verona, this creative craftsman produced a light and fluffy sweet cake, with a star-shaped cross-section, and patented it with the Ministry of Agriculture of the Kingdom of Italy. The dusting of vanilla icing sugar that adorns its top helps to make this delightful Christmas cake well known even outside Italy. The Arena of Verona, built in the 1st century AD, between the reigns of Augustus and Claudius, is one of the best conserved Roman theaters in Italy. It originally stood on the outskirts of Verona but has been gradually absorbed by the expansion of the city, so much so that it is now in the heart of the old city center. Albeit in different forms, it has never ceased to be a perfect setting for spectacular events: gladiatorial contests and popular shows mentioned by Pliny the Younger, medieval jousting and tournaments, circuses, theatrical performances and even bullfights. Since 1913 it has been home to the city's operatic season, including some memorable performances of Verdi's *Aida*.

By Francine Prose

TRIESTE,
Where Vienna Meets Venice

May 13, 2001

THE HOWL OF THE WIND AND SEA

Piazza Unità d'Italia (on the preceding pages) is flanked on three sides by imposing buildings from the 18th-19th centuries, while the fourth side borders the sea. When the icy winter wind known locally as the bora begins to blow, the large square offers no resistance and the end result, as Trieste's finest novelist, Italo Svevo, put it, is: "an immense howl composed of the union of various smaller voices."

Elegant buildings overlook the seafront (above). Facing page, the Serbian Orthodox church of Saint Spiridion.

From across the Caffè San Marco, the most splendid and theatrically Old World of Trieste's historic coffeehouses, I find myself unable to stop staring at the elderly man who, like certain figures you see when you are traveling, seems conjured up, by magic, to enhance the ambience of a place. Perhaps it's just the setting – the glossy, dark wood paneling, the golden walls, the marble-topped tables, the paintings of masked revelers, the uniquely Triestian mix of Vienna and Venice – but it's easy to imagine that the elegant coffee drinker has been at that same table with his newspaper for the century or so since the cafe was founded.

I keep thinking of the characters of Trieste's greatest novelist, Italo Svevo, gathering in coffeehouses like this one to discuss their romantic and financial affairs: businessmen-artists, cosmopolitan hicks, patriots who love their city yet fear that it has somehow fallen off the edge of the known world, isolated by its position on the border of Italy, Austria and the Balkans, cut loose by its years as a bargaining chip in the forging of treaties and alliances. Colonized by the Romans in the second century B.C., Trieste was taken over by the Venetian Republic in 1202. In 1303 it placed itself under the protection of the Hapsburgs and remained part of the Austro-Hungarian Empire until the end of World War I, when it was returned to Italy, only to be overrun again, first by the Nazis, then by Marshal Tito of Yugoslavia. Not until 1954 did the city again become part of Italy. This troubled history has left its scars on Trieste's landmarks (the Caffè San Marco, which opened in 1914 and was restored after being damaged in World War I) and on its older residents, many of whom have the haunted, slightly otherworldly look of the elderly man in the cafe. When at last he rises, folds his paper and leaves, I half expect to see the filtered late-morning light shining through his ethereal frame.

Trieste is proud of its melancholy ghosts. At the time of my visit, the tourist office has run out of brochures that direct visitors to the locations frequented by James Joyce during the 11 years he lived here with his family, taught English at Berlitz, finished *Dubliners* and nearly starved to death. But at the Museo Sveviano – a modest collection of mementos and vintage photographs housed on the second floor of the musty, fabulously old-fashioned public library – you can pick up a map of the places where Svevo lived and wrote the bittersweet

THROUGH DESERTED ROOMS
All Maximilian of Hapsburg
wanted from life was "a castle
with a big garden overlooking
a beach." He got his wish, but it
didn't last long. Miramar castle
(below) was finished in 1864;
that same year the archduke
boarded ship for Mexico, where
he briefly became Emperor.
The adventure came to a tragic
end three years later with his
execution by a Mexican
republican army firing squad.
Maximilian's wife, Charlotte
of Saxony, lost her mind
and ended her days in Belgium,
at her father's court. The
sumptuous rooms of Miramar
were left desolate and empty.

novels that themselves function as guides to this moody
and beautiful port city on the Adriatic.

In Svevo's fiction, the climate is often inclement, a further torment to his brooding heroes as they wander the
rainy, windswept waterfront in search of impossible
loves. But during the bright early autumn days I spent
in Trieste with my husband, Howie, the Adriatic was
tranquil and blue, the hills surrounding the city a sort
of silvery California green, and the weather couldn't
have been balmier.

Everything in Trieste and in the surrounding
province of Friuli-Venezia Giulia reminds you of so
many disparate places and historical periods that the
result is like nothing else, like nowhere else. Unlikely
combinations crop up in every aspect of the life of the
region, from its local cuisine to its urban and rural
landscapes.

In trattorias that resemble Tyrolean chalets, you can
order pasta with goulash, prune gnocchi, ravioli sauced
with butter and cinnamon, a delectable sort of potato
pancake (called "frico") filled with melted cheese. The
hills of the Collio, north of the city, one of Italy's major
wine-growing areas, look — except for the onion-domed
churches — like Tuscan vineyards. In Trieste itself, it's
possible to wander along a wide canal (the Canale
Grande) past a 19th-century version of a Venetian
palazzo, then past the blue-domed Serbian Orthodox

church of San Spiridione and into a small square lined
with brightly painted houses reminiscent of Ljubljana,
in Slovenia, or Prague. Alternately, you can wander the
Borgo Teresiano, a Hapsburg grid of orderly streets,
banks and office buildings decorated with heroic,
aggressively Rococo nude statuary and then, minutes
later, enter the mazelike alleys of the medieval city.
They wind beside a well-preserved Roman amphitheater and up the hill of San Giusto to a cathedral decorated with 12th-century mosaics, smaller, plainer versions of those at Ravenna.

The trip up to San Giusto is particularly rewarding. The cathedral is very much a work in progress,
still under renovation when we visited; successive
revisions and additions range from the Roman portrait
busts embedded in the facade to mosaics from the
1930's. In the churchyard are the ruined pillars of the
Roman basilica and forum, as well as a rugged castle
begun in the 14th century — only serious medieval
armor buffs will want to linger in its museum — surrounded by walkways and turrets offering spectacular
views of the sea, the busy harbor and the limestone
hills beyond. You can feel the energy rising up from
the city, the hum and buzz of Trieste's reawakening
from its postwar torpor, partly thanks to the computer
industry, drawn to the area by factors that include the
physics center down the coast at Miramare, not far

Ettore Schmitz and Italo Svevo

As far as the people of Trieste were concerned, for most of his life he was merely Ettore Schmitz (1861-1928), a comfortably well off gentleman, an honest businessman and a good family man. He had a sole vice, literature, cultivated by writing short stories for *L'Indipendente*, a small Trieste-based newspaper, and publishing novels at his own expense. Apparently an unknown amateur writer, he was hailed at his death as one of the pioneering novelists of the last century. The son of a wealthy Jewish merchant (his father, who was in the glass business, was German; his mother, Italian), he went into the family business. But bankruptcy forced him to find employment with the Banca Union in Trieste, where he worked for almost 20 years. Marriage to Lidia Veneziani, the daughter of a paint factory owner, led to his joining his father-in-law's company in 1899. There he spent the rest of his life, making only a few business trips abroad and giving himself over to his all-consuming passion for literature, cultivated semi-clandestinely under the pseudonym of Italo Svevo.

And if, in 1925, the Italian poet Eugenio Montale and James Joyce had not turned a literary spotlight on the "Svevo case" in the most influential magazines, the employee Schmitz would have always remained exactly that. His talent would have never emerged from an office where all one seemed to breathe was the vapors of solvents and other chemical products, and certainly not the air of the most important cultural currents in Europe. Yet his tormented, painful novels, which unfold to the rhythms of a poignant and occasionally ironic disenchantment, convey the speculative thinking of Schopenhauer and Freud, Darwin and Marx. Svevo also probed the barely explored field of the subconscious. He introduced the new technique of the interior monologue, which ventures deeply into the characters and exposes their neuroses and tendencies toward self-deception.

The difficulties of leading a double life emerge in a brief autobiographic profile in which Schmitz/Svevo explains that the chilly critical response to his first two novels, *A Life* and *Senility* very nearly put an end to his literary vocation: "I resolved to give up literature as it evidently weakened my commercial capacities and I devoted what little spare time I had to the violin in order to repress my literary dreams. The war caused me to lose business and this was probably the reason for the lengthy break that, in 1919, led to my writing *The Conscience of Zeno*, which I published in 1923." Recognition, so long delayed, soon followed but the novelist did not enjoy it for long. It was only after his death in an automobile accident five years later that Svevo was lauded as a brilliant exponent of the early 20th-century European novel.

WHERE HISTORY WEDS POETRY

The order, a coffee or an aperitif, is merely an excuse. People crowd Trieste's historic cafés to experience an atmosphere, to leave one world behind them and plunge into another, more diaphanous but no less real for all that – a world that breathes the same air that seduced Italo Svevo (above) and James Joyce, Umberto Saba and Stendhal. In the 19th century Trieste was crammed with hundreds of cafés; today only a handful like the Caffè degli Specchi, the San Marco (left), the Tommaseo and the Tergesteo bear the standard of a blend of past and present, culture, art and everyday life – a little more stimulating than just drinking a coffee.

A RECORD BREAKING CAVE
The Grotta Grande at Sgonico, near Trieste, made the Guinness Book of Records in 1995 as the world's largest tourist cave. It was opened to the public in 1908, after four years of preparatory work. On inauguration day the gloom of the cavern was banished by the light of 4,000 candles, while the band cheered the huge crowd of onlookers with the music of Wagner. Postcards from the period showed side-by-side photos of the main part of the cave and St Peter's in Rome, implying that the latter could have easily been contained by the former.

from the castle at Duino where Rilke was inspired to write his elegies.

Even on the sunniest days, Trieste casts deep shadows. A few steps downhill from the cathedral, the Civico Museo di Storia ed Arte contains a fine collection of antiquities, Egyptian mummies and treasures from Roman tombs. On the grounds is a chapel housing the remains of the archaeologist J. J. Winckelmann, who was killed while on a trip to Trieste in 1868. According to one story, he made the mistake of showing off some gold coins to an acquaintance and was murdered – presumably for his art treasures – by an eavesdropping waiter. A charmingly and romantically gloomy garden – the Orto Lapidario, or Stone Garden – is decorated with sculpture and features a large structure, a sort of shed, sheltering tombstones and votive objects exhumed from the graveyards of the ancient and medieval world.

As we walked the trail that winds through the attractively shaggy garden, church bells began to toll, disturbing the dozens of semiferal cats who make their home there. Like a feline version of the elderly coffee drinker at the Caffè San Marco, a black cat appeared and ran just ahead of us, pausing every so often to look back over its shoulder. The whole scene – the funerary monuments, the tomb of the murdered archaeologist, the gauzy greenery, the tolling bells, the cat – had the obvious but effective spookiness of a dream sequence in an early Bergman film.

Yet another attractive aspect of Trieste is that you never feel the guilt-inducing pressure of a long list of art sites you think you should probably visit. Most of the city's museums, in former private houses, still retain their original furnishings and architectural details, which are generally more interesting than the art – the result of the somewhat spotty collecting tastes of the city's princes of commerce and finance. The Museo Revoltella, in particular, is a kind of wonderland of 19th-century kitsch, displaying paintings with titles like *Listening to Beethoven* and *After the First Communion*. Like Marseilles and Miami, Trieste is not a city to which you go to see much of anything in particular but rather just to be there, to experience the pulse and rhythm of the place: dodge its swarming Vespas; browse

Gallerie del Tiepolo, a section of the Museo Diocesano in the Palazzo Patriarcale, in which there is also an engaging collection of Friulian religious sculpture from the 13th through the 18th centuries. Commissioned by the region's archbishop, Dionisio Delfino, the frescoes of the gallery and the ceiling over the staircase were painted between 1726 (when Tiepolo was about 30) and 1730. Representing his first major commission, they have the assurance and the exuberance of a great artist proving himself, and coming into his own. The colors in the Old Testament scenes that cover the gallery – *Sarah and the Angel*, *Rachel Hides the Idols*, *Abraham and the Angel*, *Jacob's Dream* – are splashier and livelier (and the human drama more individual and intense) than in Tiepolo's earlier work.

In the so-called Red Room, you can almost watch him discovering the fun that can be had with perspective, trompe l'oeil, the viewer's position in relation to the image. In *The Judgment of Solomon*, the baby (whose mother pleads for its life with the cruel soldier who holds her child nearly upside down) seems to dangle, terrifyingly, directly over our heads. These daring experiments with the energies and dizzying possibilities of space seem already perfected in *Banishment of the Rebel Angels*, a portrayal of the guilty and unhappy angels repenting – too late! – as they are sent spinning through space, sprouting bat wings and tails. The painting's placement, over the staircase descending several stories, dramatically increases our sense of the distance that the angels are going to have to fall as they plummet past us down the stairwell.

To see the frescoes in this setting is very different than viewing Tiepolo among the dutiful crowds in Venice. On a Saturday morning, Howie and I spent an hour and a half, mostly in the gallery, and in that entire time, only one other couple came into the museum. The privacy and quiet also made it possible to see *The Rebel Angels* as we did – lying flat on the stairs and looking up at the ceiling.

the antiques shops on the Via dei Rettori; walk the Corso Cavour at dusk when the whole population, it seems, turns out for a leisurely stroll; look out your hotel window to see the last rays of sunlight strike the golden mosaics on the facade of the Palazzo del Governo, across the grand sweep of the monumental Piazza dell'Unità d'Italia; or eat fritto misto at a waterfront restaurant, watching ships come and go and listening to your fellow diners switch effortlessly back and forth between Italian and Slovenian.

There are great art treasures in Friuli. About 45 miles northwest of Trieste, the prosperous, sleepy, immensely pleasant – and rarely visited – city of Udine calls itself, with good reason, the "City of Tiepolo." The Duomo contains several works by the Venetian master, as does the nearby small Oratorio della Purità, where the ceiling is decorated with Tiepolo's newly restored *Assumption*. On the day we visited, the chapel was being prepared for a wedding; bouquets of white roses and ribbons adorned the pews and a tenor, a violinist and an organist were rehearsing the *Ave Maria*. By far the most numerous and magnificent frescoes are in the

The pace and the prettiness of Udine make you fantasize about living there, visiting the Tiepolos every now and then, and in the evenings going out to eat (or even to stay) at one of the agriturismo farm-inns that dot the Friulian countryside, cooking and serving up extraordinary meals, with many locally grown ingredients. But in case you are eager to see another major wonder of the world of art, less than an hour south, the third corner in the triangle of short drives from Trieste – you can proceed to Aquileia.

Once the fourth-most-important city of the Roman Empire, a regional capital of about 100,000, Aquileia never quite regained its prominence after being sacked

**BENEATH THE SIGN
OF THE STAR**

Built between 1906 and 1912 by Ruggero and Arduino Berlam, the synagogue of Trieste bears witness to the presence of the city's large Jewish community at the time.

CITY OF TIEPOLO

The Bishop's Palace in Udine, the seat of the Patriarch of Aquileia until 1751, is an authentic sanctuary dedicated to Tiepolo. In his *The Fall of the Rebellious Angels* the artist used stucco to represent one of Lucifer's arms and a strip of clothing that protruded beyond the frame, lending the picture a three-dimensional effect. *The Judgment of Solomon* (left), on the ceiling of the Sala Rossa, has a similar effect on the viewer thanks to Tiepolo's use of perspective.

163

THE SOUL OF UDINE

This square was once called Piazza Contarena, in gratitude to the lawyer Girolamo Contarini who had it paved in the 15th century. It was also known as the "piazza del vino" as it resounded with the cries of wine merchants as they made their deals. Finally renamed Piazza della Libertà, today it is considered one of Italy's finest squares in the Venetian style. The place of honor is occupied by the 15th-century Loggia del Lionello with its alternating bands of white and pink stone.

by Attila, and gradually dwindled into a small provincial town. It has an amazing archaeological museum, and there is a walk you can take along the Via Sacra, once the principal street of Aquileia's important river-port system and now an astonishingly beautiful lane lined with cypresses, lush lawns, a canal and archaeological fragments. The floors of private Roman houses remain in a field near the Via Sacra and across the main road; these well-preserved mosaics depict animals and geometric forms that give you a sense of the domestic architecture and of the layout of a neighborhood in ancient Rome.

Any of this would be enough to merit a trip to Aquileia, even if it weren't for its real eye-popper: the patriarchal basilica, founded in the fourth century and worked on for almost a millennium, with a floor the size of a soccer field and a fourth-century pavement, more than 800 square yards, completely covered with a prodigious mosaic portraying writhing animals, faces, birds, a fight between a rooster and a turtle, a detailed and animate fishing scene. These images out of some paleo-Christian Looney Tunes assume the additional weight of being early Christian symbols. There are two crypts, one painted with 12th-century frescoes of the life of St.

Hermagoras, a martyr and an early bishop of Aquileia, and another in which you can see, through a plexiglass floor, more recent excavations exposing yet more mosaics.

Just outside the basilica, I watched a group of men working in a cordoned-off area, carefully digging and brushing dirt and dust off a mosaic floor. It is possible, given Aquileia's remoteness, that these workers were the direct descendants of the original Romans who lived here, or of the invading Huns, or both. But who knows if they were thinking about any of this on a warm cloudy September morning, as they labored to unearth what has been buried for centuries beneath the layers of history that underlie so much of Friuli, and Trieste?

_____

FRANCINE PROSE is the author of 12 novels, including the National Book Award finalist, "Blue Angel," and the forthcoming "A Changed Man" (HarperCollins). She is also the author of "Sicilian Odyssey," a work of nonfiction.

BASILICA OF THE PATRIARCHS
The slender columns of the
Roman Forum and a row of
svelte cypresses look like maids
of honor to the towering bell
tower of the basilica of
Aquileia. The church, founded
in the 4th century by Bishop
Teodoro, destroyed by the Huns
in 452, rebuilt and redesigned
many times, was the most
important religious symbol
of the Patriarchate of Aquileia.
Excavations beneath the floor
of the basilica have revealed
the most extensive mosaic
decorations in western
Christendom (above, a detail).

165

By Elisabetta Povoledo

In Bologna
A Grand Plaza Defines the City

September 24, 2000

A PLACE TEEMING WITH MEMORIES

Between piazza Maggiore and piazza del Nettuno (right), the people would assemble to hear the town crier read out proclamations and new laws. Here, too, knights staged tournaments and justice was meted out. This small area has witnessed nothing less than the history of Bologna, from condemned men hanging from the balcony of Palazzo della Podestà to the ill-fated prisoner-king Enzo, the son of Emperor Frederick II of Swabia, who tried to escape his jailers by hiding in a wine barrel.

Few Italian cities still live in their main squares as intensely as Bologna does. Since the 13th century, the Piazza Maggiore has served as the city's social, administrative, political and commercial heart. Milestone events that have marked Bologna's history – from the celebrations for the coronation of Charles V as Holy Roman Emperor in 1530, to the city's collective rage after a extreme right wing terrorist bomb killed 85 people at the train station in 1980 – have been commemorated there.

From morning to night, the sounds of Bologna overlap and merge in the square. Mornings bring the soft prayers of the devout in the Basilica of San Petronio at early Mass, the clamor of the nearby food market and the shuffle of briefcase-carrying civil servants on their way to the Palazzo d'Accursio, the original part of Bologna's immense city hall, the Palazzo Comunale.

As the day progresses, the shouts of schoolchildren visiting the Municipal Collections of Art or the Morandi Museum become more boisterous, and eventually the piazza becomes an after-school playground where passers-by duck flying soccer balls.

Around sunset, the square fills with clusters of older Bolognesi – mostly men – animatedly discussing the latest soccer match, and cafe-lounging people-watchers savoring aperitifs at tables in front of the Palazzo del Podestà. At night, students from Bologna's renowned university – dating back to the 11th century, it is one of the oldest in the Western world – gather for concerts, street performances or just hanging out.

The square was built by the Commune, or town council, so that Bologna's citizens – at the time 50,000, more than Rome, Paris or London – had a place to meet. Over the centuries, the Piazza Maggiore has reflected the

changing city. Today, another transformation is under way, sparked by Bologna's selection as one of nine European Capitals of Culture for the year 2000.

Bologna has many nicknames. It is known as "la grassa" (the fat), for its love of food and physical pleasures. It is known as "la rossa" (the red), not because of its political inclinations (from the end of World War II until last year it was governed by Communist or post-Communist administrations), but because of the distinctive russet red brick that has shaped much of its architecture. And it is known as "la dotta" (the learned), because of its university.

Although it has the lowest birth rate in Italy, Bologna is a city of young people. The presence of the students is felt everywhere, from the profusion of funky clubs and well-stocked bookstores, to the enormous outdoor market selling used just-about-everything that takes over the central Via dell'Indipendenza every Friday and Saturday. Bologna takes its role as a center of education seriously. Of the many projects associated with Bologna 2000, one in particular is intended to encourage the Bolognesi to remain "dotti," and that is the transformation of the so-called Ex Sala Borsa, or Former Stock Exchange, into Italy's largest multimedia library. Part of Palazzo d'Accursio, the Stock Exchange, just off the square, was built in the late 19th century, when the city administration decided it would be more dignified for farmers to do their haggling inside rather than on the streets. The farmers snubbed the offer (they were too attached to their beloved piazza) and after various incarnations, the building has been restored. The enormous central hall has retained its 19th-century look, ringed by arcades on three levels, but to be fitted out with 900 work stations and some 300 computer terminals.

The restoration brought to light Bologna's distant past. Traces of Etruscan wells and of the Roman forum and basilica were found, leading archaeologists to conclude that this spot was once the heart of the ancient city. The remains of these foundations are visible through the glass floor in the main hall of the Stock Exchange. The building reopened with an exhibition on Charles M. Schulz and "Peanuts" (Italians love Snoopy).

If you ask a Bolognese to meet you somewhere downtown, he is likely to suggest the enormous 16th-century fountain of Neptune, just outside the front door of the Sala Borsa. Certainly, the gigantic bronze sculpture of the god of the sea, by the Flemish sculptor Giambologna (the fountain itself was designed by Tommaso Laureti) is hard to miss and there are steps to sit on and people to watch should your date be late. The statue is a symbol of the city, as are two imposing early

12th-century towers in the nearby Piazza di Porta Ravegnana, the Garisenda and Asinelli. The former, in particular, leans at an ominous, Pisa-like angle, but unlike the one in Pisa, their stability does not seem in question. Eight hundred years ago, there were more than 100 such towers peppering the Bologna skyline, like so many clunky red-brick reeds growing skyward. A few others still exist, scattered throughout the center, but only Asinelli, at 318 feet the tallest remaining one, can be climbed – on rickety, well-worn wooden steps – for a spectacular view of the city.

Many of the buildings of the Piazza Maggiore look medieval, with pointed gothic arches and crenelated parapets. How odd, then, that one of the most authentic medieval buildings – the 13th-century Palazzo di Re Enzo – was essentially reconstructed in the early 20th century. Its transformation into a fairy tale castle was based on turn-of-the-century notions about the Middle Ages.

Attached to it is the Palazzo del Podestà, a 15th-century reconstruction of the 13th-century original. After a lengthy restoration, its high Renaissance arches again provide a fitting backdrop for the piazza's better cafes. Along with the Palazzo di Re Enzo, also restored, it is used for exhibitions, conferences and congresses; Bologna is an important city for trade fairs. The impenetrably fortress-like Palazzo d'Accursio, is one of the largest building complexes in Italy. Almost a small city within the city, it has been since the 13th century a seat of power, both secular and papal. Today, the municipal government is gradually moving out of the palazzo, making room for new exhibition halls and expanded art galleries. The restored Sala d'Ercole – so called for a gigantic statue of Hercules by Alfonso Lombardi (1519) that dominates the room – is used for photography exhibitions. The impressive municipal art collections on the second floor of Palazzo d'Accursio have been reorgan-

STROLLING UNDER COVER
Bologna enjoys more than 23 miles of cool, dry arcades (facing page), built when the city's population boomed in the Middle Ages. In order to preserve the road system only the upper floors of buildings were enlarged, with overhanging parts supported by columns. Below, the *Lamentation over the Dead Christ* by Niccolò dell'Arca, in the church of Santa Maria della Vita.

THE CRADLE OF SCIENCE
According to tradition, in 1088 an independent institute of learning free of ecclesiastical influence was established in Bologna, marking the birth of the city's renowned university. Leading scholars of grammar, logic and rhetoric such as Pepone and Irnerius laid the foundations of jurisprudence. The teaching of medicine was authorized by a papal bull in 1219. Above, students near the university, one of the oldest in Europe.

ized and restored, and the last rooms will open by the end of 2,000. Paintings, sculptures and furniture are arranged to suggest an 18th-century private mansion; one apartment includes a charming room entirely frescoed to give the illusion of standing in an outdoor garden. Bird songs from the piazza complete the fantasy. Since 1993, the palazzo has also housed works by Giorgio Morandi, one of Italy's modern masters.

On the Piazza Maggiore, the comune built an immense gothic basilica to commemorate Bologna's independence and dedicated it to San Petronio, a fifth-century bishop of Bologna who is the city's patron saint. Statues of the Virgin Mary and child and of two saints, and pilasters with scenes from the Old and New Testaments, sculptured by Jacopo della

Quercia, decorate the main portal. It is easy to see why the young Michelangelo was impressed by the portal's dramatic intensity and technical virtuosity. The 15th-century masterpiece lightens San Petronio's massive facade, which was left unfinished – a foretaste of heaven perhaps.

Already one of the largest churches in the world, legend has it that San Petronio was to be even bigger than St Peter's. But the city's ambitious plans were thwarted by Pope Pius IV, who in 1562 ordered the building of the Palazzo Archiginnasio to the east of the basilica, effectively blocking further development.

The interior walls of the Archiginnasio, once the principal seat of the university, are entirely covered with the coats of arms of cardinal legates, rectors, priors and students, artfully arranged in frescoed commemorative

memorials. The theater where doctors held anatomy lessons (only in winter because in summer the corpses would smell), was bombed during World War II, but faithfully reconstructed with as many original pieces as were salvageable.

Covering the intricately carved wood ceiling are astrological figures; in the 16th century, doctors used astrological calendars to decide which days were best for operating. Happily for the advancement of science, the medical school in Bologna was the first to question this widely held practice.

For a city that isn't particularly rainy, Bologna is well endowed with arcades. There are an astonishing 23.6 miles of these "portici," tall passageways that originated in the Middle Ages as do-it-yourself home-expansion projects to house students pouring into the city. The

longest is the Portico di San Luca, whose 666 arches extend nearly two and a half miles.

The portico that flanks the Archiginnasio is a mere 456 feet long, so the walk isn't strenuous. Still, it is nice to know that at its end, one can stop at a fashionable bar that has not renounced its 1950's feel. Bustling at the hour of the aperitif, a Bolognese tradition, the bar offers snacks of quail eggs, cheese puffs and canapes with spinach and shrimp and sun-dried tomatoes, nearly a meal in themselves.

Attached to the Archiginnasio is a former Renaissance hospital, about the last place one would expect to find a 3,300-year-old Egyptian bas relief. But Bologna's exceptional archaeological museum, housed in the Ospedale Santa Maria della Morte, has the largest collection of Egyptian art in Italy after Turin. The original

**FROM CONSTANTINOPLE
TO MONTE DELLA GUARDIA**

Legend recounts that in the 12th century a Greek pilgrim was entrusted by the prelates of Constantinople with a sacred and delicate mission: to take to Italy an image of the Madonna painted by the evangelist Luke and to place it on Monte della Guardia, a hill just outside Bologna. A church (top left) was built on the hill to accommodate this holy image. Above and top, scenes from the feast day dedicated to Saint Luke.

171

**BOLOGNA,
THE CITY OF TOWERS**

Of the hundreds of medieval towers that have stood guard over Bologna only about a dozen survive. Two, built very close together between the 11th and 12th centuries, became symbols of the city: the leaning Garisenda and the Torre degli Asinelli, over 318 feet high and the fourth tallest tower in Italy. The Garisenda, originally about 196 feet high, was shortened by about 30 feet in the mid 14th century because it was in danger of collapsing. The angle of tilt, which today exceeds 9 feet, impressed Dante, who wrote in the *Divine Comedy* that the tower looks as if it is actually falling down if observed when the clouds are moving in the direction opposite to the tilt.

19th-century wood-and-glass display cabinets give you the feeling that Howard Carter could saunter through the door at any minute bearing a statuette from Tutankhamen's tomb.

They don't call Bologna "la grassa" for nothing. One of its principal attractions is food, and the city is renowned for delicate meat-filled tortellini; plumper, ricotta-filled tortelloni; passatelli (pasta made with bread crumbs, eggs and Parmesan); and mortadella, the scrumptious sausage that bears little resemblance to American baloney.

Behind the 16th-century Palazzo dei Banchi, dominating the eastern end of the Piazza Maggiore, is a picturesque cluster of narrow streets, packed with opulent small shops bursting with a fantastic variety of fruits, vegetables, cheeses and cured meats. You may have to fight for walking space, but a stroll through the market's fresh produce is key to understanding why the Bolognesi eat so well.

Tucked inside the market – and eerily silent compared with the cacophony outside – is the recently restored church of Santa Maria della Vita. In a dimly lighted chapel on the right is one of Bologna's greatest art works, a 15th-century life-size terra-cotta group sculpture, *Lamentation Over the Dead Christ*, by Niccolò dell'Arca (Nicholas of the Tomb), – one of the most touching and horrifying depictions of raw grief imaginable.

The artist was known by his somber name because of his other masterpiece: the upper sections of the tomb of St. Dominic, who is buried in a church dedicated to him just a few blocks south of Piazza Maggiore. Three youthful works by Michelangelo are also part of the monument. Another Michelangelo work, a bronze sculpture of Pope Julius II, had a short life on the facade of San Petronio. After three years there, it was destroyed in 1511, when the pope lost control of Bologna, ousted by the French, who reinstated the Bentivoglio family to power. The Piazza Maggiore was a principal stage where that power struggle was acted out, just another chapter in its 800-year history as the city's vital heart.

_____

ELISABETTA POVOLEDO reports from Italy for the "International Herald Tribune."

QUALITY GUARANTEED

Mortadella, often known as "bologna", is perhaps Italy's most renowned sausage. It is certainly one of the oldest, whether its name derives from the Latin mortarium ("mortar") or from myrtle, which the Romans used to add to sausages in order to enhance the flavor. The fact that modern mortadella originated in the Emilia region is confirmed by a proclamation issued in Bologna in 1611 by Cardinal Farnese, whereby production criteria were established in order to ensure quality. One of the first examples of quality control in the history of gastronomy!

Emilia, auto country

THE DRAKE

Above, a photo of Enzo Ferrari (1898-1988). The "Drake", the nickname that Italian auto racing fans invented for him many years ago, was also good driver. Between 1920 and 1931 he chalked up 31 victories. He also founded the Scuderia Ferrari (facing page, top, a period picture), which competed using cars provided by Alfa Romeo, another renowned Italian marque.

A strange alchemy transformed a small patch of the Po valley between Modena and Imola into the cradle of Italian auto engineering.

Ferrari, De Tomaso, Lamborghini, Maserati and Ducati are marques that immediately call up the legend of speed, excitement, technical excellence and perfect styling. At the same time they also represent a wholly Italian synthesis of traditional "hand made" craftsmanship and painstaking attention to detail with the race to be first with the latest electronic wizardry or aerodynamic refinements.

In recent years these companies have also become important tourist attractions. The trend was begun by Ferrari, which opened its own museum in 1990 at Maranello, a few miles outside Modena. Here everything reflects the spirit of the marque, which is to progress, to improve, in the awareness that the best car is one that still has to be built. This was the maxim of the legendary Enzo Ferrari, whose office has been faithfully reconstructed in the first section of the exhibition. Through photos and mementoes visitors can follow Ferrari's career: first a driver and owner of a race team, then director of Alfa Romeo racing and finally the founder and manager of the company that bears his name to this day.

The visit continues with the section devoted to the world of Formula 1 racing. Single-seaters of yesterday and today can be admired in a setting similar to a Grand Prix event, with reconstructions of the pits, the pit lanes, pit walls and the track. In the third section visitors can see the modern road cars, the sophisticated mechanical and electronic components designed for competition and the wind tunnel with some scale models.

A visit to the Ferrari Museum is not important only for those interested in knowing more about the development of the marque; it is also a full immersion in the history of motoring, which owes so much to the company, whose technological inovations have often filtered down from racing cars to the cars we all use every day.

A few miles from the Ferrari Museum, in sant'Agata Bolognese, we find the headquarters of Lamborghini, another marque much admired by racing buffs. Next to the works, an elegant steel and glass building contains the family jewels – dozens of cars starting from the models of the 1960'S, some Formula 1 vehicles, auto

and marine engines (including Class 1 Offshore engines, world champions in 2001 and 2002), old tools and hundreds of models from various countries. The stars of the show are the most important Lamborghinis, from the Countach to the legendary Miura, from the 350 GT to the Espada, down to the Diablo – of which there is also a wooden prototype.

From four wheels to two. In the Ducati Museum in Bologna about 30 racing bikes built from 1947 to the present day symbolize the story of the technical and design development of the marque, which is still represented in the World GP and World Superbike Championships, wining many victories. Together with the bikes and mechanical equipment, archive materials, original designs, period film clips, the leathers and the helmets of the riders combine to tell the story of the men whose ingenuity and courage led Ducati to the pinnacle of success.

To continue this pilgrimage, visit Modena, the home of Maserati, another glorious marque recently acquired by Ferrari, as well as the Museo De Tomaso, a company that produced cult roadsters such as the Vallelunga and the Mangusta.

Near Imola, in the Santerno hills, there stands a race track built in the 1950'S where the first winner of an official race was the legendary Jim Clark. Since 1980 Imola has been the venue for yearly Formula 1 Grand Prix, World Motorbike Championship and World Superbike Championship events. The circuit has been renamed in memory of Enzo Ferrari and his son Dino.

GEMS FOR A CHOSEN FEW
On the facing page, bottom,
the Lamborghini Miura, a model
built in 1966 whose name derives
from the famous breed of bulls
that confront the red capes
of matadors. Admirers
of this car included the Shah
of Persia, the Aga Khan and Frank
Sinatra, who once turned up
at the Lamborghini plant with
a pile of leopard skins which
he wanted used as upholstery.
On this page, the Ferrari works
and a recent Ducati street bike.

By Olivier Bernier

A Tale of
TWO DUCAL CITIES

December 5, 1982

THE MOST BEAUTIFUL BEDROOM IN EUROPE

Facing page, the cupola of the Camera degli Sposi (the Bridal Bedroom), also known as the Camera Picta (the Painted Room): Ludovico II's bedroom. Entirely frescoed by Mantegna, the wall still holds the hooks used to support the canopy above the bed.

Above, via Mazzini, in the center of Ferrara; the cathedral bell tower is in the background.

After five centuries, the Italian Renaissance has lost none of its magic. Its thirst for art, knowledge and the pleasures of life still haunt our cultural memory; and luckily for us, two of its cities have survived, virtually unchanged, in northern Italy.

To take a walk anywhere in the center of either Ferrara or Mantua is to go straight back into the past. Palaces fronting on narrow streets; doors opening to reveal green, arcaded courtyards; a big red dog fast asleep on his cushion at an open ground-floor window; even a little girl dressed in a pink sweater, a purple skirt, white lace stockings and black patent leather shoes – all seem to belong in the background of a Renaissance painting. And just in case we had any doubts, within seconds we are bound to pass a church where the bells that once beckoned Renaissance worshippers still ring at the same times to call the faithful.

Both Ferrara and Mantua owe much to that most famous of Italian families, the Este. They built and, when needed, tore down to rebuild, Ferrara. When Isabella d'Este, the first lady of Italy as her contemporaries called her, married Francesco II Gonzaga, the ruler of neighboring Mantua, she brought the Renaissance along in her train. It was hardly surprising: besides being beautiful, elegant and learned, she was also the daughter of Duke Ercole I, a collector of paintings, antiques and books whose palaces bore names like Schifanoia, away with dullness. His court was unusually splendid and, because he liked architecture, his city offered the first example of large-scale urban planning in Europe since the fall of the Roman Empire.

Ercole d'Este, who ruled from 1471 to 1505, started with a project that might have seemed unpromising to just about anyone else: in the midst of a small medieval city stood a menacing massive fortress, complete with a moat, drawbridges, towers and machicolations. It had been built in the l4th century as a warning to rebels at home and enemies abroad, and was hardly a pleasure dome. By the time the Duke finished with it, Este Castle had white marble balconies, a loggia and, most important, a passage leading to a new, Renaissance palace opposite the cathedral. He left it to his son Alfonso I to order the sumptuous, frescoed rooms we can still see today: the ceiling of one illustrates a Renaissance vision of every kind of athletic game played by the ancient Romans, another bears representations of the four seasons. Later, Renée of France, the daughter of Louis XII and wife of Ercole II, had the jewel-like chapel built. This tiny oratory, enriched with polychrome inlaid marbles and lit by windows with alabaster panes, represents the happiest of compromises between the old Catholic tradition and Lutheran austerity. The Duchess followed the new dispensation but obviously felt that banishing the images and replacing them with geometrical patterns was sacrifice enough; she wasn't about to give up beauty as well.

Hidden deep in the newer town hall just across the street is another Renaissance masterpiece. First, walk up the majestic open staircase built for Ercole I in 1481; then cross a series of rooms in which officials go about their very desultory business. Ask for the "Stanzina delle Duchesse," and they will keep you going in the right direction until you reach a smaller office; repeat your query. One of the clerks will happily inter-

PARVA, SED APTA MIHI...
"Small but fit for me..."
Thus reads the Latin tag
inscribed on the poet Ludovico
Ariosto's home in Ferrara.
The quotation from the Latin
poet Horace has become a
proverbial way of describing the
sober life style of noble spirits.
The inscription was already
present when Ariosto acquired
the house and he found it so
congenial that he made
it his own motto.
The city of Ferrara named
piazza Ariostea (above) for one
of its most illustrious sons.

rupt his "far niente" to unlock a little door. Walk in, and you will find yourself in the most civilized of retreats, a little sala, with grotesques frescoed against gold ground, pilasters of marble inlaid with mirrors, a gilt-and-sculpted cornice. And there are also allegorical figures and putti and garlands and trompe-l'oeil sculpture: after 400 years, the Duchess's favorite salon has lost none of its charm, grace or sophistication.

Grace, in fact, and moderation are characteristic of Ferrarese architecture. The palaces, never very large, are built of brick, not stone, and are adorned with terra-cotta reliefs, not marble. A five minute walk down the Corso della Giovecca, starting from the castle, will take you past several of these harmoniously weathered houses to the Palace of Marfisa d'Este, a one-story villa built in 1559. On the street, there is only a plain brick facade, with a rhythm of terra-cotta pilasters and a doorway chastely adorned with two marble Corinthian pillars. But inside, the square rooms boast carved marble mantles and frescoed ceilings decorated with all the enticing fantasy of the late Renaissance: grotesques,

garlands, herms, vases, flying deities. Trompe-l'oeil curtains and climbing vines set off here a Diana of Ephesus, complete with eight breasts, there animals springing through the decor. The colors are light, the mood cheerful, yet civilized. And since this is in Italy, there is a loggia opening onto the garden: It must have been quite idyllic to sit under its triple arcade and look away toward the summer house crowning a little hill in the middle distance. This, along with many other secret enclosed gardens, is one of the great charms of Ferrara. When you tire of the narrow streets and their cobblestones, walk into any of the doorways you pass: almost certainly, you will discover an arcaded loggia and a miniature park whose quiet is doubly refreshing after the city's bustle.

Like the palazzina, the Romei House was a retreat for a worldly lady, the (unjustly) infamous Lucrezia Borgia. That it should stand on the Via Savonarola is perhaps ironic: no one could have been more different from the austere and fanatical preacher than the pleas-

Connected to the castle by
a covered walkway, the Palazzo
Comunale in Ferrara is a 13th-
century building that has been
reconstructed many times.
In the Corte Ducale (top left)
is an outstanding 15th-century
covered staircase.

Above, the tomb of the writer
Giorgio Bassani in the Jewish
cemetery of Certosa. His novel
The Garden of the Finzi-Contini,
was the basis for the famous
film of the same name.

ure loving Lucrezia; but then, the street is one of the prettiest in Ferrara, a fact of which, no doubt, the Duchess was aware. She was married to Duke Alfonso I, Isabella's brother, and although he was her third husband (No. 1 was repudiated, No. 2 poisoned at the behest of Lucrezia's brother, who, no doubt, was following orders of their father, Pope Alexander VI), he not only survived the match, but grew to be very fond of his elegant, literate, artistic wife. Because splendor, in the 16th century, was just as much a weapon as missiles are today – it overawed the enemy – the Duke and Duchess lived in a spectacular style, but it was to this small, simple house and its arcaded courtyard that Lucrezia came to rest, read and meditate.

Built in 1445 around a small, light courtyard, it was designed for every kind of weather: on a hot day, you can sit under the groundfloor cloister-like arcade; on a sunny winter day, you can move to the top floor. There, the frescoed gallery runs around three sides of the court, while on the fourth side the wall is adorned with six marble medallions. Today, the house is a museum for frescoes rescued from collapsing churches and objects transferred from vanished buildings; but even that kind of hodgepodge is reminiscent of the collecting done by Renaissance grandees, and the little frescoed rooms on the ground floor bring back the atmosphere so dear to Lucrezia.

After this, there is more to be seen: the cathedral, with its Romanesque facade and Baroque interior; the art museum in the Palace of Diamonds, a Renaissance building made of stones shaped like diamonds in which the shimmering quality of white and pink marble blocks seems to abolish the very notion of wall; the so-called Palace of Lodovico il Moro (it actually belonged to a Ferrarese ambassador, not the Duke of Milan) with its two-story arcade, stone-and-brick loggia, 16th century formal garden and garden room, where life-sized portraits peer down at us from the frescoed ceiling.
And still there are squares and hidden churches. Just forget your map, allow yourself to get lost and you will find them. There are Este palaces everywhere, and

179

Renaissance city gates nobly framing the edges of Duke Ercole's grand design. And at the edge of town (a brisk half-hour walk will take you from one end to the other), there is the Schifanoia.

It is not easy to see how life could ever have been dull for the dukes of Ferrara: endemic wars, a splendid court, the hunt, collecting and womanizing should have been enough to keep even the most energetic of rulers occupied; not, however, Duke Borso, Ercole's father, who, in 1470, built himself a palace specifically to keep boredom at bay. And just so that no one would miss his point, he had one room in particular frescoed with his activities. At the bottom, the Duke goes about his business: hunting, receiving ambassadors, holding court. In the middle of the walls, the signs of the Zodiac show the passing seasons while at the top symbolic representations of the months mix classical mythology with the court of Ferrara. In this wrap-around masterpiece, the artist Francesco Cossa gives a clear, immediate and glamorous idea of the Early Renaissance.

When the 18-year-old Isabella d'Este moved, just before the turn of the century, from this avant-garde city to Mantua, she found a town where, by comparison, time might have stood still. Here was a medieval city with crooked streets, Gothic palaces and no master plan. As it turned out, she was too busy to do much about it. Her husband, Francesco II, although a courageous warrior, was all too glad to let his wife take care of the Government; so Isabella merely set about rearranging a section of the huge, rambling palace. Naturally, she wanted to have pretty, comfortable rooms, but she also had to house a growing collection of paintings, antiques sculpture, precious objects and dwarfs.

First, she tackled her own quarters, which soon grew splendid enough to be called "del Paradiso," the paradise. We can still see today the blue-and-gold coffered ceilings, the carved marble lintels and the little music rooms paneled with inlaid precious woods, as well as her own arcaded courtyard; but the Mantegnas and the Leonardos are gone, along with the Roman marbles and the famous Majolica service, some to the Louvre and others to museums throughout Europe. At least, by dint of bending nearly double, we can explore the dwarfs' apartments, a warren of little rooms built to one-quarter scale and imagine them, once again, filled with quarrels and laughter.

The rest of the Ducal Palace also deserves a stroll. There is the famous marriage chamber (Camera degli Sposi), frescoed by the great Andrea Mantegna between 1471 and 1474 to celebrate the splendor of the

THE FORTRESS
OF SAN MICHELE
When the starving people
of Ferrara rebelled against the
ruling Este family in 1385 Duke
Niccolò II decided to build
a fortress that would do double
duty as a defense against riotous
mobs and as an intimidating
symbol of ducal power. The
architect Bartolino da Novara
designed and built three new
towers and linked them to form
a quadrilateral structure with
the pre-existing Rocca dei Leoni
fortress, adding walls and other
defenses. The new construction
was emblematically dedicated
to Saint Michael, who defeated
the rebellious angels.
Facing page, the palace
of Sigismondo d'Este, called
the Palazzo dei Diamanti, which
today houses the National
Art Gallery.

**THE PALACE
WITH 500 ROOMS**

The Sala degli Specchi, or Room
of Mirrors (above), one of the
500 rooms in Mantua's Palazzo
Ducale, was an open loggia
before it was converted into
a gallery in the 17th century by
Federico Gonzaga. The frescoes
on the ceiling are attributed
to the school of Guido Reni.

On the preceding pages,
a view of Mantua, which made
a big impression
on Charles Dickens.

Gonzagas; and rooms hung with some admirable 16th
and 17th century tapestries, whose compositions and
bold colors display classical themes as revised by the
Rennaissance. There is also the enchanting Rococo
Sala dei Fiumi with its mirrors, light-colored stuccoes
and frescoed river gods. A walk through the apparently
endless edifice, in fact, while requiring some stamina,
amply repays the visitor by making him feel like a week-
end guest of the Gonzagas: the hosts are busy elsewhere and have left us run of the house.

Architecturally, too, the palace is a fascinating hodge-
podge. It starts with the crenelated 14th century facade
of the Piazza Sordello; suddenly, on the second floor, it
produces an enchanting little cloistered garden; throws
off a spectacular mannerist courtyard on the side of yet
another wing; and is closely tied to the grim, medieval
fortress of San Giorgio, complete with slit-windows,
moat and towers, only to turn around and present us
with the classical Chapel of Santa Barbara designed in
1562 by Bertani.

The city of Mantua itself is not unlike the palace.
Its three central, communicating piazzas – delle Erbe,
Broletto and Sordello – reflect the accretions of some
seven centuries, but from the Church of San Lorenzo,
a rotunda completed around 1040, to the cathedral's
Baroque facade, built in the 1760's, a complete, harmonious architectural landscape is formed. A stroll
through Mantua, in fact, is a little like looking at a book
on the development of Italian taste; here, too, it pays to
get lost.

Naturally, there are surprises. Behind the cathedral's
Baroque facade is a splendid interior by Giulio
Romano, cool, grand, almost awesome in the perfection
of its proportions and the dignity of its colonnades.
Around the corner from the 14th-century Hall of
Justice is a milestone of Renaissance architecture, the
Church of Sant'Andrea. Its architect, Leon Battista
Alberti, died in 1472 while it was still being built, but
he knew he had once and for all buried the Middle
Ages. The church is only of middling size, but Alberti,

who was clearly thinking of the Romano's grand basilicas, managed to make it look immense. The facade, with its massive arched doorway and giant pilasters, is impressive enough, but it is the interior volume which is literally awe-inspiring. There is just one enormous nave, topped by a massive coffered barrel-vault. At the sides, the chapels give this austere space a feeling of openness. All is grand, simple, glorious and rational. Alberti had written the first modern treatise on architecture before he designed Sant'Andrea and here he offers us the result of a lifetime's study, a volume as clear and as well defined as the minds of the great Renaissance creators.

Of course, there's still much more to Mantua. You might like to wander into the charming small 18th century Teatro Scientifico, for instance, or follow the Rio Canal which crosses the city; you might want to look up, now and again, at the stern brick towers silhouetted against the sky; you can enter any of a dozen splendid churches, drift into palace courtyards. In any event, you must not miss a country villa, a full 15-minutes' walk from the cathedral, built by Isabella's son, Federigo II, as a place where he could conveniently see his mistress. The masterpiece of Giulio Romano, the one-story Te Palace, with its rusticated, trompe-l'oeil courtyard, grand loggia but generally modest appearance does little to prepare us for the wildly inventive frescoes decorating the walls and ceilings of its rooms. There, all kinds of mythological characters play and struggle before us. Bold, over-life-size figures, odd perspectives (in one room, we find ourselves under the hoofs of huge horses), all combine to create new, exciting spaces. In this house more, perhaps, than anywhere else in Italy, we know what it was to be a Renaissance prince.

OLIVIER BERNIER is the author of 12 books, most recently "The World in 1800." *He lectures at the Metropolitan Museum of Art in New York and in museums across the country.*

CITY OF ROMANCE

"The most romantic city in the world" was how Aldous Huxley described Mantua after a visit in the 1920's. And even though more than half a century has gone by since then, the romance lingers on in piazza Sordello, piazza delle Erbe (above) and in the medieval alleys festooned with flowers in window boxes high above the cobble stones.

By Rachel Billington

TUSCANY'S
Timeless Landscape

October 20, 1985

THE GREEN SENTINELS OF TUSCANY

"The cypresses at Bolgheri stand tall and pure..." In his opening line of a famous poem, Giosué Carducci bequeathed us a masterly sketch of Tuscany as it has always been. First imported to the region by the Phoenicians, these compact, tapering evergreens stand like silent sentinels along the roads that wind their way through the countryside. Tradition associates the cypress with cemeteries, which are frequently adorned with them, but their austere calm, regal bearing and aromatic scent are well suited to the meditations of the living. In fact, it's hard to imagine Tuscany without its characteristic cypresses. The photo shows a panoramic view of the Valle d'Orcia, in the hills around Siena.

Imagine first a rose-colored city, sitting atop a small mountain. It is circular and bounded by a crenelated wall. Bunched within its confines are a multitude of palaces, fortresses, churches and towers. Each one has its own decoration of arched windows, tiled roofs, mosaiced walls, buttresses, domes, verandas and pillars. It is a child's picture of fairyland, an unforgettable image of order and design.

Imagine next a pattern of fields and woods, spreading across small conical hills. Streams and lakes glitter in the valleys. Vineyards are embroidered across fields. Somewhere there is a copse of pines, somewhere else a line of cypresses — or one alone, tall, dark, very Italian. For this is Tuscany, a small part of Italy below Milan and above Rome, an even smaller part of the world, yet holding in its towns and hills a great inheritance of art and beauty. During the 13th, 14th, 15th and, some would say, 16th century, a prosperous and energetic community created for itself an idyllic setting.

This was not so extraordinary. More extraordinary is that, owing to the sudden decline from prosperity to penury, the buildings and countryside are still almost unchanged. The two scenes I described, of city and countryside, were painted by Ambrogio Lorenzetti in the first half of the 14th century as a background to his fresco, *Gli Effetti del Buongoverno* (The Effects of Good Government). But the same scenes can be enjoyed by the tourist as he travels across hillside or through ancient town.

There are many ways of discovering the past, but to find a direct link between the present and the landscape of an artist who lived more than 650 years ago must be the most exciting. Lorenzetti was a Sienese painter and in

WELL-ORDERED COUNTRYSIDE

Facing page, a detail from the cycle of frescoes by Ambrogio Lorenzetti that shows the results of wise land management: orderly cultivated fields, well kept vineyards and a feeling of prosperity. A similar image is called up by the undulations of the "crete" (literally, the clays) of the Siena district (above): farms and crops wrested from grudging terrain that took centuries of tenacious toil to make fertile.

the top left of his city there is a campanile marked with the distinctive horizontal stripes made by the white marble and the very dark green, known as "verdescuro di Prato." Beside the tower is the dome of a cathedral. *Gli Effetti del Buongoverno* hangs in the Palazzo Pubblico of Siena's Piazza del Campo and, as one walks away from the piazza, there arises ahead the same tiger-striped campanile and unmistakable dome.

Lorenzetti was one of the world's great landscape painters roughly 200 years before anyone else thought of landscape painting as an art form. In Siena's Pinacoteca Nazionale his two fresco panels, *Città sul mare* and *Castello in riva ad un lago*, are astonishing for a time mostly dominated by large figurative religious subjects. They are supposed to represent the harbor of Talamone in the Maremma. Matching painting to reality, naturally enough, cannot always be exact, but an eye looking from the 14th-century viewpoint soon picks up interesting details.

Inside the duomo itself is the Piccolomini Library, whose walls are decorated with frescoes by Pinturicchio depict-

ing delightful scenes from the life of the humanist and diplomat Enea Silvio de' Piccolomini, later Pope Pius II. Every scene has a landscape background. In No. 5, our hero, now Bishop of Siena, introduces Emperor Frederick to Princess Eleonora of Portugal against a background of a vast column bearing their two coats of arms. The column can still be seen outside the Porta Camollia, which itself appears in the painting, plus a very small and distant cathedral.

Examples of exact architectural reproduction are fairly rare. More often it is the general features and feeling of Tuscany that are reproduced. For example, most paintings of towns show a mass of tall towers that to the modern eye either seem fantastic or some strange forecast of skyscrapers in Manhattan. It is only when one visits the tiny hilltop town of San Gimignano that this particular aspect of the scene comes to life. San Gimignano has 15 remaining towers that look, as D.H. Lawrence wrote, "like an angry porcupine." In the town's wealthy

Piazza dei Miracoli (the Square of Miracles) was how the poet Gabriele D'Annunzio dubbed Pisa's piazza del Duomo (on the following pages). D'Annunzio's statement was typically emphatic, but it is not untrue. The green lawn of the square can boast more than one miracle: the Cathedral, the Baptistery, a majestic jewel of Romanesque architecture, the Camposanto and the leaning Tower, which in its eight centuries of existence has tilted about eight feet owing to ground subsidence. No small problem, but no Pisan would ever dream of exchanging the tower for a perpendicular one!

years, 600 years ago, there were many more towers as the rich wool merchants competed for height and breadth. In the Church of St. Augustus, Benozzo Gozzoli painted a magnificent fresco behind the altar, depicting the life of the Saint. Wonderful though the foreground figures are, the towns and countryside that track his way as he leaves for Milan are almost more appealing.

The *Life of St. Augustus* is a secular approach to what might be roughly termed a religious subject. But most paintings of the period were purely religious. Those tranquil Madonnas and Child by Simone Martini or Duccio are usually painted against gold or bands of choiring angels. But more formal scenes such as *The Adoration of the Magi* by Bartolo di Fredi (in Siena's Pinacoteca Nazionale) have a detailed landscape background with, once again, the tiger stripes of the campanile and duomo clearly identifiable and farther off a much turreted hilltop town that looks remarkably like San Gimignano. Bethlehem, in its moment of triumph, has been transported into a Tuscan landscape. Once one identifies this

in one painting, it seems repeated, though perhaps in a more general way, on other canvases, other walls.

In the same gallery, Giovanni di Paolo's *Flight Into Egypt* is nearer a landscape painting than anything else, with Tuscan hills lighted by a golden evening sun. In Sansepolcro, the *Resurrection* by Piero della Francesca, who was born in the town, shows the risen Christ against a background of Tuscan scenery. In Arezzo at the Church of San Francesco, the same artist painted a fresco of the identification of the true cross with the walled city of Arezzo detailed behind it. In San Gimignano the lovely *Annunciation* by Ghirlandaio painted on the wall beside the cathedral shows a view of three tall cypress trees and the green-clad conical hills, so typical of that part of Italy. In Pisa the Camposanto has Gozzoli frescoes of scenes from the Old Testament that, though fire-damaged in the war, still show Pisan hills and trees. In the Uffizi Gallery in Florence the beautiful *Annunciation*, now thought to be an early work of Leonardo da Vinci, has a magnifi-

189

San Gimignano (above)
is recognizable thanks to its
silhouette, marked by 15 towers,
the sole survivors of a 13th
century epoch when the city had
72 of them. More than defensive
structures, the towers were
symbols of prestige and authority,
so much so that after the podestà,
the ruling authority of the town,
built a tower that was 167 feet
high he then forbade the
construction of anything higher.
On the facing page, top, Arezzo;
below, the same city as seen in a
detail from the cycle of frescoes
by Piero della Francesca about
the *Legend of the True Cross*.

cent set of cypress and pine trees as background. Not
far away the public Boboli Gardens give just the same
atmosphere of peace and order.

Suddenly the magic feeling of familiarity with the
Tuscan scene as one drives through its endlessly winding
roads – three-fifths of it is hill country and only one-
tenth plain – finds a possible explanation. This children's
picture-book world has come to us, bowdlerized through
the centuries, as an image of the Holy Land, more real
than the original. We have learned to put a Tuscan setting to the life and death of Christ and his disciples and
saints. Even if this Christian orientation fails to appeal,
or perhaps to convince, few would not admit to entering
a world in which real and created merge, making every
new sight take on a particular intensity.

Volterra, like San Gimignano, sits atop a hill, but this
time the slope is steeper, the walls thicker, so that it
seems like a fortress hanging in the sky. Sitting in the

Piazza dei Priori, one expects the brilliantly robed figures
painted, perhaps, by Sodoma (1477-1549) to step out of
the tall doors of the Palazzo dei Priori. In Florence a walk
across the Ponte Vecchio seems trailed by the ghosts of
Dante and Beatrice – as painted at a much later date by
the pre-Raphaelite, Edward Burne-Jones.

In Arezzo and San Gimignano and many other
towns, ancient stone wells, sometimes roofed with pink
tiles, stand sturdily in central squares just as they do in
paintings of the period. In Cortona the *Deposition* by
Luca Signorelli shows Christ lying at the foot of a cross
which is in the foreground of a little town on a lake very
much farther west than Jerusalem. All over Tuscany
there is a wealth of ancient towns and fortresses quite
apart from the famous and much visited. The problem
for the driver is when to stop, or rather when to strike off
the excellent autostradas and brave the small roads that
curl up to hilltop encampments. On my last stay, I went

up to Sunday mass at Barbischio, a tiny village near Gaiole in Chianti. Typically, it had a small solid church and a large fortress shaped like a tower. Vineyards crowded down the slopes, pines and cypress marked boundaries. It could have been 600 years ago – until the priest changed into his T-shirt. At Poppi, in the northeast of Tuscany, there is a crenelated castle that might well have served as a model for Lorenzetti. It was built by the Counts Guidi in the 13th century and has a superb view over the Casentino. At Prato there is another 13th-century castle, the Castello dell'Imperatore. Other castles or fortress towns look over the sea – another image from our paintings, although there are no longer sailing boats billowing out to sea and the coastal regions are most altered by tourist requirements. There is the medieval village of Castiglione della Pescaia, or Forte delle Rocchette, in the south near Grosseto. Everywhere one comes across lines of dark cypresses, planted as if for a stage set, like a particularly impressive

row near Bolgheri. Any route, though the smaller the better, has its share of viaducts or bridges that only seem real when you get out of the car to touch them. The Ponte della Maddalena, also called the Devil's Bridge, was built over the Serchio River in the 14th century. With its huge hump and four asymmetrical arches, it looks as if it were drawn with a child's crayon.

Landscape into art. Even the crudest postcard of, for example, the turreted walls of Monteriggioni near Siena or the strange red tower in the middle of Lucca that is crowned by a flourishing pine tree, seem closer to those paintings of the past than our world of offices and airplanes. Tuscany is one of the very few places where one can view the present with the eye of the past.

———
RACHEL BILLINGTON is the author of 16 novels, the latest being "A Woman's Life" *and* "The Space Between." *She has also published three children's novels.*

Siena in its glory days

By Paul Chutkow
May 11, 1986

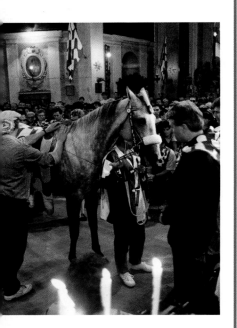

FROM THE TOP OF THE TOWER
Piazza del Campo is dominated by the Torre del Mangia (facing page), whose name derives from that of a bellringer nicknamed "Mangiaguadagni" (Spendthrift) for his reputation for wasting money. In the other pictures, scenes from the Palio.

Around the ancient piazza the horsemen paraded, children pressing against the rail of the track, flags saluting from the balconies above, the stone face of the Tuscan belltower rising flame-orange in the late afternoon sun. Around, around, until – KABOOM! – the cannon exploded, jolting the horses, startling the crowd and, with swords flashing silver, the commander crying "Charge!", every heart in Siena kicked into a gallop.

This was it, the moment quiet little Siena lives and works for all year, the opening of another Palio. In the next 90 minutes of spectacle and rising passion, the 17 rival districts of Siena, each colorfully named and known collectively as "contrade," would parade in the piazza in full medieval regalia. Out would come drummer boys and trumpeters, flag twirlers and horsemen laden with armor, all in the blazing colors of their home contrada, all in total concentration to do honor to their contrada and to keep the flame of Siena's medieval glory and tradition.

When the clock overlooking the piazza marked 7 P.M., 10 chosen contrade would send out their horses, their riders and their last-minute prayers for the climactic showdown. The rest of the Palio is spectacle, ritual and medieval myth, but this is the moment when the Palio is high-stakes politics and business, with fortunes to be won or lost in the next few minutes. Just as it has been twice a summer for more than 400 years, this is the race for the prized banner known as the Palio, three wild laps around the majestic, screaming Piazza del Campo, bareback, no holds barred, winner take all.

Unlike Rome, Florence, Milan and Venice, Siena is not cosmopolitan, outgoing, multilingual or accustomed to the comings and goings of international travelers. A walled city, perched high in the nexus of three hills overlooking Tuscany and Chianti country, Siena is insular and inward-looking.

But in the summer, in the high spirits of Palio time, the Siena you discover basks in that special light of the Mediterranean sun, its skirts are the lush green of the surrounding fields and vineyards, its narrow streets combine business with the final drum and flag drills for the Palio. This is Siena the eternal university town, vivid and magnetic, a center of art and music, a treasure of small riches, a taste of unspoiled Italy. There are few greater pleasures than idling in the Piazza del Campo over a Campari or cappuccino and contemplating just what it is that makes Italy Italy, what makes Italian life so agreeable, so civilized.

Because the Sienese had the wisdom to keep cars out, the Piazza del Campo retains a timeless feel. Nine lanes of cobblestones fan out from its clocktower, each supposedly representing one of the nine generals instrumental in the founding of the Siena Republic. The Palazzo Pubblico, an Italian version of the town hall, borders the oval piazza, and in the middle is the Fountain of Joy, actually a copy of the original by Siena's most celebrated artist, Jacopo della Quercia. At Palio time, when the outer rim of the piazza has been made into a dirt track and flags and banners hang from many of the balconies, you can easily imagine the glory days of Siena.

In Siena, it is only natural that history is recounted not just in major events and years but in Palios lost or won, sometimes by cheating. Here births and marriages are not just family occasions but contrada occasions; every schoolchild plays with 17 big marbles painted in the colors of the contrade and most know too the year their contrada last won the Palio. Every schoolchild also knows the date 1260, the year the Sienese crushed their archrivals the Florentines in the Battle of Montaperti. Even today the rivalry continues between the two Tuscan cities, and the great battle lives on in the work of della Quercia, Duccio and Simone Martini, and in its portrayal as a centerpiece event in the *Divine Comedy* by the Florentine Dante Alighieri. If you want to relive the spirit of Montaperti, take a Florentine to the Palio.

Siena's conquest of Florence proved short-lived, as did peace generally in the history of Siena. The city knew empire and wealth, and the success of today's banking powerhouse Monte dei Paschi reflects Siena's long history of banking and financial influence in central Italy. But prosperity and peace were usually just interludes in Siena, and its history from the Middle Ages is more a story of war and betrayal, foreign occupation and plotting, even plague. The Black Death of 1348 is reported to have wiped out 65,000 Sienese, just about the city's entire present population. Reading the history of Siena, it seems that at one time or other every major ruling family in Europe ganged up on the little Tuscan enclave.

PAUL CHUTKOW is a journalist and author. His books include "Harvests of Joy," the memoirs of Robert Mondavi, and "Depardieu," a biography of the French actor Gérard Depardieu.

**THE EMBODIMENT
OF VIRILE ELEGANCE**
The dazzling white marble
of the *David*, sculpted by
Michelangelo in 1504, it is the
first statue of the Renaissance
period to portray manly
strength and elegance in
complete nudity. The block of
marble from which it was made
has a singular history.
In 1464 it was given to the
sculptor Agostino di Duccio
for a statue of a giant, but he
ruined it and it lay abandoned
in the storehouse of the
Cathedral for 37 years.
Then Michelangelo saw the
marble block and asked if he
could retrieve it for a statue of
David. In some places the artist
deliberately left his
predecessor's clumsy chisel
marks in plain view.

By Frank Bruni

Sublime
FLORENCE

December 8, 2003

It is impossible to walk around, talk about or even summon a fleeting mental picture of Florence without focusing on the Duomo, so it makes sense to begin there, with the city's most ineluctable landmark, the candy-striped architectural confection to which so many of its cobbled streets lead. Vast in size and busy with detail, it hypnotizes the viewer, and it seems constantly to change form, or at least to change effect. At midday, in sunshine, the pale green and red of its exterior almost shimmer, and the Duomo comes across as the preening peacock of Italian cathedrals, flaunting its marble plumage. At dusk, under the cover of clouds, those colors fade, so that the Duomo reverts to a simpler, more somber play on bright and dark, black and white, the stern umpire of Italian cathedrals, asserting its authority over all others.

Then there is its soaring, bulbous, red cupola, erected in the 15th century and still breathtaking after all these years. Its architect, Brunelleschi, meant for it to leap over the boundaries of what was considered possible and to dazzle, and he ended up with an apt metaphor for all of Florence. From medieval times through the Renaissance, over centuries of formidable wealth and power, Florence was the canvas on which successive generations of artists and aristocrats sought to outdo one another, upping the ante on splendor and accomplishment. They stuffed it with treasures, turning it into a synonym for beauty itself. The Duomo was — and is — one chapter in that narrative, the most eye-catching evocation of an enduring theme. In a country with stiff competition, Florence remains the capital of indulgence.

It is no longer the center of artistic, commercial or intellectual life in Italy; other cities, like Milan and Rome, have claimed and now carry those mantles. In size and present-day importance, bustle and hustle, they eclipse Florence, which has only about 360,000 residents. At night, when many of the tourists retreat — and there are many, usually too many, tourists — Florence falls into an almost otherworldly quiet, a reminder that it has become, by some present-day yardsticks, a sleepy place. But it still exerts a special pull on the imagination and tug on the heart, and it exists even now as a shorthand for all in this world that should and can be relished and savored. Small wonder that when the fictional character Hannibal Lecter slipped his cuffs and made his jailbreak, it was Florence to which he fled. Although a few of Hannibal's appetites were unorthodox, many others were refined. He knew that in Florence, he would find a good meal, a good suit and a sublime setting in which to enjoy both.

Among Florence's promiscuous blessings is its location: a dimple of land between the rolling green and golden hills of fabled Tuscany. Those hills rise steeply from the flanks of the city, neatly framing it, as if an artist had actually arranged them just so. They are quickly accessible and easily scaled, especially on the far side of the Arno River, away from the center of town, and they allow anyone with sturdy legs and hungry eyes to find plenty of vantage points from which to admire Florence. The city, in turn, seems to bask in that attention. My favorite perch is the grounds around Fort Belvedere, whose name literally means "beautiful view." I have spent many hours here, at eye level with Brunelleschi's red cupola, tricked by its scale into the giddy belief that I could jump over the Arno and land atop it. Sometimes, after several glasses of Chianti, I am very close to trying.

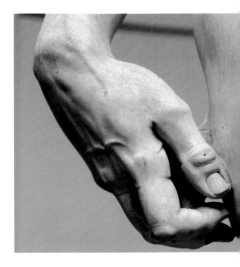

RETURN TO FORMER GLORY

On 16 September 2002 work began on the restoration of the David, a task concluded in the summer of 2004. In the course of its history, the statue — which was on display in piazza della Signoria until 1873 — has been subjected to all kinds of abuse, from air pollution to vandalism.

197

GUARDING THE TREASURE
The Forte di Belvedere, which provides excellent panoramic views of the city, is an imposing star-shaped fortified structure built at the end of the 16th century by the architect Bernardo Buontalenti. The treasure of the Medici family was kept in a secret well, protected by a death trap that was always primed to spring – and instantly eliminate any thief foolish enough to think of robbing them.

I have friends who deem Florence too perfect, too composed. They may be right, or they may simply be responding to how endlessly and tirelessly its praises have been sung. It is no longer possible to "discover" Florence, free from all the impressions that other visitors have passed down, all the images that have been captured in paintings and photographs and movies, all the descriptive prose that has been lavished on it. To travel to Florence is to brush up against sights and scenes so familiar that they seem not like memories in the making but like memories already made, and yet this provides its own kind of pleasure.

It is one thing to examine a picture of Michelangelo's *David*. It is quite another to be confronted with the statue itself, finished in 1504 and ensconced in the Galleria dell'Accademia. How did Michelangelo manage this? How did he make marble such a pliant, uncanny mirror of flesh? Cords of sinew emerge from the statue's neck. A bulging vein runs down its right wrist. At the knees and knuckles, hips and calves, there are ripples, furrows, knots and curves of a precision that only a close, immediate examination reveals. It would be worth visiting Florence for the David alone, but the David is only one masterpiece among many that Michelangelo left here. He also sculpted the statues in the Medici Tomb here, and he designed, again for the Medici family, the flawlessly proportioned, gently curving staircase for the library above the San Lorenzo Basilica. Such is the near-ly insane artistic wealth of this city that it has things as mundane as staircases by artists as magnificent as Michelangelo. For many of the masters, especially during the Renaissance, Florence was a principal source of commissions, a main theater for performance. It is an art history class come to life, a textbook unfurled into galleries and palaces and squares through which a visitor can wander and rummage, for days on end.

The most famous may be the Uffizi, which lies just to the side of the enchanting Piazza della Signoria, between the 14th-century Palazzo Vecchio, with its crenellated turret of a belltower, and the Arno. Titian, Botticelli, Giotto – all are represented here, in a collection so bounteous that paintings shoved into corners or placed high on walls would command center stage in most other museums. On a recent visit here, I played a game with myself and focused only on pieces that other visitors quickly passed.

There is a depiction of *Adam and Eve's exile from the Garden of Eden*, by Jacopo Carucci (called Il Pontormo), that conveys a degree of misery and desolation beyond comprehension. The fallen pair look more than just ashamed and regretful. They look positively petrified as they step into a grave new world. There is also a take on the *Annunciation*, by the painter Lorenzo di Credi, that can make the viewer giggle with delight. The angel here seems to be begging Mary to consider her assignment,

FIVE ARCHITECTS
FOR ONE CHURCH

At least four architects worked
to give Florence and the world
that matchless expression of
Gothic art represented by the
church of Santa Maria del Fiore:
Arnolfo di Cambio, Giotto,
Andrea Pisano and Francesco
Talenti. To their number
we must add the name
of Brunelleschi, who designed
the magnificent dome.
Standing alongside the church,
Giotto's impressive tower
is proof that the great painter
was also a skillful architect.

Above, a detail of Botticelli's
Spring, in the Uffizi.
On the following pages,
the Ponte Vecchio with its rows
of traditional goldsmith's shops.

199

FINE ART IN AN ARTISTIC BUILDING

The 16th-century palazzo degli Uffizi, designed by the legendary Vasari, is the ideal setting for the art collections of this celebrated gallery, one of the best in the world. It was probably also the first museum to be opened to the public; since 1591, the Grand Duke graciously granted permission to those who asked to view the collections.

while Mary seems too distracted or disbelieving to be bothered with it. She exhibits no awe – just amusement, aloofness and maybe, just maybe, a trace of curiosity.

The Uffizi is more frequently visited, but I prefer the Pitti Palace, despite its lesser collection and its too-imposing, too-imperial aspect. In Florence, sadly, the visitor must hatch strategies to establish some distance between himself and the thickest of the ever-present crowds, and going to the other side of the Arno, where the Pitti is located, sometimes does the trick. I like the history of the Pitti, which underscores the dynamics that gilded Florence. Originally, Brunelleschi was commissioned to build it in the mid-15th century by the banker Luca Pitti, who wanted something big, bulky and bullying enough to rival anything that the Medici clan had. Pitti ultimately lost his fortune before the palace could be finished. The work on it was reprised many decades later, under the orders of its new owners: the Medici family itself. There are some fine paintings here, like a Caravaggio of a sleeping Cupid in which the cherub seems more conniving than playful, more cruel than kind. Perhaps better yet, there are a succession of rooms so posh and gaudy that they tell the visitor precisely what Florence was once about. And then there are the Boboli Gardens out back, a verdant slope of meticulously maintained land that is latticed by trees and punctuated by pools and fountains. Take that slope and those trails in the right direction and a surprise awaits: a link and entrance to Fort Belvedere. It is hard to imagine an afternoon more pleasant than one that begins at the Pitti and ends at Fort Belvedere.

Most of Florence's sumptuousness belongs to the past, but an ethic of luxury survives and thrives in the present, and it is most conspicuous in the city's shops. Florence is finery: stationery and notebooks that qualify as art forms all their own; silk ties and silk scarves in scores of colors; and leather, always leather, which means shoes and more shoes. During a long hiatus before he acted in the movie *Gangs of New York*, Daniel Day-Lewis chose Florence as his hideaway and shoemaking as his hobby. At the foot of Via Tornabuoni, which is like Florence's Madison Avenue, Ferragamo has its headquarters and its signature store. They occupy a riveting 13th century building that looks like an architectural companion piece to the Palazzo Vecchio, and it seems utterly fitting that one of Italy's premiere purveyors of sumptuous footwear would be coddled in a Florentine landmark. I usually stay on Via Tornabuoni, in a charmingly chopped-up hotel that spreads out over many floors and half-floors, twisting corridors and narrow staircases. Florence abounds in such places, designed from the start

or carved up later on with an eye toward whimsy and an aim of cozy warmth. It also has more conventional, up-to-the-minute lodgings and every other option in between those extremes. That is the upside of being a tourist mecca. As a practiced and popular host, Florence knows how to cater to almost any taste.

What holds true for hotels holds perhaps less true for restaurants. Italian cities do not usually excel in a variety of cuisines, because they excel in a cuisine that is the envy of most of the rest of the world: Italian. So Florentine trattorie and osterie pump out the pasta and the risotto, the veal and lamb. To my taste buds, fish is not a Tuscan standout, but beef, well, that is a different, sublime, exalted story. Tuscany is the home of many a specially-fed cow, and Florence is their afterlife. The tables here practically groan under the weight of mammoth porterhouses, or "fiorentine", that can make a grateful, Atkins-exonerated carnivore weep with joy. Tuscany also lays claim to being one of the most important regions for Italian wine-making, and the fruits of those endeavors are also abundant in the restaurants of Florence, many of which provide a selection of wines by the glasses that is much longer and more diverse than the norm. I remember – or, to be honest, only half remember – a night on the edge of Piazza Santa Croce, in a restaurant whose manager unleashed a cavalcade of vintages on a friend and me. An astringent white was followed by a smoother one. Then the reds sauntered along, something fruity followed by something peppery. Finally, with dessert, something golden and sweet galloped to the fore. It was pure overkill, which may just be another way of saying it was pure Florence.

Rain poured down that night, so my friend and I could not walk back to his home, which was two miles away. Under other circumstances, we would have, because Florence begs to be strolled. It has a pattern, a Rhythm: narrow alleys give way to broader streets while brooding dark stone from five or six centuries ago yields to the creamy pastel hues of more recent eras. A stretch of shade leads to a patch of sunlight, and then a piazza pops up precisely when it is most needed and appreciated. Or, suddenly, the Duomo looms, and no matter how many times it has brashly presented itself before, it demands – and wins – new attention. The patterns and figurines on just one of its many sets of metal doors, or on one of the columns of marble that frame those portals, could absorb a viewer for hours. As many angels hover here as on the head of a pin. They are magical creatures, and Florence never could get enough of them.

_____

FRANK BRUNI, restaurant critic of The Times, *recently completed a two-year assignment as the paper's bureau chief in Rome.*

MICHELANGELO REGRETS
"O my poor Ammannato, what a fine marble you have ruined!", remarked Michelangelo on seeing the statue that adorns the Fountain of Neptune (top) in piazza della Signoria. Actually, the work of Ammannati is well respected in the history of Florentine art, the opinion of Michelangelo notwithstanding.
Above, a group of tourists rounds off a day spent admiring Florentine art in a local restaurant.

203

ANCIENT STONE STREETS
Sovana, a short distance from the border with Lazio, contains some exceptional Etruscan remains in its "cavoni" or "hollow streets" (right). These are ancient pathways carved out of the rock, perhaps to shelter travelers from inclement weather; a few stretches are still used by farmers today to reach their fields. The darkness and the dank, silent atmosphere have given rise to thousands of legends about mischievous gnomes and elves, lying in wait to play tricks on the unwary who walk along these paths at night — which explains why the town's medieval inhabitants carved out little tabernacles in the walls to protect themselves from evil spirits.

By Beth Archer Brombert

MAREMMA,
Where Etruscan Ghosts Linger

June 7, 2004

"Maremma l'amara" it was called, Maremma the bitter, for the harsh life of its inhabitants, their unforgiving lands, their ruined villages. Of all the well-traveled regions of Tuscany, it was the most feared and remains the least known. Yet it is the one that most captivated the Tuscan imagination from Dante's lugubrious evocations of violent death and disease in the region made to symbolize human vanity and eternal despair, to Giovanni Fattori's desolate land-and-seascapes in the 19th century. Deserted after the fall of Rome by all but wild horses and long-horned cattle, the once-fertile plains reverted to mosquito-infested marshlands. What man abandoned, the sea reclaimed. Yet it was here, a thousand years before Rome was built, that a great nation of 12 city-states mined the hills for iron, copper and silver, tilled fields drained by ingenious canals, produced the finest weapons in Europe, and traded with Phoenicia, Egypt and Greece.

This was Etruria, land of the Etruscans, who gave Rome her first kings. By 600 B.C. the central half of the Italian Peninsula, from the Bay of Naples to the Po Valley, was under their dominion. In 90 B.C. the *Lex Julia* (a law promulgated by the Roman consul Lucio Giulio Cesare) imposed the laws and language of Rome on Etruria, and in 83 B.C. the Etruscans were definitively conquered by Silla who divided their lands among his faithful commanders. The Maremma (said to be a corruption from the Latin for Maritime Provinces) became the necropolis of Etruria's cities, temples and tombs.
Etruria was not merely conquered. Its books, except for those devoted to its religion, were destroyed, its culture travestied by Greek and Roman historians who por-

trayed Etruscans as pirates, worshipers of cruel gods, sybarites. Since necropolises were all that remained of their civilization, it was seen as obsessed with death.
Only in the last few decades have many of the mysteries of this people begun to be unraveled. The language of the Etruscans – unwritten until their contact in the 8th century B.C. with the Greeks, whose alphabet they adopted – is being arduously compiled from the limited vocabulary found in tomb inscriptions and still awaits its Rosetta stone. What has been determined is that few ancient civilizations had so rich an artistic, political or religious history, and that Rome may have learned more from her immediate Etruscan neighbors than from the more remote Greek colonizers in Sicily and on the mainland. Even the *toga*, so emblematic of Rome, was borrowed from the Etruscan *tebenna*. Not by accident did the Etruscan civilization fall into near oblivion. When it was finally conquered by Rome, every effort was made by the victor to obliterate its traces by prohibiting its language and absorbing its culture. Like the Maremma, now rescued from its long abandon, Etruria is being resurrected.

Geographers trace the Maremma from the Cecina River on the north to the Fiora on the south, and from the western coast up to the Colline Metallifere and the Mount Amiata. Historians necessarily include Tarquinia and Volterra in Maremman Etruria, while Tuscans regard the southern half, with Grosseto at its center, as the real Maremma. Here, two hours south of Florence, one enters a world of silent cities, medieval strongholds, forests roamed by wild boar and deer, sand beaches fringed with miles of umbrella pines. Here too is the land of the "butteri," the ranch hands of the Maremma who in 1887 challenged and defeated

THE ASHES OF A CIVILIZATION
Traces of a people, probably cattle herders, who lived between the 7th and the 1st centuries B.C., are to be found in the numerous Etruscan necropolises in Tuscany. One of the most important tombs, near Sovana, is known as "Hildebrand" in honor of the town's most illustrious son, Hildebrand, who became Pope Gregory VII. Above, the interior of another tomb near Sovana. This one is known as "dei Colombari," because of the ranks of "pigeon holes" that contained the ashes of the deceased.

205

**DANCING INTO
THE AFTERLIFE**

The tombs discovered around
Tarquinia boast a wealth of
pictorial decorations that have
provided precious information
about the everyday customs of
the Etruscans and their notions
of the hereafter. There are
a large number of convivial
scenes (above, a detail from
the Tomb of Triclinius) showing
singing and dancing, almost as if
they were intended to remind
the deceased of the happy
moments of their earthly
existence. Only after the 3rd
century B.C., with the decline of
Etruscan civilization, were
the tombs decorated with
disturbing figures, an evident
sign of the disquiet and fear
that had seized the population.

Buffalo Bill's cowboys in a test of rodeo skills. In those
days, as in Etruscan times, when horses and cattle were
an important part of the region's economy, "la merca,"
the branding of herds, gave rise to the same skills practiced in the American West. In the protected wilderness
of the Maremma, butteri are still roping and herding.
For the traveler already familiar with the itinerary of
the Grand Tour, Maremma is a fascinating change
from the crowds and optical fatigue of Italy's art centers. Volterra, an hour's drive from Florence, is a good
place to begin. *Velathri*, its ancient name, was the the
northern bulwark of maritime Etruria. Almost uni-
formly medieval today, Volterra has one of the finest
collections of Etruscan art in Italy, begun in 1732 with
pieces taken from local sites, displayed in the least tiring of museums (Museo Etrusco Guarnacci, 15, via
Don Minzoni). Some 600 carved funerary urns are
arranged by theme (Trojan cycle, the netherworld,
heroic figures, marriage), making it possible for the
non specialist to become acquainted with Etruscan art
and culture in an hour. There are also two famous
Etruscan statues that will immediately remind viewers
of Giacometti.

A two-hour drive south brings one to Roselle, little
known even to Tuscans, who at best may have heard of
it (six miles from Grosseto, a sign on Route 223, the
main road between Siena and Grosseto, indicates the
turnoff for "Rovine di Roselle," ruins of Roselle.) One
of the twelve Etruscan city-states, Roselle was at its
peak during the sixth and fifth centuries B.C. Despite
its conquest by Rome the city was not destroyed and
continued to flourish. Most of its ramparts, 23 feet high
and almost 2 miles around, are still intact. Paradoxically,
later Roman structures, built on supports, protected
the ancient city, which permitted the total excavation
of an Etruscan urban center, where previously all
knowledge of Etruscan life came from tombs. A complete Etruscan city, surveying the entire plain to the
sea, lies open to the visitor – streets, baths, houses,
even clay pipes for municipal water and sewage.
Perhaps the only benefit malaria brought to the region
is the survival of Roselle.

Though a dozen miles south of Tuscany's borders,
Vulci, Tarquinia and Tuscania are nonetheless officially
and historically part of Maremman Etruria. Vulci was a

A PEOPLE OF GHOSTS

The historian Dionysus of
Halicarnassus (1st century A.D.)
described the Etruscan people
as "different from any other race
in language and customs." The
Greeks called them "Tyrrhenians,"
the Romans "Tusci," while they
called themselves "Rasenna."
Perhaps they were a migrant
people, or native, or perhaps
descendants of the legendary
Pelasgians; in any event we know
little about them. The Emperor
Claudius, who married an
Etruscan, wrote at least 20 books
about them, but all have been
lost. The tombs, walls and jewels
that remain render the Etruscans
even more evanescent and
mysterious. Above, the necropolis
at Populonia. Left, the remains
of Etruscan walls at Pitigliano.

207

THE WINGED HORSES

This Etruscan clay statue from the 4th-3rd century B.C. is the main attraction in the National Archaeological Museum in Tarquinia. Originally the two horses were part of the ornamentation of the façade of the so-called Ara della Regina (the Queen's Altar), the largest Etruscan temple so far discovered.

mighty Etruscan city that in the seventh century established trade with the rest of the Mediterranean world. Over the next two centuries Vulci, while exporting its own bronze sculptures and wine, imported so great a number of both black- and red-figured vases from Greece that Etruria came to have more examples of this art than Greece. Today, a small museum with few but well-chosen pieces is housed in an ancient fortress that stands at the edge of a gorge worn by the Fiora River. A bridge on Etruscan foundations, barely wide enough for a mule, spans the gorge. Vulci, which D.H. Lawrence found so suggestive in *Etruscan Places*, is still a place of haunting strangeness. Storm-laden clouds hung over windswept fields the day I was there, while arrows of golden light fell on a browsing mare and her foal.

The still bright wall paintings in Tarquinia's sixth- and fifth-century B.C. tombs offer a vivid record of Etruscan customs, dress, physiognomy, furniture, food, even animals. Some 300 tombs have been now opened, out of the 6,800 that have been identified (by electrical sensing devices) in the necropolis, of which 15 can be visited. Unlike expressionless Egyptian figures, these look like real people who enjoyed the pleasures they are engaged in on the walls of the tombs: eating, drinking, watching jugglers, embracing their wives.

Etruscan women held a position in society unequalled in Greece or Rome: they shared banquet couches in life and sarcophagi in death. One of them, Tanaquil, the wife of Tarquin the Elder, was known as "the kingmaker" for having made her husband and his successors kings of Rome, who ruled from 616 to 509 B.C. Judging from the wall paintings, Etruscan women also attended boxing matches and chariot races, which no respectable Greek or Roman would have been allowed to do.

The Greeks accused the Etruscans of *truphé*, dissipation. Pleasure-loving they were, but to have wrested vineyards and olive groves from primeval forests, fields of grain from malarial swamps drained by an intricate system of canals, to have mined the hills for copper, iron and silver, smelted and exported ore, built ships to trade with the rest of the civilized world, hardly suggests a dissipated people. One has only to visit the Maremma to appreciate the diligence of the Etruscans. Under the more combative Romans, the lands so painstakingly cultivated by the Etruscans fell into disrepair. The sea reclaimed the drained marshes and the sludge grew weeds.

The Etruscans cultivated not only natural resources but the arts and letters as well. It was from them that the Romans acquired the concept of government and law. At a time when primitive tribes roamed Europe, the Etruscans lived in a federation of urban centers,

MAREMMA,
WHERE ETRUSCAN
GHOSTS LINGER

READY FOR THE RODEO
Giovanni Fattori represented with poetic realism the rugged lands known as the Maremma (above). The subjects of his paintings are local cowherds, peasants, horses and oxen, symbols of a simple and straightforward lifestyle, bound up with the land. The cowherds (left) descend from ancient herdsmen of the Maremma, when it was a vast, uninhabited region where untamed cattle roamed freely.

some of which still thrive today under other names: Volterra, Cortona, Arezzo, Perugia, Fiesole, Orvieto, Bologna. Piombino continues to be a port as it was under the Etruscans, now hauling tourists to Elba or Corsica instead of metals, wine and weapons. Etruscan jewelers taught the rest of the world how to make filigree – lace made of minuscule grains of gold. And Etruscan artists produced statues and vases to rival much that was made in Greece.

If tourism is the quest for *dépaysement*, removal from one's time and place, Maremma can amply provide it.

———

BETH ARCHER BROMBERT, author of "Edouard Manet: Rebel in a Frock Coat," *spends summers in a village near Siena. She is presently working on a memoir of her years in Italy.*

By Bernard Holland

Within the Walls of
LUCCA,
Both Mystery and Music

August 13, 2000

Lucca in September can make one forget the Renaissance ever happened. Situated just above the knee of the Italian boot barely 20 miles from the Mediterranean, this Tuscan city of 87,500, long prosperous and well pleased with itself, uses the beginning of autumn to celebrate what it was and what in good part it still is.

The dour beauty of the old city is medieval. Florence is 50 miles to the southeast but even more distant in spirit. The Romans gave the town its enduring roots although Lucca (probably from *luk*, the Ligurian word for marshland) had residents going back to Paleolithic times. The marks of an economic boom during the first two centuries of the Christian era have not gone away. The great amphitheater in the center of old Lucca is Roman to this day, as are some of the surviving walls around the city.

Lucca became both a crossroads for trade and more important a purveyor of silk, which it sold to both Europe and Asia. The feudal struggles that followed were not good for business, ending in some ugly 15th-century episodes during which Florence and the hated, nearby, Pisa moved in and established rule. There was also an unfortunate takeover by Napoleon and his sister Elisa in the early 1800's, but Lucca — handsome and livable — eventually retook and retained its air of independence and hard work. The mulberry trees that ring the ramparts remind the visitor of the city's silk trade. The banks that seem to occupy every corner of the old city today testify that the Lucchesi have found new ways to make money.

If the ancient buildings and the narrow streets of old Lucca act as physical reminders, it is the enduring attitude toward art and religion that makes this city feel so medieval. The Renaissance told us that painting, architecture and music could exist away from the church, where it had been so at home. In the third week of September, Lucca has the festival of the Volto Santo to remind us of old unities, beginning with a midmonth procession of solemnity and beauty to make its point.

"The Wandering Saint" (loosely translated) is a life-sized crucifix that was carved, according to legend, by Nicodemus from a cedar of Lebanon. It is said to have arrived in Lucca on a cart drawn by untamed oxen after having come ashore on an unmanned ship at some shadowy time a millennium ago. Legend says that boatmen from Pisa were the first to spot the floating crucifix, but broke their oars trying to approach it. The Lucchesi had no such problem, hence their current ownership. The Pisani, I am sure, have another story.

Ownership seemed to have had its problems early on. Apparent inanimacy did not keep this dark and fierce-eyed image of Christ from walking periodically from its perch at night and reclining in adjacent fields. There, the ancient Lucchesi would find it in the morning and restore it to its church. Now elegantly housed at the Cathedral of San Martino within a small 15th-century octagonal temple designed by Matteo Civitali and set in an enclave to the left of the main altar, the *Volto Santo* has stopped its wandering ways.

Yet with a little help, it makes a yearly sacred promenade, the Luminara di Santa Croce. Outfitted with a crown, the simple robe on the Christ figure covered with elaborate ornament, this object of continued and sincere devotion waits every Sept. 13 for sundown. Streetlights are turned off and torches lighted, and the ancient crucifix is carried for about two hours across

THE COPSE ON THE TOWER
On the top of the 24th century Torre dei Guinigi, also known as the "Wooded Tower," stand centuries-old ilex trees.
The Guinigi, a family of nobles and merchants, erected the tower to proclaim the family's prestige and opulence to posterity.
The view of the city from the tower is superb (facing page).

A DISPLAY OF ARCHES AND COLUMNS
The church of San Michele in Foro, completed in the 14th century, owes its name to the fact that it was built on the site occupied in ancient times by the Roman forum.

Facing page, views of Lucca's historic city center; below, the via Fillungo, the heart of the medieval city.

the half-mile width of Old Town from the Church of San Frediano to the cathedral. Good deeds and good fortune are attributed to the Volto Santo, and in gratitude gold plaques from citizens are hung for display in the cathedral, or cash is donated.

For this slow march, clergy from local and nearby churches is joined by squadrons of parishioners, all in full regalia. Windows along the Via Fillungo are embellished with richly decorated cloth and carpet. The procession, slowed by the narrowness of the streets, passes the Piazza San Giovanni and then reaches the cathedral. Participants keep up their strength with nut candies called "croccanti," which are made and sold for the occasion from the "bancarelle," or street carts, set up along the way.

At San Martino, high Mass is celebrated and a motet, written annually for the occasion, is sung. For the last decade the composer has been one of the city's musical activists, Msgr. Emilio Maggini. His predecessors include the father, grandfather and great-grandfather of the opera composer Giacomo Puccini, all of them church musicians. If the cathedral is filled to capacity, which it usually is, loudspeakers on the piazza outside convey the proceedings. Two to three hours can pass from start to finish, by which time Lucchesi are ready for dinner.

For the immediate celebrants the church lays on a banquet; restaurants are filled, or else families go home to dinner. This has been an evening when art serves the church, but in multiple events lasting through October, the church opens its doors to art and music. The La Scala Orchestra's concert last fall of nonoperatic Puccini conducted by Riccardo Muti was held, for example, in San Frediano. Art exhibits are everywhere. It is at this time of year that theater and opera also come to life.

If culture begins to wear on you, restaurant and hotel comforts are to be had. At one hotel frontdoor you can soak up music history with no effort whatsoever. Look straight ahead to the Giglio where Gilbert Duprez in 1831 introduced Italian opera to the first tenorial high C sung from the chest, thus changing the medium forever. Turn your head to the right and contemplate the stately Palazzo Ducale, where Paganini, wizard of the violin, had apartments and was said to frolic illicitly with his landlord, Maria Luisa of the Parma Bourbons.

The city walls, most of which were built in the 16th and 17th centuries, help modify the corrosive traffic plaguing most Italian cities. Many thoroughfares and byways are for pedestrians only, and this is truly a walkable

town, especially along the tops of the walls themselves. One stop on almost every pedestrian tour is the cafe on the Via Fillungo where Puccini and colleagues gathered. It has its glossy charm, but odd and accidental discoveries on aimless walks are often more interesting. I was struck by the postered death notices found on walls all over town. Paid obituaries in local newspapers, I was told, are expensive; these "manifesti per lutto" are the medium of choice.

The towers are fascinating. Where 130 once existed, only about nine remain, some four and five stories high. Rich homeowners once used towers to compete among themselves: the higher the altitude, the more potent the family. That the Torre delle Ore on the Via Fillungo survives has to do with its clock, deemed a practical necessity.

Wandering through the Roman Amphitheater, laid out in the first century A.D., one comes upon ancient houses now being peeled to the original brick. The smooth facades we associate with old Italian cities were in fact a product of the plague. Stucco, it was thought by 14th-century Lucchesi, sealed off disease.

The Renaissance did pay rich visits to Lucca. See especially Tintoretto's *Last Supper* at San Martino, the cathedral built in the sixth century, rebuilt in the 11th and notable for its stacked arcades and sculpted pillars. A lot of Lucca's striking pictures, facades and sculpture are older. In San Martino, spend time in two places. First, before the Volto Santo. If the glaring eyes of the Christ figure follow you too closely, find relief and calm in the extraordinarily beautiful Sarcophagus of Ilaria del Carretto, young wife of the powerful Paolo Guinigi, carved by Jacopo della Quercia in 1405.

Mystery and something vaguely disquieting inhabit the first image, utter serenity the second. A few moments with both might help prepare the visitor for the people out there on the streets of Lucca. They have been good businessmen for several millenniums, yet it is these same shrewd and practical people who hold firmly to the city's mysterious Christian legends. The thoughts may be new, but they are informed and colored by old beliefs.

If the Lucchesi dream of the past, they also insist on time to live right now. The growing, cooking and consuming of food is discussed in bars and cafés as rabidly as baseball is in the Bronx. This city must have its workaholics, but the flow of pedestrians in the streets at noon and late-afternoon reflects a citizenry that knows when to put business behind it and to enjoy friends and family. Creating space for both enterprise and relaxation is a life's work here.

BERNARD HOLLAND is national music critic of The New York Times.

WITHIN THE WALLS OF
LUCCA,
BOTH MYSTERY AND MUSIC

IN THE ANCIENT AMPHITHEATER
Piazza Anfiteatro (left) was built in the 19th century by enlarging the area once occupied by the Roman amphitheater and modifying it to accommodate houses and shops. The ancient arches were used to make the shops.

In piazza Cittadella there is a bronze statue of the musician Giacomo Puccini (above), the work of the sculptor Vito Tongiani.

By Barry Unsworth

UMBRIA,
Timeless and Enduring

September 13, 1998

**QUENCHING
THE CITY'S THIRST**
In 1254 Perugia set about
constructing a monumental
aqueduct to channel water from
the slopes of Mount Pacciano
to the city's Fontana Maggiore.
In the 19th century the fountain
was remodeled and the final
section became a spectacular
elevated walkway (facing page).
Above, the self-portrait
of Perugino in the Collegio
del Cambio.

We knew the landscape before we came here. We had seen it in London, Paris, New York. It is the world that opens beyond casement windows in Umbrian and Tuscan paintings of the early Renaissance, a background, never there for its own sake, never the center of interest, sometimes no more than an exercise in perspective, a world where those dreaming Madonnas and attendant saints could not really be imagined as ever setting foot, but intensely real to the imagination of the spectator, the walls and bell towers of some fortified town, the folded ranks of hills, with their dark, slender cypresses, as sharp and symmetrical as spear blades, and their steep terraces of olive and vine.

It is six years since we bought the house here in the hills south of Lake Trasimeno in western Umbria, halfway between Florence and Rome, but that sense of delighted recognition has never worn off. It is 600 years since the paintings were made, and that there should be any recognition at all says a great deal about the nature of the land and its history. These high-walled towns that surround us, Spello, Bevagna, Bettona, Montefalco, Corciano, Panicale, grew up in times of insecurity difficult now for us to imagine, a period of extreme violence and rapacity, constant strife between Guelph and Ghibelline, the forces of Pope and Emperor. As usual, it was the peasants who suffered most. They took refuge from marauding armies within the walls of the towns. The war zones shifted, the people came out to their ruined fields, patiently began again. Those centuries of conflict are over, strife takes different forms in Italy now, the hill towns of Umbria sleep within their walls, most of them hardly changed in appearance – too high, too far away, too

difficult of access for the dubious benefits of modern development and often protected by strict building regulations. The terraces of vine and olive below them, narrow and steeply sloping, are not much changed either. Much of the work on them is done as it always has been: on foot, by hand and laboriously.

Identical terraces surround us now, in our house here, with its five acres of land –warmly colored, fertile land, as good for zucchini as it is for roses. It was a typical Umbrian farmhouse when we bought it, the ground floor used for keeping animals, storing grain, making wine, an outside stairway to the upper floor, where people lived. The small village where we get our mail and buy most of our groceries is a couple of miles away, our nearest neighbor a 10-minute walk up the hill. There is no local industry and almost no traffic — nothing that could really be called a road anywhere near us. The sort of silence reigns here that is only deepened by sound. Sounds are seasonal events, the nightingales in May, the crickets a bit later, the cicadas in the full trance of summer, the ruffling wind from the north, the tramontana, that brings cold weather. Sounds the Etruscans listened to, long before the Romans came; and before the Etruscans the shadowy Umbri, original inhabitants of the region.

This constant feeling of intimate connection between the present and the past has always been of first importance to me as a writer. My themes, the sort of meanings that interest me and wind through the texture of my novels, are concerned with the influence of history and landscape on human character and behavior and the ways in which old patterns are repeated in new forms. I feel privileged to be able to live in a place

SWEET TEMPTATIONS
Sweets with exotic names
like "mostaccioli"
and "pinocchiate" and other
succulent delicacies, local and
otherwise, are the staples
of the Pasticceria Sandri,
established in 1860 and
a genuine institution in Perugia.
Beneath its frescoed ceiling one
can meet at any hour of the day
for an aperitif, a snack, or a
tasty tidbit to be savored in a
truly timeless atmosphere.

that is beautiful in itself and at the same time so suited to my temperament and imagination. I look out from the windows of my study across a broad valley planted with corn and sunflowers to the foothills of the Apennines, a landscape shaped and molded by many centuries of human habitation.

Some three miles away lies the reed-fringed southern shore of Trasimeno, the biggest lake on the Italian peninsula, always a surprise when you come upon it, by turns leaden and sullen, softly luminous, brimming with light, responsive to shifts of weather too delicate for the eye to register. If you stand here on a summer day and look northward, beyond the three green islands of the lake, you can make out the pale shapes of the hills above Tuoro, half hidden in the haze. Here, on a summer morning 22 centuries ago, Hannibal waited in ambush with his Carthaginians, fell on the Roman legions under Gaius Flaminius as they passed through

the narrow defile between lake and hills. Floundering in their heavy armor among the marshy verges of the lake, the Romans were slaughtered in their thousands — it was one of the bloodiest defeats of their history. The local place-names still testify to it: Sanguineto, where the blood ran, Ossaia, place of bones. Tranquil places today, no hint of violence about them.

The nearest town of any size is Perugia, capital of the province, about half an hour's drive from home. If you walk along Corso Vannucci toward the cathedral you see on your left the great curving facade of the late-medieval Priors' Palace, with its beautiful patterning of pink and white stone, its rows of lancet and mullioned windows. Here is housed the National Gallery of Umbria, recently extended and enlarged, containing what is arguably the greatest collection of Umbrian masters anywhere to be found. In one corner of the cathedral square, there is a pasticceria with a few tables

THE QUIET OF THE EVENING
At dusk in the ancient piazza Grande the hum of conversation from nearby cafés and bars blends with the murmuring of the Fontana Maggiore. Created toward the end of the 13th century by Nicola and Giovanni Pisano as the end point of the Mount Pacciano aqueduct, it is considered the finest surviving medieval fountain in Italy. The three nymphs in the center of the bronze basin were once surmounted by three griffons, the heraldic symbol of Perugia.

219

THE LEGEND OF THE LAKE
Prince Trasimeno, son of the
god Tyrrhenus, fell in love with
the nymph Agilla. When his
love was not requited, the
Prince pined away and died.
Even today, from the waters
of the lake (top right),
around twilight, there rises
a tenuous soughing similar
to muffled sobbing.

Perched on a hilltop above the
plain, the natural defensive
situation of Panicale
(bottom right) was reinforced
when the town was surrounded
by a robust wall, against which
many attempted conquests
and sieges of the past
were defeated.

Located in the center of Italy's
"boot" and surrounded by
three regions that prevent
access to the sea, Umbria
instead enjoys cultivated fields,
hills, mountains, plains, valleys
and vineyards (facing page).
Not just a trove of natural
beauty, but an authentic
source of everyday life.

set outside. This is where I generally have my coffee when I come to Perugia; in fact it is my favorite corner of the city. On one side there is the north flank of the cathedral with its Renaissance loggia and a section of Roman wall below. Immediately before you is the circular Great Fountain with its marvelous decorative sculptures of the seasons and their labors, done in the late 13th century by Nicola and Giovanni Pisano. And on your right the southern side of the Priors' Palace, the massiveness of the architecture lightened by the asymmetry of the levels at the sides of the fan-shaped staircase. With the pigeons strutting about on the cobbles and the life of the city going on around you, this is a place where an hour can go by like a minute.

The Priors, 10 in number, were drawn from the merchant class and they governed the Commune of Perugia in the time of her greatness, the 13th and 14th centuries, when she was a free republic. Things got worse after that, much worse, with first the murderous power struggles of the noble families, then a long Papal tyranny. The administration of the Priors was perhaps the most enlightened that the city knew until the 19th century. But enlightenment is a term that has to be understood relatively. In the labyrinth of medieval streets behind the Palace, many of them alleys so narrow that their upper stories almost meet overhead, there is the Via della Gabbia, the Street of the Cage, so called because an iron cage was hung high on the wall, and criminals were locked up in it and left to the sun and the wind. You could hear them crying day and night like mad people, says a contemporary chronicle. These cries would have come to the ears of the sober merchants as they balanced their books in the Collegio del Cambio, the counting house alongside the Palace, with its superb coffered ceilings and paneled walls and frescoes by Pietro Vannucci, called Perugino, the city's greatest artist. What is probably the only Perugino self-portrait in existence hangs in the Audience Room. Contrast of another kind can be found by strolling over the way from the Cambio to Sandri's Café, which is long and narrow and has an atmosphere of Central Europe of some earlier age. They make a most wonderful apple strudel there – a very un-Italian thing. The owner is Viennese and very old, and there is a general fear that the secret of the apple strudel will not be passed on.
Just around the corner, in Piazza Raffaello, there is the Church of San Severo, which has a fresco in the shape of an arch, divided in two by a horizontal line. The upper painting is by Raphael, the lower by Perugino, who was Raphael's teacher. Raphael was commissioned to do the whole work, but halfway through he was

THE PALAZZO DEI CONSOLI

The 14th-century Palazzo dei Consoli in Gubbio is one of the finest public buildings in the country. The Museo Civico, inside it, contains a unique exhibit: seven bronze tablets (the "Eugubine Tablets") from the 1st and 2nd centuries B.C., engraved with descriptions of rites of expiation and purification, as well as religious ceremonies, in Latin, Etruscan and a local dialect. The tablets are thus of exceptional importance, since the literary works of the Etruscans have been completely lost.

called to Rome by the Pope and never returned. He died young, amazingly so when one thinks of the volume and achievement of his work, at 37. The teacher outlived the pupil and Perugino, then in his 70's, completed the painting in 1521, two years before his own death. For anyone interested in Italian painting, it is a unique opportunity to compare and contrast the work of the two masters.

One of the great advantages of living in a place, any place, as opposed to merely visiting it, is that you have stores of time at your disposal; time to discover what you particularly like, time to return to it and return again. The lower basilica of the Church of St. Francis at Assisi (now open again to the public after some damage to the vault caused by the recent earthquake), with work by Giotto, Cimabue, Lorenzetti, Martini, all more or less contemporary, a truly astounding concentration of genius. The Campo in Siena, seen from above – the perfect early-Renaissance city square.

And since man does not live by beauty alone there is a trattoria in Castiglione del Lago, on the western side of Lake Trasimeno, which serves the best pizza – in my view at least – to be found north of Naples. The true pizza, the thin-crust sort. The place is an old wine-cellar with splendid vaulted brickwork ceilings and some enormous ancient vats still lining the walls. In summer you eat in the courtyard under pergolas of wisteria and grapevines; in winter – temperatures commonly fall below freezing in December and January – there are log fires and the warmth of the great stone oven in which the pizzas are made. One of these, perhaps preceded by bruschette and accompanied by one of the light local wines, and you have a true feast. It is a good place to visit, in any case: built on a promontory that thrusts out into the lake. You can stroll below the medieval city walls – there is only a footpath, no road – climb to the castle, which affords splendid views, the silver-green of the olive groves, the warm reddish brown of the earth, the changing colors of the lake.

Another favorite excursion, especially if one wants to avoid cars for awhile – and Italy has more of them per capita than almost any other country – is to the Isola Maggiore, largest of the three islands in Lake Trasimeno. The ferry goes from Passignano, on the eastern side, and the crossing is short – about 20 minutes.

The one village on the island is known for its lace-making – delicate white webs of lace are displayed on either side down the main street. Once this is left behind there is silence and peace. Even at the height of the holiday season you can feel alone on these wooded slopes, a seclusion that perhaps St. Francis was looking for when he came here, something like 700 years ago on a visit of 40 days, during which time he is said to have consumed just half a loaf of bread. If you follow the path that winds upward to the island's highest point you come to the Church of Sant'Arcangelo, which has a crucifix painted by Bartolomeo Caporali, another fine Umbrian painter.

Places where you like to eat, places where you can walk and think in peace, you get to know them in the course of time. Also important to know is a source of good wine. We drive north to Greve in Chianti, in Tuscany, to a vineyard there and spend an agreeable time talking about wines, tasting them and learning something about the process of making them – an extremely difficult business. Then a leisurely choice and home again, well provided – at least for awhile. If there is time we can stop in one of the numerous thermal pools scattered throughout Tuscany and Umbria, bathe in the warm springs, perhaps have a meal before getting back on our way. The trips one makes, the home one comes back to, these are the patterns that shape our lives. You move somewhere else and the shape changes. But we are not thinking of moving.

BARRY UNSWORTH, who won the Booker prize for "Sacred Hunger" in 1992, is the author of 14 novels, most recently, "The Songs of the Kings." He lives in Italy.

THE EPIC OF ST FRANCIS
Scenes from the life of St Francis are portrayed in Giotto's frescoes in the Basilica Superiore in Assisi.
Top left, the story of the miracle of the source: to refresh a thirsty disciple, St Francis caused fresh water to spring from the living rock.
Top right, Pope Honorius III gives his approval to the Franciscan Rule.
On the following pages, the Piazza Inferiore of the Basilica of St Francis in Assisi.

223

Jazz, Italian style

Thirty years ago few would have bet on its success. It was a period of crisis both economically and musically: gasoline was in short supply and after the Beatles it looked as if nothing would be the same anymore. In 1973 the birth of the Umbria Jazz Festival looked like a colossal gamble. Such an "American" show in the heart of a country dominated by the sugary melodies of Sanremo (the historic festival of traditional Italian popular music), couldn't possibly have a future.

Yet it grew more and more successful, one year after the next. Today it can be said that Umbria Jazz has introduced at least two generations of Italians to Afro-American music, two generations weaned on bebop, cool, hard and free jazz played by the greatest masters of the 20th century.

Chet Baker, Gato Barbieri, Michael Bublé, Miles Davis, Gil Evans, Stan Getz, Dizzy Gillespie, Herbie Hancock, Keith Jarrett, Charlie Mingus, Jerry Mulligan, Gary Peacock, Michel Petrucciani, Wayne Shorter... this is the sequence (rigorously alphabetic, because authentic fans disdain merit rankings) of artists who have played onstage at this event. The successful staging of the annual show, held during the first two weeks of July, does not involve smoky cellars (commonly required by a rather dated iconography) but is a festive mix of cultivated, refined music played indoors, and a less elitist music, but by no means inferior in quality, played in the streets and the squares – from noon to the small hours – for 10 straight days.

During the concerts Perugia puts all its venues at the disposal of the organizers: from the central Corso Vannucci to the evocative Piazza IV Novembre, where a stage is set up between the cathedral, the Fontana Maggiore and the nearby Palazzo dei Priori. Open air sessions are also held in the Giardini Carducci or on the field of the old soccer stadium, while purists prefer to make a rendezvous in the city's two theaters or in the Oratory of St. Cecilia. It's as if the medieval nucleus of the city were transformed into one great stage teeming with fans of jazz and all its offshoots. So blues and soul musicians are also welcome (B.B. King and James Brown have played here), not to mention the masters of swing, Big Band music, jive or Latin jazz (Tito Puente and Milton Nascimento).

Italian artists of the caliber of Paolo Fresu, Enrico Rava, Roberto Gatto and Rita Marcotulli are also greeted enthusiastically. Umbria jazz has even become the promoter of Italian jazz in the USA, with a recent session at the Blue Note club in New York, From America to Umbria and Back. This, too, is the path of jazz.

UNDER THE STARS OF JAZZ
Every year, for 10 days in July, Perugia welcomes old and new stars of jazz with vast crowds, both for the free shows held in the squares of the city, and for the theater events. From the left, Herbie Hancock, Tony Bennett, Chick Corea and Bobby McFerrin.

ORVIETO
Marvel of the Middle Ages

By Olivier Bernier

November 4, 1984

The plateau that time forgot: there can be few more alluring notions, and Orvieto, perched above a green, wine-growing valley in central Italy, fulfills it perfectly. The city, on its tall, sheer cliffs, is still almost as hard to reach as it was in the 12th and 13th centuries when, in a series of wars with its neighbors, its site served a strategic purpose. It also turned out to be a convenient refuge when, as often happened in the Middle Ages, the Popes found it politic to retreat from Rome; so, for quite a few years, Orvieto was actually the capital of Christendom. Much later, in the 19th century, the same lofty site precluded the building of railroad tracks (the station is down in the valley), superhighways, shopping centers and other similar blessings of the modern age. So the city has remained much as it was centuries ago, when it was part of the pontifical States.

Yet this seeming permanence is threatened: the passage of time and the vibrations of the traffic have undermined the city, and the soft volcanic stone of the cliff on which it stands has begun to disintegrate. It is no wonder, really: under all those imposing monuments, an endless warren of caves testifies to the fact that Orvietans always understood that good wine needs to be aged. Even worse, the caves are connected by apparently endless tunnels: digging down, in Orvieto, is not at all encouraged.

That great, towering cliff in itself would make a visit to Orvieto worthwhile; but because of a miracle – or so they thought in the 13th century – this little city also draws us with a large and utterly resplendent Gothic cathedral adorned, inside and out, with the very best the Italian art of the time had to offer. The story of the miracle in question, which actually took place in nearby Bolsena, has all the appeal, and the veracity, of a me-

dieval romance. In 1263, a priest, it seems, had lost his belief that the host, when consecrated during the mass, was actually the body of Christ. One day, when he was celebrating that rite, blood began to drip from the host he was holding up before the altar, staining the altar cloth. Although this is not, in itself, a really appealing phenomenon, it served the purposes of the papacy in the right way and at the right time.

The Pope, Urban IV, was both personally and politically committed to the doctrine of transubstantiation; he also knew a good thing when he heard it, and immediately declared that a major miracle had taken place. The next step was the building of a cathedral to enshrine the relic, and since Urban IV was then residing in Orvieto, the city was chosen as the site. In 1264, Urban signed the papal bull declaring Corpus Christi a feast day. The grand processions that mark the event, which usually falls in early summer, are still a part of life in Orvieto. And for all those who would like to see a striking depiction of the event, the Raphael fresco, in the Vatican, adds the undoubted truth of art to the rather less certain accuracy of the event itself.

The cathedral, happily still in top condition, is a church of extraordinary beauty, in which all the many resources of the richest Gothic came together to produce something more like a jewel than a building. From the moment the first stone was laid on November 13, 1290 by Pope Nicholas IV, money was spent freely. More important, in 1309, the Sienese sculptor and architect, Lorenzo Maitani took over. Blending complexity of form and lush color, he achieved the impossible: everything should clash and nothing does. Each of the cathedral's three great doorways is surmounted by an

A HEROIC COAT OF ARMS
Above, the arms of Orvieto. The lion holding the keys and the motto *Fortis et fidelis* (Strong and Faithful) were given to the city by Pope Hadrian IV in token of his gratitude for the welcome he received there. The red cross on the white field was added by the men of Orvieto on their return from the Crusades.

Facing page, a detail of the side of the cathedral, with the characteristic green and white "stripes" of the marble cladding.

A BONUS FOR THE ARTIST
Two scenes from the frescoes
by Luca Signorelli in the chapel
of San Brizio in the cathedral.
Above, the *Last Judgment*:
top, right, *Paradise*.
It seems that Signorelli's
contract included, as well
as cash, a supply of 1,000 liters
of wine a year for the artist
and his helpers.

elaborately Gothic gable crowned with a bronze statue;
then comes an open arcade, so that at the top of the
building, already pushed upward by the powerful thrust
of the gables, seems to float on air. Four pinnacles,
framing the doors, rise up to tall conical crowns; above
the arcade, on either side, two more mosaic-filled
gables are silhouetted agains the sky.

So far, although complicated, all the forms have followed
the same logic, but here comes the touch of genius: in
the central panel of the second level of the façade,
Maitani placed a circle within squares. First, there is a
lacy rose window; then comes a carved round frame contained by an even richer square that is in turn surrounded by smaller square niches, each sheltering a head
sculpted in full relief; then there is another sumptuous
frame; then, going up the sides and across the top, a
gallery sheltering full-size figures of saints and prophets.
All this is surmounted in turn by the tallest of the gables
on which, in mosaics, we see Christ crowning the Virgin.
The whole is awash with color. In every gable and around
the doors biblical scenes in bright blues, greens and reds
stand out against a gold ground. The gables and pinnacles are edged with pink and green marble, laid out in
thin stripes, and are surrounded with bands of the same
marbles carved to look like twisting ropes and openwork
lace, enclosed within two wider bands of geometric motifs. All this would have satisfied most designers; not
Maitani, however, who proceeded to adorn the piers between the doorways with carved bas-relief scenes from
Genesis and the New Testament, from the lives of the
Prophets, and, finally, of the Last Judgment. The quality

of the sculpture is extraordinary, the composition full of
movement and emotion. Here, for all to see in a world
where very few could read, was the Bible writ large.
We have yet to see the best. The interior of the church
blends sumptuousness and grandeur in an even more
striking way than the façade. As we enter, we find ourselves at the beginning of an immensely long nave, made
even longer by its gray and white stripes; on either side,
an arcade opens into a narrower aisle that makes the
nave look wider and taller. Here, as in all successful
Gothic churches, the roof seems impossibly high, impossibly light. Then, straight ahead of us, we see, behind the
main altar, a tall, narrow window flanked by 14th century frescoes and topped by a clerestory. The clerestory is
surmounted by another fresco; even from the back of the
nave we are conscious of the richly colored glow.

This, however, is merely the beginning. Even
greater riches await us in the two side chapels. The
chapel on the left is covered with frescoes representing
the miracle of Bolsena. They were painted between 1357
and 1363 by two local artists, Ugolino di Prete Ilario and
Domenico di Meo, and are clearly marked by Giotto's influence. No matter where we look, every image belongs
to the 14th century. Clear color, volumetric form, emotion visibly expressed, all help to draw us into this still
medieval world, and we enter it all the more readily because the walls and ceiling of the chapel are still in good
condition. A marble tempietto over the main altar holds
the reliquary of the Corporal, one of the most important
pieces of gold and enamel work in existence. The reli-

THE PERFECT WORK

The façade of Orvieto cathedral
is breathtaking. The series
of vertical lines, the symmetry
of the structures, the colors
of the decorations
and the mosaics: the eye
quickly recognizes a marvel.
That this harmony has survived
is even more remarkable if you
consider that it is the end result
of the work of many different
artists and trends that followed
one another during three
centuries of construction.
Above, a detail of the mosaics
on the façade showing
the Baptism of Christ.

231

quary, which is almost five feet high, was made in 1339 to hold the piece of cloth on which, that day in Bolsena, the host is said to have bled.

The chapel on the right represents a completely different world. Although it was built in 1397, the chapel of San Brizio was not entirely frescoed when, in 1499, Luca Signorelli was called in to complete the ceiling, which had been begun by Fra Angelico. In 1500, Signorelli was commissioned to paint every available inch of wall. Keeping the strong color scheme originated by his predecessors, he set about creating the scenes of the last days of the world, the resurrection of the dead, heaven and hell that constitute his masterwork. In these paintings, all belongs to the Renaissance, from the figures and clothing – the man in the brightly striped tights, the young noble in red cap and laced velvet jerkin – to the classicizing architecture. But most striking is the grand sweep of the composition. The crowds pressing around the Antichrist (one black-clad figure is a self-portrait) and the picturesque confusion of the Last Judgment, with the damned being herded about by highly colored demons, forecast the Raphael Stanze in the Vatican; the coronation of the elect, with its musical angels and ecstatic listeners introduces the kind of three-layered composition found in such later works as Titian's *Assumption of the Virgin*. All here is full of exuberance, of the joyful and inquiring spirit of the Italian Renaissance.

Although one might spend all day in the cathedral, there is still more to see. To one side of its piazza, for instance, is a splendid Gothic palace, built between 1281 and 1285 for pope Martin IV, that houses the Museum dell'Opera del Duomo. As you enter its large hall, you will first see bits and pieces – carved stones, wooden statues – that were once part of the cathedral. Toward the back, however, there are three long rows of vitrines protected by faded curtains. Push these aside and you will find yourself looking at an extraordinary collection of ecclesiastical vestments: Renaissance figured damasks in still bright deep colors seem to have come right out of the portraits of the time and make it clear why these fabrics were so enormously expensive. The palm and leaf patterns are grand and complex; the shimmer of the silk reminds us that this was once the rarest of fabrics; and it is easy to imagine them, worn by popes, bishops and priests, adding their glow to the color of the cathedral. There are 17th-century copes stiff with gold embroidery meandering all over their surfaces (and, no doubt, adding greatly to their weight), gold-lace capes of amazing delicacy and richly embroidered 18th-century figured silk vestments which could just as well have served for the hooped skirts of a fashionable noblewoman, and offer us the tender colors – pale blues, greens, pinks – we can still see in the works of Boucher. Directly across the cathedral, the Museo Archeologico Claudio Faina, installed in a 17th-century palace, is also worth a visit. The museum, which was begun in 1864 as a private collection, contains a great many of the Etruscan pieces found in or near the city. Orvieto was, before Rome took it over, a major center. Etruscan tombs in great numbers are dug into the hills; and so the objects which come from that necropolis are numerous and high in quality.

There is every kind of object here, terra cotta portraits of extraordinary immediacy in which the influence of Greek art blends happily with that feeling for precision

THE CITY ON THE ROCK

Top, a view of the houses of Orvieto on the edge of the travertine crag. Above, the Corteo Storico, celebrated annually on the occasion of the Corpus Domini religious holiday to commemorate the city's establishment as a free commune.

Facing page, the dizzying shaft of the Pozzo di San Patrizio (St Patrick's Well), built to guarantee the city a supply of fresh water in case of a siege.

and recognizability which the Romans then inherited; carved stone sarcophagi, colored glass vials and, as a bonus, a vast quantity of Greek vases, with black figures on red ground portraying the gods, athletes and mythological scenes; and some of these are absolutely first-rate. Look out of the window in any of the front rooms: there, before you, the cathedral stands glistening against a ground of distant green vines and a vast blue sky. After that, nothing could be more appropriate than a walk through the city, whose narrow streets, opening from the Piazza del Duomo, are lined with shops full of all kind of treasure. Orvieto is known for its earthenware, decorated with blues and ochers with scenes and motifs that reflect Renaissance models. Walk on and you will pass stone palaces, some of them adding a note of 17th-century majesty to the picturesqueness of their Gothic neighbors. There are tiny brick houses from which a medieval artisan could emerge without seeming out of place. Here and there, square or octagonal towers rear up into the sky. Churches, some of them Romanesque, but most of them with animated 13th-century facades continue, in a simpler way, the note struck by the cathedral, and as the streets wind and twist, as grand facades suddenly appear around a corner, you will know exactly how it felt to stroll in a medieval city.

All that is above ground; but, of course, what has been dug down matters in Orvieto – not just the many caves but also the spectacular well of San Patrizio. Designed in the 1520's by Antonio da Sangallo the Younger on the order of Pope Clement VII de' Medici, it is about 200 feet deep; two helical staircases, lit by windows that look out into the central shaft, take two hundred and forty eight steps to reach the water at the bottom, a great convenience, apparently, for the donkeys who brought the filled urns back up. When you re-emerge from the well, just walk on; eventually you'll end up at the Piazza del Popolo. There, massive but graceful, is one of the most striking buildings in Italy, the Palazzo del Capitano del Popolo. A perfect example of what the local guidebooks refer to as "Orvieto Romano-Gothic," it is half-palace and half-fortress, with a wide outer staircase, stepped vaults on the lower floor, a broad terrace at the top of the stairs, Gothic windows and the most decorative of crenelations. It is a good place to pause and drink in the atmosphere of this enchanting city; and the next step can only be to one of the local restaurants, where the light Orvieto white wine will complete the picture.

OLIVIER BERNIER is the author of 12 books, most recently "The World in 1800." He lectures at the Metropolitan Museum of Art in New York and in museums across the country.

By Dan Hofstadter

THE MARCHES
Italy as It Used to Be

May 17, 1992

A MOUNTAIN IN THE SEA
Mount Conero (facing page) plows into the Adriatic like the prow of some gigantic ship. Rocky, even grim in places, it confines the beaches to small hidden coves, where they await discovery by the most adventurous tourists. Its slopes are clad in vineyards that produce the delicious wine named for the mountain.

Many italians speak of their loss of innocence during the 1960's. During this period, they claim, the elemental passions were diluted by psychobabble, the charming old songs were replaced by rock music, and certain graceful and unquestioned habits, like cooking well or dressing attractively, became infected by a painful self-consciousness. Yet one region, the Marches, is widely believed by Italians to be far less "contaminated" than other, equally prosperous areas. Situated between Umbria and the Adriatic Sea, the Marches has a long coast, filled with fashionable beaches, resorts and hotels. But if the coast is sophisticated, the ancient virtues of familial piety and spontaneous generosity may still be encountered in the sparsely populated hill towns a few miles inland, where the earth's crust rumples into hills like shirred green velvet.

The curious name "Marches" is related to the German word *mark*, meaning frontier domain; in the Middle Ages such territories were ruled by marquesses, margravines and other picturesquely titled feudal worthies. For long periods the Italian Marches lay along the outer rim of the Papal States, but in the 1860's, when Italy was conclusively reunified, they were grouped into a single region. Cut off by the Apennines, the Marches is readily accessible by car from only one major Italian city, Bologna, and so is not as popular with tourists as the other regions of central Italy. It is Tuscany, however, that the Marches most resembles, with its hazy sunlight, gray-green tonality – perhaps less gray than around Florence, since the olive is not widely cultivated here – and for-

tified hill towns bristling with churches and palazzi. The region is a sort of eastern companion piece or pendant to Tuscany, as visiting Tuscans readily observe; and if it is not so splendid or various, it still offers a parallel sense of civilized refinement, of cultural achievement at the highest level. Bramante was born in the Marches, as were Raphael and Barocci; one of Italy's greatest poets, Giacomo Leopardi, was a Marchigian; so were Rossini and Beniamino Gigli. Of the many gifted outsiders lured into the region, one, Lorenzo Lotto, stands out: this Venetian master left a large number of pictures both in Recanati and in the pilgrimage town of Loreto.

Like most Marchigian towns, Recanati rises from a verdant setting. It is paved in bricks and little square stones, and shaded by fragrant oleanders, and the meadows round about are filled with flowering broom in spring and poppies in summer. If Loreto is the center of the cult of the Madonna (according to legend, her house, the Santa Casa, was miraculously transported there in 1291), Recanati is a Mecca for the literary – no academic tourist would be caught in this spot without a battered copy of Leopardi's verses poking out of his tweed jacket pocket. The 19th-century bard's shade seems to haunt the place, emitting angry, bored and melancholy vibes, and his palazzo is on most days open to his devotees. Entering an atrium, you behold a large Baroque staircase – its proportions seem to suggest poetic glory – which leads up to an enormous library. With its precious furniture, family portraits and collection of antiquarian books and autograph manuscripts it is perhaps a perfect funerary monument for a writer of the Byronic age.

AMONG THE HILLS OF THE POETS AND THE PAINTERS
The hills of the Marches, which inspired many painters of the Italian Renaissance, have also provided poets with immortal words. Giacomo Leopardi, perhaps the greatest of the Italian Romantic poets and the author of the renowned poem *L'infinito,* was born in Recanati, a small town clinging to the hillside.

Some 50 miles north of Recanati is Urbino. The jewel in the Marches' crown, it is a perfect hill town, wall-girded, rosy-gray, ringing with belfries, free of gross suburbs from any approach you choose. The classic approach is from the Colle delle Vigne, where, rounding a bend, you suddenly behold a gift assortment of turrets and spires and domes suggesting a Renaissance model maker's ideal city. There are many different shapes of Italian hill town – disks and cones and long, thin lozenges – and Urbino may be described as camel-like, for it occupies two tall humps and the hollow in between; the charm of this arrangement is that you can climb to the top of either hump to contemplate the other. Visiting Urbino in the early 1950's, the writer Edith Templeton offered this description of its stubby streets in *The Surprise of Cremona:* "They are so narrow that two people leaning out of opposite windows could shake hands, and they are so short that, looking down each of them, one finds that it opens on to the

wonderful panorama of green hills and blue ridges. This is moving; those dark alleys, which seem like the beginning of a labyrinth full of poison cups and daggers, breaking off almost as soon as they have started, and forming windows for the blue-green loveliness of the Marches."

Up and down go the alleys, as if tossed upon stone waves. Those of the western hump tend toward the city's most famous building, the Palazzo Ducale, built by Duke Federico da Montefeltro in the late 15th century. It was Federico who created the Urbino that we see today – he fashioned the most refined court in Italy and attracted the most brilliant artists of the age to decorate his reception rooms and living quarters – and his mutilated nose, immortalized by Piero della Francesca, still seems to dominate the town. Federico's architect, Luciano Laurana, redesigned the palace as a sort of monumental Janus with two distinct

236

facades, imaginatively remote from each other. One, in brick and lacy carved travertine, is elegantly sober; the other, flanked by two spire-capped towers and decorated by two superimposed loggias, suggests a fairy-tale castle from the medieval past. The result is a building dreamlike and expressionistic beneath its apparent classicism.

The Duke was a man of notable valor – his nose had been broken in a joust – but when he came to commission his study, the "Studiolo," he had it covered in trompe l'oeil inlaid wooden paneling that shows his armor put away in a closet, while all the paraphernalia of the arts lie strewn about, and a squirrel, emblematic of nature, stands upon a windowsill devouring a nut.

In the 17th century, when Urbino passed to the papacy, the palace was emptied of its art and left to fall into desuetude; not until modern times was it restored and a portion of its treasures recovered, with

the aid of the Italian Government. Today, the palace still possesses one of the noblest courtyards in Italy, Laurana's "Cortile d'Onore," with its arresting Roman-style inscriptions; it also houses the National Gallery of the Marches. This name suggests an offbeat provincial showcase, but in fact it is one of the great museums of Europe, packed with enough masterpieces to require several visits. Among other things, there are two works by Piero della Francesca, the *Madonna of Senigallia* and the *Flagellation of Christ* (both displayed in one room, which is mobbed in high season). The *Flagellation*, whose subject remains obscure, may be the most perfect of Piero's smaller paintings: five of the figures are seen at a distance, through atmosphere, and the the exquisite calm modeling of their garments suggests some mysterious grace in the otherwise gruesome action. The National Gallery also holds a matchless Raphael portrait (*La Muta*, The Silent Woman), a superb *Madonna and*

MAY THE BEST MAN WIN!

The Giostra della Quintana (the Quintana Tournament) was born in Ascoli Piceno in the 15th century when, between one war and the next, mounted knights kept themselves in training with simulated combat. The event begins with a spectacular historic procession (right), then the flag wavers hurl their standards into the air before the real Tournament finally begins (above). Citizens from the town's various neighborhoods take turns to charge a revolving puppet that represents the ferocious Saladin.

Fermo is one of the most characteristic towns of this region. The maze of cobbled streets of the city center suddenly open up before the 16th-century piazza del Popolo (facing page), where visitors can relax in the many cafés.

Child by Orazio Gentileschi and a huge roomful – the great collection – of Baroccis.

Federico Barocci is regarded by Italians as one of the major painters of the late cinquecento. To get acquainted with this obsessive, darkly religious, somewhat out-of-the-way talent is surely one of the pleasures of a first trip to the Marches. Barocci was born in Urbino in 1535, and during his 20's went to work and study in Rome. From an early age he drew like an angel, in a style that would soon become astonishingly proto-Baroque – his spiralings and shallow curves and long, soft brush strokes seem to prefigure Rubens. Yet Barocci's promise was just what got him into trouble and ruined his health. According to an early biographer, a number of other painters, "agitated by envy," invited him for a meal and then poisoned his salad, whereupon he fell so ill that no doctor was able to help him, and in the end he was advised to go back up into the hills, to Urbino, whose beneficent winds might bring him some comfort. This he did, and in time he regained enough strength to paint one hour in the morning and one in the afternoon for the rest of his life – he lived to be 84. Barocci took a house in town (still to be seen on the street that bears his name) where he dwelt in a permanent depression, wracked by stomach pains and plagued by such unremitting insomnia that he would lurch through his rooms all night, muttering and lamenting his fate. But beneath his irascibility lay monumental patience, and young men flocked from afar to study under him; his students were innumerable and spread his style through central and northern Italy.

Wandering around Urbino you find Barocci's large religious compositions everywhere, and if you walk through the fine wrought-iron gate before the Chapel of the Sacrament in the Duomo and continue inside you will see his greatest masterpiece, the huge *Last Supper*. In it, all the beautifully drawn and brilliantly colored figures seem to be caught in a high wind, like one of those gales that rip through Urbino and make it a center for kite-flying contests. Barocci was the only Italian painter who could fill a big canvas like this with 20 or 30 figures – angels, apostles, dishwashers – and get all the frenzied action convincingly choreographed, psychologically credible and devotionally decorous. All, that is, but Jesus's own gesture, a blessing that is saccharine and over-holy, so that you feel that there must be some morbid sadness at the heart of Barocci, some shrinking away from the salt of truth – this Christ seems made of marzipan.

THE BADGE OF FAITH

The story goes that angels transported the Holy House of the Madonna of Loreto from Palestine to its present location on December 10, 1292 in order to prevent profanation at the hands of infidels. In the past it was customary for friars of the sanctuary to tattoo pilgrims with some religious subject, as a token of their undying faith.

The Marches, music and Rossini

The Marches have an outstanding musical tradition. The most famous local musician, Gioacchino Rossini (Pesaro 1792-Passy de Paris 1868), enjoyed immediate popularity. His father, Giuseppe Antonio, the town crier of Pesaro, earned some extra cash by playing the horn in the theaters and public academies; his mother Anna Guidarini, was a singer who enjoyed a brief career in the theaters of the Marches and Bologna. It was in this climate that little Gioacchino first came into contact with the world of opera. In 1802 Rossini's family moved to Lugo where the young man studied in the house of the brothers Luigi and Giuseppe Malerbi, who introduced him to the works of Mozart and Haydn. Rossini himself wrote six sonatas for two violins, cello and double bass when he was only 12 years old and had not yet taken, to use his own words, "any lessons in accompaniment." A few years later he enrolled in the Bologna school of music and by the time his studies were over he could play the viola and other stringed instruments, the harpsichord and the piano. He was also an accomplished singer.

Rossini's arrival on the operatic scene was electrifying. In 1810, still very young, he made his debut in Venice with *La cambiale di matrimonio* and in 1812 he made his debut at La Scala in Milan with *La pietra del paragone*. After huge public successes with *Tancredi* (1813) and *The Italian Girl in Algiers* (1813), in February 1816 Rossini staged *The Barber of Seville* in Rome. But the Roman public failed to appreciate this masterpiece, even though Beethoven was quite won over by it. Later, things went better with *Armida* (1817), *The Thieving Magpie* (1817), *Moses in Egypt* (1818) and *Zelmira* (1822), just to mention a few of the works that express all of Rossini's art: simple, linear writing allied to the physical exuberance and joviality of the famous crescendos. The year 1824 found him in Paris but contact with German Romantic opera provoked a reaction that left Rossini at loggerheads with the musicians of the new generation. His Parisian works include the outstanding *William Tell* (1829) performed at the Opéra to a wildly enthusiastic audience.

A late work with which Rossini laid down the groundwork for modern musical drama, *William Tell* is devoid of all 18th-century structure and represents Rossini's challenge to the Romantics, a last powerful blow on the part of the great composer. Immediately afterward Rossini returned to Italy and he lived for a time in Bologna, but his health gradually began to deteriorate. In 1846 he married Olimpia Pélissier, a beautiful socialite, and he settled down with her in Milan where he opened his home to famous musicians, including Liszt. Then he passed another spell in Bologna, moved to Florence and then, for health reasons, went back to Paris where things seemed to improve for a while. Rossini continued to organize his famous musical soirées, attended by the best known singers and composers passing through the French capital. But his health, already precarious, suddenly deteriorated and in 1868 Rossini died in his villa in Passy.

GENIUS AND LAZINESS

It is commonly believed that great artists are forever creating and polishing their masterpieces. But the cliché definitely does not apply to Rossini, whose indolence was proverbial. Stendhal left us an amusing anecdote according to which the great musician, who was composing in bed, preferred to rewrite a duet rather than pick up the sheet of music that had slipped to the floor. Right, the interior of the Teatro Rossini in Pesaro.

CALLIOPE'S FORGE

"I nominate the city of Pesaro, my birthplace, as heir to my estate with the proviso that it establishes and equips a school of music in the city after the death of my wife..." With these words Gioacchino Rossini willed his hometown a school for aspiring young musicians, now the Conservatory. Founded on November 5, 1882, the Conservatory has been directed by prestigious musicians such as Pietro Mascagni and Riccardo Zandonai.

243

Leaving Urbino, you find attractive cities and towns in almost any direction. I have mentioned Recanati and Loreto; there is also Pesaro with its Renaissance piazzas, Jesi with its 18th-century theater and hoard of paintings by Lorenzo Lotto, Urbania with its distinctive churches and sweeping vistas of the River Metauro. San Leo, a village that is about a two hours' drive to the north, has not made it into English-language guidebooks. This part of the Marches is a craggy blue-green fantasy, a landscape out of Mantegna: rocky pinnacles soar into the sky, each one

more vertiginous than the last, perfect sites for world-shunning conventual orders – but the pinnacles are uninhabited save for the one surmounted by San Leo and its impregnable Renaissance fortress, the Rocca. The sight is breathtaking, a chunk of superb military geometry atop a dizzying precipice.

It was here in the clouds, far from the gullible race of men, that the Inquisition imprisoned Giuseppe Balsamo in 1791. He is better known as Count Alessandro di Cagliostro, the most brilliant charlatan in history – magician, alchemist, clairvoyant, miracle

worker and founder of the Egyptian branch of the Masonic movement. Cagliostro was a gifted confidence trickster who grew enormously rich on his mesmerized followers' donations to his cult. At the same time, he bravely defended certain values that he believed in, and ended up more dangerous to himself than to anyone else. The Inquisition threw him in a tiny cell in the rocca, with a scrap of a view through three iron grilles, down upon San Leo. One pictures the charlatan laughing contemptuously through his triple bars, but, in reality, he was utterly wretched, surveilled day and night from a hole in the ceiling of his oubliette; after four years and four months of imprisonment he died of an apoplectic fit.

San Leo has two fine churches. The smaller, parish church, which contains the sarcophagus of St. Leo, the Dalmatian who helped convert the region to Christianity, was built in the ninth century; it has the irregular lines and perfect proportions common to buildings of this period. It is faced, outside and in, with undressed stone blocks of a warm, tawny color, and the size of these blocks – about that of a big loaf of the local bread – is exactly scaled to the size of the building, giving it a rugged, slightly shadowy texture. The Duomo is a later edifice, part Romanesque and part early Gothic, but it, too, is tall and slender and inviting to the palm of the hand, and its apse has the same shallow form as that of the parish church, only

stretched – drawn upward – into a an elegant, sliced-cylinder shape. Inside the Duomo a fragment of the saint's occipital bone is lovingly preserved.

The respect for tradition that characterizes the Marches is abundantly evident in its food. The region has two notable specialities. One is a flaky flat bread, made of unsweetened pastry dough, that goes by various names ("cresce" in Urbino). The other is "brodetto," the fish soup of the coast, of which there are two types: the northern (served from Numana upward), prepared with 13 types of fish, and the southern, prepared with 9 types of fish, plus saffron. Another seafood dish, "garagoli," cone-shaped mollusks harvested from May through August, tastes good with wild fennel. The Marchan lasagne, called "vincisgrassi," is an unusual and delicious combination of chicken giblets and black truffles.

Throughout the Marches there are many comfortable and reasonably priced small hotels. You should expect to sleep well in this most tranquil of all central Italian regions, dreaming of dukes and poison cups, honey-tongued magicians and the bones of wandering saints.

DAN HOFSTADTER's most recent book, "The Love Affair as a Work of Art," a volume of criticism, was nominated for an award by the National Book Critics Circle. He spends much time in Naples.

THE WIZARD'S CITADEL

The Rocca di San Leo (above), a papal prison since the 17th century, owes its fame to its most celebrated inmate: the self-styled conjuror, physician, thaumaturge and alchemist known as Cagliostro.

Facing page, the Palazzo Ducale in Urbino, a Renaissance masterpiece built by Federico da Montefeltro and designed mostly by Luciano Laurana. The cylindrical towers of the façade, which culminate in a cusp, are reminiscent of Oriental minarets.

By Muriel Spark

My
ROME

March 13, 1983

I settled in Rome long ago in 1967 because I found myself returning there again and again, staying longer and longer. I think what attracted me most was the immediate touch of antiquity on everyday life. If you live in central Rome you have only to walk down the street and you come to a fountain by Bernini in which children are playing or a Michelangelo embassy or some fine 15th-century building with today's washing hanging out. The names Bramante, Raphael and Borromini become like those of friends. One comes into the territory of the Republican ages, the Caesars, the emperors or the medieval popes at any turn in the road. Here is the Rome of Garibaldi's troops, of Keats and Shelley, of Arthur Hugh Clough (whose narrative poem *Amours de Voyage* contains one of the funniest descriptions of the English in Rome during the troubles of 1848); Byron's Rome, Henry James's Rome and Mussolini's big fat dream Rome with grandiose popular centers and concepts.

The first apartment I occupied was in the Piazza di Tor Sanguigna, not far from the Tiber on the corner of Via dei Coronari, an ancient street of antique furniture shops. I was at that time dazzled by the adjacent Piazza Navona (as indeed I still am), and I greatly desired a permanent home in the piazza. I did find a flat there, with a picturesque view of Bernini's marvelous Four Rivers fountain, but devoid of everything else, including water. The bathroom and the kitchen, explained the landlord, and the plumbing, electricity and other trivialities, were to be laid on by the lucky tenant who succeeded in obtaining from him a contract limited to one year's residence. The rent alone was high, and I knew right away that the project was impossible, but I still enjoy the memory, as I did the experience, of standing in that dark, vaulted, cavelike apartment while the landlord explained in a mixture of Italian, French and English those terms which I discerned, by careful deciphering, were exorbitant.

I fairly egged him on, as far as my powers in Italian permitted, so keen was I to see with my novelist's curiosity how far he would go. The tenant had to be an American, he said. I was a Scot, I informed him, and I doubted that he would find an American to pour capital into his property with a tenure of only one year. He replied that the apartment was in a famous 15th-century building in which many famous lords had lived, which was true enough. So he went on, while I looked out the window, watching the fountain playing in the fine October light of Rome. The theatrical figure representing the Nile, his hand held up as if to ward off some falling masonry, seemed apt to my situation. "Speak to me," Michelangelo is said to have challenged his Roman statue of Moses; and indeed, the sculptures of Rome do speak.

I moved to an apartment full of history in the Palazzo Taverna, and I radiated out from there. The

FROM IMPERIAL MAUSOLEUM TO PAPAL PRISON
The Emperor Hadrian wanted his remains to be preserved in a monumental cylindrical mausoleum crowned by the statue of Helos, the sun god. This imposing structure forms the first nucleus of Castel Sant'Angelo, which over the centuries became a fortified bridgehead, a refuge for popes under siege, the papal court and the papal prison. According to tradition, during the plague of 590 Pope Gregory the Great had a vision of an angel, high on top of the building, who announced the end of the scourge. This is why the fortress was named for the archangel Michael. In the 13th century a fortified corridor was built, the so-called "passetto", which provided a direct connection between Castel Sant'Angelo and the Vatican to allow the pope to reach safety in case of danger.

247

Along the median line of piazza
Navona three splendid Baroque
fountains are lined up:
the Fontana del Moro,
the Fontana del Nettuno,
and the Fontana dei Fiumi.
The renowned architect Bernini
had a hand in all of them, albeit
sometimes only
for reconstruction
and modifications.
But the Fontana dei Fiumi was
entirely designed by him.
More than 45 feet high, the four
marble statues symbolize four
rivers and their respective
continents: the Nile for Africa,
the Danube for Europe, the Rio
de la Plata for America and the
Ganges for Asia (above).

palazzo was at the top of the Via dei Coronari overlooking Castel Sant'Angelo. The main room was enormous, a Renaissance Cardinal Orsini's library, and the upper walls and the ceilings were painted with classical scenes and Orsini emblems. I didn't try to furnish it, but made a sitting room in a remote corner while the rest of the room, with its polished Roman tiles, was for going for walks (it would have made a good skating rink). In one of the corridors a Roman pillar had been let into the wall. By this time I was getting used to permanent residence in historic Rome – part of the excitement of visiting one's friends was to see what portion of history their living space occupied. The Palazzo Taverna, with its fountain in the great courtyard, its arches and small courtyards, was fun to live in, and my echoing cardinal's room was to many of my friends one of the wonders of the world. My cats used to love to sit on a rug while we whizzed them round the vast floor. After dinner everyone in the palazzo would go down to the courtyard to take the air with the neighbors. One of the fascinations of Old Rome is that there are no exclusive neighborhoods. Rich and poor live on top of each other.

The wives of ambassadors to Rome are hard put to seat their guests according to protocol; there are several different hierarchies. In the first place, Italy is a republic, but of course the Vatican cardinals and ambassadors top the cake. Then there is the Old Aristocracy, whose ancestors were Popes; they stood, up to the early 1970's, very much on ceremony if they deigned to go outside their palace walls at all. The New Aristocracy comprise the hurly-burly of princes and counts who have sprung up since the time of Napoleon – Bourbon descendants fall somewhere among this category, but I know neither where nor who does know. And ex-monarchs usually find their way to Rome, which is another headache for the embassies (fortunately these were not my problems, for whenever I throw a party, high and low as it may include, I make it a buffet).

Nowadays there are fewer ex-royals. But I remember once having stopped by the office of Jim Bell then in charge of the Rome bureau of an American news magazine, who often played golf with exiled Constantine of Greece. Before we left for lunch a secretary put her head round the door. "The king wants to speak to you," she said. "The king of what?", Jim Bell wanted to know.

I always go to the Rome Opera in the winter. Each year on the night the opera opens there is a great embracing and greeting of fellow ticketholders and "Bentornato" (Welcome back) all round. One never sees these people anywhere else; they are one's opera friends. On one special evening when Montserrat Caballé was singing in a Bellini opera, the rain started coming through the roof. Now, a well-known Roman of that time was the late Mario Praz, a critic and scholar of English literature (he wrote *The Romantic Agony*). He was said to have the Evil Eye and was known as the Malocchio. This nickname wasn't attributed with any repugnance, but rather as an affectionately recorded and realistic fact (for such people are regarded as carriers rather than operators of the Evil Eye). Naturally, everyone noticed when Mario Praz was present at a party, and waited for the disaster. There was usually a stolen car at the end of the evening, or someone called away because his uncle had died. Well, when I saw the rain coming in the roof at the Opera, and heard the commotion behind me, I looked round instinctively for Mario Praz. Sure enough, there was our dear Malocchio sitting under the afflicted spot. He died recently and was mourned on a national scale (the Italians put their artists and people of letters on a higher level than anywhere else I have known). Before his house could be unsealed for his heirs, robbers got in and looted his lifetime collection of museum pieces and memorabilia.

In the summer I always try to see the open-air performance of *Aida* at the Baths of Caracalla. These mighty ruins are extremely well adapted to the mammoth spectacle with its superabundance of camels and cavalry, its luxurious scenery and massed troops. The ancient Romans, for whom the Baths were built as a social and cultural center, would have loved it. But I think it is a great blessing to us that the Baths have fallen into ruin, nature's magnificent sculptures that they are. The originals must have been of decidedly totalitarian dimensions. Against a late afternoon light all Rome looks sublime, and especially the ruins of Caracalla. They are floodlit at night; the environs used to be a favorite night walk, but nobody takes lonely walks in Rome any more. The footpads are rife. Even the girls of the night, with their picturesque roadside bonfires, have deserted the vicinity of the Baths, and the nightingales sing to the ghosts.

My stay at the Palazzo Taverna came to an end after three years, when the landlady wanted the flat "for her daughter." My next flat looked out on the Tiber at the front, and at the back on the rooftops and winding alleys of ancient Trastevere. Here again I had one big room surrounded by a few small rooms. The best thing about it was the view of the river at night with a moving bracelet of traffic on either side of the Tiber and over the bridges; and if I was working very late at night I loved to go for a walk in my big room and look out at the three floodlit monuments of my window view: the clocktower of Santa Maria in Trastevere; up on the Gianicolo the Fontana Paola; and behind it the church of San Pietro in Montorio. Eventually my landlady wanted this

TWO MILLENNIA OF AMUSEMENTS IN THE SQUARE

Piazza Navona lies in an area once occupied by the Emperor Domitian's arena, of whose dimensions and rectangular form (with one of the short sides curved) the modern square is a faithful copy. In its long life the square has witnessed events of all kinds, even naval battles. Its concave bottom was flooded to enable war games between crews of nobles and prelates. Also, tournaments, races, historical pageants and, in early January, the annual Festival of the Befana — a brightly colored toy market.

**A STAIRWAY OF FLOWERS
TO PARADISE**
When the French diplomat
Stéphane Gouffier died in 1660
he left a bequest for an
imposing flight of steps to
connect piazza di Spagna and
the church of Trinità dei Monti.
Another 60 years went
by before the work was
completed, to a design
by Francesco de Santis. Today
it can fairly be described
as the "floral stairway." Spring
is celebrated each year with
a magnificent display
of azaleas, then with a blaze
of roses timed to coincide with
a prestigious international
competition for new
varieties of roses.

On the preceding pages, the
Anfiteatro Flavio, better known
as the Coliseum, a symbol of
the grandeur that was ancient
Rome. Work was begun under
the Emperor Vespasian
in 72 A.D. and the arena was
inaugurated by Titus eight years
later. According to the Roman
historian, Suetonius, the
emperor ordered games to be
held there for 100 days straight,
with naval battles, hunting
and killing wild beasts
and gladiatorial contests.

apartment, too, "for her daughter." Tired of landladies' daughters, I acquired for my own the apartment I live in now, a small but very exciting place just emerging from slumdom. It is in a little street between Piazza Farnese, where Michelangelo added a floor to what is now the French Embassy, and the great Campo dei Fiori, the colorful flower and fruit market. This is deep in the Rome of the Renaissance. My apartment dates from the 14th century at the back and the 15th at the front. It belonged to an inn called "La Vacca" owned by La Vanozza, mistress of Pope Alexander Borgia and mother of Cesare Borgia. Her coat of arms, those of her husband and those of the Pope, all three joined, are set in the outside wall near my windows. When the workmen were getting this apartment ready for me they tore down some paper which covered the ceilings to reveal beautiful woodwork. A window was found in a wall leading to the main part of La Vanozza's property. Embedded in the old tiles of the floor they found the remains of a speaking tube that communicated with the street door.

Whether or not this was used by La Vanozza's 15th century call girls, I will never know. Wherever I live I am in the writer's condition: work is pleasure and pleasure is work. I find Rome a good place to work. The ordinary Roman is nearly always a "character," which is to say there are no ordinary Romans and therefore life among them, although it may be exasperating at times, is never boring. The extraordinary, Byzantine bureaucracy of Italian living and the usual bothers of life are always present, but if I can get, say, a glimpse of the Pantheon – even passing in a taxi on my way to fulfill some banal commission – I find the journey worthwhile. At night, if I go to dine near the Pantheon, I love to walk around with friends in the great, solid portico for a while. It is sheer harmony; the bulk is practically airborne.

_____

MURIEL SPARK is the author of 22 novels, most recently "Aiding and Abetting" *and the forthcoming novel,* "The Finishing School." *Her most celebrated works include* "The Prime of Miss Jean Brodie," *and* "Loitering With Intent." *She lives in Tuscany.*

MICHELANGELO'S PIAZZA

The Campidoglio (the Capitoline Hill), the smallest of the seven hills on which Rome was built, was also the steepest. For this reason it was the city's stronghold from earliest times. It later became a sacred place, crowned by the Temple of Jove, the god of war (Giove Capitolino). The Campidoglio, which slowly fell into ruin after the fall of the western Roman Empire, was reborn in the 16th century, a grandiose architectural project whose guiding hand was Michelangelo.

By William Weaver

The City
BENEATH ROME

October 6, 1985

ST PETER'S CHAINS

Above, San Sebastiano, a detail
of the 7th-century mosaic
in the church of San Pietro
in Vincoli. The building was
erected in the 5th century
to house the chains
that bound St Peter,
a prisoner in Jerusalem.

Those who venture into the
ground beneath Rome will
discover the inimitable
superimposition of styles that
also can be seen in this view
of the Forum (facing page).

Nobody seems to know how many catacombs there are in Rome: one of my guides said 60, another said more than a hundred. Besides the Christian catacombs, there are also pagan and Jewish ones. More are being discovered all the time, but many – for reasons of economy – are not regularly open to the public. Cynical travelers say that if you've seen one catacomb, you've seen them all. This is partly true, but the effect of visiting them is cumulative. In any case, asked to recommend one catacomb to stand for all, I would suggest the vast cemetery under the church of San Sebastiano, on the Appian Way. It is not the richest catacomb, but it is certainly the most famous; during the Middle Ages, while the other catacombs were forgotten, pilgrims still came to this spot to pay homage to the early martyrs.

The entrance to the catacomb is through a doorway in the walled forecourt of the little Baroque church of San Sebastiano. Descending to the first chamber, is the tomb of St. Sebastian himself. The room is plain, except for a simple table altar and a marble bust of the saint, somewhat dubiously attributed to Bernini. Long a place of worship, the chapel is still the site of an annual pilgrimage on St. Sebastian's feast day, Jan. 20. From there the real catacombs begin: rows and rows of shelf-like niches carved out of the porous tufa rock. Bodies were simply wrapped in shrouds, then sealed in a niche with a slab of marble or, with poorer families, brick. These graves can easily be dated, since Roman tax laws required brick makers to stamp their bricks with a device bearing the emperor's name. The San Sebastiano cemetery was in use from the first to the fifth century A.D.

Since the San Sebastiano catacombs were always known, they were subject to vandalism and are relatively bare (though some interesting and beautiful wall decorations do survive, including a charming fresco of an appetizing bowl of fruit with a plump bird pecking at a grape). But the San Callisto catacombs, nearby, were lost for more than a thousand years and rediscovered only in 1849 by the pioneering Italian archeologist Giovanni Battista De Rossi, who found them while visiting a vineyard. Pope Pius IX bought the land at once, and excavations began.

The San Callisto catacombs are a short, pleasant walk from San Sebastiano. After crossing a busy road, you enter the Vatican's property, a flourishing farm, where you proceed between fields of corn and wheat, past a luxurious kitchen garden (I paused for an envious inspection of the fat artichokes and luxuriant tomato plants).

One of De Rossi's early discoveries was the important crypt of the popes, with loculi containing the remains of nine pontiffs from the third century, identified by marble plaques. He went on to bring to light frescoes, mosaics and carvings. Among the most striking are the frescoes showing six praying figures (in a cell curiously misnamed "The Five Saints") and an early third-century fresco of Christ, the *Good Shepherd*, a favorite theme in several catacombs. The excavation was fresh when Nathaniel Hawthorne visited the catacombs in the late 1850's and used them for a scene in his Roman novel, *The Marble Faun*: "They went joyously down into that vast tomb, and wandered by torch-light through a sort of dream, in which reminiscences of church-aisles and grimy cellars – and chiefly the latter – seemed to be broken into fragments... The intricate passages, along which they followed their guide, had been hewn, in

A SUBTERRANEAN CHURCH
The church of San Clemente,
built in the 4th century
(there is an even older
1st century layer), was badly
damaged by the Normans
of Robert Guiscard in 1084.
A few years later, Pope Pascal II
decided to construct a new
church over the ruins.
The parts of this ancient
church were not
rediscovered until 1857.
Right, 11th-century frescoes
portray episodes from
the life of St Clement.

some forgotten age, out of a dark-red, crumbly stone. On either side were horizontal niches, where, if they held their torches closely, the shape of a human body was discernible in white ashes, into which the entire mortality of a man or woman had resolved itself."

Torchlight has been replaced by electricity, but otherwise today's experience is much like Hawthorne's. His stern puritanism often made him an unsympathetic tourist: the accent on the grimy cellar is indicative. But catacombs are, indeed, not to everyone's taste. In 1788, the more sympathetic Goethe went to San Sebastiano, meaning to visit the catacombs, but he reported: "I had hardly taken a step into that airless place before I began to feel uncomfortable, and I immediately returned to the light of day and the fresh air."

The grottoes of St. Peter's are not catacombs exactly. Originally they were a cemetery in the open air, then buried for centuries. What we see today is the result of excavations begun in 1940 at the command of Pope Pius XII and concluded in 1965, after the discovery not only of the grave of St. Peter but also of most of a skeleton that is generally accepted as the saint's. Visit is by appointment, since groups have necessarily to be kept small.

As you explore the substrata of Rome, it is often hard, even impossible to grasp the architectural sense of a complex site. To assist the visitor, in the anteroom of the grottoes there is a scale model, showing the relationship between the first basilica of St. Peter's, erected by Constantine in the fourth century, and the earlier aedicula, the little monument built to protect the remains of St. Peter not long after his death. The aedicula stood within a necropolis bounded by the so-called "red wall" of monumental niches that together with the "graffiti wall," named for its early Christian inscriptions, provided evidence essential to authenticating the site of St. Peter's grave. Visitors are invited to take a long look at this model, which makes the subsequent progress through the excavations more rewarding.

To build his Basilica, Constantine had to level the Vatican hill, covering an ancient graveyard that had occupied the southern slope since the first century A.D. The tombs — like so many little houses — were lined up along narrow streets. The excavations disinterred two of these streets, parallel to each other; and if in your imagination you can remove the dark ceiling over your head (and the huge basilica above it), you can believe you are walking through a cemetery in the first century, when people who had witnessed Peter's martyrdom were still living. The red brick facades, after a millennium and a half, still have a warm glow, and here again, the sound of voices — those of the party of tourists ahead or behind your own — echoing along the street reinforces the sense of life.

For there is nothing gloomy about these tombs: some are bright with frescoes of birds and fruit and animals, or with mosaics (one shows Christ as the sun, driving a chariot like Apollo's, against a glowing gold background), or with stucco decorations. The inscriptions tell us that most of the tombs are pagan, but some are Christian and some are both, suggesting that the family owning the little temple was converted.

Finally, you come to the Clementine chapel, built over St. Peter's grave (and directly below the great main altar of today's basilica) by Clement VIII at the end of the 16th century. This is where the excavations ordered by Pius XII began, and it is the heart of St. Peter's. Above the altar is a vertical porphyry slab, flanked by slabs of plain white marble. This was the rear wall of Constantine's monument over the tomb of St. Peter. From the chapel, one person at a time can go and peer through a grille and see the site of the tomb, the simple, rough wall in which the bones were found and in which they rest today. At this point, the visitor's religious convictions (or lack thereof) are beside the point. You know you are in a holy place.

———

WILLIAM WEAVER is a biographer of Verdi, Puccini and Eleonora Duse. He has also translated many works by Umberto Eco, Italo Calvino, and Alberto Moravia. He resides at Bard College.

THE NECROPOLIS OF THE POPES

Built on four levels, the catacombs of San Callisto are among the most important and venerated in the city and cover an area of 120,000 square yards. Many of the early popes were buried in the Crypt of the Popes (above), decorated by order of St Damasus in the 4th century. The body of the young martyr St Cecilia was found in the Crypt of the same name and her remains were later removed to the church of Santa Cecilia by Pope Pascal I in the early 9th century.

257

**AN ENDLESS FLIGHT
OF COLUMNS**
Bernini's spectacular colonnade
represents a brilliant
architectonic solution to the
problem of delimiting piazza
San Pietro without modifying
the surrounding buildings
and without exceeding them
in height. In addition, the two
sides that connect the piazza to
St Peter's are divergent, creating
an evocative perspective.

258

By Malachi Martin

From the
POPE'S WINDOW

April 4, 1982

Even with all the wonders and marvels and spells of Rome to pull the visitor in this direction or that, there is one magnet that draws nearly everyone. Whatever takes you to Rome, business, pleasure, or lifelong dream, you will find yourself in a Vatican-centered – a Pope-centered – city. "Did you see the Pope?" strangers ask each other, gazing upward from St. Peter's Square to a window where a moment before, at noon, a white-clad figure smiled and raised a hand in universal blessing.

At other times of day, that window is unremarkable, one of 10 on the third floor of a 15th-century Vatican building that stands looking in a southeasterly direction over Rome, over its river, the Tiber, out to the distant hills and beyond. That building is part of the Apostolic Palace, a jumble of buildings begun six centuries ago and on which construction is still in progress. Nothing is done hastily in the Vatican. Indeed, that window is only one out of a total 12,523 windows in the Palace – which, in addition, houses more than 10,000 rooms, suites, halls, cellars and passages and two or three elevators, as well as 997 flights of stairs. The Pope's window is one in the papal study. His living quarters are on the fourth floor. But his daily work is done on the third, in that study.

If you or I, tourist or pilgrim, could stand for a moment beside him at that window, we would receive mainly two impressions: of shimmering expanse and of mysterious detail. We would see Rome as it lies in the region of Lazio, with the sky seemingly lifting away from the city and countryside in a fashion that suggests some invisible highway joining Rome with the distant high country far beyond the Campagna plain, the mountains and the sea. The world of man and something of the mystic country above the world of man rush in to greet you through that window. It becomes a transom opening on the infinite and the eternal.

Then details crowd in on us. The gaze falls over Rome to find a hundred hooded domes glinting in the sun and a myriad of spires, towers, monuments, hemmed in with palazzi, parks, supermarkets, shops, simple houses, all connected by streets of every kind, long, straight, curving, short, narrow, broad. And, night and day, even from that Vatican window, the ear picks up the unceasing hum of Rome. For the city sits on top of hardened, echoing volcanic ash, the tufa. Even a visitor, versed in the rolling syllables of the Roman dialect, can converse in the quiet of an early morning with a friend five streets away, if he has learned to throw his voice "alla Romana." These are the things about which we might chat afterwards, if we could stand beside the Pope at his window for a minute or two.

But when the Pope looks out that window, he has none of our ease or fascination. Every detail he sees fits into the template of his duty. What he sees first is not that wide expanse, the city and its monuments. It is, directly, beneath the window, the piazza or "square" of St. Peter's. We, his momentary visitors, would have noted from our guidebooks that it measures 215 yards in its greatest breadth, is flanked on two sides by the colonnade of Bernini, itself a complex of 284 columns and 80 buttresses surmounted by 162 statues, each 12 feet high. In the center of the piazza, a 132-foot Egyptian obelisk weighing 320 tons.

The Pope would remember, rather, that over 1,900 years ago, they ran chariot races below in that ellipse.

SIGNED, MICHELANGELO
The Chapel of the Pietà in St Peter's contains Michelangelo's famous *Pietà*, the only work ever signed by the master. The sculptor, then 25 years old, was commissioned by Cardinal Jean Bilhères de Lagraulas, the French ambassador to Rome.

THE PAPAL MILITIA
Julius II, the pope who signed
Michelangelo to decorate the
ceiling of the Sistine chapel,
established a tradition that
endures to this day.
In 1503 he recruited a company
of soldiers from the Canton
of Zurich for the defense
of the apostolic buildings
and the pope himself.
The proverbial loyalty
of the Swiss Guards extended
to the point of self-sacrifice,
as was demonstrated during
the Sack of Rome in 1527.

On the two pages, crowds
of the faithful invade
piazza San Pietro.

And, one night after the races, in a narrow street running across the Vatican hill, they killed an aging Jewish fisherman called Simon Peter, in order to delight an emperor called Nero and his girl-friend, Poppea. Peter's friends hurriedly buried his body in a shallow grave at the top of the hill, because at that time Roman eagles were screaming victoriously all over the world, the hob-nailed boots of Rome's legionnaires were beating out a firm imperial tramp on Roman roads that ran all throughout the empire and civilized Rome had absolutely no use for one miserable fisherman. Not yet.

With a shift of your gaze to the right, but in a direct line of about 1,200 feet from that third floor window, you can see Michelangelo's dome. Under it, that shallow grave of the fisherman lies beneath the high altar of St. Peter's Basilica, where the Pope says mass. We, standing at that window, will marvel at that basilica, at its proportions – 651 feet long, our guidebook tells us, 435 feet high, with 777 columns, 44 altars, 395 statues and a bronze ball on top of its dome in which 16 persons can fit comfortably. But the Pope will not for-

get that, even when the Roman Empire ceased to be, and Peter became the Great Fisherman, still it took over 1,000 years for his successors, each one of them wearing the Fisherman's Ring, to create this basilica as the focal point of a new empire, Christianity; and that it was scarcely finished when that Christian heartland was torn irreparably to shreds by wars, hate, animosity and self-perpetuating divisions.

We can see much from that window – the American College on the Janiculum hill, the roof of the Sistine Chapel, in which the Pope was elected by the Cardinals, the round red brick Castel Sant'Angelo built by the emperor Hadrian. But the Pope sees chiefly the robust reminders of the principal elements of his Roman organization with which he must govern his church and perhaps reduce the hate, eliminate the animosity, heal the divisions.

The Secretariat, headed by the Cardinal Secretary of State, normally the closest advisor and collaborator of the Pope, maintains its own diplomatic representatives in over 100 countries. Representatives from about the same number of states are accredited to the Holy See.

Vatican Radio, call letters HJV, faithfully broadcasts the encoded messages awaited by Vatican representatives and emissaries in all five continents.

Directly across from the Apostolic Palace, on the south side of St. Peter's Basilica, are two other principal elements of papal government. The more important one is concerned with the preservation of Roman Catholic belief and the correct observance of the church's moral law. Formerly called the Holy Office, it is now known as the Congregation for the Faith (a Congregation is the Roman term for what we call a government ministry or department). It is housed in a centuries-old building, a former monastery, enclosing an inner courtyard entered by an arched portal. More than any other component of the Vatican, this is a quiet place, full of discreet silences and memories of ancient disputes and struggles stirring in every room and throughout its austere corridors.
Within a stone's throw of the Congregation for the Faith stands the Vatican bank in a relatively modern building, complete with all that makes for a bank – managers, vice presidents, tellers, messengers, investment experts, accountants, vaults. Here all financial transactions of the Vatican and the Roman Catholic Church as a worldly institution are performed. It would be crass to think that the only *raison d'être* the bank has is to make money. For one thing, the [over $170 million] annual budget of the Vatican must be met regularly. For another, the Vatican directly supports hundreds of colleges, schools, orphanages, universities, clinics, leprosaria, philanthropic institutions and some thousands of bishops and priests and nuns all over the world. But, as with the Secretariat of State, there is a nice calculation to be made by the Pope, as he gazes across at the Vatican bank: in managing its material wealth, his Vatican must not allow spirit to suffer nor faith to be diminished. For the only wealth brought to Rome by the Great Fisherman consisted of spirit and faith planted with his blood on this same ancient Vatican hill one night long ago.
"When I step away from that window," Pope John XXIII said, "and sit at my desk, I need consolation. I need strength at my back." It is symbolically significant that behind the Apostolic Palace, behind the Pope's back as

THE FOUNTAIN OF DREAMS
Created between 1699 and 1751 and designed by the architect Nicola Salvi, the Trevi Fountain is the most famous fountain in Rome.

Facing page, the interior of the Lateran palace, originally destined to be the pontiff's summer residence. It stands alongside the basilica of St. John Lateran, the cathedral of Rome, that is to say the church of the bishop to the city, in other words the pope himself.

he sits at his desk, lie most of the great treasures the Vatican has preserved from the past, its irreplaceable library and archives, its fantastically rich museums, its long galleries of ancient, medieval, Renaissance and modern art, its vast, vast storage rooms, its collection of paintings and frescoes. And, also, some of the Vatican's more mysterious parts that are unknown to most people – the Tower of the Winds, for example, and the Room of the Meridian with its zodiac mosaics and ancient frescoes.

Before you leave that papal window, glance out one more time. Let your eye travel. Past the sluggish gray-green waters of the Tiber. Past the nearest of Rome's seven hills, the Capitoline. Past that pile of brilliantly white Brescian marble, the Victor Emmanuel Monument, nicknamed "il peccato mortale" by the Italians and "the wedding-cake" by generations of English-speakers. Out over the other six hills of Rome, northwards to the Pantheon and southwards to the opening of the old Appian Way. Over all the monumen-

tal fountains, massive churches, towering columns, monasteries with flaming frescoes, palatial houses and gardens. Over all the staircases by which you can climb and view this Rome. Feel the indefinable – and, at first, puzzling – pull this Rome of the Popes can exert on you. But do not be afraid of it. Everywhere you can look from this window, great and renowned men and women have been before you and have felt that same mysteriously gentle attraction of Rome and its pope. John Keats died in a house at the foot of the Spanish Steps. James Joyce spent one winter of his discontent on the banks of the Tiber. Rome's streets and Vatican have been trod by Robert Adam, Elizabeth Barrett Browning, Thackeray, Hans Christian Andersen, Lizst, Buffalo Bill, Queen Cristina of Sweden, Nathaniel Hawthorne, Rubens, Stendhal, even the pope-baiting poet, John Milton (he attended theatrical performances in the palace of the Barberini popes surrounded by red-robed cardinals). And the sad-faced Sigmund Freud, for many of his last years, wrote about "going home to Rome..." Romans can better explain what he meant than most

Freudians can! The truth is that all these people, as you, could feel at home in Rome. For Rome is not Italian. It is uniquely itself. And universal.

May is the month to be here. It is the month when Rome blossoms anew and welcomes. Winter bitterness and spring uncertainty are no more. The choking sirocco wind rarely blows over from the African deserts to the south. There is scarcely one "temporale," that sudden downpour of sheet-rain bringing with it a fine red tufa dust. The sky of Lazio smiles with that singular luminosity – an amalgam of loveliest blue and transparent light and the white fleece of shapely cloud – that poets and painters swear can be found nowhere else on earth, and that Raphael described as "the casement of Heaven itself."

Rome is filled with flowers and sparkling fountains in May. Restaurant tables and chairs are moved out onto every pavement. The marble statues and the earth-brown palazzi bask in the caressing warmth of the new sun. And every soft evening, above the Spanish Steps, around the fountains and colonnades of St. Peter's Square, up on the ancient Capitol and out around the tombs and ruins lining the old Appian Way, the swallows have arrived from North Africa; they dive and soar and bank in the chase of invisible mayflies.

Before you leave that window in this May of your mind's eye and your desiring, before you leave Rome – if you really must leave – remember to toss a coin in the Trevi Fountain, a short mile from here. It insures that you will come back. But Romans have long memories; and they well remember that once before when popes deserted Rome, this city became the refuge of robbers preying on a few dirt farmers and gypsies, its monuments overgrown with weeds and grass, and that it earned the nickname "cow-patch" all over Europe, so dank and smelly and dangerous did it become. And so Romans reckon that one major reason why Rome persists and will persist is the charismatic man up at that window who talks with Brezhnev and with God, the man present-day Romans refer to as "il nostro polacco romano," our Roman Pole, much as they speak familiarly of Julius Caesar as "il nostro Cesare" and their dead national hero as "il nostro Garibaldi." They, and he, know with surety Rome will always house the Great Fisherman. Or cease to be Rome.

MALACHI MARTIN, was a priest, theologian and author of 16 books of non-fiction and fiction. Among those still in print are "Hostage to the Devil," "The Jesuits," "The Keys of This Blood" and "Windswept House: A Vatican Novel." He died in 1999.

The Roman castles

A CARPET OF FLOWERS
For the Corpus Domini holiday, the rendezvous is held at Genzano di Roma for the "Infiorata" (top, left). For more than two centuries, the town is transformed for the occasion into a multicolored palette, with the petals of 350,000 flowers forming a spectacular mosaic. A festive invasion of children marks the end of the spectacle and the destruction of the floral carpets (facing page).

Top, right, the 16th-century Villa Aldobrandini at Frascati.

On its southeastern boundary the city of Rome is sheltered by rolling high ground generally known as the Colli Albani (the Albani Hills), which are the remains of intense volcanic activity eons ago. Over the centuries the capital city drew shepherds and artists, intellectuals and peasants, nobles and plebeians, who colonized the area well beyond the inhabited center. Here, it was far from the marshes of the plain and favored by a pleasant climate. Later, in Rome's Republican period, the aristocracy spent their energy and their money on building grand villas in these hills to bear witness to their refined tastes and wealth.

In the medieval period there appeared numerous castles, around which clustered bustling villages, which were later to become free Communes, which is why the little towns that grew up from these settlements are known as the Castelli Romani. During the Renaissance, wealthy Romans and aristocrats built a large number of beautiful villas all over this region. Surrounded by luxuriant gardens, they are one of the prides of the region.

While many of the local place names recall the noble origins of their first inhabitants, Castel Gandolfo, overlooking Lake Albano, is perhaps best known because it has been the papal summer residence since 1597. Less well known is that this location has been identified by some experts as the site of the ancient Albalonga, which according to tradition was founded by the descendants of Aeneas, in Greek mythology the Trojan warrior whose mother was the goddess Aphrodite and whose feats were immortalized by the Roman poet Virgil.

Lake Nemi, the other crater lake in the Albani hills, measures about 3.5 miles in circumference. In ancient times it was sometimes called the "Mirror of Diana," for the goddess of hunting who was particularly venerated in that area. In fact, there is a fascinating story in this regard. It had long been known that two Roman ships had sunk in the lake almost two thousand years before, but all efforts to raise them had failed until 1929, when the two galleys were finally recovered following a spectacular salvage operation that involved partially draining the lake. They were pleasure craft used by the Emperor Caligula for festivals and ceremonies in honor of the goddess. Many of the objects found on the ships are now in local museums, but the ships themselves were unfortunately burnt and almost wholly destroyed by the retreating German army in 1944.

Nowadays, the Castelli Romani are a popular destination for Sunday excursions, often enlivened by a drop of the local wines – always drawn straight from the keg – to which the volcanic soil has lent a particularly vigorous bouquet.

By David Laskin

River Gods and Grottoes:
Four Italian
RENAISSANCE GARDENS

August 24, 2003

A WORLD OF WATER

Water plays a starring role in the gardens of Villa Lante, and not only for the imposing presence of fountains and waterfalls (above, the Water Chain). Well hidden and scattered in the greenery are remote-controlled jets of water that were used to spray unsuspecting party guests.

"Perhaps, on the whole, the most enchanting place in Rome," the 30-year-old Henry James sighed after visiting Villa Medici in January 1873, and indeed, I felt like something out of Henry James as I stood, dazed with awe and jet lag, before the villa's arched and studded door on a hot July morning. I was in Rome to see four Renaissance gardens that have been preserved in the city and within a few hours' drive – gardens inspired by the stately villas of classical antiquity but tricked out with all the competitive splendor, aquatic panache and passion for mythology typical of 16th-century potentates. Somewhere behind that door, I knew, lay one of those gardens – a geometrical pleasure ground of terraces, allées and peerless views created by Cardinal Ferdinando de' Medici in the 1570's to house his vast collection of classical statuary.

My first impression – after mounting the grand staircase, pausing to admire the statue of Louis XIV in Roman imperial garb, emerging on the dazzling white loggia and hurrying past the dainty bronze Mercury – was that these paths had not seen a lick of pruning or weeding since Velázquez painted here in 1630. The Roman version of crabgrass all but strangled the immense parterre. A pink granite obelisk rose from a basin of green slime. The hedges of laurel, boxwood and holly that line the long, straight, intersecting paths of the "bosco" (woodland) have grown into shaggy walls.

Set high on the Pincian Hill, Villa Medici was one of the first "gardens to look out from" – a garden of carefully stage-managed views. You walk in the dark of a leafy tunnel for a score of paces and then, at the juncture of two paths, you get a circle of dappled light set with benches, herms (busts set on stone pillars) and vis-

tas terminating in a goddess, a glimpse of St. Peter's or a classical arch rising before a stand of velvety cypress trees. A gardening friend remarked that Italian gardens are not about plants and flowers but about theater – and I began to see the Villa Medici as one of the world's great horticultural stages, its drama compounded of the very best bones and the very worst maintenance.

The next morning, after a two-hour drive north through city sprawl that soon shaded into the tawny fields, rolling hills and ancient towns of Lazio, I presented myself at the gates of Villa Lante. This was the garden about which Edith Wharton raved in *Italian Villas and Their Gardens* – "so perfect is it, so far does it surpass, in beauty, in preservation, and in the quality of garden-magic, all the other great pleasure-houses of Italy, that the student of garden-craft may always find fresh inspiration in its study."

I was not disappointed. The moment I stood before the statue of Pegasus shooting water over the heads of a solemn company of drooling muses mounted on towering pedestals, I felt as if I'd stepped into the pages of Spenser or Ariosto. Up a flight of mellow stone steps, past a stand of Italian cypresses glowing in the midday sun, through a gate, and I burst upon the great water parterre. Intricate compartments of boxwood embroidery framed a square pool set with ascending rings of balustrades. In the center, four naked stone youths held aloft a heraldic device of stylized mountains capped by a star, all of it glistening with arcs of water.

Presiding over the scene were the twin toylike pavilions that Cardinal Giovanni Francesco Gambara commissioned the fashionable architect Jacopo Barozzi da Vignola to build for him in the 1560's. Vignola's mas-

A POPE AMONG THE GIANTS
In a natural area of great beauty,
fenced as a hunting reserve
since the 19th century, Villa
Lante in Bagnaia is one of the
jewels of the Tuscia region.
Pope Leo X frequently came
here to rest and relax away
from affairs of the Vatican.
The Fontana dei Giganti (left)
represents the Tiber
and the Arno.

267

terstroke was to set the houses in the grounds like a matched pair of garden ornaments so that the whole space is a symmetrical composition fixed on an axis of flowing water. The terraces that rise in tiers behind the houses have been softened with hydrangeas, camellias and plane trees. Though it could stand a bit of grooming, Villa Lante still casts an exuberant spell. This quintessential Renaissance pleasure ground glorifies pagan sensuality, the rules of proportion and the rebirth of hydraulic ingenuity (even 440 years later one wonders how the Sienese engineer Tommaso Ghinucci got water to rise and fall from so many orifices simultaneously – though sadly some of them no longer run).

At the end of the topmost terrace, past the immense stone table set with a gently flowing canal, above the river gods furred in moss, beyond the water staircase in the shape of an elongated crayfish (a play on the cardinal's name), the garden's rigid symmetry finally disintegrates in the Fountain of the Flood, a dripping ferny grotto that rises into a precipice of untamed woods.

Like Villa Lante, Villa Farnese at Caprarola sits on a rise overlooking the narrow streets and rooftops of a medieval town – but everything about Caprarola is a couple of notches grander. The ascent through the town is steeper, the surrounding landscape more rugged, the view from the entrance more mountainous, and the villa itself far more imposing. The house here is a true palace with acres of frescoed and gilded chambers that fit together in a complex pentagonal design. From the rear of the palace a stone bridge over the (dry) moat leads to a walled garden with four tree-shaded squares outlined in waist-high boxwood. Before I could quite absorb the aura of the place, the guard was prodding us up past a "secret garden" (trellised climbing roses and grapes) and then on to a series of rough earthen steps bordered by soft masses of camellia and rhododendron. Nice, I was thinking, if a bit predictable – until the trees parted and we emerged on the first fountain of the Casina del Piacere (Cardinal Alessandro II Farnese's pleasure house). My eye fell first on a goat's head gushing clear water from its mouth, nose, ears and eyes. I traced the flow up the water stairs fed by a cascade spilling off a colossal goblet to a pair of river gods reclining amid bubbling stone pots.

As the next level up, the swirls of stone and spray gave way to the serene geometry of meticulously clipped foliage. I had reached the famous terrace of the herms – two squares of smooth grass and clipped box edged with a low stone wall on which high pedestals set at regular intervals support a collection of 28 male and female herms, each with an urn balanced on its head. I've been in Japanese gardens that attain this kind of eerie stillness by paring down nature to its essence, but I never dreamed that severe formality and rampant pomp could create so surreal a space.

**OPULENT
AND BEAUTIFUL RESIDENCES**
In 1540, when Cardinal Camillo Crescenzi took possession of what is now Villa Medici, it was no more than a modest country cottage. The work of Nanni di Baccio Bigio, Annibale Lippi and other exceptional artists transformed it into a gem (right).

Facing page, below, the unmistakable pentagonal plan of palazzo Farnese in Caprarola, a 16th-century masterpiece by Vignola.
Facing page, top, the Viale delle Cento Fontane in Villa d'Este, at Tivoli. This sumptuous residence was built by Cardinal Ippolito d'Este and designed by Pirro Ligorio.

After a few days back in the splendor and heat of Rome, I was ready for another garden, and so one warm and breezy morning I headed out to Tivoli, site of Villa d'Este, a public park and the final Renaissance garden on my list. It proved to be the perfect day trip, easily accessible in under two hours by public transportation, and absolutely ravishing. The spectacular fountains that the architect and antiquarian Pirro Ligorio and other artists fashioned here for Cardinal Ippolito d'Este between 1550 and 1569 deserve all their fame – but the garden is much more than a series of hydraulic show-stoppers. At Villa d'Este Ligorio enlisted "caprice and cunning," as one writer put it, to turn a challenging site into an exciting and inspiring garden.

With no guard to slow me down, I breezed by the sunny courtyard, through a series of frescoed but otherwise bare rooms, and out to the terrace. The sweeping view stopped me in my tracks. In the distance, the hazy plain of the Roman campagna; to the right, a clump of knobby hills; and directly beneath my feet, the treetops, urns, pots, statues, stairs and ramps of the garden, which covers almost nine acres. I could hear the ceaseless rush of water below, but from this first perch over the precipitous face of the upper garden, the only fountain in sight was a delicate tripod that Ligorio pinched from the nearby villa of the Roman Emperor Hadrian. I was itching to plunge right in, or rather down – but which way? Every juncture, every tier, every nook and

niche of Villa d'Este confronts you with multiple choices. Descend directly to the scalloped prowlike lip of the Fountain of the Bicchierone (big goblet) created by Bernini, or angle off to the foaming oval basin in which the infant Venus hatches from her scallop shell? Proceed along the Pathway of the Hundred Fountains, the villa's trademark water feature of spouting masks, boats and eagles, or skirt the grandiose Fountain of the Dragon? And what about the Staircase of Bollori, a seemingly infinite series of steps lined with clipped hedges and carved masks and shaded with huge cypresses (reputed to be the tallest in Italy)?

I did it all, prancing up and down the terraces, until I finally came to rest where the steep slope subsides in a chain of three rectangular fish ponds. As I gloried in one of the great vistas of Western garden art, I tried to recall the lines from Anthony Hecht's poem *The Gardens of the Villa d'Este*. I knew it was something about sex, which seemed odd when I read it but apt now. One solace of returning home was to open Hecht's poem again: "There is no garden to the practiced gaze/Half so erotic: here the 16th century thew/Rose to its last perfection."

DAVID LASKIN is co-author of "Artists in Their Gardens" *(Sasquatch). He lives in Seattle.*

By Michael Mewshaw

PONTINE ISLANDS,
A World Away in Six Shades of Blue

June 14, 2004

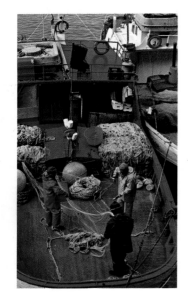

ONCE UPON A TIME THERE WAS A VOLCANO...
Born eons ago from volcanic lava, Palmarola (facing page) is a strip of contorted, rocky land barely half a square mile in area. Uninhabited for most of the year, its enchanting silence invites the visitor to rent a small boat and draw near in order to contemplate the bizarre creations of the fire god such as the rock known as Suvace, which looks like a whale; the Faraglione (the stack); and the Grotta di Mezzogiorno, a monumental Cathedral of lava.

At first it seems enough simply to be in Italy, especially in Rome with its dense golden light and terra cotta-colored buildings. Even so, there eventually comes over a traveler a powerful craving for the authentic Italy reduced to its essence – a land of classical lines, serenity, timeless ritual and fragrant countryside. In short, that's the time to leave urban civilization and its discontents for the island of Ponza and its archipelago of islets.

Located about 60 miles south of Rome off the coast of the Circeo Peninsula, the Pontine Islands can be reached by hydrofoil in less than an hour and a half from Anzio or Formia and a handful of other ports. While part of the Region of Lazio, this scattering of craggy Mediterranean specks is largely populated permanently by families that hail from Naples, and the food, the pastel facades, the fishing culture and care-free "ambiente" recall the warmth of their ancestral hometown.

The day I arrived on Ponza, an old man on the wharf tending a hand-held fishing line roused himself just long enough to help tie up the hydrofoil before returning to his indolent search for that evening's meal. Doubtful that I would ever see anything more folkloric – had the Chamber of Commerce arranged the scene to delight visitors? – I was later amazed to watch another old salt spring to his feet on the quay, hurl a trident into the water and haul in a foot-long fish. It should be emphasized that I came to Ponza in early May, before the tourist crush. By any measure, spring and fall are the best seasons to visit. In September in particular, the sea is warm, the weather clear and the beaches blessedly uncrowded. By con-

trast, in July and August the island's population of 3,000 or so often finds itself submerged in a tide of 10,000 day-trippers. On weekends so many luxury yachts and runabouts and rubber dinghies squeeze into the port it appears that a nimble-footed pedestrian could hike from one deck to the other across the harbor. There's even a helicopter service that flies in rich folks from Rome at a cost of $2,000 a trip.

Much as one might regret the droves of summer tourists, Ponza's attractions are undeniable and impossible to resist. The crescent-shaped port, with sailboats bobbing in their wavery reflections, is picture perfect, as is the spill of sugar cube houses tumbling down toward the water. Wildflowers star the hillsides, geraniums crown each window ledge and swags of royal purple bougainvillea cloak the walls.

All the towns on the island, bunched in valleys or beside bays shielded from the wind, are built on an intimate human scale, and most streets are inaccessible to cars. Sometimes there don't even seem to be any streets, just hallways and staircases leading through an immense rambling palazzo owned by a lively family that has offered outsiders free rein of the place. Each miniature piazza gives the impression less of a public square than of a living room where a party is in progress. Sometimes an impromptu soccer game between kids replaces the party, and tourists have to step lively or get tackled.

More than anything, though, it's the sea which draws boaters, swimmers and skin divers to Ponza. Remarkable for its clarity, the water has colors that range from Robin's egg blue to della Robbia blue to azure, turquoise, cerulean and cobalt. No one descrip-

**IN THE SHADOW
OF THE TOWER**
Perched on a rocky spur above
the port of Ponza is the Torre
dei Borboni, erected in the 18th
century over the ruins of
a Roman site and transformed
into a hotel in the 1960's.
Surrounded by the typical local
buildings, the structure's simple
architecture is enhanced
by its delicate pastel tones.

tion is sufficient since the sea here changes chameleon-like according to its depth, the weather and the time of day.

If Ponza sounds paradisiacal, it must be remembered that it has endured a tumultuous history – which perhaps explains why its inhabitants have little trouble putting up with a peaceful annual invasion. They have suffered far worse. Indeed, the island, with its volcanic origins, was born with a bang, and the remains of a crater loom around the port and along the coast farther north at Cala Inferno. But after the lava cooled into a thorny spine of land four and a half miles long, Neolithic people started settling here.
They were followed by Phoenicians, Greeks, Romans, Saracens, and French Bourbons, each of whom arrived with grasping intentions. Some wanted access to Ponza's fresh water to resupply their ships. Others

used the island as a military base for attacking the mainland. Pirates found hiding spots in its caves and grottoes. Like the Romans who dispatched trouble-makers and enemies of the empire to these stony shores, Italy once sent Mussolini here. On Sept 11, 1943 British and American troops liberated the island without opposition (Ponza was antifascist) and a memorial outside the church of S. Silverio and Domitilla bears the names of dozens of local men who died at sea when British fighters planes attacked their ships. An inland community still is named Campo Inglese but according to a local official, it has nothing to do with World War II. In the early 1800's, it turns out, two English frigates captured the strategic location from the French and the name stuck.

The peace and beauty of the countryside I hiked through can seem part of ancient times. On one walk,

THE ISLAND OF THE BOURBONS

Only two villages grace the island of Ponza. Le Forna and Ponza Porto (above) were founded in the 18th century when the ruling house of Bourbon, then the owners of the island, decided to repopulate it by relocating fishermen and peasants from the Campania region. The construction of the harbor, also from the Bourbon period, was ordered by King Ferdinand IV.

PRISONERS OF THE SEA
The Pontine islands were once
a dismal prison colony.
A Roman cistern, built
originally to solve water
shortages in Ventotene
(top right) was converted
to house the prisoners of the
Bourbon regime. Then, toward
the end of the 18th century, the
island of Santo Stefano became
a gigantic prison for convicts
serving a life sentence (facing
page). Still functioning until
a few decades ago, one of its
most infamous prisoners was
an Italian-American anarchist
from New Jersey, Gaetano
Bresci, who assassinated King
Umberto I in 1900.
Right, rural homes
on the island of Ponza.

I tried to reach Chiaia di Luna, Ponza's best known beach, which is connected to the port by a 2,000 year-old tunnel first constructed by the Greeks, then expanded and improved by the Romans. But the tunnel is currently closed for repairs, and the beach is off-limits to sunbathers because of the danger of rocks falling from the yellow and white tufa cliffs that line the shore. Still, one can reach the bay there by boat and dive down to ancient ruins and the fragments of amphorae.

This is the case with many of the beaches; they are best approached by boat. From the port, ferries service almost all of them, and in a spirit of perfect democracy, the water makes no distinction between people who jump off dinghies and those who plunge from elegant schooners.

After hiring a taxi to take me to the far end of the island, I decided to walk back to the port. Sometimes I followed the main road. Sometimes I strolled over well-marked paths that honeycomb the hills, passing through yellow splurges of scotch broom and between red and pink hedges of oleander. At the town of Le Forna, I stepped into the church to escape the sun, and watched a lizard amble up the aisle in front of me, as leisurely as a businessman returning from a three-martini lunch.

Back on my way, I descended through vineyards that had been terraced from the highest hilltops down to the shore in what looked like steps for a giant. Although I was 500 feet above it, the sea exerted an inexorable pull. It wasn't simply that I was never out of sight of it. It wasn't just that I could gaze down at sailboats bobbing at anchor in glassy pools, at tiny beaches digging like fingernails into the coastline and at the afternoon "aliscafo" from Anzio leaving what looked like jet contrails on the Mediterranean. It was that even up in the hills, there were constant reminders that farmers on Ponza remained first and foremost oceangoing men. Many kept boats in their back yards or out in the middle of their cultivated fields, and I noticed that one scarecrow wore an orange life jacket. To understand Ponza properly, it occurred to me, I'd have to put to sea myself.

The island swarms with all manner of craft — clunky fishing boats, sleek yachts and rubber zodiacs — that can be rented by the day, with or without a hired hand to navigate. By no means a competent sailor — to be honest I don't know port from starboard — I chose to depend on the Cooperativa Barcaioli Ponzesi which offers group trips at reasonable prices, with a knowledgeable local captain at the helm. The first morning, we cruised across a rolling sea to Palmarola. A small

NATURE'S PALETTE

The spontaneous vegetation on Ponza (top) is largely Mediterranean maquis, or brush, liberally sprinkled with Indian figs, spurge and agaves. Also widespread are various species of broom, known in the local dialect as "vastaccedo" (the hatchet breaker) because of the hardness of its wood. Cultivated species also do well on the island and luxuriant cascades of bougainvillea (above) enliven the panorama with bright patches of color.

island west of Ponza, it is inhabited only in summer and takes its name from a dwarf palm found there. But whatever the singularity of Palmarola's flora and its copious bird life, its true uniqueness lies in its landscape, a kind of lunar terrain tortured into phantasmagorical shapes by wind and rain. Some rock-falls along the coast resemble Roman ruins that have been half-swallowed by the sea, leaving visible what might be the crenelated walls of a castle or the lonely arches and columns of a collapsed temple. One imposing cliff face is called the Cathedral because its spires and pinnacles resemble a Gothic church. It certainly left my boatload of pilgrims close to a state of religious awe.

In season, with permission, trips can be arranged from Ponza to the much smaller islet of Zannone. Now a national wildlife preserve, Zannone boasts 138 varieties of birds, including hawks, African nightingales and white storks. It was once home to a Cistercian abbey,

but the monks have long since departed, and only a lighthouse keeper and a flock of wild goats remain.

My next maritime adventure took me on a slow and thorough circumnavigation of Ponza aboard a boat whose skipper managed to guide us safely through shoals, past prickly outcroppings of rocks, in and out of grottoes and caves, and, like the camel and the needle's eye, through a natural arch called Spaccapurpo. At the same time as he manned the wheel, he regaled his passengers with anecdotes and arcane information. The arch was called Spaccapurpo, he explained, because fishermen used it as a landmark, and before they lowered their nets there, they cried out, "Spacca u purpo." That is, cut up the octopus for bait.

If that weren't enough esoteric knowledge for us, he said the arch sported some rare specimens of the "pasquini" lizard, as it is known locally. I confess I saw not a single one of them. But I did spot something just

as surprising – nude sunbathers lounging on spiny rocks, like swamis on beds of nails.

The captain also showed impressive dexterity at inserting and extracting us from La Peschiera Augustea, an ancient basin that Romans carved into the Promontorio della Madonna. But his lecture, as I understood it, suggested that the basin had been a combination swimming pool for people and aquarium for moray eels. That sounds like a bad mix to me.

A much better mix was whatever I chose to eat for dinner. There was always excellent mozzarella from the mainland, and fish from the Mediterranean. Some evenings my dinners seemed to replicate the chart of evolutionary chain demonstrating the development of sea life from simple flaccid organisms to mollusks and bivalves and scuttling crustaceans and finally to finned creatures. From squid to clams to shrimp and lobster and tuna, I ate my way back into the future. But I must admit that what I liked best was a hearty local dish of lentil stew.

It might sound macabre to admit that I spent my last day in the cemetery. But the one on Ponza isn't in the least bit depressing. To the contrary, it commands a sublime position above the port, looking out toward the mainland. Many of the mausoleums are the size of modest homes, and are painted in fresh pastels. In a way, the cemetery is a miniature of the island's villages. Only here, instead of an address, each door has a picture of the deceased and an uplifting epitaph such as "Lived humbly, died serenely." I couldn't help thinking, What a way to go and what a place to reside for eternity. Ponza!

_____

MICHAEL MEWSHAW is the author of ten novels ("Island Tempest," most recently) and six books of non-fiction. He divides his year between Florida, England and Rome.

IN THE ARMS OF CIRCE

According to Homer Ponza was the home of the sorceress Circe, who used her arts to seduce Ulysses and try to persuade him not to return to his native Ithaca. But perhaps he was seduced by the wild beauty of the island, an outpost of twisted rocks amidst a boundless sea.

The promontory of Punta La Guardia (above) looks like a dinosaur that has just emerged from the waters.

By Susan Lumsden

EASTER DRAMA
in the Piazza

April 7, 1985

THE GREEN OF HOPE
The brotherhood of the Madonna of Loreto, who carry the statue of the Virgin on the Easter Day procession, wear typical short green cloaks known as "mozzetti." Once her black robes have been removed, the Virgin also appears dressed in green, the color of hope.

In northern Italy, the death and Resurrection of Christ is celebrated symbolically at Easter mass, followed by a huge family lunch and the cutting of the "colomba," an Easter cake shaped like the dove of peace. In many parts of southern Italy, Easter is not only celebrated but also lived, starting at the latest on Holy Thursday, which is when I arrived in Sulmona, the ancient capital of the mountainous Abruzzo region. "You've returned for the procession," exclaimed one of my host's delighted friends as I entered the crowded Piazza XX Settembre. To all appearances, Sulmona's medieval Easter procession had already begun, so many people were gathered there under the brooding statue of Ovid, the Latin poet, born in Sulmona in 43 B.C. But no, the friend went on to explain: "It's always like this after 5 P.M. This is the daily passeggiata, not the processione. If you don't see someone for two days here, you know something's wrong."

Easter processions are still staged in various parts of Sicily and Calabria. And in all of southern Italy there may be nothing quite as popular, elaborate and dramatic as Sulmona's feast of La Madonna che Scappa in Piazza – the Madonna who races through the square – which takes place annually in this market town of some 20,000 inhabitants, about a two-hour drive from Rome. Four days of events culminate in an Easter Sunday procession in which life-size polychrome wooden statues representing the characters in the Resurrection are paraded through the Piazza Garibaldi, one of the largest marketplaces in Italy.

The celebration begins on Holy Thursday. Small models depicting the preparation of the tomb of Christ – "allestimento del sepolcro" – could be seen in nearly a dozen churches, some of which date back to the Middle Ages. On the night of Good Friday there is the procession symbolizing the deposition and burial of Christ in which statues of the crucified Jesus and the mourning Madonna are paraded through the town.

This procession is organized by the Confraternita della Trinità, a lay brotherhood that dates from the Middle Ages when such associations were formed throughout Italy to assist in the work of the Lord.

The Confraternita della Trinità began in the 13th century as an association of noblemen whose purpose was to help the needy and bring the dead to the cemetery. In the country's industrial north, such brotherhoods have shrunk to folkloric remnants. But in the more traditional south, they still represent the main divisions of social life.

In the medieval version of the Good Friday procession, the personalities of the Crucifixion were portrayed by townspeople. The event became so emotional and often violent, particularly for the character of Judas, an original member of the procession, that statues had to replace human beings as the protagonists. Yet standing in the dark, medieval streets, one could see the pathos painted on the faces of the statues reflected in the faces of the Sulmonesi. The main exception was the well-known and obviously well-loved town tippler, who swayed and joked with the crowd. As the statues of Christ and the Madonna loomed up in front of him, he suddenly yanked his cap from his head, made the sign of the cross and began to weep silently.

This eternal dialogue between the sacred and the profane was echoed in the music of the Good Friday procession, performed on brass instruments by members of

FROM THE DARKNESS TO THE LIGHT

The symbolic change from night to day marks the phases of the celebration. The nocturnal Good Friday procession is a gloomy one and the members of the brotherhood bear ornate lamps to symbolize the light of faith, while the Easter ritual (left) is pervaded by joyous light.

279

**IN THE PRESENCE
OF CHRIST RESURRECTED**
In back of the square the statue
of Christ emerges in triumph
from the tomb and is revealed
to the crowd. It is a moving
moment – a meeting
of orthodox faith
and popular beliefs.
This is not merely folklore,
but a display of spontaneous
religiosity in which all the
inhabitants of the city take
an equal part in the sacred
celebration of the
Resurrection.

280

the Confraternita della Trinità. The music was brassy, even raucous, and not in the least religious to one brought up in the well-tempered tradition of Bach. It was modified, however, by the dragging step of the brothers, intended to evoke the sound of the chains of prisoners bearing their own crosses. To expiate their sins, the nobility of Sulmona used to parade naked to the waist and be flagellated or flagellate themselves as part of the Good Friday procession.

On Saturday evening, there was another procession. Though I was only a visitor, I was invited to join the townswomen who were carrying candles and accompanying the statue of the Madonna to the Church of San Filippo Neri, where she would wait until Sunday. The only other outsider in this female ceremony was a man, the town character, who rushed about constantly asking the time. In Sulmona, he is known affectionately as "Seikoquartz."
Another local personality is Ferdinando D'Eramo, an 83-year-old carpenter who has inherited the task of dressing the Madonna for the Easter procession. He must do so in such a way that her black robes of mourning fall away with the first gust of wind, revealing a green dress that signifies the arrival of spring. The secret of how he manages this is shared only by his nephew, Ennio, 50, who will ultimately take over the task, as will Ennio's 17-year-old son, Gaetano.
The statue bearers are chosen in a "sorteggio," or lottery, of the young and athletic members of the Confraternita di Santa Maria di Loreto, Sulmona's working-class brotherhood. Just as the rival and more aristocratic Confraternita della Trinità is responsible for the events related to the death and deposition of Christ on Good Friday, so the laboring brothers of Santa Maria di Loreto, including Ferdinando D'Eramo, are responsible for those related to the Resurrection.
Easter Sunday dawned bright and sunny, and we made our way through the narrow, gray streets to the Piazza Garibaldi. Had I not actually seen the spectacle before me I never could have imagined it. Thousands of excited Abruzzesi had filled the piazza and were packed shoulder to shoulder – on the ground, on the rooftops, in every window and even on the large, medieval aqueduct that borders part of the square.
On the open side of the Piazza Garibaldi, the magnificent snow-capped Apennines provided a backdrop to the people and the architecture. Miraculously, it seemed, the piazza had been transformed into a larger-than-life theater. Shortly after 10 o'clock, there appeared the brothers of the Confraternita di Santa Maria di Loreto, robed in green and white, bearing the statues of St. Peter, St. John and a triumphant Risen

EASTER DRAMA
IN THE PIAZZA

TENEBRAE FACTAE SUNT
Good Friday represents a moment of sorrow and grief. Red is the color of the blood shed by the Redeemer, red are the insignia and red the color of the habits of the brotherhood of the Santissima Trinità, who sing the *Miserere* as they walk in procession.

On the following pages, this is the culmination of the celebration. The Virgin, overjoyed by the sight of Christ resurrected, lets fall the black cloak of mourning and drops her white handkerchief, a symbol of mourning. In its place, as if by magic, there appears a blood red one. It is no longer the red of suffering, however, but of redemption and life.

Abruzzo: one region, many parks

Three national parks (The National Park of Abruzzo, Lazio and Molise, The National Park of the Gran Sasso and the Monti della Laga, and the National Park of the Majella), one regional park (the Sirente-Velino Park) and dozens of oases, reserves and protected areas comprise a region synonymous with nature.

As the name suggests, the National Park of Abruzzo, Lazio and Molise extends over a good three regions and is a fine example of intelligent management of the territory and its natural heritage. Two thirds of the park are covered with beech forest, one of the largest unbroken expanses of this kind in the entire Apennine chain. Here live various species of deer, the rare and elusive wildcat, wolves and Marsican bears, all hard to see but reasonably tolerant of pacific intrusions on the part of humans. Higher up on the more inaccessible mountain peaks, the elegant chamois of the Abruzzo shows off its acrobatic skills by leaping from ledge to ledge among the ravines.

The National Park of the Gran Sasso and the Monti della Laga culminates in the peak known as the Corno Grande – at over 9500 feet the highest peak in the Apennines – and includes the Calderone glacier, the only one in the Apennines and the southernmost glacier in Europe. The calcareous environment of the Gran Sasso, an area with a wealth of karsic phenomena such as subterranean caves, ravines, pot-holes and ponors, deep holes that swallow the waters of streams or lakes, is set off by the extensive forests of the Monti della Laga: beech, chestnut, and oak trees whose forerunners were planted back in Roman times. There are large numbers of endemic species, and even some exclusive varieties.

According to Pliny, the Majella was the "Father of Mountains." Imposing and wild, since Paleolithic times it has sheltered and nourished hunters and gatherers, hermits and later brigands and robbers. Near Mount Cavallo visitors can see the "Tavola dei Briganti" (The Brigands' Table), with inscriptions bearing the signatures, dates and graffiti written by the outlaws.

THE EMPEROR'S MOUNTAINS
Campo Imperatore, the best known ski resort in Abruzzo (below) is named for the Holy Roman Emperor Frederick II. Below, right, the moonlight works its magic on the houses of Pietracamela, a small village nestling among the most beautiful mountains of the National Park of the Abruzzo.

WHO'S AFRAID
OF THE BIG BAD WOLF?

In the heart of the National Park
of the Abruzzo there is a hidden
sanctuary, inhabited by
mysterious divinities that
cannot be seen by the eyes
of men. This is the Camosciara
Nature Reserve, established in
1921 and the first protected area
in Italy. Here the Marsican bear,
the Apennine chamois and the
wolf, rediscovered divinities
of primitive nature, have
found their last refuge.

285

THE BURDEN OF SANCTITY

The Cathedral of Sulmona is dedicated to San Panfilo, whose relics are kept in a bronze urn in the crypt. Legend has it that the priests who were bearing the remains of the sainted bishop back to his birthplace suddenly felt their burden become unbearably heavy. Completely unable to proceed, they realized that the Divine Will had decreed that the church destined to honor him was to be built on that very spot.

Lord, a crown atop his head. First, St. Peter was paraded from one end of the piazza to the other, symbolically bringing the news of the Resurrection to the Madonna mourning in the church. Then came St. John, to confirm the message.

When the black-robed statue of the Madonna finally bobbed through the portal of the church to face the statue of Christ at the opposite end of the piazza, an audible wave of emotion swept through the crowd. The brothers holding the statue of the Madonna, who had been pacing carefully in front of the church, broke into a run. As their shoulder-borne Madonna was raced across the piazza, her black robes of mourning fell cleanly away to reveal a bright green dress, symbolic of fertility and spring. With the ascent of 12 doves, symbolic of the 12 apostles of peace, the crowd burst into applause, hugs, tears and kisses.

After four days of mournful masses and sonorous processions, I, too, felt a great relief, perhaps even joy,

never quite experienced at Easters elsewhere. If the black veils of mourning had remained stuck to the Madonna, it is said, crop failures and general bad luck would have been in store for Sulmona. In 1913 and 1930, when some of the black fabric stayed fixed, there were earthquakes.

On Easter Monday, the Sulmonesi traditionally pack a picnic and head for the countryside for an "al fresco" celebration of spring. Ideally, the picnic takes place near the ruins of the massive Roman Temple of Hercules or in the Campo di Giove – the Field of Jupiter, father of all the gods.

Delicious and brightly colored, "confetti," or sugared almonds, are the specialty of Sulmona. Their name comes from the Latin *confectum*, which means, "prepared," and indeed their preparation requires a patience little short of Biblical.
It is no surprise, therefore, that they are said to have been made for the first time by nuns in the 15th century.
Top, left, the so-called "Complesso dell'Annunziata," which comprises the building that is now home to the Museo Civico and the church.

_____

SUSAN LUMSDEN, a Canadian journalist and broadcaster, spent the last 15 years of her life as a free-lance journalist in Italy writing about travel and art history. She died in 1994.

Where eagles fly

L'Aquila (The Eagle), is a city named for the monarch of the skies; it is also a city that endured a troubled and adventurous existence for many centuries. It arose in the 13th century through the unification of numerous local castles – 99 of them according to tradition. Founded by the Holy Roman Emperor Frederick II, it was destroyed over and over again. Guilty of remaining faithful to the Church in the clash between the Papacy and the Holy Roman Empire, in 1259 it was razed to the ground by Frederick II's son Manfredi, barely a decade after its foundation. As if stunned, the abandoned city lay in ruins for years. Then pride prevailed. Charles II of Anjou reorganized the local nobility and ordered the construction of a new circle of walls and seven monumental gates thus confirming an indomitable spirit that endures to this day. The symbol of this alliance, the peerless Fountain of the 99 Spouts, is the work of the master Tancredi da Pentima. For centuries this fountain has been used by everyone from washerwomen to the powerful wool merchants' guild. But from the unusual stone spouts (each one different from the next) there emerges something far more important: the life-giving waters of solidarity.

The name of this city is indissolubly bound up with that of Pietro Angeleri, who went from his quiet hermitage on Mount Morrone all the way to the Papal throne in Rome, with the name of Celestine V. But caring for the souls of the faithful was too grievous a task, or perhaps he simply found it too hard to maintain his purity of spirit amid the whirl of corruption and compromise of the papal court. In any event his pontificate lasted only a few months and on 13 December 1294 Celestine publicly read the Bull of Renunciation thereby consigning his name to history as the first – and so far the only – pope ever to have resigned.

In the centuries that followed, the city's loyalty to the ruling House of Anjou earned it many honors and rewards, while the production of saffron, a highly prized spice used both for cooking and dyeing, gave it an important commercial position. But after many earthquakes L'Aquila was seriously damaged by a particularly powerful tremor in 1703. Once again a patient and laborious task of reconstruction brought the city back to its ancient splendor, an effort crowned in 1860 by its "election" as the regional capital of Abruzzo. We don't know with certainty if the name L'Aquila derives from the humble village of Acculi – which stood on this site in ancient times – or from the emblem of the Imperial House of Swabia, but it is a fine thing to see the Eagle soar, today as in the past, the lord of the winds and the storm.

THE CITY OF 99

L'Aquila is also known as the "city of 99." It is said to have 99 squares, 99 churches, 99 fountains and that it sprang from the union of 99 local castles. These symbolic connections were behind the decision to build a great fountain with 99 spouts (facing page). Interestingly, the provenance of the water that feeds it has always been kept secret so that no one can lay claim to it. The construction of the basilica of Santa Maria di Collemaggio (below) was begun in 1287 by order of Pietro da Morrone, who seven years later was crowned Pope with the name of Celestine V.

By Michael Frank

A Rarity Among Roman Towns:
SAEPINUM

December 23, 1990

**FROM SANNITES
AND ROMANS**

Lying at the outer offshoots of
the Matese massif, surrounded
by mountains, hills, woods and
springs, Sepino (above) is an
attractive resort whose roots
are sunk deep in Sannite and
Roman culture. The curative
qualities of the waters that
spring from the locality known
as Tre Fontane (Three Fountains)
were known to the Romans,
who used them
as thermal baths.

It is a place that whispers history in the way ruins
must have a century ago, before armies of tourists
arrived in stone-splitting buses and archeologists
had to guard their treasures with spiked fences and
wire ropes. Four hours southeast of Rome, three hours
northeast of Naples, Saepinum is tucked into a corner of
the Molise, one of the least populated and least known
districts in all of Italy. Even for the Molise, Saepinum is
a rarity: an ancient Roman town that is preserved rather
than embalmed, seldom but easily visited, alive despite
the tenets of museology.

Although guides cluck with disapproval, a handful of
farmers, whose forebears have worked this land since the
Iron Age, continue to tend fields bordered by ancient
walls and to inhabit houses that incorporate ancient
stones, at times even older than Roman. Saepinum is full
of such pairings: ancient and contemporary, urban and
rustic, it is among the country's most evocative, unspoiled sites.

In Saepinum, chickens feed alongside chariot-pitted
Roman roads. Apples ripen and drop into the remains of
Roman houses, stocking the larders of a vanished civilization. Grasses regularly sprout in the forum, a tenacious, earthy reminder of Saepinum's origins as a key
crossroads amid fertile pasture land. Here, it seems, man
has always lived in close rapport with nature: Saepinum
was no Rome, muscling the landscape, everywhere flex-
ing its might. It was a provincial city, modest in both
scale and scope. Never grand, always accessible,
Saepinum is the kind of place where it's easy to add a few
imaginary bricks to broken walls, fill the air with clap-
ping hoofs and creaking carts, and fool yourself into believing – for a moment anyway – that you can catapult
backward to the city's heyday.

290

Saepinum is situated at the intersection of two roads of age-old significance: the tratturo Pescasseroli-Candela (a tratturo is a cowpath or sheepway) that links the Abruzzo and Apulia regions, and the road that crosses the plain of the river Tammaro and climbs up into the nearby Matese hills. They are just a tangle of place names until you realize that for millennia the shepherds transformed these dry roads into rivers of undulating wool as they moved their flocks across these pastures and that their livelihood depended on meeting at this junction to trade with local farmers. Here, through commerce and conversation, a community set down its first fragile roots.

A small settlement is thought to have existed on the site before recorded history. At the beginning of the Iron Age (circa 1,000 B.C.) the Petri, a tribe of Samnites, the indigenous people of the region, founded a village at Saepinum called *Saipins* in Oscan, the language spoken locally until the second century B.C (official and educated classes continued to speak Oscan until the Social War of 88 B.C.: the language was still spoken at Pompeii at the time of its destruction in A.D. 79). *Saipins*, in Oscan, is linked to the Latin *saepire* – to hedge in, to enclose – and indeed this sense of enclosure is palpable in the ruins as they stand today, with their 275 yards of Roman walls that protect the city against attack and hug the valuable crossroads for which they serve as a kind of immense, ferocious toll booth.

In the fourth century B.C., threatened by the expansion of Rome, the Samnites withdrew to the nearby hills to fortify themselves against the new powers. Famous for their cyclopean walls throughout the Molise, they barricaded themselves at Terravecchia, one and half miles southwest of Saepinum. But in 293 B.C., during the Third Samnite War, the fierce Samnites, whom Livy called the strongest and the mightiest, fell to the Roman

The basilica of Saepinum once stood in the city center, where the two main Roman roads (the *cardus* and the *decumanus*) crossed each other. Below, the remains of the colonnade, which divided the interior of the building into naves; little remains of the perimeter wall. In Roman culture the *basilica* was a rectangular space intended for civil purposes, such as business dealings and the administration of justice.

consul L. Cursor Papirius after a battle that left 7,400 dead and 3,000 prisoner. The few survivors crept down into the plains and once again settled around those essential crossroads. The territory was annexed by Rome during the first century B.C. The first stones of the walls were laid at the end of the Social War (88 B.C.), but most of Saepinum was built during the reign of Augustus (27 B.C. to A.D. 14).

The best way to orient yourself at Saepinum is to have a sense of the crossroads and the walls with their four heroic doors. The old tratturo became the Roman *decumanus* (or east-west road, though at Saepinum it's quite a bit skewed) and is demarcated by the Porta di Bojano to the northwest and the Porta di Benevento to the southeast. The road that led down from the Matese into the plains became the *cardus* (or north-south road) and is bound by the Porta di Terravecchia to the southwest and the Porta del Tammaro (northeast). Arriving from Campobasso, you park outside the Porta del Tammaro and enter Saepinum through its crumbling remains. Almost at once you should have a sense of the modest proportions of the city, which covers an area of 29.6 acres within the walls, and can be traversed, along the *cardus* or the *decumanus*, in fewer than 10 minutes in either direction. Saepinum is small but not parochial. An active commercial center for more than 400 years, the city mimicked Rome's urban customs and imperial architecture, though naturally on a diminished scale and with local stone instead of marble as the principal building material.

It has the feeling of a diorama in the way it gives an elegant overview of the elements that were essential to any Roman city – the *forum* and *basilica*, the market and theater and necropoli, the walls and shops and houses – only it is a diorama you can enter, often virtually alone and always with a tangible sense of the proximity of the past. The theater, just off the *cardus*, is one of the city's best preserved structures. It is quintessential Saepinum: ancient Rome combined with modern Molise (that is, of the 18th and 19th centuries), urban dash joined with country frugality: surely this is the only theater in antiquity whose *summa cavea* (roughly our loge) has been swallowed up into a crescent of rustic farmhouses. It offers a queer, compelling sight, Piranesi merged with Escher: the nine rows of seats, which include the *ima* and the *media cavea* (roughly our orchestra and mezzanine), are divided by two aisles. This is quite normal. But instead of rising gracefully, the steps stop and disappear into a semicircle of buildings made of the local grayish-white stone, creating an unlikely union of mood, style, and use: if they returned today, ancient actors would play to an audience of farmhouses rather than farmers.

These structures, which were inhabited until 20 years ago, incorporate stones from the Roman theater, which at full capacity could seat 3,000 spectators. And they are balanced, where the *scena* (or stage building) once stood, by another farmhouse, which now contains a handsome museum of Roman objects, chiefly funereal, that were found on the site.

Another unusual characteristic is the theater's location against the city's walls, where a gate leads directly into the open countryside. It has been hypothesized that theatrical productions coincided with fairs held outside of the city walls; in any event, crowds were easily managed, and kept out of the center of town, by this clever arrangement. Continuing along the wall toward the Porta di Bojano, you will soon come to the public baths, with their characteristic succession of *calidarium* (sauna), *tepidarium* (a transitional room of medium temperature), and *frigidarium* (an unheated room for cooling off). Faded scraps of mosaic flooring are still visible here, as are pipes that conducted hot air to the sauna. Closest to the door are the remains of a public latrine.

The partly reconstructed Porta di Bojano at the foot of the *decumanus* is the most intact of the city's four majestic gates, which were all built along the same model and were all strongly influenced by Rome's triumphal architecture. As an introduction to Saepinum, the gates were not exactly welcoming. The whole mentality of the city — and in a way, the civilization that produced it — is revealed before you see the first scrap of street or glimpse of shop.

The gates proclaim the city's strength with their two circular towers of reticulated stone whose thickest sections face the open countryside. They invoke a god: Mars or Hercules, who glares at you from the keystone in the arch that links the two towers. The gate intimidates you into good behavior: the god is flanked by two seminude barbaric prisoners in chains, a reminder of the city's reputed — and demonstrable — bellicosity; if you try anything devious, it is suggested, these manacled figures will be your fate. Then there is the inevitable inscription mentioning the benefactor (at Bojano, there were two: the imperial princes Tiberius, the future emperor, and

WALLS, TOWERS AND THEATER
Facing page, a part of the walls
and the remains of a few
homes. The defensive circle,
built in the early years
of the Christian era, was more
than 1,300 yards long
and had 29 circular towers
linked by walkways.
The theater (below) could hold
3,000 spectators. The lowest
tiers, reserved for the nobles
of the city, are larger and more
comfortable than
the upper tiers.

A GATEWAY TO HISTORY
The Porta di Bojano (the Bojano
Gate), crossed by the Roman
road (above), was one of the
four monumental gates giving
access to the city.
There was also a smaller fifth
gate, which served as a direct
exit from the theater.
The Roman town plan made
no significant modifications
to the older Sannite one.

his brother Drusus, who also paid for the city's walls).
Few public edifices or monuments were ever completed
without acknowledging who footed the bill, which alert-
ed a visitor to the man in power in either the city or the
empire or both.

Finally, of course, the most physical message was carried
by the two sets of doors. The first, facing the countryside, was a metal gate operated from a control room
above the arch. Then, on the city side, there was a massive wooden door of two leaves. A heavy slice of metal or
chunk of wood was always ready to slam down during
times of strife or, more likely, when a recalcitrant shepherd refused to pay the stiff tithe Saepinum exacted be-

fore he could pass through the city. These Saepinese
were not a people to fool with.

What follows is altogether more friendly. The terror
of the gates, once overcome, gives way to the texture of
the decumanus, Saepinum's once hopping main street.
Although only about a third of the city has been excavated, most of its public and a healthy sample of its private
buildings are grouped along this narrow stone avenue.
Flat, grayish circles, the ghosts of columns that once
lined the road, draw you through the commercial district.
On both sides of the decumanus are shops with residences behind. Ruts in the foundations indicate gates or

BY ORDER OF THE EMPEROR
The Porta di Bojano is topped
by a statue representing
a protective divinity whose
identity is uncertain (top).
At the sides of the single arch
of the gate are two figures of
barbarian captives (left) in
commemoration of the Roman
general Drusus's military
successes in Germany.
In all probability, the cost of
constructing the imposing walls
and fortifications of Saepinum
was met by dipping heavily
into the spoils of war brought
back from Germany
by the Roman legions.
The inscription at the top of the
gate (partly visible in the photo)
is a paean of praise and thanks
to Drusus and his brother
the Emperor Tiberius,
who "saw to the construction
at their own expense."

counters that faced the street for ready commerce. Much more modest are the private rooms outlined beyond. They suggest that the small-businessmen of Saepinum put business before domesticity in nearly every case.

The first public building of any size, the *macellum*, or market, is on the right just before the crossroads. Like many buildings in Saepinum, the *macellum* was trapezoidal, a shape dictated by the slightly off-kilter intersection of the *decumanus* and the *cardus*. It was a preceded by a pillared portico; inside, there was a hexagonal courtyard lined with shops or stalls that faced a hexagonal basin, which was made from the millstone of an olive press and used to capture rainwater.

Still embedded in the crusty earth, the millstone was the precise center of the district's agricultural community. Here, every morning, farmers gathered to hawk their produce, and here the ladies and servants of Saepinum gathered to provision their daily meals.

Next to the *macellum* is the *basilica*, which could be entered from either the *decumanus* or the *cardus*. It was a rectangular building, internally subdivided by a peristyle of 20 columns. Nine of these, with their smooth shafts and their elegant Ionic capitals, have been raised. The floor was once paved with mosaic. Built in the first century A.D. and later reconstructed and enriched with marble, the *basilica* was a center for town meetings and demonstrations, a place where political issues and economic problems were debated and philosophical lectures presented. This juxtaposition of basilica and market — high and humble — is typically and quaintly Saepinese. Nowhere in the big city would you find potatoes and philosophy sharing a common wall.

Beyond the basilica, the *decumanus* opens into the *forum*. It is paved with rectangular limestone and slopes gently, and ingeniously, to catch the rainwater; a sewer inlet in the shape of a pierced grid is visible near the fountain of the griffin. The *forum* bears the imprints of many monuments — a column dedicated to Constantine, equestrian statues, votive offerings — and was certainly the most active outdoor space in all Saepinum. Along its left side are a succession of important public buildings: the *curia*, or town hall, where the local senate met; the *comitium*, an assembly hall, where elections were held; the *capitolium*, a temple believed to have been dedicated to the capitoline triad of Jupiter, Juno and Minerva; and a second set of baths, for private, or noble, use.

At the far (eastern) corner of the forum is the graceful griffin fountain, which was paid for by Caius Ennius Marsus, a magistrate who followed the local custom of financing a public monument upon taking office.

The *decumanus* resumes at the far end of the *forum*, and the buildings that line it are once again of a private nature. Of particular interest is the "casa dell'impluvio sannitico," the house with the Samnite impluvium, a basin for collecting rainwater. Under the Roman impluvium an earlier, third-century B.C. Samnite impluvium was identified by a stone chiseled with letters in Oscan, once again testifying to the pre-Roman origins of the city. Just beyond it are the remains of a building that once housed an olive press; it is not clear whether it was meant for the use of a single family or to produce inventory for a shop. Immersed in the ground are four brick jars, originally lined with lead, for the storage of olive oil. Only half of the fourth is visible; its other half disappears behind a low wall and into an embankment of earth. It is a reminder of the lost — or, possibly, the still undiscoverd — Saepinum. The *decumanus* continues past farmhouses. Some are still inhabited by local farmers; some house offices for archeologists; one has

**ON THE TRAIL
OF THE SHEPHERDS**
The importance of Saepinum
as a commercial center
was mostly due to its position
on the intersection of the
Pescasseroli-Candela main road
(right) and a minor one that
wound its way up toward the
Matese area. These two tracks
became the Cardus and the
Decumanus, the basis of the
city's street plan.
The main roads are wide tracks,
in places over 100 yards across,
created by animal herds during
migrations between
the mountain pastures
and the plain.

been turned into a second museum, which tells the history of the digs at Saepinum. Soon the *decumanus* passes through the Porta di Benevento and into one of the city's two necropoli. Here is the striking tomb of Ennius Marsus, the man who gave Saepinum the griffin fountain: its large cyclindrical drum rests on a square base, where four crouching lions once crushed warriors with their paws. No matter by which door you enter or leave Saepinum, your final sign of civilization is inevitably a monument, which never fails to invoke the man or family in power.

During the late empire, as traffic diminished and city dwellers were replaced by rich landowners, Saepinum went into decline. After the fall of Rome in 476, its buildings were abandoned and the surrounding farmland was left uncultivated. In 667 the city was ceded by the Lombard Duke of Benevento to the Duke of Bulgari, who tried to revive it. In 882 Saepinum was sacked by the Saracens, and the remaining inhabitants once again returned to the hills, taking refuge this time in *Castellum Sepini*, the site of today's village of Sepino.

As soon as it leaves the Porta di Benevento, the *decumanus* becomes a dirt road and stretches deep into the Molise, once again recalling the tratturo it was from before the beginning of history.

Here, at the edge of Saepinum, the air has an animal pungency. Twentieth-century twig fences are propped up against first-century stone walls. Students of archeology bathe shards of pottery and lay them out in the sun to dry; a few yards down the road, weatherbeaten farmers heft bales of hay and feed their chickens and stake their tomatoes against a strong wind. One civilization investigates, interprets, protects and visits another, while the people who resided here before the Romans built their walls and their towers and their baths continue as they have for millennia. Somehow, one feels, they always will.

_____

MICHAEL FRANK's essays, articles, and short stories have appeared in The New York Times, Travel & Leisure *and* The Yale Review, *among other publications. He divides his time between New York and Italy.*

By William Murray

Variations on a
NEAPOLITAN AIR

November 19, 2000

THE CITY AND THE VOLCANO
Looming in the background
of the Bay of Naples, behind the
Castel dell'Ovo, like a sly old
dog Vesuvius absently surveys
the bustling city.
The Neapolitans respect the
mountain, they are not afraid
of its tremors even though they
have caused destruction and
grief. Vesuvius is a friend, a
capricious one, perhaps, and the
local people have never
hesitated to build houses and
plant vineyards on its slopes.
It is said that God wept on
seeing the Bay of Naples, which
the Devil had stolen from him;
and where His tears fell a vine
sprang up. This is why the wine
of the Vesuvius area
is called "Lachryma Christi "
(the Tears of Christ).

In Naples, everyone lives in an inebriated forgetfulness of himself, Johann Wolfgang Goethe wrote in *Italian Journey*, an account of his travels in Italy between 1786 and 1788, when he was in his late 30's. "That also happens to me. I hardly recognize myself and I feel myself to be an entirely different man. Yesterday I thought 'Either you were mad before or you are now'."

Naples has long had this effect on people, and I am no exception. I'm astonished, every time I visit the city, by the extraordinary, almost insane vitality of the place – the cheerful clamor in the streets, the music in the air, the purposeful energy of its citizens in pursuit of their often chaotic lives, the dark dramas and comic scenes played out daily in its ancient streets and grand piazzas. It is not by accident that Italy's most popular 20th-century playwright was Eduardo de Filippo, a native Neapolitan whose bittersweet comedies, written in the local dialect, express the joys and sufferings of a population that has survived 2,500 years of history.

"See Naples and die," goes the old saw about the place, alluding to the beauty of the city's incomparable setting in the shadow of its volcano and the blue waters of its enormous bay. "See Naples and live!" is how I prefer to think of the city, because, quite apart from the artistic, archaeological and historical rewards Naples provides to even the most casual tourist, the humanity and good humor, even in adversity, of its citizens is one of its main attractions. Strike up a conversation anywhere with anyone in the streets of Naples and you are likely to be rewarded with a bit of wisdom or an observation that will startle by its originality or make you

laugh. Not long ago, on a visit to the top of Vesuvius, Europe's smallest but still active volcano, I commented to an old guide seated at the edge of the crater that the mountain seemed to be dormant. "He sleeps with one eye open," the old man answered. More recently, after I'd been regaled by an outpouring of detailed information from a bright young man giving me an unsolicited tour of the exquisitely beautiful Chapel of Sansevero, the vendor of postcards at the exit explained cheerfully that my guide was "a well of science." It helps to be able to speak at least some Italian to appreciate such linguistic subtleties, but many Neapolitans get along very well in English and are eager to be helpful, which they express by the small touches of gentility that dignify public life.

I often find myself marveling at this, because surely no major city in the world has survived more calamities than Naples, from volcanic eruptions and earthquakes to floods, plagues, wars and foreign occupations. The most recent of these was an earthquake in 1980. Centered in an area some 50 miles to the southeast, it shook the city hard enough to crack the facades of many of its most splendid palazzi and to force about 50,000 people to leave their homes for temporary shelters. The tourist industry, a mainstay of the local economy that had long suffered from a high rate of unemployment, ceased practically overnight to exist. It has taken nearly a generation to build it up again, but any traveler interested in the arts, architecture, archaeology or history will rejoice in its recovery (even at the lowest ebb in its fortunes, I myself never missed an opportunity to revisit the city). Naples is like a great courtesan dressed in the tattered finery of her past and with a great story to tell.

PLACES OF THE MEMORY

Above, the dolls' hospital, an old workshop where for four centuries craftsmen have been repairing puppets, dolls and toys. Right, a view of Spaccanapoli, the sequence of streets that follow the route of the old Roman road that once ran clear across the center of the city, dividing it into two almost equal parts. Facing page, the crowded market in via San Gregorio Armeno, which offers a wide range of figures for crèches over the Christmas period. As well as the traditional holy figures, they also produce figures of famous modern characters, such as actors, sportsmen and politicians.

The man most responsible for the city's rebirth is Antonio Bassolino, an independent, forceful politician who was elected mayor in 1993 and devoted most of the seven years he was in office, until he recently became president of the entire region, to what he himself defined as a "cultural and civic awakening." Not only did he oversee the repair and reopening of many of the most damaged private and public buildings – among them the great Bourbon palazzi in the heart of town, the museums and the exquisite 17th- and 18th-century theaters – but he also sponsored a vast cleanup of areas once much favored by foreign visitors but allowed for decades to decline into crime-ridden filth and despair.

The section of the waterfront stretching for several miles from the Santa Lucia district, with its luxury hotels and popular restaurants, to the verdant peninsula of Posillipo has been restored to its former glory and partially closed to traffic; parts of the once badly polluted waters of the bay have been cleaned up and reopened to swimmers; and the dark volcanic rocks of the long scogliera, over which fishermen, bathers and picnickers once had to scramble through discarded rubbish, now

gleam pristinely in the sun. Under Bassolino's enlightened regime, the municipal government also began closing piazzas and entire neighborhoods to traffic, creating large pedestrian islands where everyone can shop, eat, drink, sightsee and stroll without having to hug building walls to avoid a honking automobile or a noisy motor scooter. A walk along the entire length of the Via Roma and Via Toledo, with their luxury shops and inevitable franchise outlets, past the vaulted arches of the Galleria Umberto I to the Piazza del Plebiscito, in front of the Palazzo Reale (Royal Palace) and the San Carlo Opera House now provides visitors with a perfect symbolic view of old and new Naples.

To the left are mostly modern office buildings, but to the right, threading their way up the steep slopes of the Vomero district to the Castle of Sant'Elmo and the Carthusian Monastery of San Martino, are the vicoli of the Quartieri Spagnoli (Spanish Quarter), where for centuries the poor of Naples have lived in noisy squalor in their tottering but picturesque tenements. So it's fine these days, using ordinary prudence, to take a walk up the Vico della Tofa, the Via Trinità degli Spagnoli or,

EMBRACED BY COLUMNS
Piazza del Plebiscito
is the "true" square of the
Neapolitans, the semi-elliptical
venue for shows and popular
assemblies of all kinds.
On the straight side stands the
immensely long façade of the
Royal Palace while the curved
side lies in the gentle embrace
of a monumental concave
colonnade. The center of the
colonnade is occupied by the
church of San Francesco di
Paola, whose construction was
decreed in 1816 by Ferdinand I
of Bourbon who had sworn
to build it if he managed
to reconquer the throne.

especially, the Vico d'Afflitto (the Alley of the Afflicted) and you will see life as it has been lived here since the mid-18th century – but now partly gentrified by a new generation of Neapolitans. There is so much to see in Naples that a week seems barely enough, especially if the plan is also to take in the nearby ruins of Pompeii and Herculaneum, where teams of archaeologists are still unearthing ancient Roman and Greek treasures buried for centuries under volcanic ash. But this "famous, stupendous city," as my long-out-of-print Italian guidebook defines it, "is noted in the world for her artistic treasures and her long past." Beautifully put, because Naples can date its first flowering to its beginnings as a Greek city, *Neapolis*, back to the seventh century B.C. It blossomed under the Romans and has continued, despite periodic cataclysms, to remain "world famous" until the present day. To an extent matched only by Rome, Naples is a hub of museums and churches, 104 of the latter by my count. The great palaces and castles, such as the Castel Sant'Elmo, the Castel Nuovo, the Palazzo Reale and the Castel dell'Ovo, are architecturally and historically worth a visit, quite apart from their function as museums.

Another royal palace, built between 1738 and 1838 in the spacious hilltop park of Capodimonte, with its dramatic view over the whole city toward the dark mass of Vesuvius, houses one of the world's great art collections – works by Giovanni Bellini, Lorenzo Lotto, Mantegna, Titian, Raphael, Vasari, Botticelli, Dosso Dossi and many others, as well as my personal favorite, Peter Bruegel the Elder's haunting depiction of *The Blind Leading the Blind*, painted in 1568, a year before the artist's death. Many other cities have great art museums, but none more important or fascinating than the National Archaeological Museum, with its huge collection of treasures – paintings, sculpture, mosaics, jewelry, household objects, coins – assembled from the diggings at Pompeii and Herculaneum. Newly refurbished and partly restaffed by multilingual bright young people, many of them students hired specifically to cater to foreigners, the Museo Archeologico quite simply overwhelms the senses. Among the hundreds of enthralling objects is a huge dramatic mosaic depicting a battle between the armies of Alexander the Great and King Darius of Persia, in which, as my wife, Alice, pointed out, Alexander behaves like a typical Neapolitan: "He isn't wearing a helmet." Long closed to the general public, the museum's pornographic collection, first put on limited display in 1845 and only periodically made available ever since to scholars and small groups of privileged visitors, has been permanently reopened in a special wing. Groups of 25 to 30 people at a time, of all ages and sexes, including children, are given a guided

**AMONG THE VINES
OF THE CLOISTERS**

The Santa Clara complex, built in the 14th century by Robert of Anjou as a mausoleum for his dynasty, is one of Naples' best loved symbols, immortalized by the words of a popular song. The cloister garden (left) with its pergolas, vines and lemon trees is characterized by the majolica decoration of the columns (above, a detail), designed in the 18th century by Domenico Antonio Vaccaro.

Pompeii and Herculaneum: saved from the lava

Not far from Naples, at the foot of Vesuvius, the two cities of Pompeii and Herculaneum owe their "survival" – that is to say their extraordinary state of preservation – to the catastrophic eruption of 79 A.D. when Pompeii, with all its inhabitants, was destroyed in a few minutes. Streets, houses and monuments remained sealed for centuries beneath a blanket of ashes and lapilli that was several yards thick in some places. The inhabitants met a terrible doom, as can be seen today by observing the casts of some bodies, made by injecting plaster into the cavities left by decomposition in the surrounding volcanic material. Men, women, children and animals were thus immortalized.

The city of Pompeii, whose origins date to the 5th-4th century B.C., was an important Etruscan and Sannite settlement before its colonization by the Romans. When the volcano erupted, the city was just recovering from a violent earthquake that had struck in 62B.C.; the new catastrophe revealed to archaeologists a town in the process of reconstruction. The excavation has brought to light the small details of everyday life in the city, the kind of things that are normally lost during archaeological digs.

Nearby Herculaneum met its fate very shortly afterward. Like Pompeii, originally Etruscan and then Sannite, it came into the orbit of Rome in the 3rd century B.C. In 79 A.D. it was a renowned holiday resort. During the eruption it was largely spared the ash and the lapilli, but a few days later it was suddenly engulfed by a sea of mud that, as it solidified, sealed the city with all that it contained, preserving even the upper floors of the houses and some of the organic matter that was there at the time, from wooden structures to papyruses and other perishable objects that in Pompeii were consumed by the heat of the eruption.

A city that had disappeared for centuries, Herculaneum was rediscovered accidentally in the early 18th century. In the course of the first digs the ancient theater was despoiled of its precious statuary before official excavations began in 1738, by order of the Bourbon King Charles III. But these were not open air digs: the vestiges of the city were reached through deep underground passages in the volcanic rock, the sole aim being to enhance the king's art collection in the nearby Villa Reale at Portici. The excavations went on intermittently throughout the 19th century. It was only in 1927 that work began according to modern criteria, and it is still going on to this day. Although the ruins of Herculaneum are less extensive than Pompeii, it is in far better condition, with paved streets, houses with porticoes resting on pillars, spas, public buildings and a superb theater, as well as large and comfortable homes. So far, a good quarter of the southern part of the city has been recovered, including two spa facilities, a large gymnasium, a sacred suburban area and a part of the neighborhood around the Forum. In recent years archaeologists have resumed digging in the city's most famous building, the Villa dei Papiri, so called because in the 19th century a large library of papyrus scrolls written in Greek was found there.

THE VILLA OF MYSTERIES
The evocative Villa of Mysteries in Pompeii is decorated with pictorial compositions showing initiation ceremonies of the Orphic Mysteries or of the cult of Dionysus (above, a detail). Right, the remains of the Teatro Grande, which could accommodate 5,000 spectators.

tour of the roughly 100 objects on display — out of a collection that now numbers in the thousands. What is most striking about the exhibition is not its often cheerfully obscene nature, but the startling beauty, more sensual than sexual, of many of the pieces, such as the white marble statue popularly known as the "Venus in a Bikini," with its traces of gilding and gold paint.

No one can claim to have truly enjoyed the best of

and called after his name saint. He left his personal stamp upon the city to an extent unmatched anywhere else, for which we can forgive him his excesses.

Spaccanapoli itself has been closed to traffic, the whole area is safe to wander in and the rewards, visual and cultural, for a sightseer are many. Most of the restored palazzi, such as the elegant Carafa and the Spinelli, with its strangely beautiful elliptical courtyard and bas-reliefs, can be visited and carry identifying placards beside their front entrances. Well-marked accesses to the archaeological sites are situated conveniently near the Duomo and other churches. They offer tantalizing glimpses into the Roman and Greek civilizations that underlie the whole city and one, Napoli Sotterranea, provides a spooky, comprehensive hour-and-a-half tour of these long-vanished worlds.

The churches themselves are wonderful in their variety, ranging from the fantastically ornate to the austere Gothic of the Monastery of Santa Chiara, destroyed by incendiary bombs during World War II but rebuilt exactly as it had been. In contrast is the Church of Gesù Nuovo across the way, with its rich mosaics, inlaid marbles, paintings and sculptures and, in a side chapel, the busts of 70 saints perching serenely on top of their reliquaries as if in miniature opera boxes. The privately owned little Chapel of Sansevero is a cornucopia of treasures, including the piece known as the *Veiled Christ*, made in 1753 by Giuseppe Sanmartino, a statue so technically amazing that another accomplished sculptor, Antonio Canova, on a visit to Naples, reportedly attempted to buy it for himself. Less well known, the Church of San Gregorio Armeno provides an oasis of cool silence from the hubbub outside in the street of the same name, where for generations Neapolitans have manufactured their "presepi," or Christmas mangers. The last time I visited San Gregorio Armeno, a baby was being baptized, the child's family the only others present, while from high above the nave a cluster of beaming, bare-breasted angels gazed down upon the scene, a reminder that the church was originally founded as a convent for the wayward daughters of the nobility.

And then, in isolated splendor, its elaborate decorated ceiling supported on 16 piers incorporating more than 100 antique columns, there is the great Duomo of San Gennaro (St. Januarius), known affectionately to Neapolitans as "San Gennà." Indifferent to the fact that under Vatican II San Gennà was inexplicably demoted from the Holy See's official calendar of saints, his constituents still consider him the city's guardian angel and his dried blood, kept in a couple of ornate vials in a side chapel, continues miraculously to liquefy several times a year, most notably on his feast day, Sept. 19. Visitors can

THE MIRACLE OF THE BLOOD
For over 16 centuries (since 315 A.D.) San Gennaro (St. Januarius), the patron saint of Naples, rewards his city with a recurrent miraculous event. The blood of the martyr, collected by the wet-nurse Eusebia after his decapitation and today kept in a reliquary (above) undergoes a process of liquefaction three times a year. The miracle is enthusiastically invoked by the crowds, who yell, weep and pray for it to come to pass. This is also because a failure of the blood to liquefy – which occasionally occurs – is seen as an omen of ill luck.

Naples who hasn't spent at least a couple of days in the section of town known generically as Spaccanapoli, or "Split Naples," so named after the long straight progression of narrow streets that bisects the Centro, especially in the area between Piazza del Gesù Nuovo and the Via del Duomo. Important not only for the presence here of distinguished churches, monuments, statues and archaeological sites, Spaccanapoli, with its grandiose Baroque palazzi and warren of colorful vicoli, recalls Naples as it was under the reign of the Bourbons, from 1734 to the arrival of Garibaldi's liberating Redshirts in 1860. The Neapolitans rightly consider Spaccanapoli, in all its noisy confusion and exhilarating vitality, to be the city's soul.

The Bourbons were a dismal ruling family, corrupt and cruel, but the first of them, Charles III (1734-59), was a tremendous builder and patron of the arts. An indifferent ruler, he spent lavishly to make Naples a great cultural center that would justify his exalted opinion of himself, and hired the architects and artists to carry out his many projects, among them the building in 1738 of the splendidly Rococo San Carlo Opera House, all cream and gold

**A COFFEE, AN APERITIF,
A RUM BABA**

A coffee, an aperitif and a stroll
to admire the shop windows.
What better place to enjoy
these than the Galleria
Umberto I? Beneath the 19th-
century glass and iron dome,
on the elegant inlaid marble
floor, the daily round of
socializing unfolds. And where
else to find the best rum babas
— sweet chunks of soft sponge
oozing with rum — in Naples?

309

reserve early for good seats at the event. San Gennà's most vocal supporters maintain that the city's well-being depends on the speed of the liquefaction, a phenomenon no one has yet been able to debunk. Older Neapolitans tend to believe in miracles and, given their city's tumultuous history, why shouldn't they?

Naples still sings, though not as preeminently as it used to. There is, of course, the San Carlo, less celebrated internationally than La Scala, but larger, equally impressive and steeped in tradition, the house where Rossini and Donizetti scored their early triumphs. Tickets here are cheaper and easier to come by than in Milan, and the year-round repertory of operas, symphonic concerts and ballets ranges from the traditional to the adventurous. Last May, I attended a terrific production of Donizetti's rarely performed *Anna Bolena*, sung by a first-rate international cast and directed by Jonathan Miller. The popular music industry that brought such classics as *O Sole Mio* and *Turna a Surriento* into the world no longer dominates the national scene, but the tradition is still very much alive, and lovers of the old songs have only to ask where they can be heard to be rewarded. The traditional popular music of Naples calls for accompani-

ment by such stringed instruments as the mandolin and guitar. A recently formed group for solo voice and six instrumentalists calling itself Almalatina has already won awards for putting on programs of Neapolitan songs dating back to the 16th century that speak for the heartaches and longings of an entire population. Street musicians, as they can in every tourist hub, can become a nuisance, but less so in Naples, where at least one is less likely to be assaulted by boom boxes and raucous attempts at rock. Neapolitans have subtler ways to separate people from their small change. Luciano De Crescenzo, a well-known chronicler of Neapolitan life, recalls a time he was having lunch with a friend at an outdoor restaurant table. They were approached by a man carrying a guitar who parked himself close to their table, then held up a sign saying, "I don't play in order not to disturb." Amused and relieved, De Crescenzo tipped him and the man bowed and left. The waiter appeared. "Poor man," he said, "the sole support of four children and he can't even play the guitar." So Neapolitan.

_____

WILLIAM MURRAY's most recent book is "City of the Soul: A Walk in Rome." His book on young opera singers will be published next year. For many years was a Staff Writer for The New Yorker.

**CHARLES OF ANJOU'S
NEW PALACE**

In the 13th century the House of Anjou, succeeding the Dukes of Swabia as the rulers of southern Italy, moved their capital from Palermo in Sicily to Naples. Charles I of Anjou built a new royal residence in a strategic position near the port and, to distinguish it from other fortresses in the city, he called it Castel Nuovo (facing page); it is also known as the Mastio (or Maschio) Angioino. Above, a detail of the interior.

By Shirley Hazzard

POSILLIPO,
A Scene of Ancient Fame

March 7, 1993

THE UNFINISHED PALACE

In 1642 the viceroy of Naples, Ramiro Guzman, the Duke of Medina Coeli, decided to build a luxurious palace for his wife Anna Carafa, but with her untimely death work came to a stop. Later damaged during a popular uprising, then by an earthquake, Palazzo Donn'Anna stands silent and mysterious beside the sea, a disenchanted witness that none will question further.

I am standing on a terrace in Naples, on the headland called Posillipo, looking at the bay. To my left, through umbrella pines, the city – red, ocher and a centuried sepia – forms a crescent toward Vesuvius. The volcano, in turn, sweeps down to the long arc of the Sorrentine peninsula, which, constituting the southern arm of this gulf, faces me across a few miles of water – clear enough, in today's pure light, to distinguish towns and villages and the old tower at the tip of Cape Minerva, where, in past ages, a great bell was rung to give warning of Saracen ships. On the right, in the open sea, Capri and its mountain lie on the horizon. Such clarity can last for days, or announce a sudden storm; and there are times when the south wind, the humid sirocco, drops its curtain of warm wool over all the incomparable scene.

Immediately below me, close to shore, there is a scattering of traditional Neapolitan fishing boats with worn indigo hulls, sometimes under erratic motor, more often silently propelled by the standing man at the oars, whose partner casts or retrieves the net. On fine nights, such boats use lamps to attract the fish that come – said Shelley in Italy – "to worship the delusive flame."

Terse words in dialect then rise to us in darkness and, once in a while, the rhythmic slapping of a paddle used to scare schools of tiny fish – sardines, anchovies – into the net. Fishing from small open boats is the old, hard life of these waters, plied without interruption since this shore was a Roman resort and its sea – none too clean this morning – so thick with the detritus of grandiose new houses that, according to Horace, even the fish complained.

Trawlers also pass here, their catch escorted by flocks of gulls. These larger boats come from as far as Sardinia seeking varieties of bass and grouper – and the bream

POSILLIPO

Enchanting and prestigious, the hill above Posillipo conceals stately villas and steep paths that lead down the rocky shore and the sea. On Cape Posillipo, the outermost offshoot of land that encloses the Bay of Naples, stand the terraces of Parco Virgiliano, a splendid belvedere recently enhanced by a painstaking renovation program that has equipped it with lighting, new floors and furnishings as well as freshly planted trees and colorful new flower beds. The "hill of repose" beloved of the Ancients will still seduce those in search of peace and beauty.

called "orata" associated with a Roman entrepreneur, C. Sergius Orata, whose innovative fishponds and oyster beds, at nearby Baia, attracted the attention of Cicero 2,000 years ago.

A regatta of small yachts with colored spinnakers has glided by. Far out, there is a ketch with reefed sails making south, for Amalfi or Salerno. And a huge old three-master, her canvas furled, has left the port of Naples for southern France: with her long bowsprit and the mighty masts that justify their Italian name "alberi" – trees – she has, even under engine, the spectral composure of old barks that move as if unmanned and self-aware.

Not far from land, but in deep water, the wave rises and withdraws over a reef capped by an outcropping known as the Salt Rock, the "Pietra Salata." In Naples, things are seldom what they seem; and the reef, the rock, are in fact remnants of Roman structures gradually submerged by coastal change. When summer comes, the Roman reef will be active with young swimmers who, coming out from the city in boats and rubber dinghies, use it as a diving board. On warm weekends, the hydrofoils for the islands – for Capri, Procida, Ischia and even Ponza – pass here constantly; and, late on summer Sundays, this stretch of sea along Posillipo becomes an autostrada of ferries, motor cruisers and small craft streaming back to Naples. By nightfall, the churning subsides. A few fishermen return, looking for "totano," the

seasonal squid. An old motorboat with colored lights takes families out to dine at the nearby cove of Marechiaro. The measured sound of the ocean resumes on the sea wall. There is the turning, barely perceptible, of the negligible tide.

Now, however, as the wave recedes from the Salt Rock, divisions of stone foundations can for a moment be seen, heavy set, abraded and purple with encrusted mussels. Ruins of the kind are plentiful round the Neapolitan coast, both above and below water – arches, porches, parapets, the enclosures of ancient baths, docks, fisheries. Farther out on this promontory, there are extensive remains of the Roman villa called *Pausilypon* – in Greek, "a pause from care" – that gave name and fame to the entire headland of Posillipo. A complex of pleasure buildings constructed in the first century before Christ, during the reign of Augustus, *Pausilypon* was sumptuous even by standards of the place and era. The villa was left by Vedius Pollio, its cruel and wealthy owner, to Augustus himself – a prudently announced intention that possibly saved Pollio from the hard consequences of imperial envy in his lifetime. Augustus was entertained here – notably, on an occasion when Pollio ordered that a slave, who had broken a goblet at table, be fed to a tankful of carnivorous eels. Having remonstrated at first in vain, the emperor smashed the rest of the costly dishes and invited the host to impose the same penalty on his sovereign. All told, one feels, not a successful party.

314

When, during World War II, Naples was bombarded, Vesuvius erupted and the Allied front inched northward, with grim suffering, to Monte Cassino, Posillipo — at a short distance from the city's heart — remained a safe haven. Monarchs, generals, statesmen were billeted on the farthest of the great Posillipo properties: Winston Churchill cruised about the harbor from Villa Rivalta; the vacillating king of Italy fished, from a cockleshell, off Villa Rosebery; and a sergeant from Ohio scratched his name into the terrace tiles at Villa Barracco — where King George VI was also a wartime guest. Naples absorbs the exotic easily — having, even to excess, the gift of taking strangeness for granted and balking only at system. The host of Allied troops, departing, gave place to the emissaries of NATO — who furnished, with all the wonders of the PX, their modern apartments in blocks newly pitched on the Posillipo hill.

When I first came to Naples in the 1950's and lived for a year at Posillipo, in a red, romantic house that rises from the sea on Roman foundations, this district was still recognizably close to the scene of past centuries — not only in appearance, but in its expansive relation to the intensity of the city. Naples then was a blitzed town of large-eyed, overburdened, resilient people. Many of its great churches and palaces lay open to the elements, its waterfront was a shambles. To drive out from the shattered city after work, to the colors and flowers of Posillipo and old walls hung with plumbago, bougainvillea and jasmine; to swim from inlets and grottoes of the blond tufa of which this cape is composed; to watch, from any balcony or shop front or curve of Via Posillipo, the unfolding light and adventure of the bay, was to achieve tranquillity without tedium: a life always animated by the energy and curiosity, the capacity for humanity and vitality, that pervade the Posillipo community no less than all the rest of this extraordinary metropolis. In the 1860's, when the Bourbon Kingdom of Italy evaporated in the unification of Italy, Naples lost the territory, influence and revenues of south Italy and Sicily. Unlike other dispossessed powers, however, the city itself did not languish or repine. The Neapolitan vitality turned — as E.M. Forster wrote of ever analogous Alexandria — inward: the vigor and ingenuity and, above all, the temperament, formerly exercised in a large realm were concentrated in these few miles of land and sea, known locally as "the Crater." In that unique, civilized and sometimes explosive liveliness, Posillipo plays its immemorial part.

"Rends-moi le Pausilippe et la mer d'Italie" — this was the cry of Gerard de Nerval. Posillipo begins with poetry, at the Roman tumulus long venerated as the tomb of Virgil, in a garden near the Mergellina station. This little hillside park, which contains, also, the austere tomb of the Romantic poet Giacomo Leopardi, who died at Naples in 1837, culminates in the Grotto of Posillipo, the entrance to a road tunneled, in Roman times, through the rock, from Naples to the neighboring Gulf of Pozzuoli. Nearby, the Renaissance poet Jacopo Sannazzaro — who, in his *Arcadia*, presciently dreamed of visiting the vanished cities of Vesuvius — is buried in the red waterfront church of Santa Maria del Parto. In an upper reach of Via Posillipo, Piazza Salvatore di Giacomo — with its simple restaurant "Al Poeta," where James Merrill has dined, and where once a Scottish bard, wandering south Italy, sang to us the songs of Robert Burns — commemorate the poet whose verses in dialect inspired many of the tender Neapolitan songs.

From antiquity, writers, artists and esthetes have sought pleasure and inspiration, and solace, at Posillipo. In 1880, Henry James was scandalized by "the fantastic immoralities and esthetics" of an émigré circle here; and declined, for linguistic reasons, to meet another foreign resident, Richard Wagner. In 1897, Oscar Wilde, staying, impecunious and heartsick at Posillipo, completed *The Ballad of Reading Gaol*; while Norman Douglas, living farther out, at lovely Villa Maya, studied marine life along Posillipo in scientific expeditions of a kind charmingly recorded, in frescoes by Hans von Marees, in the Naples Aquarium. The ghosts of this region are too many, and too vital, to sadden us: rather, they create a company, ironic and benign, to which we ourselves may ultimately hope to belong.

Like much else at Naples, Posillipo is best explored on foot. The uneven paving of Via Posillipo slopes upward from Mergellina past the enfilade of old villas that, on the left, line the shore. To the right, the 19th-century palazzi, with their shops and fruit stalls and cafés, and their hung laundry, line the street. On the hillside above, among modern blocks, some countryside can still be seen, and an occasional splendid house, such as the neo-classical Villa d'Angri, now in disrepair. But it is the seafront that enchants — even the scruffy stretch of red wall that all but conceals the skeleton of Sir William Hamilton's seaside retreat, the little Villa Emma, where, on hot days of the late 18th century, Hamilton escaped the rigors of court and city. Here, from a shaded, elliptical terrace, whose outline is still discernible, Hamilton's celebrated visitors enjoyed the spectacle of the bay and Goethe exclaimed: "There is really no more glorious place in all the world."

———

*SHIRLEY HAZZARD's most recent novel, "The Great Fire,"
received the 2003 National Book Award. Naples and its seaside
district of Posillipo are the setting of an earlier novel,
"The Bay of Noon."*

**MARECHIARO, THE
FISHERMEN AND THE MOON**
A short distance from Posillipo,
Marechiaro was made famous
by the eponymous Italian song
written by the local poet
Salvatore di Giacomo,
who imagined the village
illuminated by moonlight
and thoughts of love.
Although no longer a silent
fishing village; the romantic
appeal of the Neapolitan song
and the scent of the night
on the sea have all the allure
of times gone by.

By Susan Allen Toth

A Tranquil Side of
CAPRI

March 18, 2001

On our first morning in Capri, I stepped onto our sunny terrace, looked beyond our yellow-splashed lemon tree to a blue-green sea, and immediately felt as if I had stepped into a frame of *Enchanted April*. In this 1992 fairy-tale movie, several unhappy, chilled Englishwomen, fleeing the rainy gloom of London, open the shutters of their Italian villa to an astonishing flood of sunlight and lush greenness. The promise of romance floats in the air almost as tangibly as the lacy swaths of wisteria.

It is easy to feel star-struck in Capri. Ever since Caesar Augustus discovered the charms of this small, flowering island in the Bay of Naples and purchased it in 29 B.C., the rich and famous have moored in its two inviting harbors, climbed its steep streets to admire its cascading flowers and plants (more than 800 species), taken in dazzling views of the bay and neighboring islands, sat on its sun-baked terraces, or swum in its clear turquoise waters.

Between Easter and November, tourists arrive in boatloads from Naples or Sorrento, only 20 to 75 minutes away via frequent ferries. Yet we discovered to our delight that Capri has not been spoiled.

For 10 days we explored the island from a rented house, visiting viewpoints, Roman ruins, grottoes, churches and other landmarks. Taking long walks every morning, we felt we could treat ourselves to sybaritic lunches, always cheeringly inexpensive, at restaurants that offered spectacular views toward the sea. Most afternoons we read or dozed on one of our private terraces, shopped a little for groceries, and walked some more.

Much of the pleasure of an extended stay on Capri lies in not having a car (though residents own cars, tourists usually cannot take them onto the island.) Minibuses ply between several key locations, including the two main towns of Capri (population 8,000) and Anacapri (7,000), and a fleet of taxis, including vintage convertibles called bathtub taxis, hover near the main port, Marina Grande, and close to the two town squares.

Although several main streets connect key points on the island, most other lanes, narrow and twisting, are necessarily traffic free, except for occasional motorized carts ferrying heavy goods. With trails criss-crossing the hills, and a maze of intriguing lanes, this is a walker's island.

Most of our walks ended somewhere high on a limestone cliff overlooking Capri's glinting waters. On such a compact island – 4.2 miles long, 1.7 miles at its widest point – we were never far from a glimpse of the sea. One favorite short walk took us from Anacapri's main square along a paved path carved into the side of Monte Solaro, the island's highest point (1,932 feet). Passing secluded houses and intensely cultivated vineyards and gardens wedged into the hillside, we were soon out of sight and sound of the busy small town, surrounded only by lemon trees, tiny sunbathing lizards and bees humming among the fragrant flowering bushes. In half an hour, we arrived at the Belvedere della Migliara, a terrace with views of Capri's lighthouse, and a few steps farther, of the Faraglioni, rock outcroppings rising dramatically out of the waves.

Another walk, beginning at Capri town's Piazza Umberto I, the island's most celebrated gathering place and known simply as La Piazzetta, took us along Capri's elegant shopping street, the Via Camerelle. The windows of its boutiques, often built into an old Roman wall, glittered with Gucci, Ferragamo and other design-

AN UNFORGETTABLE AZURE MEMORY

The Grotta Azzurra was well known to lovers in ancient Roman times. In fact, the discovery of statues and other artifacts suggests that the cavern was once a nymphaeum. Before the writer August Kopisch fortuitously rediscovered it in 1826 the people of Capri called it the Grotta di Gradola. They were afraid to explore it believing it to be inhabited by witches.

317

er confections, as well as sleek Italian shoes ostentatiously displayed like jewels. This promenade ended above the Punta Tragara, a promontory with more sweeping views of sea and sky.

Much of Capri remains surprisingly wild, rocky land left to goats and sea gulls, maritime pines, semi-tropical shrubs and windswept scrub trees. One strenuous but rewarding walk plunges down what seem like hundreds of steps almost to the sea, past a grotto called Matromania, an ancient sacred site dedicated to the Great Mother. Then it winds among brush and woods, with occasional peeks at the sea, including the Villa Malaparte, a strikingly red Modernist house built on a rugged point, until it climbs back up, and up, to the Tragara belvedere and then blissfully downhill to the Piazzetta.

There, we toasted our stamina with delectable pizza at da Gemma, Graham Greene's favorite restaurant during his many years in Anacapri (the novelist's former home, Il Rosaio, was the focus of another Anacapri walk.)

A steady uphill climb led us in an hour to the heights of Villa Jovis, an extensive ruin where the Emperor Tiberius once held court. Capri was his capital of the Roman Empire between A.D. 27 and 37, and remnants of Roman rule – walls, odd bits of ruins, ongoing excavations – crop up all over Capri. Villa Jovis became famous when Suetonius, a Roman popularizing historian, described with relish Tiberius's bizarre orgies and cruelties. Local guides still gleefully point out the Salto di Tiberio, a towering cliff where Tiberius is supposed to have pitched victims of his vicious whims into the sea.

Although Capri has its evil emperor (perhaps, historians now suggest, unfairly maligned), it also has a kind of modern saint. Every evening, we took a leisurely sunset saunter to the Villa San Michele, a striking whitewashed structure built by Axel Munthe (1857-1949), a Swedish doctor and humanist, whose many acts of generosity included tending the victims of plague and cholera in Naples. His memoir, *The Story of San Michele*, is a minor classic.

Struck by the beauty of this hilltop site with an abandoned chapel, Munthe restored the chapel and built an extraordinary house. Furnished sparely but with discerning taste, it almost glows with marble mosaic floors, antique sculptures and ornaments, and other works of art. Surrounding the house is a luxuriant garden, with a colonnade leading to a panoramic view over the whole Bay of Naples. Guarding this view is a small Egyptian sphinx, dating from the 11th century B.C., that now appears on many postcards and posters as embodying the elusive, almost mystical spirit of Capri.

A TRANQUIL SIDE OF
CAPRI

A SWEDE IN CAPRI

Axel Munthe first set foot on Anacapri in 1884 when it was struck by an epidemic. He was a young, highly esteemed doctor and such was the charm of the neighboring island of Capri that he abandoned his native Sweden and his illustrious Parisian patients to become a general practitioner on the island. He bought an entire mountain, which he designated a bird sanctuary, while he built his home around the ruins of a medieval chapel dedicated to St. Michael. At his death he bequeathed the villa (left), which stands in a bright, colorful spot, to the Swedish state. Above, the exclusive elegance of the Grand Hotel Quisisana.

319

**A PIONEER OF ENVIRONMENTAL
CONSERVATION**

Pizzolungo (below) is a rocky
stretch of the southern coast
of the island. In the early years
of the 20th century, several villas
were constructed here
in an environment of rare and
wild beauty. These villas include
Villa Solitaria, built by Edwin
Cerio, an engineer who
developed an architectural style
in harmony with the
characteristics of the
surroundings. A genuine
forerunner of environmental
conservation, Cerio set up
a watchdog commission aimed
at preventing unauthorized
building on the island.

Besides walking around the island, we wanted to
see it by water. An otherwise pleasurable adventure by
boat, past hidden grottoes and fantastic rock formations,
included a stop at the Blue Grotto, an amusingly weird
experience. Since more than a dozen tour boats (and this
was off-season) hovered outside the entrance, we had to
wait almost an hour to be precariously downloaded into
small flat rowboats. These boats, riding so low in the
water they seemed about to sink, could ferry only three
or four passengers at a time through the entrance, which
looked but inches high (on windy days, with high waves,
the grotto is closed).

Once we paid a special fee to yet another boatman, we
took our place in a further floating queue. Then, suddenly, as our guide shouted again, we whizzed at high
speed toward the impossibly low, narrow, dark entrance.
I gasped and shut my eyes. A few seconds later, we were
safely inside, bumping gently into several other boats.

At first I could see nothing in the darkness. Then I
managed to make out strange glints of blue, shifting
and winking as light flashed through the opening.
Before I could absorb the magic of this eerie, changing
color, all the milling boatmen broke into clashing ver-

sions of *O Sole Mio*. One or two minutes later, we sped
toward the entrance again — and out under the sunny,
welcoming sky. Our guide halted to request a tip; then we
were free to reboard our excursion boat. The Blue Grotto
seemed to us the least characteristic feature of this unex-
pectedly restful, seductive island. On our last day, after a
farewell walk through the maze of lanes in Capri town,
we headed down toward Marina Piccola, the smaller of
Capri's two harbors. Our pedestrian path provided tantalizing glances past elaborate wrought-iron gates guarding
domed, vaguely Moorish villas, their whitewashed walls
and tiled terraces shaded by lemon trees, wisteria and
flowering shrubs. A few people strolled by us, but otherwise the lane seemed asleep in the quiet sunshine.

After lunch, we walked across some flat rocks where a
woman was sunbathing to the edge of the water.
Looking up at the rocky, pine-strewn cliffs which now
seemed so familiar, we felt as if we owned the island.
And in a way, we did.

———

SUSAN ALLEN TOTH's *most recent book is* "Leaning into
the Wind: A Memoir of Midwest Weather" (*University
of Minnesota Press*).

THE HEART OF SOCIAL LIFE
Crammed with tables,
overlooked by the Moorish-
style church of Santo Stefano, is
Piazza Umberto I, universally
known as the "Piazzetta" (left),
where all the island's social
rituals are held. The VIPs simply
choose which of the four highly
exclusive bars will have
the honor of serving them an
aperitif or a coffee in the shade
of the Torre dell'orologio.

321

Ischia, the spa island

While Capri is an enchanting limestone rock, Ischia, which lies at the opposite end of the Bay of Naples, is a mountain forged by fire and lava. Over the centuries, volcanic activity has modeled the land, creating cliffs, natural terracing, rocky promontories and sheltered coves. That same activity has left the soil extremely fertile, and the island is for the most part covered with woods, orchards and vineyards.

But the main inheritance of the volcanoes takes the form of the healthful muds and spa waters, an immense treasure that since Roman times has contributed to the fame of the island. In the 19th century, it was an obligatory resort for the élite of Europe, who flocked to enjoy the therapeutic waters.

Today, those who wish to spend a reinvigorating vacation may choose from a large number of hotels equipped with spas, open-air and indoor swimming pools and beauty farms. The most luxurious of these are on Ischia, the capital of the island, at Lacco Ameno and Forio. This area also boasts the Giardini Poseidon (the Poseidon Gardens), one of Ischia's principal "spa parks," an extensive green space overlooking the sea where – in exchange for a small payment – visitors may use the spa and beach facilities and, in summer, enjoy evening concerts and dances.

Visiting Ischia is a tiring but rewarding enterprise: narrow roads wind their way among archaeological remains and fishing villages, springs and fumaroles, vineyards clinging to the rocky hillsides, and cool pinewoods from which one glimpses the occasional panoramic view. It's not worth taking a car to the island; it's more convenient to take one of the local micro-taxis, brightly colored and spartan little vehicles that can take tourists almost everywhere. They have been used by Cary Grant, Rock Hudson and Jack Lemmon in some of the many films shot on Ischia. Ask the "cabbie" to drive to Castello Aragonese, a small fortified island connected to the main island by a bridge built in 1438, to the Sanctuary of Santa Restituta, a religious complex whose roots are sunk in the early centuries of the Christian era, and to Sant'Angelo, a lovely small fishing village. And for those visitors undaunted by a strenuous walk, it is well worth visiting the hamlet of Fontana, where the path begins to Mount Epomeo, the highest point on Ischia at 788 meters (over 2,500 feet). The view of the island of the Bay of the Naples from the summit is matchless.

THE FACTOTUM CASTLE

The first construction on the islet on which the Castello Aragonese (facing page, below) stands dates to 474 B.C. The castle proved an exceptionally effective stronghold against enemies and pirates alike, but it was only in the 15th century, under the rule of Alfonso I the Magnanimous, that this rocky outcrop became the center of public and social life. Here churches and offices sprang up, attracting clerics, soldiers and politicians; here too came artists like Michelangelo, Tasso and Ariosto. Abandoned at the end of the 18th century, the islet first became a prison under the ruling House of Bourbon before it was finally sold to a private person. Top right, a view of the village of Sant'Angelo. Right, a church in Forio d'Ischia, a fine example of Mediterranean architecture.

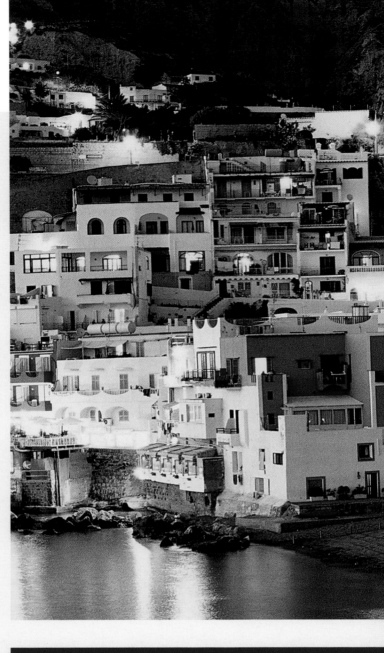

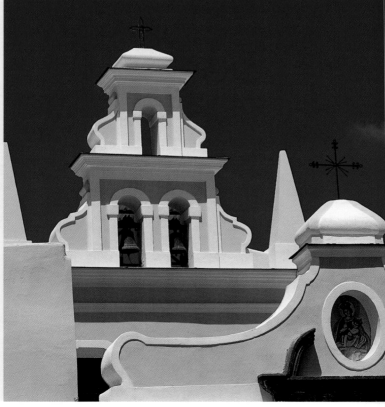

AMALFI, THE SEA AND LEMONS

In Amalfi the beach umbrellas have been furled by now and a mild breeze carries the scent of the sea. After a good fish dinner it is hard to resist a chilled glass of "limoncello", a liqueur made solely with the local variety of lemon known as "sfusato amalfitano." The disinfectant, astringent, digestive and regenerating properties of this fruit were known to the "Scuola Amalfitana", the renowned medieval school of medicine that prescribed this fruit for the treatment of a wide variety of disorders. In short, a lemon a day keeps the doctor away.

324

By Jane Shapiro

Above All,
RAVELLO

February 27, 2000

Ravello is all vantage points, a town where everything overlooks something else. Above Amalfi on the southern coast of Italy's Sorrentine peninsula, this ancient village sits high above the Gulf of Salerno, perched on a rocky green spur between two mountain valleys and between two vast bluenesses, sea and sky. The entire village of Ravello overlooks the towns of Scala and Atrani and busy Amalfi, and, from some standpoints, Maiori down the sea road. The road descending to Amalfi twists and turns so radically that it regularly overlooks itself.

The first settlement in Ravello is said to date from the sixth century, when a few Romans arrived on the slopes of the Lattari Mountains – as the guidebooks tell us, in flight from barbarians; since then, it's been a resort. Well into the 20th century, when the redoubtable man of letters Gore Vidal looked around for a country place – deciding, I like to think, to leave behind many barbarians of his own – he moved in here. Ravello is the sort of Italian town that is justifiably called a jewel; small and elegant and serene above its sweep of glimmering sea. Here are lovely complicated gardens, and concerts under the sky in the 11th-century Moorish Villa Rufolo (Wagner's model for Klingsor's magic garden in *Parsifal*), and a splendid cathedral, and sea breezes in summer, and locally produced buffalo mozzarella and tart, sweet limoncello liqueur and locally produced calm.

The drive down from Ravello – like the famous Amalfi coast road below – is a remarkable series of hairpin turns and narrow escapes (alternatively, you can walk down a meandering stairway, hundreds of steps, in a brisk hour or so). Perched on the coast below, Amalfi, once a city with 80,000 inhabitants, a major center of the medieval world, is today an insistently lively town of some 5,000 year-round residents, filled, of course, with motorbikes and seafood restaurants, tourists and their buses, and beach umbrellas and chaise longues lined up on small gray beaches, six-deep in the Italian way, row by tidy row. At the center, as usual, sits the Duomo. Crowded below the cathedral, like tiny saints around the feet of the outsize Madonna in a medieval painting, are the customary various establishments: cafes, butcher shops with impressively hefty veal chops and giant's tongues, leather stores wafting the scent of their vests and jackets into the summer air, small shops selling the local Vietri pottery, sunglasses pricey or cheap, Kodak color film, tuna in jars. At one fruit-and-vegetable store, dried hot peppers hang on strings, labeled with a succinct sales pitch: "Viagra Naturale." And from an upper story drifts the scent of cumin, reminding you that Amalfi, like other southern Italian cities, lives with the memory of its nearness to North Africa. Above it all, the cathedral, begun in the 9th century and finished in the 12th, with its Arab-Norman facade, is most reminiscent of Muslim Spain: four tiers of variously colored arches like lace carved in stone.

Sixty steep steps lead to the entrance. And here, too, is Africa: the Chiostro del Paradiso, a whitewashed cloister fairly stuffed with plantings and palm trees. The museum of the Duomo holds the remains of the cathedral's 12th-century pulpits, these in the style of Campania influenced by Muslim style from Sicily. The pulpit arch with marble and mosaic decorations in gold, greens, red, black, white. Two peacocks with green and aquamarine mosaic feathers, ingesting flowers in unison. Wonderful pulpit pillars crowned by vegetables of Islamic influence; and a geometric pulpit arch, with lines of deeply colored

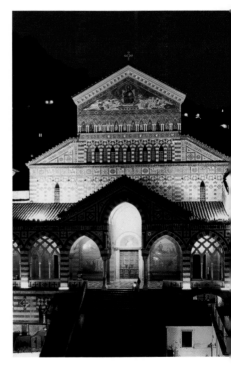

THE CATHEDRAL OF AMALFI
From the heights of a steep stairway the cathedral of Amalfi watches over the sleeping city. Dedicated to St. Andrew, whose relics are kept there, the cathedral also boasts a colossal statue of the saint donated by King Philip III of Spain.

325

CLASSICAL AND NEOCLASSICAL
We owe the rediscovery of Paestum to the poetic sensibilities of Goethe and Shelley, who visited Italy's ancient ruins in the 19th century. The Doric style of the temples influenced Neoclassical architecture in both Europe and America.

interlocking triangles of asymmetrical design. A sign informs us that glass was used in place of marbles, leading to greater variety and vivacity of color, and concludes by protesting that the Arab-Sicilian influence in these mosaics is absolutely secondary to the local tradition.

One day, ranging afield, we make an excursion to see the Salerno ivories. We descend from Ravello early in the morning, driving south along the coast, through Cetara, with its houses pressed higgledy-piggledy

against the road, and on into the city of Salerno (this early in the day, the spectacular twists of the coast road seem almost navigable; on the way back, it'll be an automotive nightmare of cars, buses, trucks and darting motorbikes jockeying for position – typical of this route in summer). We park in the Piazza Cavour, ascend the hill to the museum and climb its stairs. Inside, in two simple glass cases, is the largest unified series of ivory carvings preserved from the pre-Gothic Middle Ages, depicting scenes from the Old and New Testaments.

Some 36 small, low-relief panels (along with two colonnettes and a few fragments of decorative borders) tell that marvelous story, from the separation of light and darkness and the creation of the world to the Ascension. Plants and animals abound.

In *The Spirit Over the Waters*, the dove, wings outstretched, rests on the calm surface of a simple incised ivory sea; in *Creation of Birds and Fish*, a small ocean appears, crowded with turtles, squid, schools of delicately marked fish and, on the sea floor, a sort of wolf-fish, both monstrous and benign; in *Creation of Plants and Trees*, the Creator, accompanied by angels, calls forth two flowering, berry-laden trees, whose branches entwine as they rise.

Almost all the panels are in fine condition, only continuing to glow more warmly golden with age. Robert Bergman, the late director of the Cleveland Museum and the Byzantine scholar who wrote *The Salerno Ivories*, believed the ivories were actually made not in Salerno but in Amalfi, near the end of the 11th century, when Amalfi was still one of the four or five most powerful cities in Italy. But whatever their provenance, these are the most significant existing medieval works of art from southern Italy; and almost nobody visits them.

On the way back to the car, we stop at the Duomo, where we observe the ubiquitous scaffolding and, in June here as in America, one of the ubiquitous bridal couples. They're posing for photographs, she in truly form-fitting ivory satin with her skirt arranged in an insistent swirl like precise marble drapery. As one can observe repeatedly in front of the Pantheon in Rome, Italian brides and grooms often stand for photographs as though born to it, with a kind of provocative serenity. This particular bridal couple, on the steps of the Duomo in Salerno on a 90-degree morning, is the image of voluptuousness: she leans back into him with her blonde curls dangling; he rests his cheek against her hair with wonderful louche insouciance. Watching, a middle-aged woman, one of the wedding guests, comments on the bride's expression: "A beautiful glance!" The bride, suddenly, as if wrenching herself awake: "Basta." And we disperse.

Go early enough to Salerno and you'll be able to press on to Paestum. You arrive through fields – cows and corn and Queen Anne's lace – until you come upon a huge field in which sit several remarkable Greek temples. A few steps and we're in imposing and utterly lovely Paestum, founded by the Greeks in 600 B.C., and ruled by the Romans beginning some 300 years later. Paestum was then abandoned for centuries, increasingly hidden in marshland and deep forest, by chance to be rediscovered in the 18th century in its remarkable state of preservation, like some awakening sleeping beauty. The town's four major temples are Doric and simple, singularly intact and eloquent, set out amid carpets of fuchsia flowers, butterflies and grasses, wind in the cypress trees.

ABOVE ALL,
RAVELLO

DREAM VACATIONS

Relax on a terrace embellished with hand-painted majolica tiles and admire the Bay of Positano (below).

THE VILLA OF TEMPTATION

For over 50 years Villa Rufolo has been staging a festival of Wagnerian music. The garden inspired the German composer to create the garden of Klingsor, the wizard in *Parsifal* who vainly tries to tempt the hero with the aid of his magical flower-maidens.

Above, red hot chili peppers (the sign says "better than Viagra"), lemons from the Amalfi Coast and a cool spring to quench visitors' thirst.

Returning to Ravello, we conclude with the second most obvious activity (the most obvious is to sit on the terrace): there's very little more delicious on a summer day than a stroll in the cool and rustling garden of the Villa Cimbrone, a simple Renaissance-style villa with Moorish-influenced cloisters, from which the garden cascades, a complicated park filled with flower beds and small temples and statuary, paths and groves and thickets.

You enter the garden in birdsong, past a bank of pink and blue hydrangeas, under a canopy of pale green frosted-looking grapes. Along the tree-shadowed path to the promontory: spiked purple acanthus, orange heads of tritone, little bursts of petunias and masses of white daisies leaning to catch some sun. Step into the small Doric Temple of Ceres, where the harvest goddess stands as serene in her marble drapery as our Salerno bride, inclining her smartly coiffed head. At last you emerge from the enveloping shade of the tree-lined path onto the most astonishing promontory in this town of overlooks, guarded by its seven white marble busts. Here we shall turn for our description to Gregorovius, in the 19th century: "Right at the edge of the crag there was a terrace commanding an enchanting view; it was surrounded by horrible marble statues which, however, from afar, had a sort of appeal." Well, they're not really horrible, they're O.K., lining the seaside edge of the Terrace of Infinity, where you gaze not into infinity but over Amalfi below, to the sweep of Tyrrhenian Sea and the Cilento mountains beyond: the most enticing, exhilarating view in a town composed of views.

Then a stroll into the piazza, perhaps a coffee under an umbrella, a peek into the Cathedral, certainly a nap; then dinner on a terrace, above the water, beneath the sky. Late at night in Ravello, one simply sits, on one of the town's terraces genuinely at the top of a world. Lights below in the darkness describing the curve of coast, and the broad glittering sea stretching out in the moonlight. My son tells me that one night, late, in magical Ravello, he heard four churches toll midnight in turn. That's what night sounds like here: a bell from a church in the valley, a dog's bark somewhere down the mountain, a distant motor scooter in full cry, making a hairpin turn. Amalfitan dogs, motorbikes, church bells — always, in this tiny orchestra, the same three instruments: at least once in life, you should hear this music.

JANE SHAPIRO is the author of two novels, "The Dangerous Husband" and "After Moondog." Her short fiction and journalism have been published in The New York Times, The New Yorker, Harper's Bazaar, *and* Ms., *among many other publications.*

By Frederika Randall

A Busy Crossroads
of History

March 31, 2002

STONE AND NUMBERS

Crowning a hill near Andria, Castel del Monte is pervaded by the mystical recurrence of the number eight. The castle is octagonal as are the towers and the inner courtyard. There are eight rooms on the ground floor and eight on the first floor; the decorative patterns on the portals and columns are almost always repeated eight times. The octagon was held to be a symbol of resurrection, as well as the link between the Earth and the Heavens, so perhaps the Emperor Frederick II, a man of wide-ranging interests, conceived the castle as a kind of symbolic alchemical laboratory.

331

HOMELAND OF THE TRULLI
The Valle d'Itria, in the province
of Bari, is a highly fertile area
whose orchards, vineyards and
almond and olive groves form
a small Mediterranean paradise
amid the surrounding
pastureland. The valley is also
the homeland of the trulli,
small stone houses with conical
roofs that are found all over
the local countryside and
especially in the districts
of Monti, Aja Piccola
and Alberobello (top right).

The sun is homing in on the mountaintop, an
alien spaceship docking, red as a huge San
Marzano tomato. It hovers there above us as
we coast down the Apennine foothills onto
the Tavoliere, the great agricultural plain of Apulia.
It's a gorgeous late December sunset as such sunsets
go — but also a bone of contention. I prod the accel-
erator and squint sideways at my husband, Vittorio,
who sits in the passenger seat, a sphinx. Whose fault
is it that we'll be arriving in the dark? Well, let's just
say we disagree on that point.

It wouldn't really matter except that Apulia's daylight
is special, even here in the Mezzogiorno, the sun-
washed southern half of Italy. Elsewhere light glows;
here, especially as you move south into the part of the
region known as the Salento, the point of the heel of
Italy's boot, light hums with charged particles, it
crackles with electricity — so potent you want to bottle it and take it home.

In its weightless, immaterial way, light is one of the
elemental forces shaping the landscape, the architecture and the anima of this corner of southeast Italy,
known to Italians as Puglia. The light is different here,
a native of the region once explained to me, because
the long, level spur of land, with its miles of silvery-
green olive groves, sits between two seas — the cobalt
blue Adriatic, and the lapis waters of the Ionian — that
mix their reflected sparkle in the limpid Apulian air.

The autostrada runs along the Adriatic side of the
peninsula to Bari, then swings west toward Taranto:
we'll take the highway down the east coast toward
Brindisi. We've seen those three cities — among the
region's largest — previously. This time we're heading
more out of the way.

What's out of the way depends on your perspective, of
course, and that applies to the whole of Apulia: a
place on the far fringe of Western Europe that's a per-

STONE HUTS

It is not clear whether the name "trullo" derives from the Latin *turris* (tower) or from the Greek *tholos* (dome), but the sense is almost the same: the trulli are cylindrical constructions topped by conical roofs. They look like primitive dwellings, but there is nothing primitive about the technique used to build them, which ingeniously solves all structural problems without wooden structures or cement.

Above, the tomato crop. The Puglia region is one of Italy's major tomato producers.

333

CITY LIGHTS

Ostuni is known as the "crèche city," as the photograph makes clear. But in order to understand its other nickname, the "white city," visitors must venture into its oldest neighborhoods in full daylight to feel all the impact of the dazzling brightness of the houses, inimitable examples of Mediterranean architecture.

manent gateway to the Balkans, the Middle East and Asia beyond. Not by chance is this an area criss-crossed by historic roads, whether they be the wide, grassy tratturi – the hundreds of miles-long routes along which sheep made the seasonal journey from the mountain pastures of Abruzzo to the Apulian plain – or the basalt-paved Via Appia, the consular road down to Brindisi, where the Romans launched their ships for the East.

It's a gateway still very much traveled today. In the shadow of the ferries and freighters plying the Adriatic, clandestine vessels of fortune dart across the narrow Strait of Otranto – the Rio Grande of Southern Europe – bearing would-be immigrants who have come halfway around the world. Over the millenniums, Apulia's fer-tile plains have been settled and resettled, fought over by Greeks and Romans, Orthodox and Roman Catholics, Christians and Muslims.

The history books usually begin with the colonists from Sparta who arrived in the 8th century B.C. and built a flourishing center of *Magna Graecia*. But the "indigenous" Daunians, Peucetians and Messapians they found here were also colonizers, migrants from the Balkans and Crete. The Romans made this their territory at the end of the third centu-ry B.C. But not before losing a horrific battle to the brilliant general from Carthage, Hannibal, leaving more than 25,000 of the Roman legions dead at Canne della Battaglia.

When, six centuries later, the Roman Empire shrank to its close, Apulia was swept into the Greek-speaking Eastern Empire. Some Apulians – half easterners, half westerners – had never stopped speaking ancient Greek. Their Byzantine governors hung on for some 600 years, trading territory with Longobard invaders and Arab raiders preying on the Apulian coast. In 846 the Aghlabid conquerers, the ones who occupied Sicily, got a toehold here, seizing the port of Bari and holding it for 25 years. The West reasserted control in the 11th century, when the Normans arrived.

Not long afterward, ragtag bands of Crusaders pledged to the Norman Prince Bohemond sailed off from here to wreak havoc on Muslims in Antioch and the Holy Land.

After the Normans came the Swabians, the Angevins, the Aragonese, the Bourbons and finally the "Piedmontese" as the southerners thought of the new Kingdom of Italy under the House of Savoy. And that's not to mention the incursions made by the Venetians and the Ottomans in their prime. All those great powers left their mark on the landscape, so every town has its own archaeological or architectural style. Today a few people here are finally thinking about conservation, after the running river of postwar real estate development spread concrete around the big cities and down part of the coast. Not much harm ever came to Martina Franca, midway down the region in the stony Murgia highlands. We won't get a good look at it until the following morning.

THE ANCIENT HEART OF OSTUNI

The cathedral of Ostuni, built in the Romanesque-Gothic style between the 15th and the 16th century, features a remarkable rose window portraying Jesus giving his blessing, surrounded by God the Father and the 12 apostles. The Terra district, the nucleus of the old city that first grew up around the cathedral, is still entirely surrounded by 15th-century Aragonese walls.

Virgin forests, sandy beaches

By Robert Riche
June 27, 1993

BY LAND AND BY SEA
The hinterland of the Gargano peninsula is a succession of mountains and plateaus, broken up by ancient woodlands (above). Over 120 miles of coastline and superb beaches offer a wide variety of charming seaside resorts. Below, a view of Peschici; facing page, the beach at Vieste.

Along the southeastern coast of Italy, a little more than a quarter of the way up the Italian boot, a spur of land juts into the Adriatic Sea, looking out across the clear blue-green waters that separate western Europe from the Byzantine east. It is a chalky limestone massif known as the Promontorio del Gargano, or Gargano Peninsula, and it offers many of the finest sandy bathing beaches, spectacular seaside vistas, and some of the most beautiful mountainous forests in the whole of Italy. The 2,000-square-mile Gargano is about 250 miles slightly to the southeast of Rome. Although its southern boundary presents a flat and rather severe rocky landscape alongside the sea, the terrain rises up in its central mass to a densely forested mountain plateau 3,200 feet above sea level where some of the oldest trees in Italy stand in the Foresta Umbra, a 30,000-acre virgin national forest of soaring oak, beech, maple and pine trees. In spring the ground under the trees is carpeted with blue, white and pink wild anemones, marsh marigold and cyclamen.

Farther out on the peninsula, to the east, an irregular jagged coastline is punctuated by promontories that rise hundreds of feet above the Adriatic along sheer calciferous cliffs, then slope down through olive and orange groves, the road plunging and winding around hidden bays and inlets where waves and wind have, over millenniums, carved out subterranean caves and grottoes. There are more than 20 grottoes along the coast of the Gargano, accessible by boat from the sea, some of them beautiful, with centuries of inscriptions and archeological evidence pointing to habitation by people from the Stone Age.

The easternmost point on the peninsula is Vieste, a town with a year-round population of 13,000, and a long history. Many of the early Crusaders passed through the region on their way to the Byzantine Empire and the Holy Land, taking time along the way, as pilgrims and tourists still do today, to visit the Santuario di San Michele and its grotto in the nearby hill town of Monte Sant'Angelo, where the Archangel Michael was supposed to have visited in A.D. 490.

The ancient Greeks traded with Vieste and other towns along the Gargano. But before the Greeks there were the Phoenician traders and fishermen, whose influence is still apparent along the coast in the form of "trabucchi," platforms erected above the sea on stilts. From the platforms nets attached to booms are lowered into the water to catch schools of fish. You find them staked out in isolated areas, always with a lone patient fisherman sitting in a shed tending the equipment.

Between the 15th and 17th centuries, Vieste was repeatedly invaded by the Turks. A rock in the heart of the old town center, Chianca Amara, is dedicated to those thousands of townspeople captured and decapitated in 1554 during an invasion by a Turkish pirate and his men.

The road to the village rises up to the main street, Corso Fazzini, with lovely public gardens along the wide avenue

in full bloom to the left, then arrives shortly in the town's central plaza, Piazza Vittorio Emanuele II. Nobody, however, seems to refer to the piazza by its name. Instead, because it is at a level lower than the original medieval old town, where the fortified castle stands, it is known as Piazza del Fosso or Il Fosso (the ditch). Facing the piazza are several terrace sidewalk cafes, and in the center is an octagonal bandstand where concerts are held during feast days and on some summer evenings.

We eventually emerged into a charming tiny piazza with a stone fountain in the center, crowded by buildings on three sides, looking on the fourth side over a low wall onto the Adriatic 100 feet below.

At the top of the cliff we circled the fortified castle, with its stunning views of Vieste and the distant slopes of olive groves inland and the sea to the east. The fort was built by the Romans and expanded and strengthened in the 13th century at the direction of Frederick II, the eccentric and enlightened Swabian emperor who occupied Apulia at the time, parading through its towns with his elephants and dancing girls and Arab and Italian court. The alleyways are lined with private apartments, with drying laundry like flags waving from lines overhead. Ceramic artisans and other artists work in shops along these alleyways, displaying their glossy, stylishly colorful creations in the windows. The art of shaping clay on the potter's wheel to make bowls and flasks for water, wine and oil is an ancient tradition in the region.

The old town, including the buildings of its 17th-century expansion, clings to the edge of the cliff, the narrow alleyways extending out onto a tongue of land at the point of which is another church, San Francesco — a modest, straightforward structure, once part of a convent that was closed by the French under Napoleon in 1811. From here one can look back along the southern coast with its limestone cliffs, or along the other side to the north of the town with its harbor and its esplanade under a sweeping canopy of palm trees.

It is but a short walk back to the Piazza Fosso, where a sidewalk table at the cafe is a perfect vantage point for observing the pedestrian life of the town's citizens going about their daily business very much as they always have.

ROBERT RICHE, a playwright and novelist,
travels to Europe frequently. His second novel,
"The Vision Thing" (Publish America), appeared this year.

AN EVOLVING LANDSCAPE

The Murgia plateau, which lies in southwestern Puglia, was formed about 60 million years ago and has never ceased to evolve. The winds, seismic activity, atmospheric agents and the hand of man have all molded it at will, while the geological phenomenon known as karsic erosion has carved out ridges, caves and the typical "gravine," deep narrow valleys cut out by the waters.

It's a brisk day with bright blue skies and a northern wind that bites and the ladies of Martina Franca have tossed on their furs to go to market. Mink may sound over the top for southern Italy, but it's right in keeping with the luscious Rococo building fronts of this improbably pretty little town, which took its current shape between the 17th and 18th centuries. The secret of Martina Franca, according to the Italian art historian Cesare Brandi, is that its Baroque design contains no grand palazzi, just humble cottages and streets as narrow as the crooked back alleys of Genoa or Venice. It's a whole city carved up and channeled with Rococo details, like the tracings of a rambling vine, he said.

The other secret is that it's so extravagantly different from the surrounding countryside, the green and rustic Valle d'Itria, which runs north toward Locorotondo. The Valle d'Itria takes its name from a Byzantine cave chapel nearby that was said to hold a magical image of the Virgin Hodegetria, the protectress of imperial Constantinople.

The basic element around here is the rough gray limestone that litters the fields. It is fitted together without mortar to make the stone fences that crisscross the valley, as well the distinctive local housing unit, the trullo, a white-walled, dome-roofed hut decorated with a whitewashed pinnacle. The trullo's mortar-free vault, made of rings of stone that narrow to the top, predates Roman construction and is similar to dwellings found in Cappadocia in Turkey, Sardinia and elsewhere around the Mediterranean. Nobody knows when these picturesque houses came to Apulia, nor whether the name comes from the Greek *tholos* (designating a cupola found on a tomb at Mycenae) or the Latin *turris* (tower). Despite their certainly archaic origins, the oldest trulli standing today seem to have been built in the past three or four centuries.

The triumph of the trullo is to be found in Alberobello, where the whole town, some 1,400 dwellings and the church, is composed of trulli. How huts that belonged in a field came to make up a village is a matter of dispute. Alberobello, literally "beautiful tree," was once a

A GROTTO BY THE SEA

The entry to the grotto of Zinzulusa is at sea level in a bay between Castro and Santa Cesarea Terme. The mass of accretions terminates in a vast open space more than 60 feet high, known as the cathedral, after which the underwater part of the grotto begins. When the first explorers found themselves in this submerged basin they called it "Lago Cocito," after the icy lake described by Dante as the deepest part of the *Inferno*. Actually, only scuba divers may venture there.

A CATHEDRAL ON THE SEA
It was the year 1099 when the
archbishop of Byzantium laid
the first stone, in Trani, of what
was to become the queen
of Puglia's cathedrals; more than
80 years went by before it was
completed – even though it still
had no bell tower. Actually,
it is a complex made up
of three sacred buildings,
superimposed one upon the
other: the hypogeum
(underground vault) of San
Leucio, built in the 7th century;
the crypts of Santa Maria della
Scala and of San Nicola
Pellegrino; and finally the
cathedral itself.
The stupendous bell tower,
erected between the 13th
and 14th centuries, was the
subject of an unusual form
of restoration. Between 1950
and 1960 it was dismantled
and reassembled stone by stone
using the original materials.

341

nial holiday houses built in the roaring 1990's mix suburban-modern comfort with pointy trullo domes.

Only a few miles away, the cool, white-washed hill town of Ostuni seems like another planet. We've booked a room for a few days at an inn based in one of the old fortified farms – like haciendas – that have dominated the agricultural countryside since feudal times. Ostuni, like nearby Ceglie Messapico, traces its origins to the Messapic people, the earliest recorded inhabitants of the Salento peninsula.

From here it's less than an hour south to Lecce, a city famous for its huge population of lawyers and for some of the loveliest and most exuberant Baroque architecture in all of Italy. Rodolfo Fontefrancesco, an architect who has offered to show us around, insists, – with a pinch of provocation – that what people call Lecce's Baroque period is really its Renaissance. All this – he waves at the thick flower garlands, the gargoyle caryatids and foolish putti of the facade of the church of Santa Croce – was started in the 1500's, long before Bernini and Borromini came along, he says.

If sunlight itself had a color it would be that of the local "pietra leccese," the honeyed, golden limestone of which Lecce's many Baroque churches and palazzi are built. Rich in clay, pietra leccese is so soft when it comes from the quarry that it can be modeled like wood, and the voluptuous carving that comes forth is so fine that gilt was once applied directly to the stone. South of Lecce toward Otranto, bits of the ancient Greek presence in the Salento still cling to the language, like the dregs of resinous wine in a cup. Just a few decades ago many people here still spoke Griko, a dialect traceable in part to Doric Greek. In the Griko funeral laments collected by the folklorist Brizio Montinaro, born in the Griko-speaking town of Calimera, the dead wrestle directly with Thanatos in an underworld untouched by Christian saints. Much like the "pizzica," the time-honored local dance of seduction and sexual possession, the Griko love songs are all about hot desire. "Oh lucky little flea, what you get to do," says one song published by Mr. Montinaro, "my sweetheart is at your mercy. On her lovely white flesh you come and go – you pounce upon her bosom."

It is lunchtime and at a nearby table, gentlemen in suits (lawyers?) are devouring "cime di rapa" stewed with oil and garlic with a pleasure so fervent it's almost embarrassing to watch. In this corner of the earth, real men do like their green vegetables.

When we get to Otranto, a pretty, whitewashed city on the sea, we're unlucky to find the little Church of San Pietro, with its 11th-century Byzantine fres-

BRINY WATERS AND SPA WATERS

Built on a ledge high on the cliff top, Santa Cesarea is reflected in the clear waters of the channel of Otranto. Its fame is due largely to its spa waters, which fill four natural grottoes. The names of two of these caves, the "Solfatara" and the "Fetida" derive from the typical smell of the sulfurous waters. Above, the Moorish-style dome of Palazzo Sticchi.

forest, and the first settlers were debtors, petty criminals and other fugitives from the feudal order who hid away in the woods. Later, it seems that the local signore, the Count of Conversano, aiming to cheat the government in Naples out of its property taxes, made all his peasants live here in unmortared trulli so that the whole town could be knocked down and made to disappear overnight if necessary.

Alberobello is one of Apulia's star attractions, and we drive up nervous that we'll be put off by trullo-tourism. But we end up liking the place, even if there are too many shops and its otherworldly: Stonehenge-meets-Potemkin-village ambience. And anyway, if you want to know what real trullo-kitsch looks like, keep on driving east in the direction of Fasano, where baro-

FROM SALENTO TO PARADISE
The area known as the Salento
is the southernmost part
of Puglia, which reaches
out to divide the Adriatic
and the Ionian seas.
The eastern coast, known as the
"Riviera Azzurra Salentina"
(left, a view) and the
southwestern coast meet
at Cape Santa Maria di Leuca,
the tip of the spur of the "Boot."
Here stands a sanctuary
dedicated to the Virgin,
a popular destination with
pilgrims as it is said to be
the "antechamber of Paradise."

343

THE SPLENDORS
OF PUGLIESE BAROQUE

The 19th-century historian Ferdinand Gregorovius called Lecce the "the Florence of the Baroque" and the historic center of this city is a genuine open-air museum formed by a succession of churches, palaces, columns, spires and portals all built in that style. The church of Santa Croce (facing page), which stands in what was formerly the Jewish ghetto, is one of the finest examples of Baroque architecture in the entire region. Below, a detail from the interior of the cathedral; bottom right, two caryatids in the 18th-century Palazzo Marrese.

coes, locked up. But we do see the Romanesque cathedral, and its unforgettable polychrome mosaic floor laid down in 1165, where Norman, Greek and Byzantine ideas of fate and sin intertwine in a great Tree of Life. It hurts to look at these raw medieval images, this universe of graceful animals and rough human beings, especially when you think how much more elegant the mosaics of the Romans were. Poor, unlucky Jonah cast overboard, head down among the seaweed and the fishes.

As the sea road winds down to Santa Maria di Leuca – land's end – the coast turns steep and rocky. Near the spa town of Santa Cesarea Terme, the Grotta Zinzulusa, at sea level, is a cave full of stalactites and stalagmites where we had a wonderful swim on a previous visit. Round the point at Gallipoli, the beaches are white as salt and the sea comes in absurdly beautiful shades of violet and turquoise. We wander through the white alleyways of the old town. It's the hour of the struscio, the evening stroll. From a balcony, two teenagers who look like Britney Spears rest their elbows on pillows as they look down pitilessly on the old folks strolling below. We linger in the huge

fish market, watching gentlemen at a stall eat raw sea urchins from the shell. It's getting late. Time to begin the journey home.

On the way we swing by the caves of Castellana (not as exciting as we were led to think) and Castel del Monte, the mysterious octagonal castle built in the 13th century by the Hohenstaufen King Frederick II (not to be missed). At Ruvo di Puglia there is the Jatta Museum, a collection of Greek red figure vases and rhyton drinking cups (excellent). Up the coast past Bari, we stroll though Molfetta and Trani, each with its monumental Romanesque cathedral thrillingly perched on the very edge of the sea.

In Trani the fishermen are bringing in the afternoon catch. Octopus, red mullet, anchovies and cicale di mare, like little lobster tails. I try to remember the fish I've seen on Greek pottery. Was this what they caught in Homer's Mediterranean, or have the fish moved on, too?

FREDERIKA RANDALL is a journalist and translator living in Rome.

By Frederika Randall

ROCK HARD
and Still Untamed

September 3, 2000

THE CITY OF STONE

A spur divides the two natural limestone "amphitheaters" from which the homes of ancient Matera were dug out of the living rock: the Sasso Caveoso and the Sasso Barisano (right). The latter area, currently undergoing intensive restoration, is a hodge-podge of houses clustered around the base of the cathedral, almost as if beseeching grace and benediction. It appears that the name Sasso Barisano derives from its orientation toward the city of Bari. Above, a detail from a fresco in a cave church portraying the *Madonna del Melograno* (the Virgin of the Pomegranate).

Nightfall does not come gently to Matera. It's more like a flash flood rising from the bottom of the ravine. One minute, I am watching a couple of bats wing over the rooftops beneath the hotel terrace where I sit. The next minute, they are invisible. The houses on the hill go gray as tombstones, and all that is human and terrestrial turns pale and wan.

Up in the heavens, though, something like the Creation is happening. The sky, a dome of crazy cobalt blue, is streaked with fresh phosphorus stars. A big coppery moon is pitched on the horizon, smoldering like the halo of a Byzantine Madonna.

This must be something like the way the cosmos once unfolded every night before the watching eyes of Dark Ages villagers, or Homeric-era Greek wanderers, or the Paleolithic nomads who 15,000 years ago first burrowed in here and made their cave shelters in the Sassi, the city's distinctive limestone cliffs. Art, myth, religion — you can see how they grew out of nights like this. Some giant forces were at work out there, and it wouldn't be wise not to pay attention.

Big thoughts like these hadn't yet crossed my mind when I began the day under brilliant April sunshine, barreling along the almost empty roads of the Basento Valley into the heart of Basilicata, in southeastern Italy. I was on my way back for a return look at Matera's frescoed cave churches, and to explore some even more remote corners of this remote and rugged region.

The hilly part of southern Italy between the more populous coastlines of Campania and Puglia, Basilicata is a sort of Italian Appalachia, where nature hasn't been

MYSTIC DESOLATION

While the Sasso Barisano is, in its own way, elegant and full of fine buildings, the Sasso Caveoso is a portrait of the secluded immobility of times gone by. Visitors find themselves lost in a surreal atmosphere, swallowed up in a vortex where past and present merge. Everything is the same and yet everything is different: grottoes, porticoes, long stairways, little churches. And, in the middle of all this, are the "vicinati," the characteristic little public squares surrounded by houses. Here, movie directors such as Pierpaolo Pasolini and Mel Gibson shot their films on the Passion of Christ.

tamed by humans and the people don't like being bossed around, either. An Appalachia where at one time or another prehistoric shepherds, Greeks, Romans, Byzantines, Lombards, Saracens, Normans, Swabians and Albanians fleeing the Turks after the fall of Constantinople have passed through.

My husband, Vittorio, was actually the one pushing the speed limit, while I read out an occasional passage from our faithful traveling companion, *Christ Stopped at Eboli*, by Carlo Levi. The road to Matera from Potenza, the regional capital, coasts along the valley, and once you get past a gargantuan snake of a modern housing project on Potenza's outskirts, scarcely another building appears except for a few tiny farmhouses. There are olive groves, stands of ilex, pine and cypress, and the glint of greenhouses on the hillsides. Along the way, there's the turnoff for Aliano, the village where in 1935, Levi, a painter who was a member of the anti-Fascist group Giustizia e Libertà from Turin, was sent into confinement by Mussolini.

It was Levi, with his passionate account of his year in Basilicata, who first awakened cosmopolitan Italy to the flinty poverty and archaic dignity of this place. Trained as a physician, he went out to see the sick in their miserable homes. Many, back from America after a lifetime of hard work, now had nothing to protect them from endemic malaria but the little photo of Franklin D. Roosevelt that so often hung over a returned emigrant's bed. The reason their lives were so hard, they told him, was that Christ had never got farther than Eboli (a city toward Naples). Civilization, in other words, had never climbed these mountains.

About beautiful Matera, Levi wrote that it was a "sad, gray" city that spiraled downward like the circles of Dante Alighieri's *Inferno*, where "men, women, children and beasts" shared the same cramped caves. That vision of hell disturbed Italians from more prosperous regions, and after the war, there were calls to level the Sassi. It didn't happen, but in 1952, old Matera was evacuated.

THE ANCIENT CAVE CHURCHES

About 120 cave churches bear witness to the presence of numerous monks and ascetics in Matera from the 6th and 18th centuries. Above, the interior of the church of Santa Maria d'Idris, cut almost entirely out of the living rock. Right, a fresco showing the *Coronation of the Virgin*, in the church of Santa Lucia alle Malve, the only one of these churches still open for worship.

Then in 1993, Unesco designated the Sassi of Matera a World Heritage Site. It was an ironic and welcome turn of events.

Today, people are moving back into the old town, our guide, Giuseppe, tells us later that day as we gaze over the canyon carved by the Gravina torrent far below, before setting off on our tour. "Let's just hope they don't start painting everything up," he says, narrowing his eyes fiercely at the freshly painted facade of a cave house that is just a whisper the green side of cement gray.

He points out another one below us that has the faintest aura of yellow. "The Sassi are not in color," Giuseppe says. "The Sassi are black and white."

Ash gray inside and out, the dwellings in the Sassi were hewn out of the natural caves and water cisterns that run through the chalky rock. Blocks were cut out and used to add front rooms and facades, some quite ornate. The roofs served as the roadbed to the level above, and there were gardens and little public squares on various levels.

In a book about Matera's cave dwellings, the Italian architect Pietro Laureano shows how they were designed around a sophisticated system to capture and store water, a precious resource here after the uplands were deforested by farming and grazing as far back as the Neolithic era. The caves have affinities with those of Cappadocia and the ancient city of Petra, among others around the Mediterranean, and they are anything but poor architecture, Laureano says. The Sassi deteriorated badly under the Fascist regime, when paved roads wiped out all the green areas and public spaces, and economic conditions

WHERE TIME STOPPED
In a period in which rapid change seems to be engulfing ancestral social and cultural models, Basilicata has largely retained the proud purity of its own roots, offering the visitor living contact with the land and its origins. How else to measure "progress" without a sense of the past?

351

An Italian Olympus

**THE TREE
OF A THOUSAND SHAPES**

Frost and lightning merely graze
it, wind and storm may bend it
but it will not break. Its proud
bearing is worthy of its name.
The loricate pine wears the
armor of the ancient Romans
(lorica) and the thick hexagonal
plates of its bark protect it from
the assault of nature.
Facing page, the park contains
the highest peaks of the
southern Apennines.

traces of the southern limit of quaternary glaciation can be seen.

On the rocks of the thankless, almost lifeless, terrain grows the proud loricate pine, a Balkan species that was not believed to be present in Italy until the 20th century. Rough, knotty, sometimes gnarled and twisted, its characteristic candelabra-shaped boughs reaching up toward the sky give it a dignified bearing. In the immense beech woods and in the remains of what were once dense oak forests, wolves, otters and wildcats still survive. With luck visitors may catch sight of the majestic bearded vulture, or lammergeyer, wheeling high in the sky. The lammergeyer has a fondness for lamb, especially the head and the bones, which it drops on the sharp rocks far below to shatter them and extract the marrow.

The sanctuary of the Madonna del Pollino, towering high over the valley of the river Frido, is a first class panoramic view point; from the greenery of the woods emerge the massive bulk of Mount Pollino and the Serra del Prete. The park offers visitors a wide variety of excursions, and since the trails are not always well marked adventure is always around the corner, especially in its higher reaches.

Whether scaling mountain peaks or descending into the bowels of the earth, trekkers cannot afford to miss the breathtaking Gole del Raganello (the Raganello Gorges), which can be reached from Civita and San Lorenzo Bellizzi. The river has eroded the rocks for thousands of years, finding the line of least resistance and carving out a narrow canyon hundreds of meters deep. Birds of prey of all types soar in the crisp air; free and bold, making their nests in the steepest walls of the canyon.

But the Pollino is not only nature. The extraordinary sanctuary of Santa Maria dell'Armi, on the southeastern side, near Cerchiara, is built into the rock at an altitude of more than 3,000 feet. It includes part of the original 15th-16th century construction and traces of 15th-century frescoes.

Two small towns with a singular origin are San Paolo Albanese and San Constantino Albanese, founded in the 16th century by Albanian refugees fleeing from the city of Korone, assailed by the Turks. For feast days and weddings the people dust off their highly colored traditional costumes, decorated with ribbons, embroidery and trinkets. The older inhabitants still speak a dialect with strong traces of the speech of their forefathers.

High above the Crati and Coscile plains, the Pollino massif rises majestically between two regions, Basilicata and Calabria, to form the highest peaks in the southern Apennines. The area was declared a National Park in 1990. *Mons Apollineum* (Mount Apollo) was probably thus named by the ancient Greeks, early colonizers of southern Italy, because it reminded them of their own Olympus: a solitary and sacred mountain, an isolated observer of vast plains inhabited by mere humans. This lonely area is covered by forests and meadows, mountain springs, deep gorges and panoramas of wild beauty. The Calabrian side is steep and stark, while the side toward Basilicata is a succession of gentle slopes, meadowlands and dense woods. On this side of the Pollino

Built by the Normans in the 12th century and restored by Frederick II, who erected the "Emperor's tower" or the "eagle's nest," the castle of Melfi is a strikingly irregular and imposing structure. Its august rooms have been the site of at least four Vatican councils and it was here, in 1089, that the first crusade was proclaimed.

were so grim that people had to crowd into their storerooms and stables with their animals.

Around the seventh century, when this part of Italy answered to the Byzantine empire, Greek-rite hermit monks started to use the grottoes as primitive chapels. Those Easterners were chased away by Roman Catholic Benedictines in the 12th century, but religious art here continued to have a strong Byzantine flavor. In the wall paintings of the little Matera church of Santa Maria de Idris, a stylized Virgin appears with a precious amphora of water. One of the flanking saints is giving the Latin benediction.

Another holds his fingers in the perpendicular Orthodox way. In time, many of the chapels became houses, wine caves or refuges for shepherds. In Santa Lucia alle Malve, for example, you can see where metal rods were stuck into the decorated walls so that wool could be carded. A large piece of painted surface with a figure of St. Agatha was converted into the pillar of an old kitchen.

Next morning, up on the plain over the ravine, the air smells of wild thyme and nepitella, a kind of wild mint. Hawks are circling overhead – falchi grillai, or cricket hawks, we're told. This area, too, is honeycombed with chapels.

**ROBERT GUISCARD'S
LAST RESTING PLACE**

Above, the tomb of the Altavilla
family in the abbey of the
Santissima Trinità at Venosa,
where the Norman conqueror
Robert Guiscard is said to be
buried. In a separate sepulcher
lies his first wife Aberarda,
whom he repudiated and
locked up in the castle of Melfi.

In one low, deep cave, travelers have carved hundreds of crosses into the rock. On the wall, there's a sober, beautiful red and blue painting of the *Madonna del Melograno* (Virgin of the Pomegranate) at the Annunciation. Others to look out for include San Pietro in Principibus, Santa Maria della Colomba and the Cripta del Peccato Originale, with its delicate 10th-century frescoes on the theme of original sin.

From Matera, the road turns north toward Venosa and the traces of a different era. When the Romans first marched through these parts around 300 B.C., they found the Lucanians, a local people who roasted their meat on long bronze skewers, drank a lot of heavy red wine and celebrated Dionysus. The Latin poet Horace was born here in 65 B.C., when this was a thriving provincial Roman city. Today, it looks like a toy town, with diminutive two-story buildings decorated with iron railings, a big castle and a major archaeological site on the outskirts. On the way there, we have to stop and wait for a large, pokey flock of sheep. In Venosa are the ruins of an amphitheater, a second-century B.C. Roman domus and a thermal bath with mosaic floors from Imperial times. Down the road, several narrow tunnels and tiny cubicles are all that are left of late-Roman-era Jewish catacombs. Early Christians built a church on top of a Roman temple,

355

and on top of that stand the grandiose ruins of a unfinished Benedictine abbey, where the Norman conquerer Robert Guiscard is said to be buried.

A tour of the small but thoroughly interesting collection of the national archaeological museum in the dazzling, wind-swept Norman castle of Melfi, not far from Venosa, gives you an idea of how much wealth a fifth-century B.C. Lucanian nobleman could afford to take to the grave. He had fanciful crowns shaped of leaves of beaten gold, amber necklaces imported from the Baltic, Etruscan pottery and red-figure Attic vases, glass pitchers and bronze serving plates, and a set of bronze armor with a scary riot-gear-style helmet, made to imitate the weaponry of Greek hoplite warriors. Those luxury goods were supposed to allow the departed to carry their reputations to the beyond. And in a way they have, because we wouldn't know much about them without their tombs to dig up.

Heading south from Melfi the next day, we stop at Rapolla, a pinched, hilly little town of low white houses that looks like a village in Greece or Albania. In a tiny square, some long-legged girls are playing volleyball without a net. I wonder if they have been to the museum in Melfi to see the fine imperial Roman lady on the beautiful sarcophagus (imported from Asia Minor) that was dug up in their town. The languid, liquid marble folds of her robe suggest a level of comfort and ease that isn't known in these parts today.

Rapolla's onetime cathedral of Santa Lucia is locked, but a passer-by calls her neighbor and gets the key. The graceful, spiritual little church, built in 1200, has just been meticulously restored, with glass floor panels so that you can peer down and see the caves of the Byzantine mystics on which it was built.

Back on the road, we drive back and forth for nearly an hour looking for the turnoff to another cave chapel dedicated to Santa Lucia. We are just about to give up when we find the road, leading into the woods. Ferns, nettles and violets grow up to the door of the tiny, whitewashed church. We peer in through an iron grate: there are a couple of wooden benches and many vases of fresh flowers. The apse is painted floor to ceiling in stylized red and black scenes from the saint's life. The floor is mossy where the chapel runs back into the rock.

Our next stop is Rionero in Vulture, which like Rapolla and the nearby town of Barile (not to mention Matera) was repopulated by Albanian Christians fleeing the Turks in the 15th and 16th centuries. Today, the local dialect is heavily inflected with Albanian, one more reminder of how close Basilicata is to the Balkans.

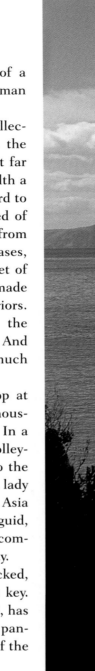

THE PEARL OF THE BAY
Here lie beaches, rocks, an enchanting undersea world for the delight of divers and caves with a wealth of strange geological formations. Maratea, a charming town overlooking the Bay of Policastro, has many strings to its bow and it is no accident that its name means "goddess of the sea." Above, the spectacular statue of the Redeemer on the top of Mount san Biagio, above Maratea. At about 70 feet high, it is second only to its counterpart above Rio de Janeiro.

Rionero, on the bottom slopes of Mount Vulture, a spent volcano, is the region's prime wine-growing area. The excellent local wine – made with the Aglianico vines imported some 2,700 years ago by the settlers of Magna Graecia – has had a DOC, an official wine denomination, since 1971.

The Aglianico del Vulture red is rich and clean, good company for the stewed wild cardoncelli mushrooms, the creamy fave e cicoria (bean puree with greens), the home-made scorze di mandorla and cavatelli pasta, the grilled sausages flavored with fennel, and the many interesting sheep and cow cheeses found here. These include the rare caciocavallo podolico, made from the exotically flavored milk of a cow that grazes only the highest pastures, chewing up rare grasses and wildflowers, tender mushroom caps or "rucola selvatica," the tiny-leafed spicy wild rocket

(we lunched on slivers of that wonderfully spicy, crumbly yellow cheese from Latteria Rizzi, a cheese shop in Matera.)

We hike partway up Mount Vulture hoping to catch a glimpse of some of those high-grazing cows, but no luck. What we can just see are the pretty Monticchio lakes nearby, where, Horace tells us, he once ran away from his wet nurse as an infant and got lost in the woods. Fortunately – befitting a baby who was going to become a famous poet – magical doves came and covered him with bay and myrtle leaves, so that the bears and vipers wouldn't harm him.

Heading back toward Potenza and Naples, we make a last stop at Castel Lagopesole, a big square reddish castle built in 1242 by Frederick II of Swabia (or of Hohenstaufen), who ruled southern Italy. It dominates the heights so absolutely that a chicken couldn't have crossed the road in the valley below without the Hohenstaufens knowing about it.

The sun is hot and a cuckoo begins to hoot, loud as a foghorn. If you think of it in premodern terms, says Vittorio, who likes to read history, Frederick was probably the most tolerant and enlightened signore who ever ruled these parts. What would Basilicata be like today if his line had survived and the corrupt, absentee Angevins, Spanish and Bourbons had never gained control?

Much more prosperous, but possibly not so wild and beautiful, I hazard.

"Hmm," Vittorio says. "Yes, that's probably right."

———

FREDERIKA RANDALL is a journalist and translator who lives in Rome.

357

By Paul Hofmann

CALABRIA
By the Sea

September 26, 1999

THE TWO FACES OF AMANTEA
Situated on two promontories of the Tyrrhenian coast, Amantea (right) is a little town with a dual nature. The silent old town, perched on the hillside, is characterized by the contrast between the mansions of the nobility and the humble homes of ordinary farmers. The new town has expanded toward the coast, kneeling before the sea that constitutes its wealth and its pride. The venerable, good-natured rivalry between fishermen and farmers is revived every August with a chess tournament held on the promenade, using a large chessboard with living "pieces".

From the parapet of the little piazza at Tropea in Calabria, the limestone cliff drops perpendicularly 150 feet, and you see the sea gulls wheeling below you. Every pebble and rock outcrop on the deep bottom of the aquamarine sea is visible. Such crystal-clear waters are an exception today off the European shores of the Mediterranean Sea. Yet Calabria, the rocky southwestern subpeninsula of the Italian peninsula, boasts many bays and coves that are still limpid. Many are now surrounded by condominium developments, shuttered most of the year, as well as by beach hotels and a plethora of recently built pizzerias.

Tropea, one of Calabria's jewels, is framed by such modern developments and by campsites. But the ancient town, high up on its panoramic promontory, has retained a measure of authenticity, and the sea is still a palette of blues, from nearly green to azure to indigo. Happily, the annual ecological surveys of Italy's 5,000 miles of seashore have up to now given the coastal waters here and in most of Calabria a clean bill of health.

That airy lookout, with its bronze cannon and its clusters of elderly men on the stone benches who discuss the catches brought in by the fishing boats and the national soccer championship, commands one of the greatest views of the Tyrrhenian coastline.

The fine sand on the beach at the foot of the towering cliff is white, in season dotted with gaudy umbrellas. A craggy rock just off Tropea, today linked to the mainland by a narrow strip of land, is crowned by an old Benedictine sanctuary, St.-Mary-of-the-Isle. A few miles to the south the green Cape Vaticano recalls the

THE SANCTUARY OF ST.-MARY-OF-THE-ISLE

In remote times a gargantuan block of sandstone broke away from the coast near Tropea, giving birth to an islet, but little by little the sand accumulated by the waves reconnected it with the mainland. According to legend, during the days of the persecution of the iconoclasts (8th century A.D.), a statue of the Virgin was found on the islet, perhaps abandoned by the fleeing faithful. The bishop wanted to set it in a natural cave, but as the cave was too small it was decided to saw off the legs of the statue. But at the first attempt to do this the bishop dropped dead. And so a sanctuary in honor of the Virgin was built on the cliff in order to provide a fit setting for her effigy.

epoch five centuries ago when the papal state had its own fleet of galleys.

On the horizon looms the cone of Stromboli, one of Europe's few active volcanoes, a 3,040-foot-high younger cousin of Mount Etna in Sicily and Vesuvius near Naples. On clear days one can see the cloud of smoke that often hangs over the crater of the small circular island. Sunsets in Tropea have the color of amethyst.

The town, which today has a permanent population of 7,000, was successively Greek, Roman and Arabic, and through the ages had to endure the multifarious invaders who passed through Calabria or occupied it. The Normans, who drove out the Saracens in the 11th century, built Tropea's remarkable cathedral with the sand-colored stone of the district.

If you hear English spoken in the narrow streets or at the cafe tables in the squares, the chances are they aren't tourists but Americans visiting relatives; enormous numbers left the region for America early in the century. The Calabrians, unlike the lively Neapolitans, are often reserved; the visitor who approaches them civilly will be met with grave courtesy. A sojourn in Tropea is particularly pleasant because it's not just a seaside resort but also a genuine old Calabrian town with an intense local life.

Many thousands of Italians from the north pour into Tropea and other Calabrian beach towns in August, the nation's hallowed vacation period, when Milan, Turin and the other big cities become deserted. During four visits to Calabria in spring 1998 and winter 1999, I avoided the summer crowds, enjoyed many sunny days, obtained favorable hotel rates and ate deliciously fresh seafood. I also saw owners of second homes on the coast who come over the weekends from Naples and Rome, and some early guests from northern Europe.

In addition to the sea, there is the subtropical vegetation – tall palms, pines, cypresses, cactuses, fig and

ON WINGS OF SONG

The citizens of Catanzaro's enthusiasm for opera was satisfied in 1830 with the inauguration of the city's Teatro Reale Francesco. Later renamed the Teatro Comunale, it housed troops during the first World War. In the 1940's the opera house was demolished, ushering in a doleful period of silence that lasted more than half a century. But in 2002 there arose the Nuovo Politeama (top left), the newest of the great Italian opera houses, and an acoustic and architectural triumph.

lemon trees and vines everywhere. A ruined castle scowls from almost every other hill, some of them like the one in Cirella, adapted as a setting for concerts, plays and other summer events. The rocky coastline is studded with ancient watchtowers that, until the early 19th century, would alert the villagers and townspeople when they sighted pirates.

In Cirella, 125 miles north of Tropea, I looked up old friends who have retired to Calabria from Virginia (they are of Northern Italian stock) to live in a pleasant whitewashed house with a flower garden and a terrace looking out on a tiny, privately owned offshore island.

My headquarters in Cirella was a new hotel in a restored seaside villa that the dukes of the Gonzaga clan built for themselves in the 18th century. The noble complex vaunts a walled garden with palms, giant cactuses, shrubbery and flower beds, and a private beach. My large room, looking out on the garden, was soberly but comfortably furnished and had a modern bathroom.

The old, still-inhabited village of Cirella, a short distance from the shoreside resort, climbs a slope below the ruins of a hilltop town that Hannibal razed 2,200 years ago, and that in later centuries was rebuilt and destroyed again, the last time by a French fleet in 1806. Nearby, a little to the south, is the beach resort of Diamante, with a tree-lined boardwalk. A jewelry trader from West 47th Street in Manhattan, who was spending a few weeks in Calabria, walked with me around the crooked streets, showing me the frescoes that contemporary local and foreign artists have painted on facades of the old buildings.

Another resort, eight miles to the north, Scalea, with ancient houses marching up a hill and a modern seaside neighborhood, has good hotels on either side of a rock with a restored medieval fortress on top; underneath are caves in which stone-age tools were found. The fortress and its fenced approaches are now privately owned.

During one of my recent trips to Calabria, I also revisited the inland city of Cosenza, 54 miles southeast. Its Old Town, a warren of lanes around the Gothic cathedral, huddles below a hill with a massive, square castle and an octagonal 13th-century tower. Modern Cosenza, with broad, regular streets, extends from the confluence of the Busento and Crati Rivers almost all the way to the village of Rende, the seat of the University of Calabria. Built in 1973, this state school is one of the very few Italian institutions of higher learning with dorms on campus.

Somewhere below the waters of the Busento the king of the Visigoths, Alaric, is supposed to be buried, along

with a fabulous treasure. The barbarian conqueror died in A.D. 412 in or near Cosenza, and his warriors are said to have forced their prisoners to divert the river and dig a royal tomb, into which they lowered Alaric's body together with spoils from their sack of Rome two years earlier. They then restored the original course of the Busento and massacred the prisoners, so that the site of the grave would remain secret.

During World War II the chief of the Nazi SS, Heinrich Himmler, dispatched a team of engineers and archeologists to Cosenza, hoping they would locate the secret tomb of the Germanic king and recover the Roman gold. They failed, as have other treasure hunters before and since.

Cosenza is the obvious starting point for exploring the sullenly mountainous Sila massif. During my latest visit, in January, when the icy wind known as the buran swept down the continent from Siberia and hit southern Italy, snow and ice on the roads made a foray into the forested heights inadvisable. During an earlier Calabrian tour, the Sila reminded me of the Alps.

The mountain area is an enormous, rugged block of granite, rising to an altitude of 6,332 feet in the Botte Donato heights, which are usually snowcapped until June. There are still patches of dense woods – pines, spruces, oaks, chestnuts and beeches – from which in antiquity the Greek city-states of Sicily and even the Athenians cut timber for their ships. Vast pastures cover the plateaus.

About 100 specimens of the light-gray Apennine wolf, a protected species, are known to be still living in the Sila, especially in its national park. A pair of wolves

ORACLE ON THE PROMONTORY

It is said that in ancient times a prophetess lived on Capo Vaticano (above) and that the name of the place derives from the Latin *vaticinium* (reply). At Paola, not far from Cosenza, stands the sanctuary of San Francesco di Paola (facing page). A hermit said to have worked miracles, the saint (1416-1507) founded the Order of the Minim friars, based on a strict way of life inspired by the ideals of St. Francis of Assisi.

Men of bronze defeat time

By Louis Inturrisi
July 8, 1984

The two great seas into which Italy dips its toe – the Tyrrhenian and the Ionian – have always been rich sources of legend and adventure. It was, after all, in these waters that Ulysses found himself in Homer's *Odyssey*, and it was in the cities along their coasts that the world first felt the expansion and surge of the art and civilization known as *Magna Graecia*.

On the Tyrrhenian side is Scilla, built on rocks that stretch out into the sea. This is the Scylla that, according to Homer, was ruled over by a female monster with six heads, twelve feet and a terrifying wail that let up only while she was devouring the unfortunate ships that had successfully made it into her territory past the harrowing whirlpools of Charybdis.

A little farther south along the eastern coast of Sicily are the Scogli dei Ciclopi, or the Cyclops Reef. These are supposed to be the rocks hurled by the giant Polyphemus after Ulysses had blinded him by thrusting a blazing stake into his huge single eye. Thousands of years after Ulysses and his brave men outlived the Cyclops and the trials at Scylla and Charybdis, the little town of Riace, 20 miles south of Scilla, is becoming famous for a similar event involving a Greek ship, brave warriors and a shipwreck along a reef that nearly – but didn't – destroy them.

The story begins on Aug. 16, 1972, when Stefano Mariottini, an amateur archeologist, was vacationing in Calabria and enjoying his favorite hobby: deep-sea fishing. On that afternoon, when Mr. Mariottini was only some 300 yards offshore and in about 20 feet of water, something caught his eye that looked remarkably like a human hand sticking up out of the sandbed beneath him. He swam closer, brushed away some of the loose sand and confirmed his suspicion.

Four days later, a crew of frogmen hoisted to the surface a life-size bronze statue of a Greek warrior that subsequent investigations would disclose was a Greek original of the mid-fifth century B.C. that had probably been lying in the same sandbed for more than 2,000 years. The next day, another statue of a warrior, differing slightly from the first, was raised from the same sandbed, thus ending the long sleep of the two statues that came to be known as the Bronzes of Riace, after the little marina town where they were found.

Because of the sand that encased them, both statues were found in excellent condition, which only improved after their restoration. One of the warriors has flowing hair tied with a headband, the other wears a helmet and has lost one eye. The restoration began in Reggio Calabria, where the initial cleaning of the statues was done, but in 1975 it was decided to send the statues to the restoration center of the Superintendent of Antiquities in Florence.

Using specially designed tools to reach the less accessible parts of the statues, such as the spaces between the hair and in the beard, the workmen removed centuries of encrusted sand deposits. It was only then that the truly remarkable features of these splendid examples of Greek sculpture came to light: the eyes, a composite of ivory, amber and limestone, are full of expression and majesty. The lips and the nipples are of copper with a reddish tint, while the teeth of one and the eyelashes of both are of silver. The veins along the calves and in the tops of the hands are so beautifully delineated that it is easy to forget that the medium is bronze and not marble. As the cleaning continued, a noble patina of shining mirror black began to emerge as the warriors slowly shook off the dullness of two millennia.

The insides of the statues were packed with sand, lime and shells. In order to empty the bronzes, an operation that could not be carried out through the existing small openings, it was necessary to remove the lead clamps that close the cavities at the feet and suck out the accumulation, which had hardened over the centuries. Finally, the statues were submitted to several conservation treatments that included immersions in special fluids to help prevent bronze disease. When the two warriors were finally unveiled to the public in their restored glory for the first time in 1981 in Florence and later that year in Rome, they drew record crowds and long lines that erupted on several occasions into minor riots among the disappointed who were unable to get into the exhibit before closing time.

LOUIS INTURRISI was a travel and food writer based in Rome. He also taught writing there at John Cabot University until his death in 1997.

**MOUNTAIN
BETWEEN TWO SEAS**
At the southern tip of the
Apennines an imposing pyramid
rises up for well over 6,000 feet
between the Tyrrhenian
and Ionian seas. This is the
Aspromonte (literally, the
"craggy mountain"), a land
of legend – brigands, ravines,
wild and impenetrable forests –
whose very name betrays
its rugged, inhospitable nature.
Today part of a national park,
the Aspromonte area is rich
in water and has many
spectacular waterfalls.
On the preceding pages, late
summer mist over the Campo
Tenese plateau on the Calabrian
side of Mount Pollino.

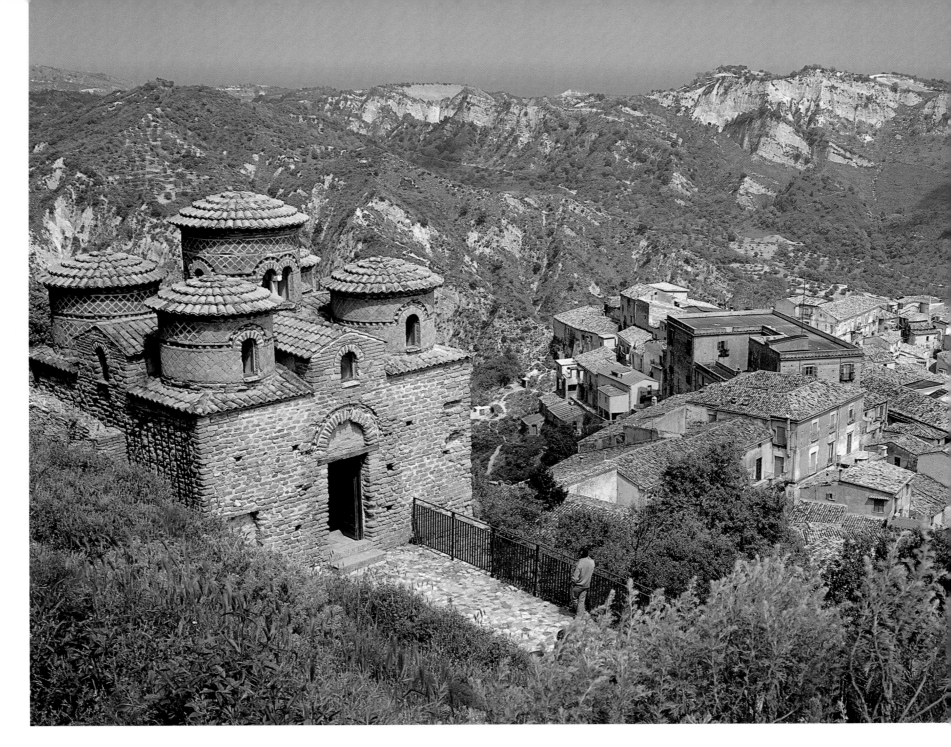

were sighted on the outskirts of Cosenza in the coldest days of January, but I saw nothing more than a few timid stray dogs. Natural and artificial lakes in the thinly populated mountains supply the water for power plants. It's a great environment for hiking, camping and, in the cold winters, skiing.

During my latest stay in Cosenza I reread chapters from Norman Douglas's *Old Calabria*, published in 1915. This intrepid and quirky Scottish traveler who, among other feats, traversed the Sila on foot, tells of villages without male adults – they had all emigrated to America – and of grinding poverty, brigandage, widespread malaria and even pockets of cholera.

Since then, Calabria has come a long way. It is as healthy now as the rest of Italy. Many Calabrians who emigrated to Germany as "guest workers" in the 1950's have returned and bought property or started businesses. The region seems ready for an economic takeoff. With the projected manufacturing plants, hotels and vacation villages, the big challenge is to keep the waters of Tropea and the other Calabrian bays and nooks as clean as they are today, and its landscape relatively uncluttered. I, for one, am reasonably confident that at least some of this beautiful coast will remain pristine; having been hooked on Calabria, I plan to return.

PAUL HOFFMAN is a former chief of The New York Times *Rome bureau. He is the author of 13 nonfiction books including* "Cento Città: A Guide to the Hundred Cities & Towns of Italy." *He lives in Rome.*

A BYZANTINE MASTERPIECE
Nestling on the slopes of Mount Consolino, the so-called Cattolica di Stilo, probably built in the 10th century, is a rare example of Byzantine art in Italy. Neat and compact, it looks like a small cube (a mere 8 X 8 yards) topped by a forest of rounded domes. Inside, the way entering light slants down from above shows how the structure's designers deliberately aimed to create symbolically significant lighting effects.

**THE SOUTHERNMOST
TOWN IN ITALY**
A rocky spur holds the ruins
of a medieval castle. Below lies
an orderly handful of houses.
Palizzi, the southernmost town
in the Italian peninsula, lies
between the Aspromonte
and the Ionian Sea.

By E.J. Dionne Jr.

Many-faced, Contradictory,
ANCIENT SICILY

June 9, 1985

Few places in the world are as underrated as Sicily. The fact is that Sicily may be the most attractive, most culturally privileged place in the complicated country called Italy. To begin with, few places have been occupied by more foreign powers. But it is also the reason why Sicily has, among other things, some of the best Greek ruins in the world; why it has Arab and Norman buildings, and why parts of Palermo look like Bourbon Spain. And whatever damage they did, the occupiers usually – although not always – respected what had been built before they came. The dialect is as much a pastiche as the architecture. Sicilian includes Greek words and French words, Arab words and Spanish; Sicilians have borrowed freely over the years.

There are many approaches to Sicily. It can be, like Cyprus or parts of southern France, a place to relax, read and stare peacefully into a sunset. It can be a lesson to be learned, a place that contains pieces of the history of so many other places as well as its own. It is an island where you can eat and drink well, swim and hike up in the mountains. You can even ski here. And whatever you choose to do, you can be certain that Sicilians will be warm and have few predispositions against whatever it was that you chose – although the friendliness toward outsiders can be matched by a certain reserve.

What follows is only one approach, with some variations. You can fly into Palermo, Trapani or Catania; then, where you choose to start, how fast you want to go, which Sicily you are seeking – these will be up to you. Taormina is carved into a hillside that drops 675 feet straight down into the warm, blue Mediterranean

COLORED TESSERAE

Villa del Casale in Piazza Armerina, in the province of Enna, has magnificent mosaics from the 4th century, among the largest ever found. Above, the *Mosaic of the Ten Girls*; their gym outfits perhaps represent the first known examples of the bikini in the history of art. "The most surprising religious gem dreamed of by the human mind" is how, in 1885, the French novelist, Guy de Maupassant, described the Cappella Palatina in Palermo, a 12th-century masterpiece with a blaze of Byzantine mosaics (left).

373

W AS IN WHITAKER
Above, the entrance hall
of Villa Malfitano in Palermo,
a magnificent 19th-century
residence in the Neoclassical
style built by Joseph Whitaker,
an English businessman who had
emigrated to Sicily. The pride
of the villa is its luxuriant garden,
whose hundreds of exotic plant
species include a clump
of papyrus growing in a pond.
A flower bed in the shape of a W
commemorates the surname
of the proprietor.

and looks up to snow-capped Mount Etna. Its well-preserved Greek Theater, set into the hills, dates back to the third century B.C. The winding drive up the mountainside at times cuts right through the rocks. To one side are the hills that rise up to the ruined walls of the village of Castelmola; on the other side, a drop straight to the sea. Along the way, you will skirt remarkable coves; rock formations rise up starkly, as if thrown out by some angry god.

The city has been amply discovered by others, notably Germans and Scandinavians, and it can be crowded, in season and out. But if you are not obsessed with getting away from other people, Taormina amply rewards a visit. Some people spend hours in the terraced gardens behind the San Domenico Palace Hotel in the late afternoon and at dusk, scanning the sky from Mount Etna to the sea. It is the sort of sunset you are unlikely to see anywhere else. The town's public gardens are a good place for an after-lunch stroll. And you can escape the crowds on the main thoroughfares by walking along

the quiet back streets that wind down the hillside, past bleached stone buildings.

Syracuse, 65 miles to the southeast, is a singular reminder of the richness and extraordinary complexity of Sicily's past. In its heyday, the city had little to do with Rome or Italy. It was founded by Corinthian colonists in 8th century B.C. and became one of the wealthiest and most powerful cities of Greater Greece (it was also the home of Archimedes, the geometrician.) For this reason Syracuse has some of the finest Greek ruins in the world. Its Greek Theater dates from the fifth century B.C., and when you look at it, you should remind yourself that Aeschylus' *Persians* had its opening night there. The theater is in the middle of an archeological park – it closes an hour before sunset – that also includes the Paradise Quarry, a series of remarkable grottoes and caverns.

The old town (*Ortygia*) is in some senses the new town. The cathedral is built on what were the foundations of

the Temple of Minerva. The cathedral and the palazzos on cathedral square – a lively place in the early evening – offer a series of journeys out of the Greek and into the Baroque. On Sunday afternoons, the whole region seems to descend on the waterfront for a passeggiata. And, as Cicero said, "There's not a day without sun in Syracuse."

If you return to Taormina and then journey north toward Messina the next day, you are in for one of the world's great coastal drives. Keep a map of Italy in your head and watch as the toe of Calabria gets closer and closer until it seems you can almost jump across. The road is a remarkable series of tunnels and clear seaside driving. At one moment, you are engulfed in darkness; then you will suddenly emerge into sunlight and yet another surprising view. At Messina, you can take a look at the straits; the town itself has suffered badly from earthquakes over the centuries and most of it has been rebuilt since the great tremors of 1908.

The northern coast between Messina and Palermo is one long run of small towns and quiet beaches. Two in particular are worth a visit. Cefalù is a small fishing town with a Norman Romanesque cathedral. In his fine book on Sicily, *The Golden Honeycomb*, Vincent Cronin reports that the cathedral was King Roger II's votive offering to God for saving him from a storm at sea. According to legend, Roger promised to build a cathedral wherever he was brought to safety and was miraculously brought to what was then the Arab town of Cefalu. "Both the vow and its fulfillment are worthy of a man who combined faith and works, love of beauty and love of battle," Mr. Cronin wrote.

Palermo is both a most modern city and a place where a noble old downtown and rambling outdoor markets beckon. It is a mad collection of blood lines, traditions, architectural styles and sensibilities, a jumble of Norman, Spanish Baroque, Fascist and modern buildings, the last thrown up over the last several

A DIVIDED CITY

Modica, south of the Iblei mountains in the province of Ragusa, is divided into two parts, Upper and Lower; "shaped like a split pomegranate," as the writer Gesualdo Bufalino put it. In 1902 the city was engulfed by a flood of apocalyptic proportions, which touched off a nationwide solidarity campaign. A new neighborhood was built, now known as "Milano-Palermo" in commemoration of the generous contribution made by the capital of the Lombardy region.

THE CATHEDRAL SUNDIAL
In Palermo cathedral (below) a large sundial was created in front of the high altar in 1801. The purpose was to accustom the faithful to the idea of measuring time according to the new astronomical rules that were then gaining ground all over Europe. But despite this profound change, the popular custom of calculating the hour starting from sunset hung on doggedly for nearly a century. Facing page, the temple of Concordia, near Agrigento (5th century B.C.). On the following pages, an abandoned tuna fishing plant in the Costa dello Zingaro nature reserve, in the Trapani area.

decades in the rush to development. The Arab influence is still felt, no more so than in the thriving street markets, offering every imaginable product, that go on for blocks and blocks in the center of town.

Palermo brings home the cyclical nature of history, the rise and fall of one civilization after another. Palermatans are often said to be cynical, a cynicism that arises from the need to adapt to a bizarre range of occupying powers. Remember, for example, that this was once an entirely Arab city with scores of mosques, far closer to Tunisia than Milan. Islam was replaced by Christianity, the Arab style by the Norman, the mosques by churches. Then it was a Spanish city – the evidence of Bourbon domination is visible in many parts of the old town – and now it is Italian. At certain times in its history, it was one of the important cultural centers of Europe.

The extraordinary contradictions of Palermo are brought home on almost every block, in almost every building. The Palace of the Normans, on the highest point of the old city, was built by the Saracens, expanded by the Normans, restored by the Spaniards. Whoever happened to be governing Sicily at any given time lived there, and it is still the seat of government. Its Palatine Chapel, built by Roger II, is regarded as one of the most

remarkable architectural achievements in all of Italy. Seen from one perspective, it is a monument to tolerance, since its mosaics are Greek inspired; its ceiling is of Arab workmanship, and its marble work is Norman. The inscriptions are in Greek, Latin and Arabic. The chapel is worth several visits, especially to be seen in different lights.

From Palermo, the inland road from Palermo to Agrigento, on the southern coast, takes you through what might be called the Wyoming of Sicily, a land of scrub brush, vast plains leading to buttes and then to distant mountains. You expect to see Clint Eastwood riding off into the sunset (which he may well have done, since this is the land of spaghetti Westerns). The drive, which takes a couple of hours, takes you far away from beach resorts and through some truly wild terrain. Agrigento itself, like Syracuse, offers a remarkable view of ancient Greek civilization. The Valley of Temples rightly draws visitors from all over the world. The Temple of Concord is the best preserved and the Temple of Hercules is believed to be the oldest, dating back to the sixth century B.C. Other temples in various states of preservation include those to Juno Lacinia, Jove and Castor and Pollux. The area is especially strik-

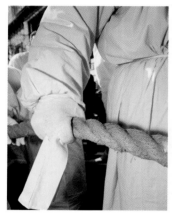

HONOR TO THE SAINT

Catania is noted for its devotion to its patron saint, Sant'Agata. In early February every year her effigy is borne in procession on a litter, drawn by ropes and followed by the dignitaries of the city and by the typical "candelore," large candles that represent the ancient city guilds. It is said that, in the 12th century, when the relics of Sant'Agata — formerly in Constantinople — were brought back to Catania, the citizens rushed to welcome the saint in the middle of the night, careless of their state of undress. That explains why the faithful wear white tunics reminiscent of nightshirts.

ing at sunrise and sunset, and to watch the spotlights flash onto the temples after darkness has fallen is to get a kind of mystical shiver.

Southeast of Agrigento is an area not often visited but worth a day trip. Ragusa has two fine Baroque churches, the cathedral of San Giovanni Battista and the church of San Giorgio. Comiso has a rich artisanal tradition; Scicli and Modica are pretty 18th-century towns. Another route from Palermo very much worth making is to Trapani and especially to Erice, perched atop Monte San Giuliano. Erice is perhaps the best preserved medieval town in Sicily. Going back many centuries, the town was a religious center to the goddesses of love and fertility of the various leading powers: Astarte of the Phoenicians, Aphrodite of the Greeks and Venus of the Romans. It reached its height of prosperity and importance in the 13th and 14th centuries, and then steadily lost influence to Trapani. Its charm lies in its long neglect; today it stands as a beautiful relic to another era, overlooking its now busier rival.

Sicily, associated with bright colors and large gestures, is in fact deceptively subtle, a subtlety related to the rococo and the Baroque and perhaps also to that sense of the absurd associated with Pirandello, who came from near Agrigento. The people, like most people, can be just as subtle: a mixture of circumspection and openness, of cunning and warmth.

But however Sicily's contradictions are turned around — whether you choose to regard it as the Orient's gateway to Europe or Europe's door to the Arab world, as the conquered island or the island that absorbed something from everyone — the island will reward those who try to understand it, those who keep searching.

———

E.J. DIONNE JR., a former Rome bureau chief for The Times, *is a columnist for* The Washington Post. *His most recent book is* "Stand Up Fight Back: Republican Toughs, Democratic Wimps and the Politics of Revenge" (*Simon & Schuster*).

WHITE GOLD OF THE SEA
The environment of the salt
pans around Trapani is at once
an ecosystem, a natural
landscape and the site of some
historical monuments. In days
gone by the coast was studded
with watchtowers (left, the
17th-century Torre di Nubia)
where fires and mirrors were
used to warn the citizens of the
approach of pirates. Above
and top, two typical Sicilian
products: Indian figs and capers.

381

**MADE FOR TOURISM
AND RELAXATION**
Lying on a natural balcony
reaching out toward the sea,
Taormina is made for
memorable vacations.
All the peoples who have taken
turns at ruling Sicily –
the Siculans, Greeks, Romans,
Byzantines and Normans –
chose Taormina for physical
and spiritual repose and
regeneration; in recent times,
many artists from different
disciplines have drawn
inspiration from it.
Above, Corso Umberto I,
the backbone of the city center.

Taormina,
an ancient and modern legend

From the Taurio, the stubby promontory that from Sicily's eastern coast extends into the Ionian Sea, the eye roams free as far as the coastline of Calabria and the Straits of Messina. And even farther into the distance, where the blue of sky and sea merge, we can imagine the columns of Greek temples, austere divinities seated on Olympus and indomitable Hellenic navigators sailing the seas. On this promontory in the 4th century B.C. the Siculans founded the city of Tauromenium, not far from the Greek colony of Naxos – destroyed by the Syracusans in 403 B.C. A half century later, Andromachus, the father of the historian Timaeus, reunited the refugees from Naxos at Tauromenium and the city become Greek.

Many peoples and cultures have passed through Taormina, leaving the traces of their glory as a kind of historical kaleidoscope and offering an infinity of reflections. The theater, for example, erected by the Greeks in the 3rd century B.C. and extensively remodeled by the Romans in the 2nd century A.D. is home to all forms of

spectacle; and the setting, needless to say, is always the "Teatro Antico."

In the shade of its austere walls even the cinema enjoys its celebratory rites, with the annual award of the Davide di Donatello prize and the Messina and Taormina Film Festival, which celebrated its 50th anniversary in 2004.

Outside the theater the show goes on, too. Goethe's enthusiasm later inspired the Prussian baron Otto Geleng who in 1868, armed with canvases and brushes, began a lengthy sojourn in Taormina before introducing his work to the artistic milieus of Prussia and France, thus paving the way for a tourist industry that has never ceased to grow.

In 1875 a terrible cholera epidemic led to an exodus from all the big cities on Sicily and the aristocratic families of Palermo found a healthy haven in Taormina, where they built sumptuous villas in line with their respective status back home.

A SPECTACULAR DESTINY

Taormina's Teatro Antico, built by the Greeks and later restored by the Romans, still stages shows of all kinds – even decidedly modern events. It is also the evocative setting of Italy's most prestigious award in the field of the cinema. In *Mighty Aphrodite* Woody Allen set part of the movie in the ancient amphitheater, complete with a Greek chorus that comments upon the story as it unfolds, a real return to the roots.

By Mary Taylor Simeti

IN THE AEOLIAN ISLANDS,
a September Song

September 29, 2002

**DEDICATED
TO THE GOD OF FIRE**

The ancient *Hierà* (meaning sacred in Greek) is known more prosaically as Vulcano, and the name is more than apt. The island is composed of various volcanic agglomerates and a narrow isthmus connects it with Vulcanello, another island that has three craters. The fire god's seething subterranean activities are visible in thermal springs, which lie in the open air in an area with many fumaroles and a hot pool. After a therapeutic bath some visitors will find it hard to resist the temptation of a second plunge – this time into the cool blue waters of the Tyrrhenian sea.

THE BIG SISTER
Lipari is the largest and most
populous island in the Aeolian
group. Less rugged than
its sisters, it has more villages.
Right, a greengrocer's shop with
typical local produce, especially
chili peppers –
an inevitable presence wherever
vegetable produce
is sold throughout
the south of Italy.
Facing page, a nighttime view of
Lipari's little harbor.

Some say that the sirens sang to Ulysses from the Aeolian Islands, a small archipelago not far from my Sicilian home, yet for almost 40 years I resisted their call. I lacked the stamina, I thought, for such a concentrate of sea and sun and bikinied beautiful people (Princess Caroline of Monaco and Cindy Crawford were among this year's visitors). When I did at last capitulate, it was in late September, after the summer crowds had sailed away. "Sail" is the operative word here, for a boat is practically the only way to reach the Aeolians, a sprinkling of dark volcanic cones that rise from the sea about 20 miles off the northern coast of Sicily. Often isolated in winter, in summer they are caught in a net of hydrofoils, ferries, fishing boats and pleasure yachts, bringing an invasion of tourists, drawn by the spectacular swimming and hiking, and by what is said to be the only permanently active volcano in Europe.

Invasion is nothing new to the Aeolians. Like their Sicilian sister hanging hazy on the southern horizon, they have been attacked and conquered and then, as a result of fire, earthquake or eruption, abandoned over and over during their long history. In the shadow of the cathedral on the fortified citadel of Lipari, excavations that start with Greek and Roman roadbeds go down through nine different cultures spanning more than four millenniums.

It was the glassy black obsidian produced by the volcano of Lipari, used for knives and weapons before the discovery of metallurgy, that first attracted settlers to the Aeolians near the end of the fifth millennium B.C. They came first from Sicily, then from mainland Italy, later from the eastern Mediterranean: cultures died out, leaving the islands uninhabited until new waves of invaders arrived. Greeks, Romans, then a Saracen attack in A.D. 836 that left the islands empty for 250 years until the Normans came. From then until the present the islands have lived on the margins of European history.

My husband, Tonino, and I decided to take the hydrofoil that runs east from Palermo to the Aeolians from June through September. Our progress through the archipelago was both geographical, therefore, and

TOURIST PARADISE
Above, a view of Ditella,
a village on Panarea, the
smallest of the Aeolian islands.
What can be seen today is only
a part of the original island,
which sank into the sea
following a volcanic explosion.
The ancient Greeks called it
Euonymos (meaning unlucky
or inauspicious) because
the shoals and the rocks around
its shores caused frequent
shipwrecks. Today the island
is a destination much favored
by tourists.

historical, for the westernmost islands of Alicudi and Filicudi remain the least changed by the modern age. Alicudi is a small and seemingly perfect cone of dark rock, dotted with pale green cactus and deeper green mastic bushes. The hillside above the tiny port is terraced, wound round with low walls built of lava and by houses in the typical Aeolian style, cubes of white and pastel-washed stucco added on side by side as the family expanded. Cane-covered porches supported by fat white pillars shade windows that look out to sea. There are no roads on Alicudi, but staircases hewn of lava thread their way through the minute vineyards and caper plantations. From the deck of the hydrofoil we could see farmers leading heavily laden donkeys — the only form of transport — up and down the steps, a time warp increased by the absence of electric and telephone poles: electricity only reached Alicudi around 1990 when, with a critical eye to the landscape, the wires were laid underground.

We left the boat at its second stop, Filicudi, an island a little bigger than Alicudi and just a little more modern. On the map it resembles a tadpole — a big

volcano long since spent, with a tail that curls up in another little hill. Houses and terraces, retreating from high seas and pirates, climb up the highlands that join the two cones, and the port of Filicudi nestles below in the curve of the tail. The small hotel where we spent the night descended the hillside in a series of terraces shaded by figs, olives and banana plants, and colored by bougainvillea and plumbago. Had I brought books I would have gladly stayed longer: deck chairs, a swimming pool and just enough distractions to keep sloth at bay.

That afternoon we hired Fausto, the brother of the two young waitresses at the hotel, to take us round the island in his motor launch. We circled counterclockwise, past cliffs of lava striped horizontally with a sulfurous yellow or split into vertical slabs, tortuous molten flows frozen and gnawed by wind and water. Offshore, pillars of lava thrust from the waves, ancient volcanoes eroded in all but their very cores, and the island itself looked like a huge, shaggy and somewhat moth-eaten bear floating on the sea, with a pelt of dried grasses and faded scrub clinging to its purple-brown flanks.

In the cool of the late afternoon, we set off to visit the prehistoric village that has been excavated on a wide plain overlooking the port: round huts of stone from about 1500 B.C. whose foundations remain.

The path to the terrace requires a stiff climb and a good head for heights. Halfway up, my vertigo kicked in, so my husband went on alone while I sat and admired the view. He returned to regale me with enthusiastic reports as I inched my way down the path on my bottom!

Our next port of call was Stromboli, the northernmost of the islands and the one with the noisy volcano. We arrived at dusk, as the main square of the town was filling up with hikers preparing to climb up to the crater to witness by night the steady putt-putt of Stromboli, the syncopated explosions of gas, ash and lava that have gone on for as long as man has been there to record them, earning the volcano the name "Lighthouse of the Mediterranean." The urge to look down into a volcano appears to be ageless: St. Willibald, on his way home from the Holy Land in 729, climbed up the volcano of Lipari in the hope of getting a glimpse of hell. On Stromboli it is possible at least to glimpse some molten lava, but this calls for a strenuous six-hour excursion, climbing more than 2,500 feet, and requires good physical condition, proper equipment and the company of a guide.

Tonino and I opted for a much gentler hike, equipped only with sneakers and a flashlight: 40 minutes of easy switchbacks to the former observatory, now a pizzeria, at Punta Labronzo, where we could sit over supper, listen to the booming of the volcano and watch the clouds above the crater glow with reflected red, the shower of incandescent sparks and an occasional geyser of red-hot gas spurting into the night sky. It was quite a distant spectacle, and I was sorry that we hadn't chosen the closer view from a boat.

We did go round the island by boat the next morning. Antonio, a sometime fisherman and mostly a supplier of rooms and boat rides to tourists, took us south on a clockwise route, stopping to chat with "the Viking," who, with his brother, was pulling in his shrimp traps, a last catch before the seasonal fishing ban went into effect. The Viking is one of the few full-time fishermen left on the island, the others having abandoned

FIRE, SEA AND WIND

Born from the primordial fires that smolder deep inside the earth, immersed in a cobalt-blue sea that stretches as far as the eye can see, the Aeolian islands are named for Aeolus, the god of the winds of ancient mythology. And the wind still tirelessly buffets the volcanic rock, eternally molding and remolding it.

Above, Cape Milazzese, on the island of Panarea, is a promontory with the remains of a prehistoric village dating from the 14th to the 13th centuries B.C.

The pillar of the sky

THE LORD OF FIRE AND SNOW
Above, a column of steam rises from the snow-covered peak of Etna. Below, a few steps from the mouth of the volcano. Facing page, molten lava forms a river of fire.

Etna is a mountain of myth and legend, one of the few places where a fifth season can reign, fire. When the ancient Greek mariners saw the mountain emerging from the sea and lighting up the night with explosions, they dubbed it the "pillar of the sky" and made it the home of the irascible god Hephaestus and the Cyclopes. Philosophers, poets and historians such as Homer, Aeschylus, Thucydides, Seneca and Virgil were inspired by its roaring flames and handed down to posterity verses that remain anchored in the memory of western literature.

Well over 10,000 feet high, the volcano dominates the eastern coast of Sicily and the city of Catania. Huddled at its foot, Catania trembles when the giant trembles, and with good reason. In 1669 the city was devastated by an immense lava flow and its history is an unnerving record of earthquakes, explosions, and sleepless nights spent observing this restless monster, which occasionally covers streets and roofs with a fine blanket of ash.

Etna's lower slopes are extremely fertile. Pear, apple, apricot, peach, cherry, almond, walnut and hazelnut trees as well as Indian figs alternate with vineyards that produce strong, full bodied wines for export all over Europe. "Etna" is a "registered" wine; white or red, its flavor seems to draw its warmth from the very deepest crannies of the volcano. Farther up the mountain slopes stand vast woods with beech, chestnut, oak and ilex trees. Above 6,000 feet the trees give way to bushes and other pioneer plants, which grow ever sparser the nearer they get to the realm of the lava. From about 9,000 feet to the rim of the central crater, the landscape is volcanic desert covered for four to five months a year with snow. Venturing into these parts is hazardous and can only be attempted with a guide, largely because the volcano is more active than ever: on all sides Etna is devastated and torn by ancient and recent eruptions. As soon as one wound heals, others open.

The southeastern slopes are deeply notched by the Valle del Bove. But don't be fooled by the term "valley," for this is no more than an immense gash in the desolate, almost lunar landscape, with steep walls and lava beds on which float the "dagale," islands of vegetation that have miraculously escaped the flames. Here, in the space of a few months between 1992 and 1993, the volcano disgorged lava flows hundreds of yards deep.

In the past Etna was also known as Mongibello, from the Latin *mons* (mountain) and the Arabic *gibel* (which also means mountain): the mountain of mountains, in other words. And that's what Sicilians still call it: the Mountain.

**THE VILLAGE BORN
IN A CRATER**

In the remote past an explosion
split a volcano on the island of
Salina. In one half of the crater,
whose semicircular outline can
still be seen in the contours of
the bay, there arose the village
of Pollara while all that can be
seen of the other half, engulfed
by the sea, is a rock (the magma
channel of the ancient volcano),
called the Grande Faraglione
(the Big Stack). Pollara became
famous when it was chosen
as the set for *Il postino*,
a film directed by Michael
Radford and starring the late
Massimo Troisi, one of Italy's
best loved actors.

their nets for the tourist business, just as the farmers have let their fields lie fallow. Antonio pointed out Punta Lena, a tableland covered with wild scrub, once famous for its fertile volcanic soil and its wheat and olives, and waxed nostalgic over the now-vanished olive harvests of his childhood.

Here, as elsewhere on the islands, the summer sun had dried and withered much of the flora, but the older lava flows were covered with "ginestra," the yellow broom that flowers in April and May, when, according to Antonio, the air of Stromboli is heady with its perfume. If the Aeolians in late September, when the water is still summer warm, are perfect for swimmers, then spring is the time for hikers to come, when countless wildflowers are in bloom.

It was windy, and the sea was rising a bit as we completed our tour, sailing past the fancy white villas that line the cliffs of Piscità, the chic neighborhood in the town of Stromboli. Here, narrow lanes wind between walled courtyards and gardens that hide gleaming white bungalows and villas belonging to the summer people, isolated from the noise and the crowds in the rest of town, where motor scooters and three-wheeled

Vespa pickups converted into taxis roar past unkempt empty lots and abandoned gardens that speak sadly of the decline of the traditional economy.

Our next landing, Salina, the Greeks called *Didyme* – the twins. It is formed by two volcanic cones joined by a high saddle. Of all the Aeolians it is the richest in fresh water, and thus the greenest: vineyards, olive groves and caper plantations are carefully farmed, and the upper slopes of the volcanoes are covered with scrub oak, arbutus and chestnut trees. Much of the island is a nature reserve with good hiking trails leading into the wooded areas and up to the top of the higher mountain, the Fossa delle Felci, whose crater is a frothy pool of green ferns.

An even closer view of traditional Aeolian life was available at the beachside town of Lingua. At the end of a boardwalk lined with restaurants and cafes (de rigueur is a stop at Alfredo's, a tiny bar famed for its granitas, with unusual flavors like fig, watermelon and prickly pear), an old residence houses an enchanting civic museum: downstairs the traditional interiors of an Aeolian house have been recreated, while upstairs

FRIENDS WITH LONG EARS
Solitary and spartan, Alicudi closes off the archipelago at its far western side. Impervious and rather inaccessible, the island echoes a time when people followed the natural rhythms of the seasons and distances were not measured in miles but in hours of travel, on foot or by mule. Donkeys and mules are the patient Jeeps of the island, only much more efficient than their four-wheeled counterparts.

model ships, documents and maps illustrate the maritime history of the island. The museum's terrace looks out over a little lake – the former salt flat, or salina, that gave the island its present name – and across to the islands of Lipari and Vulcano.

I had elected to skip Vulcano, the most unpredictable and violent of the Aeolian volcanoes, although its beaches, sulfur springs and mud baths attract enormous numbers of tourists.

Lipari, therefore, was to be our last stop: the biggest of the islands and the most populated, with about 9,000 permanent residents. I came for the archaeological museum, and was unprepared for the charm of the town of Lipari itself. The citadel – once site of the acropolis, now dominated by the cathedral bell tower – sits at the center of the harbor on a rock walled by Spanish fortifications. On the southern end of the harbor – known as the Marina Corta – is the lovely old fishermen's quarter, with streets often too narrow for cars to pass, made narrower still by large pots of geraniums, bougainvillea and jasmine vines.

Nothing had prepared me for the museum. Conceived and installed by one of Italy's great archaeologists, Luigi Bernabò Brea, it houses in the prehistoric section an amazing collection of pottery, while the classical section is dominated by vases and funerary offerings found in the tombs of the Contrada Diana necropolis, more than 2,500 sarcophagi covered over so quickly with volcanic ash that they had never been plundered. My favorites were those from the tombs of little girls – toy vases and tiny statuettes of women bathing babies or grinding wheat – and the extraordinary number of masks and statues from the cult of Dionysius, displayed so cleverly that one seemed to be looking at a Greek comedy in progress at the theaters of Segesta or Syracuse.

The attractions of Lipari are not all urban. Swimmers can choose between a variety of spectacular coves and beaches, not least the famous white beaches of Canneto. Together with obsidian, the now extinct volcano of Lipari spewed out mountains of chalky white pumice that reach down to the shore. Quarried since antiquity for artisanal and industrial use (to make stone-washed jeans, for one thing), the sandy residue from the processing, heaped in enormous piles, slithers into the sea and gets swept south onto the beaches.

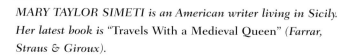

THE RESTLESS VOLCANO
Ginostra and Stromboli (above) are the only two villages on the island of Stromboli, which is dominated by the volcano of the same name. Known as the "Lighthouse of the Tyrrhenian" because of its incessant activity, at night the bright glow of its crater can be seen from great distances. Moreover, the expression "Strombolian activity" has now become the accepted technical term for the continuous emission of fluid lava, accompanied by clouds of steam and explosions.

MARY TAYLOR SIMETI is an American writer living in Sicily. Her latest book is "Travels With a Medieval Queen" (Farrar, Straus & Giroux).

THE SALT ISLAND
Since time immemorial, the
wind, the elements and the salt
spray have hurled themselves
against the rocks of the
promontory of Perciato,
on the island of Salina (left),
until they managed to carve out
the large arch from which its
name derives ("perciato" means
pierced in the local dialect).
Many beaches on the island
are black sand, proof
of volcanic origins.

By Paul Chutkow

In the Heart of
SARDINIA

September 2, 1984

THE TYPICAL SARDINIAN HAT
The hat known as "sa berritta" is the typical headgear of Sardinian men. Made of coarse black or red woolen cloth shaped like a truncated cone, its length varies from about 18 inches to a yard. It is worn folded to one side or, when very long, hanging down over the shoulders. The Sardinians' fondness for their berritta is proverbial; at one time in parts of the island peasants even wore them in high summer, topping them with a straw hat for protection from the sun. Right, the dunes of the splendid beach at Chia, on the southern tip of the island.

It begins at 5 A.M. First, a lone gull sounds forth, and then slowly up and down the coast the island birds echo the call of first light. Before long, fingers of yellow slip through the shutters, and outside the high, feathery cirrus clouds are watercolored pink. On the far horizon, beyond the two little white fishing boats that have kept their all-night vigil, out on the very rim where the Mediterranean Sea disappears east toward mainland Italy, brilliant blues, yellows, pinks and purples crowd into position.

At 6 A.M., the birds hushed and all their world at the watch, up out of the sea there comes at last that first lip of flaming orange, all liquid fire and rising majesty, until the day is born.

This is Sardinia, an island of sun and sea, mountain and pine, fish and flamingoes, citrus and bitter honey. Sardinia has many more faces, but at sunrise there is just this, the land, the sea and the sun as they have always been, and moods suggested by the seasons and decided by the winds.

So close is Sardinia to the heart of the Mediterranean that the compass of its winds spins into a lesson in Mediterranean geography. From the island of Corsica, due north, comes what the Sardinians call a cross-mountain wind. From the northeast, across the narrow boot of Italy, comes a wind from Greece. From Tunisia, due south, comes a warm noonday wind, the scirocco. From the west and northwest, from the coasts of Spain and France, comes the familiar Mediterranean mistral. There is even a dusty, suffocating blow the Sardinians say comes all the way from the Sahara, and this is called "the wind from Libya."

With foreign winds have come foreign occupiers, and Sardinia's past is unhappily stamped by Phoenicians,

Carthaginians, Romans, barbarians, Arabs, Spaniards, British and in World War II the Germans. Today Italy governs Sardinia, and although the Sardinians have special status as an autonomous region, and although their separatist voices are muted, they are not about to define themselves as Italian. Theirs is a land, a people, apart.

To those who are strangers to it, Sardinia usually calls forth an image of diamonds and champagne, an exclusive resort for the rich and aspiring. This image comes from the Costa Smeralda, the Emerald Coast, a spectacular ribbon of land and water that slightly over 20 years ago was a malaria-infested wasteland and today is just about the ultimate chic in country club vacationing.

Still, to those who know the island from the inside, and above all to the more than 1.5 million Sardinians spread across this big, thumb-shaped jut of mountain and coast, all the glitter of the Costa Smeralda has little to do with the real nature of Sardinia.

Nor is this other Sardinia for the traveler who values luxury over discovery. Even in the pockets of four-star comfort to be found outside the Costa Smeralda, this is not a place where liveried waiters deliver Campari and soda to poolside. In those areas equipped for tourists, accommodations are good, although not always available, especially in the high season of July and August. In the splendid months of June and September, though, a traveler can wander the island and be pretty sure of finding a clean roof for the night. A car is virtually mandatory, and rentals are easy, plentiful and reasonable.

It's a big island, some 9,300 square miles, ringed by several islands worth exploring, and the whole is only slightly smaller than Sicily. There is a main highway running north-south, and on it the whole island can be crossed in a leisurely three hours. Still, to get to know the whole of Sardinia takes several weeks, and that would only be a once-over.

Better to settle for a smaller taste, and for this the southernmost quarter of the island is simple and natural. Cagliari, the capital, is in the center of the southern coast, and it is linked to the mainland by daily ferry service and air shuttles to Rome several times a day. Especially for boat passages, book early.

Be it to Cagliari or to the northern ports of Olbia and Porto Torres, most of the ferry crossings are overnight, and this is fortunate, for Sardinia has not spawned easy deck chair reading for the literary traveler. Lawrence Durrell, in his peripatetic Mediterranean island hopping and resultant travel books, seems to have skirted Sardinia, and the tourist kiosks are the poorer for it.

D.H. Lawrence seems to be about the only foreign writer who has left much of an imprint, but neither

THE HEART OF ORISTANO STILL BEATS FOR ELEONORA
In the main square of Oristano (above) stands the majestic monument to Eleonora d'Arborea (c. 1340-1404), a tribute to the last ruler of an independent Sardinian state.

Facing page, top, the promontory of Torre Argentina, near Bosa in the province of Nuoro.
Below, flamingoes in the pond known as Sale Porcus, not far from Oristano. In winter this important nature reserve is home to 5,000 to 8,000 flamingoes, about one percent of the entire world population of this most elegant bird.

The bandits don't live here any more

"Barbari" was the term used by the ancient Greeks and Romans to indicate foreign peoples who had languages and customs different from their own. From "barbari" comes the name of the Barbagia, a historic region in central Sardinia, where the proud isolation of the local population has protected the area from mass tourism.

On venturing into the Barbagia from the cliffs of the Gulf of Orosei, visitors come across the Supramonte, a wild, calcareous plateau that echoes with tales of the dark deeds of brigands, bandits who became so much a part of the collective imagination that there is even a cheese named for them, Brigante Sardo (the Sardinian Bandit). In the impenetrable forests of the Supramonte live the wild sheep, which has barely survived continual poaching, and the Sardinian deer, which is endemic to the island. The skies are the realm of the rare Bonelli's eagle, the winged messenger of a boundless freedom.

The center of the Barbagia is the highest point in Sardinia – Mount Gennargentu (from *Janua argenti*, the silver gate), the heart of the Gennargentu and Gulf of Orosei National Park. "It is hard to describe the view you enjoy from this mountain: suffice it to say that you can see the sea on three sides of the island," said Alberto La Marmora, a general in the Piedmontese army of the 19th century who also was a cartographer and a great expert on the land. The highest peak on Gennargentu (about 5,500 feet) is named after him.

Orgosolo, not far north of the Gennargentu massif and about 12 miles from Nuoro, is a small town that has become a symbol of the islanders' stubborn determination to keep up their ancient traditions. But while a rather facile iconography would portray the town as an emblem of backwardness and its inhabitants as dour, silent people dressed in black, Orgosolo contradicts this image with numerous, highly colorful murals. These began to appear in the 1970s, perhaps as a bit of fun on the part of some local youngsters, but they soon found a key supporter in the person of Francesco del Casino, a painter from Siena. Since then, Orgosolo has become a living magazine, whose pages are the façades of the houses. Current events, politics, history: nothing escapes pictorial representation, sometimes sorrowful, sometimes sarcastic. The method of execution, which deliberately involves no precautions against deterioration, ensures that the pages are living and changeable: those murals that are worth maintaining are occasionally touched up and restored, while those that deserve to be consigned to oblivion are abandoned to their fate.

TALKING WALLS
Above and below, some of the murals in Orgosolo; the ingenious artists have spared no surface, not even the walls of the local junior high school. Right, the stern outline of Supramonte forms a magnificent backdrop to the countryside around Orgosolo.

WHERE THE RIVER DIES
The Barony of Posada, once
a feudal holding of the same
name, overlooks the eastern
coast of Sardinia. It is crossed
by a extremely fertile valley,
created by the deposits laid
down by the river Posada.
After about 30 miles, the river
loses its identity in a network
of meanders before it reaches
the Tyrrhenian sea in the Gulf
of Posada (right), in a series
of white sand beaches.

Lawrence nor Sardinia has much to brag about from his *Sea and Sardinia*. The way he portrays it, the Sardinians find the great writer as stiff and dyspeptic as any other stereotyped Englishman, and he in turn finds the Sardinians as overly tender and quaintly romantic as the stereotyped Italian. Match null.

As with everything else about Sardinia, when it comes to books it's better to go native. Grazia Deledda, a rebellious young woman from a grand family in the city of Nuoro, early in the century turned on the island with a scathing eye and a remarkably lucid style. She became a scandal to all Sardinia and won a Nobel Prize in the process. Her collected works are a real discovery: she does to Sardinia what Balzac did to France.

Almost all the guidebooks offer suggested excursion itineraries, and in keeping with this custom, herewith are three suggested daylong routes around which to build a personal discovery of the other Sardinia.

Day One. To the freshly arrived city slicker, full of a night's sea air and steamer fumes, the wide open spaces of the Sardinia countryside can be nothing short of nature shock. Therefore, immediately after a cappuccino and an Italian doughnut, start day one with an excursion to the rental car office in the center of Cagliari. Allow two hours, one for feeling right at home in city traffic, 30 minutes for the rental agent to finish his cappuccino and 30 minutes for deciphering the Fiat models and completing the paperwork. Then proceed to the archeological museum overlooking Cagliari. Allow two hours, one for getting lost and one for lamenting all the relics of foreign occupations. Here is the best introduction to the prehistoric Nuraghic civilization, a mysterious island culture that has left some 7,000 conical towers across the island. To get an idea why Cicero found the island's bitter honey the perfect metaphor for all Sardinia, ask any Sardinian why their finest art treasures are to be found in foreign museums.

For lunch, try following your nose, or if you want to be sure, follow the locals. The Sardinians pride themselves on their local specialties, based always on fresh, natural products. For openers, try "malloreddus" (sometimes called "gnocchetti"), small pasta curls made from hard-grained wheat and served simply with tomato sauce and Pecorino sardo or with bits of Sardinian sausage. Risotto with bits of seafood or black with the ink of octopus — "alla seppia nera" — may be even better.

Thus armed for nature shock, proceed out of town along the coast in either direction. The late afternoon light on the water or on the rocky hillsides will remind you what the Mediterranean has always held for painters and poets. At the first appetizing beach, shed all city cares and begin to experience the waters of

IN THE HEART OF
SARDINIA

**A CARPET FOR
ALL OCCASIONS**

Even though many years have passed since women in every town in Sardinia could be seen busily working their looms in the streets before their houses, carpet weaving remains an important part of the island's production of hand-crafted goods. Time-honored local traditions include the "copricassa," covers made especially for hope chests, and the "pettenedda," a reversible carpet whose particular durability is attributable to the fact that the double woolen weft completely conceals and protects the cotton warp.

403

THE "GREEN TRAIN
OF SARDINIA"
In 1885 a new law was passed
allowed the government
to contract out to private
companies the construction
and operation of Sardinia's
secondary rail network, thus
enabling a more extensive
settlement of the island.
Four of these old lines have
since been renovated to allow
visitors to reach (without too
much effort) some of the most
secluded and beautiful places in
Sardinia. The equipment was
constructed from period
railroad stock, such as diesel
and steam locomotives
and railcars from the early
20th century.

emerald water, full of sea life. In shallow water, find baby clams to eat fresh out of the shell. Along the rocks, even without a mask, you can collect sea urchins for lunchtime appetizers. Don't bother with the black ones, as they are male and not good eating. The violet and other pastels are female and worth the occasional pricked finger from their spines. Cut them open horizontally and spoon out the orange eggs for a delicate taste of the sea. Open the wine that has been chilling between sea-washed rocks, bite into a fig wrapped in prosciutto and begin kicking yourself for not having planned an extra week in Sardinia.

Once you have found beaches to your taste, day two can be effortlessly repeated and varied. The enterprising outdoor gourmet may want to purchase a little grill for an evening barbecue of veal chops, the wonderful local sausage or fresh fish from the local fisherman or a good fish market. For a real delicacy, track down a good-sized spigola, or sea bass. Fennel grows wild on the island, and once you've tasted spigola cooked on the grill over fennel, washed down with the fine light white wine called Vermentino di Gallura, you'll start to have a real appreciation of the other Sardinia.

Sardinia. Allow two hours, one to marvel at the color of the water and the fish, and one to go back to Cagliari to buy a mask, snorkel and fins.

Proceed to hotel, or to one of the many campgrounds with bungalows, if such is your taste, and then stroll on the beach for your first Sardinian sunset. Follow local advice for dinner. Suckling pig is a Sardinian specialty but not easy to find. If you find it, grab it, and follow the waiter's advice on wine. The Sardinians have several distinctive wines, one of the most popular being a light and somewhat sweet honey-colored wine called Vernaccia. Quality varies. Over a dessert of ricotta cheese and fresh figs, or the almond-based sweets known as "sospiri d'Orani," wonder again why the French think they are the only people who know how to eat. End day one with Grazia Deledda or simply with the Milky Way.

Day Two. Pack a picnic. Prosciutto and figs, olives, plenty of tomatoes and celery, fresh mozzarella or pecorino cheese made from ewe's milk, and any of the variety of local breads. Add a bottle of water and a bottle of wine, and off you go in search of your private beach. Go west toward St. Margherita di Pula or east toward Villasimius and beyond; it doesn't really matter. Either way there are long white beaches, with or without human seafront activity, and dirt roads that seem to lead nowhere may in fact lead to that deserted cove of

Day Three. Pleasantly sunburned and eager to plunge farther into the island, set out early for Barumini, inland and due north of Cagliari. Several villages in Sardinia have been promoting a revival of wall painting, and you can see some examples at Villamar, on the road to Barumini. All big and bold, a few of the wall paintings are political and crude, while others are illustrative of village life and often touching.

At Barumini is Su Nuraxi, one of the most important of the nuraghi towers. The Nuraghic civilization has been dated to about 1800 B.C., and although the secrets of these towers have not been fully decoded, the Su Nuraxi was clearly at the center of a very sophisticated village fortress. Many of the nuraghi were built around wells, to be self-sustaining in the event of a siege, and even today from the tops of Su Nuraxi and most of these towers you can spy the adjacent nuraghi, suggesting that their network served as a coordinated island defense system against invasion.

Inland Sardinia has long been fabled for sheltering bandits, but the only trace the average tourist will find of this are little banditi dolls at the corner candy and tobacco store. Tourist curio shops are alien creatures to the Sardinians, but finding native handicrafts beyond the banditi dolls is not too difficult. The persevering shopper can unearth beautiful hand-woven rugs and tapestries, and one of the places to do is Villamassargia, southwest of Barumini and en route to two little islands worth discovering – San Pietro and Sant'Antioco.

FROM THE SEA TO THE NETS
Tuna has always been a part of
the diet and culture of all the
Mediterranean island peoples.
Since ancient times this
valuable, large fish has been
caught with the aid of a clever
but cruel technique that uses
a system of nets to trap the
tuna and lead them to the
"killing rooms," the "camere
di mattanza." The tuna fishing
complexes are known
as "tonnare."
Left, a "tonnara" on the island
of Sant'Antioco.

On the following pages,
Cala di Volpe, one of the most
charming corners
of the Costa Smeralda.

405

BEWARE OF THE BEAR!
The wind plays with the rocks,
breathes life into fantastic zoos
without cages: bears and
elephants, dogs and fish are the
silent guardians of the sea,
as the wind god Aeolus never
pauses in his patient
transformation of the rocks.
Right, Capo d'Orso, on the
northern coast of Sardinia.

A 40-minute ferry ride from the coastal village of Portoscuso deposits people and cars at Carloforte, the port and principal village of San Pietro. At the height of its maritime power, Genoa controlled the island, and the Carloforte dialect is stepchild Genoese. The waterfront too has a charming touch of Genoa before the fall, and it is an ideal place to observe Sardinia's colorful daily ritual, the evening promenade, family-style or in full-dress parody of the peacock mating dance.

San Pietro is linked to Sant'Antioco by a short ferry ride, and the quiet old streets and peaceful church of the Sant'Antioco port make for a wistful stroll. On the way back towards Cagliari, off the major coastal road, a stop at Nora will round out this first taste of the other Sardinia on just the proper note.

Out on a little finger of land reaching into the sea are the sun-bleached relics of Phoenician and Roman intruders who came to make Sardinia their own. They built temples, theaters and baths, and while history notes that the Romans sometimes made use of the local nuraghi, Nora shows no signs of a fortress mentality. The native Sardinians might have roamed the mountains, but the Phoenicians and Romans apparently felt unthreatened on the coast.

Today, the winds blow dust across Roman floors of decorative mosaic, and Nora's fallen columns trace no shadow against the sun. To an outsider, Nora seems a fascinating archeological find, worth volumes of research and at least a detailed visitors' guide. As a vantage point for contemplating this land, this sea, the unshakable rising and setting of the sun, Nora's quiet grandeur would seem to merit trumpets and guidebook raptures.

But no. This is the other Sardinia, the land of bitter honey, and while outsiders are welcome to enjoy and discover, the Sardinians will just quietly bathe in the foreground of Nora and be content to keep some of their treasures to themselves.

PAUL CHUTKOW is a journalist and author. His books include "Harvests of Joy," the memoirs of Robert Mondavi, and "Depardieu," a biography of the French actor Gérard Depardieu.

THE MASTER AND NATURE

The year was 1964.

The renowned film director Michelangelo Antonioni made his first color film in 1964 in an extraordinary place – the only one, perhaps, whose magic could not be reproduced in black and white – the Spiaggia Rosa (the Pink Beach) of Budelli, in the Maddalena archipelago.

The film, *Deserto Rosso*, is considered one of the masterpieces of the cinema while Spiaggia Rosa (above) remains a masterpiece of nature.

Beyond the Costa Smeralda

By Michael Frank
April 12, 1998

THE STONE CULTURE

The most important artifacts of prehistoric Sardinia are the nuraghe (below and bottom right), truncated stone cones built for defensive purposes that gave their name to a culture that endured for over a thousand years. The giants' tombs (facing page) were cave necropolises. Above, a nuragic statuette in bronze.

Tucked in the hills above the Costa Smeralda, the village of Pantaleo lies just below a remarkable rock formation that thrusts up out of a cover of furred greenery like a set of old man's bones exhuming themselves from the grave. Much scraped and scarred by wind, rain and time, these rocks are pierced with shrubs and fissured in places with mysterious shadowy crevices and caves. They are as humbling as any of the manmade relics of the island and provide a majestic backdrop to the flowery, sun-spiked town that nestles at their base. There is not much to do in San Pantaleo itself but eat well, sleep well, buy jars of delicious local honey, and sample both archeological and contemporary Sardinia.

San Pantaleo is less than half an hour away from the town of Arzachena, which is surrounded by a scattering of important prehistoric sites of the Nuraghic people. Their legacy to the island included the extraordinary round, beehive-like stone structures also called nuraghi (singular: nuraghe), which evoke Mycenaean tombs in shape and spirit but are otherwise unique in the ancient world. There are 7,000 of these buildings on the island; their form was perfected during the early Bronze Age and consisted of internal spiral staircases, alcoves for (it is theorized) sleeping and storage, stone seats, openings for ventilation, and (on some) twig roofs and wooden battlements for defense. The Nuraghic fondness for the circle reappears in poignant necropolises, known as tombs of the giants, which are also well represented near Arzachena. Although Sardinia's grandest nuraghi are concentrated else-

where on the island, I was nicely introduced to the form at the attractive Albucciu Nuraghe (circa 1220 B.C.) on Highway 125, which is easily identifiable because of its neighbor across the street, Pizzeria Il Nuraghe (circa 1966 A.D.).

Even the most modest nuraghi produce a feeling of awe. I could not help being impressed by the considerable manpower and sophisticated engineering that went into the structures, whose stones have been meticulously stacked and shaped into a circle and held together entirely by weight. The stones are larger at ground level and smaller and more precisely laid toward the top; it is thought that, like the pyramids, they were raised with dirt ramps and (possibly in some cases) with pulleys. Inside, the nuraghi are moody, dark, damp and silent. Safe in siege and heat alike, to the modern visitor they can feel like containers of time itself.

Ancient though they are, the giants' tombs seem somehow strangely modern. Having lost all knowledge of the precise purpose of their semicircular forecourts, we are free to admire their sculptural qualities, which are considerable. Their shapes are as pure and elegant as a Brancusi, their patina rich and roughened by the wind. The atmosphere surrounding the tombs vibrates with crickets, the periodic whack of a farmer tilling his nearby field by hand, and obscure, surely reptilian, rustlings in the underbrush.

Li Lolghi, a giants' tomb off Highway 427, is in an even more remote setting than Coddu Vecchiu, another giants' tomb where the first burials took place between 1800 and 1600 B.C. An unpaved, much pitted road leads through farmland, with a narrow footpath giving access to the site itself. Li

Lolghi has a similar semicircular forecourt, and strong traces of the actual burial chambers that stretch out behind it. When intact, these collective graves would have looked like the hull of an upended boat, but one framed by stones and covered by a thatched roof. On the morning I visited, the mistral was stirring skin-stinging clouds of dust into the air, a haunting, almost Shakespearean effect. The ghost of Hamlet's father would not have been out of place among these ravaged stones and roiling winds. Another famous local sweet is honey, which is the pride of the region around Arzachena. Available in the alimentari (or greengrocer) here and in San Pantaleo are lavender honey, eucalyptus honey, wildflower honey, thistle honey and amaro, or arbutus, honey, a bitter honey known throughout the Mediterranean and mentioned by both Horace and Virgil. Difficult to produce because of the arbutus's brief blooming period, the honey has a pungent scent and decidedly bitter taste and is said (at least by one old greengrocer in San Pantaleo) to help cure asthma.

After a morning spent among the dusty relics of ancient Sardinia, a little bitter honey is just the thing to clear the chest, and the spirit, in preparation for an afternoon on one of Costa Smeralda's pristine beaches. The water's blue-green saltiness turns out to be just one among many of the island's distinctive flavors.

MICHAEL FRANK's essays, articles, and short stories have appeared in The New York Times, Travel & Leisure *and* The Yale Review, *among other publications. He divides his time between New York and Italy.*

Contributors

OLIVIER BERNIER is the author of 12 books, most recently *"The World in 1800."* He lectures at the Metropolitan Museum of Art in New York and in museums across the country.

RACHEL BILLINGTON is the author of 16 novels, the latest being *"A Woman's Life"* and *"The Space Between."* She has also published three children's novels.

BURTON BOLLAG is a reporter for the *Chronicle of Higher Education*, in Washington DC. He was a journalist in Europe for more than 20 years.

BETH ARCHER BROMBERT, author of *"Edouard Manet: Rebel in a Frock Coat"*, spends summers in a village near Siena. She is presently working on a memoir of her years in Italy.

FRANK BRUNI, restaurant critic of *The Times*, recently completed a two-year assignment as the paper's bureau chief in Rome.

PAUL CHUTKOW is a journalist and author. His books include *"Harvests of Joy,"* the memoirs of Robert Mondavi, and *"Depardieu,"* a biography of the French actor Gérard Depardieu.

E.J. DIONNE JR., a former Rome bureau chief for *The Times*, is a columnist for The Washington Post. His most recent book is *"Stand Up Fight Back: Republican Toughs, Democratic Wimps and the Politics of Revenge"* (Simon & Schuster).

UMBERTO ECO is the author of four novels as well as numerous works of criticism, philosophy and literary theory. His fifth novel, *"The Mysterious Flame,"* will be published in June (Harcourt Brace). He is Professor of Semiotics at the University of Bologna.

SARAH FERRELL is the associate editor of *The Sophisticated Traveler*, a magazine of *The New York Times* that appears four times a year. She has traveled widely in Italy.

MICHAEL FRANK's essays, articles, and short stories have appeared in *The New York Times*, *Travel & Leisure* and *The Yale Review*, among other publications. He divides his time between New York and Italy.

SHIRLEY HAZZARD's most recent novel, *"The Great Fire,"* received the 2003 National Book Award. Naples and its seaside district of Posillipo are the setting of an earlier novel, *"The Bay of Noon."*

PAUL HOFMANN is a former chief of *The New York Times* Rome bureau. He is the author of 13 nonfiction books including *"Cento Città: A Guide to the Hundred Cities & Towns of Italy."* He lives in Rome.

DAN HOFSTADTER's most recent book, *"The Love Affair as a Work of Art,"* a volume of criticism, was nominated for an award by the National Book Critics Circle. He spends much time in Naples.

BERNARD HOLLAND is national music critic of *The New York Times*.

CATHY HORYN is the fashion critic of *The New York Times*.

LOUIS INTURRISI was a travel and food writer based in Rome. He also taught writing there at John Cabot University until his death in 1997.

NANCY HARMON JENKINS is a widely published food writer who specializes in Italy and the Mediterranean. Her most recent book is *"The Essential Mediterranean"* (HarperCollins). She lives in Tuscany and Maine.

DAVID LASKIN is co-author of *"Artists in Their Gardens"* (Sasquatch). He lives in Seattle.

CAROL LETTIERI has translated three books of contemporary Italian poetry. She works in corporate communications, writing about architecture and technology.

SUSAN LUMSDEN, a Canadian journalist and broadcaster, spent the last 15 years of her life as a free-lance journalist in Italy writing about travel and art history. She died in 1994.

ALISON LURIE is the author of nine novels, most recently, *"The Last Resort."* She is professor of English at Cornell University.

MALACHI MARTIN, was a priest, theologian and author of 16 books of non-fiction and fiction. Among those still in print are *"Hostage to the Devil,"* *"The Jesuits,"* *"The Keys of This Blood"* and *"Windswept House: A Vatican Novel."* He died in 1999.

ALASTAIR McEWEN is a freelance translator based in Milan, where he has lived for nearly 30 years. He has translated works by some of Italy's leading authors.

MICHAEL MEWSHAW is the author of ten novels (*"Island Tempest,"* most recently) and six books of non-fiction. He divides his year between Florida, England and Rome.

JAN MORRIS, who lives in Wales, has traveled almost everywhere, and has also written extensively about Venice. She recently published her "final" work, *"Trieste and the Meaning of Nowhere."*

WILLIAM MURRAY's most recent book is *"City of the Soul: A Walk in Rome."* His book on young opera singers will be published next year. For many years was a staff writer for *The New Yorker*.

ELISABETTA POVOLEDO reports from Italy for the *International Herald Tribune*.

FRANK J. PRIAL has written the *"Wine Talk"* column in The New York Times for three decades. *"Decantations,"* a collection of his recent columns, was published in 2001 (St. Martins Press).

FRANCINE PROSE is the author of 12 novels, including the National Book Award finalist, *"Blue Angel,"* and the forthcoming *"A Changed Man"* (HarperCollins). She is also the author of *"Sicilian Odyssey,"* a work of nonfiction.

FREDERIKA RANDALL is a journalist and translator living in Rome.

ROBERT RICHE, a playwright and novelist, travels to Europe frequently. His second novel, *"The Vision Thing"* (Publish America), appeared this year.

JANE SHAPIRO is the author of two novels, *"The Dangerous Husband"* and *"After Moondog."* Her short fiction and journalism have been published in *The New York Times*, *The New Yorker*, *Harper's Bazaar*, and *Ms.*, among many other publications.

MARY TAYLOR SIMETI is an American writer living in Sicily. Her latest book is *"Travels With a Medieval Queen"* (Farrar, Straus & Giroux).

MURIEL SPARK is the author of 22 novels, most recently *"Aiding and Abetting"* and the forthcoming novel, *"The Finishing School."* Her most celebrated works include *"The Prime of Miss Jean Brodie"* and *"Loitering With Intent."* She lives in Tuscany.

ALEXANDER STILLE is the author of *"Benevolence and Betrayal: Five Italian-Jewish Families Under Fascism"* (Picador) and *"Excellent Cadavers: The Mafia and the Death of the First Italian Republic"* (Vintage). He is a frequent contributor to *The Times*.

JAMES STURZ is author of the novel, *"SASSO,"* set in the Basilicata region of Italy. His articles about Italy have appeared in *The New York Times*, *Travel & Leisure*, *Condé Nast Traveler* and other magazines.

SUSAN ALLEN TOTH's most recent book is *"Leaning into the Wind: A Memoir of Midwest Weather"* (University of Minnesota Press).

BARRY UNSWORTH, who won the Booker prize for *"Sacred Hunger"* in 1992, is the author of 14 novels, most recently, *"The Songs of the Kings."* He lives in Italy.

WILLIAM WEAVER is a biographer of Verdi, Puccini and Eleonora Duse. He has also translated many works by Umberto Eco, Italo Calvino, and Alberto Moravia. He resides at Bard College.

JO BROYLES YOHAY writes frequently for *The New York Times* travel section and other publications.

Photographs

The photographs in this book are by
DeA Picture Library (S. Amantini, G. Andreini,
F. Barbagallo, G. Berengo Gardin, M. Bertinetti,
M. Borchi, W. Buss, G. Carfagna, R. Carnovalini,
G. Cigolini, U. Colnago, G. Cozzi, A. Dagli Orti,
G. Dagli Orti, R. Felderer, E. Ganzerla, G. Gnemmi,
S. Lombardi Vallauri, S. Montanari, L. Pedicini,
L. Romano, D.M. Rossi, M. Santini, C. Sappa,
G. Sosio, I. Taborri, S. Vannini, G. Veggi, A. Vergani)
with the exception of the following:
85bl, br (Casinò di San Remo);
99tl (G. Lotti/Contrasto);
116l (Museo Archeologico dell'Alto Adige, *www.iceman.it*);
173 (IVSI, Istituto Valorizzazione Salumi Italiani);
175bl (Archivio Ferrari);
175br (Archivio Ducati);
226, 227 (Archivio Umbria Jazz);
302-303 (Anzenberger/Contrasto);
312-313 (Giuseppe Avallone).